Learner Corpus Research Meets Second Language Acquisition

Advances in Learner Corpus Research (LCR) and Second Language Acquisition (SLA) have brought these two fast-moving fields significantly closer in recent years. This volume brings together contributions from internationally recognised experts in both LCR and SLA to provide an innovative, cross-collaborative examination of how each area can provide rich insights for the other. Chapters present recent advances in LCR and illustrate in a clear and accessible style how these can be exploited for the study of a broad range of key topics in SLA, such as complexity, tense and aspect, cross-linguistic influence vs. universal processes, phraseology, and variability. It concludes with two commentary chapters written by eminent scholars, one from the perspective of SLA, the other from the perspective of LCR, allowing researchers and students alike to reflect upon the mutually beneficial harmony between the two fields and to link up LCR and SLA research and theory.

Bert Le Bruyn is an Assistant Professor at Utrecht University. He is an expert on semantic language variation with a solid background in corpus linguistics. He received a VENI grant in 2014 for his work focusing on the semantics and L2 acquisition of referentiality, and another grant in 2016 for his corpus-based project with Henriëtte de Swart, Time in Translation.

Magali Paquot is an FNRS research associate at the Centre for English Corpus Linguistics, UCLouvain. She specialises in the use of learner corpora to study key topics in SLA and is particularly interested in methodological issues. She is co-editor in chief of the *International Journal of Learner Corpus Research*, one of the founding members of the Learner Corpus Research Association, and a member of the IRIS Digital Repository Advisory Group.

THE CAMBRIDGE APPLIED LINGUISTICS SERIES

The authority on cutting-edge Applied Linguistics research

Series Editors 2007–present: Carol A. Chapelle and Susan Hunston
1988–2007: Michael H. Long and Jack C. Richards

For a complete list of titles please visit: www.cambridge.org

Recent Titles in This Series:

Learner Corpus Research Meets Second Language Acquisition
Bert Le Bruyn and *Magali Paquot*

Second Language Speech Fluency From Research to Practice
Parvaneh Tavakoli and *Clare Wright*

Ontologies of English Conceptualising the Language for Learning, Teaching, and Assessment
Edited by Christopher J. Hall and Rachel Wicaksono

Task-Based Language Teaching Theory and Practice
Rod Ellis, Peter Skehan, Shaofeng Li, Natsuko Shintani and *Craig Lambert*

Feedback in Second Language Writing Contexts and Issues
Edited by Ken Hyland and Fiona Hyland

Language and Television Series A Linguistic Approach to TV Dialogue
Monika Bednarek

Intelligibility, Oral Communication, and the Teaching of Pronunciation
John M. Levis

Multilingual Education Between Language Learning and Translanguaging
Edited by Jasone Cenoz and Durk Gorter

Learning Vocabulary in Another Language 2nd Edition
I. S. P. Nation

Narrative Research in Applied Linguistics
Edited by Gary Barkhuizen,

Teacher Research in Language Teaching A Critical Analysis
Simon Borg

Figurative Language, Genre and Register
Alice Deignan, Jeannette Littlemore and *Elena Semino*

Exploring ELF Academic English Shaped by Non-native Speakers
Anna Mauranen

Genres across the Disciplines Student Writing in Higher Education
Hilary Nesi and *Sheena Gardner*

Disciplinary Identities Individuality and Community in Academic Discourse
Ken Hyland

Replication Research in Applied Linguistics
Edited by Graeme Porte,

The Language of Business Meetings
Michael Handford

Reading in a Second Language Moving from Theory to Practice
William Grabe

Modelling and Assessing Vocabulary Knowledge
Edited by Helmut Daller, James Milton and Jeanine Treffers-Daller

Practice in a Second Language Perspectives from Applied Linguistics and Cognitive Psychology
Edited by Robert M. DeKeyser,

Task-Based Language Education From Theory to Practice
Edited by Kris van den Branden,

Second Language Needs Analysis
Edited by Michael H. Long,

Insights into Second Language Reading A Cross-Linguistic Approach
Keiko Koda

Research Genres Exploration and Applications
John M. Swales

Critical Pedagogies and Language Learning
Edited by Bonny Norton and Kelleen Toohey

Exploring the Dynamics of Second Language Writing
Edited by Barbara Kroll,

Understanding Expertise in Teaching Case Studies of Second Language Teachers
Amy B. M. Tsui

Criterion-Referenced Language Testing
James Dean Brown and *Thom Hudson*

Corpora in Applied Linguistics
Susan Hunston

Pragmatics in Language Teaching
Edited by Kenneth R. Rose and Gabriele Kasper

Cognition and Second Language Instruction
Edited by Peter Robinson,

Research Perspectives on English for Academic Purposes
Edited by John Flowerdew and Matthew Peacock

Computer Applications in Second Language Acquisition Foundations for Teaching, Testing and Research
Carol A. Chapelle

Learner Corpus Research Meets Second Language Acquisition

Edited by

Bert Le Bruyn

UIL-OTS, Utrecht University

Magali Paquot

FNRS – Centre for English Corpus Linguistics, UCLouvain

CAMBRIDGE
UNIVERSITY PRESS

CAMBRIDGE
UNIVERSITY PRESS

University Printing House, Cambridge CB2 8BS, United Kingdom

One Liberty Plaza, 20th Floor, New York, NY 10006, USA

477 Williamstown Road, Port Melbourne, VIC 3207, Australia

314–321, 3rd Floor, Plot 3, Splendor Forum, Jasola District Centre, New Delhi – 110025, India

79 Anson Road, #06–04/06, Singapore 079906

Cambridge University Press is part of the University of Cambridge.

It furthers the University's mission by disseminating knowledge in the pursuit of education, learning, and research at the highest international levels of excellence.

www.cambridge.org
Information on this title: www.cambridge.org/9781108425407
DOI: 10.1017/9781108674577

First published 2021

A catalogue record for this publication is available from the British Library.

Library of Congress Cataloging-in-Publication Data
Names: Bruyn, Bert Le, editor. | Paquot, Magali, editor.
Title: Learner corpus research meets second language acquisition / edited by Bert Le Bruyn, UIL-OTS, Utrecht University ; Magali Paquot, FNRS-Centre for English Corpus Linguistics, UCLouvain.
Description: Cambridge, UK ; New York : Cambridge University Press, 2021. | Series: The Cambridge applied linguistics series | Includes bibliographical references and index.
Identifiers: LCCN 2020037702 (print) | LCCN 2020037703 (ebook) | ISBN 9781108425407 (hardback) | ISBN 9781108442299 (paperback) | ISBN 9781108674577 (epub)
Subjects: LCSH: Second language acquisition–Research. | Corpora (Linguistics)–Research.
Classification: LCC P118.2 .L375 2020 (print) | LCC P118.2 (ebook) | DDC 410.1/88072–dc23
LC record available at https://lccn.loc.gov/2020037702
LC ebook record available at https://lccn.loc.gov/2020037703

ISBN 978-1-108-42540-7 Hardback
ISBN 978-1-108-44229-9 Paperback

Contents

Figures

Tables

Contributors

Philippa Bell (Université du Québec à Montréal, Canada)

Laura Collins (Concordia University, USA)

María Belén Díez-Bedmar (University of Jaén, Spain)

Robert Fuchs (Universität Hamburg, Germany)

Sandra Götz (Justus-Liebig-Universität Giessen, Germany)

Sylviane Granger (UCLouvain, Belgium)

Stefan Th. Gries (UC Santa Barbara, USA & Justus-Liebig-Universität Giessen, Germany)

Amanda Huensch (University of Pittsburgh, USA)

Tania Ionin (University of Illinois at Urbana-Champaign, USA)

Bert Le Bruyn (Utrecht University, The Netherlands)

Wander Lowie (University of Groningen, The Netherlands)

Emma Marsden (University of York, UK)

Lea Meriläinen (University of Eastern Finland, Finland)

Rosamond Mitchell (University of Southampton, UK)

Florence Myles (University of Essex, UK)

Hubert Naets (UCLouvain, Belgium)

Magali Paquot (UCLouvain, Belgium)

Charlene Polio (Michigan State University, USA)

Nicole Tracy-Ventura (West Virginia University, USA)

Marjolein Verspoor (University of Groningen, The Netherlands)

Valentin Werner (Universität Bamberg, Germany)

Martijn Wieling (University of Groningen, USA)

Stefanie Wulff (University of Florida, USA)

Hyung-Jo Yoon (California State University, Northridge, USA)

Series Editors' Preface

This volume brings into dialogue two areas of central interest to Applied Linguistics: Second Language Acquisition (SLA) and Learner Corpus Research (LCR). As the editors of this volume note in their introduction, the shared concerns of these research communities should suggest productive collaboration between the two, but in the past they have not addressed each other consistently. This can be explained at least partly by differences in their research processes: designing a corpus of learner texts is not the same as compiling a database for SLA research; the questions answered by consulting a learner corpus are not necessarily those asked in SLA.

This volume advances communication between these two areas with studies by experts who address issues of common interest. The chapters explore the challenges that corpus research poses to theoretical assumptions in SLA as well as the methodological challenges SLA offers to LCR. The volume addresses three overarching questions of substantial significance.

The first question asks the extent to which learning a second or additional language follows paths determined by universal mechanisms or by the character of the learner's L1. Several chapters in the book offer evidence from a variety of learner corpora to find the optimum fit to data between the two positions.

The second question considers how changes in learner proficiency can be measured. Here, necessary developments in corpus research come under scrutiny, in particular the need to automate measures of accuracy and complexity to take account of large amounts of data and the need to build corpora that are subdivided by time. A key issue under this theme is the interaction between individual differences and overall learner trends, and how these might be modelled.

Finally, the volume addresses the question of how the design of corpora and the statistics used to process them may be modified in order to support SLA research. Recent developments in this area are illustrated and evaluated.

The work in this volume offers an excellent example of interdisciplinary research, in which theory and methods from complementary perspectives are used to challenge and support each other. It will be of interest to students and researchers working in both SLA and LCR.

Learner Corpus Research and Second Language Acquisition: an attempt at bridging the gap

Bert Le Bruyn and Magali Paquot

1 Learner Corpora and Their Origins

Learner corpora are traditionally defined as 'systematic collections of authentic, continuous and contextualized language use (spoken or written) by L2 learners stored in electronic format' (Callies & Paquot 2015). With this characterization, it appears very clearly that learner corpus researchers have always been interested in exploring the output of the more open-ended types of contextualized production tasks assigned to L2 learners (e.g. Granger 2008; Tracy-Ventura & Myles 2015). The term 'learners' here refers to Foreign and/or Second Language learners rather than to learners acquiring their native language (L1).

The original idea behind the development of major learner corpora like the *International Corpus of Learner English* (ICLE; Granger 1993) was to enrich existing corpus collections with learner varieties and 'pass on the advances made in computerized corpus linguistics to applied linguistics', with a focus on the domains of language learning and teaching (Granger 1993). This situates the origins of Learner Corpus Research (LCR) outside the domain of theory-driven Second Language Acquisition (SLA) research.

2 From (Applied) Linguistics to Theory-Driven SLA

The fact that learner corpora systematically record learner language could have made them into a relevant resource for theory-driven SLA – much in line with the role CHILDES corpora have played in the L1 acquisition literature (MacWhinney 2000). However, a cursory look at publications in major SLA journals from the 1990s till now shows that this expectation is not borne out: learner corpus methodology has been more the exception than the rule. Looking back at the beginnings of LCR, Bell, Collins, and Marsden (in this volume) attribute LCR's lack of popularity within SLA research to its 'preoccupation for coding errors, L1 transfer errors, and deviations from a target-like norm' at a time when SLA research took pride in having moved beyond surface generalizations.

Over the years, LCR and theory-driven SLA have started to interact. In *The Cambridge Handbook of Learner Corpus Research* (Granger et al. 2015), Myles shows that LCR can interact with a range of SLA theories, citing examples like Rankin's work on the Interface Hypothesis (Rankin 2009) and Bonilla's work on Processability Theory (Bonilla 2015). She also highlights, however, the fact that SLA studies require different corpora to answer the questions they raise. For example, whereas the ICLE is a good choice for checking certain predictions of the Interface Hypothesis, its focus on essays by advanced learners would make it irrelevant for testing predictions of Processability Theory.

Myles's (2015) conclusion on the interaction between LCR and SLA is a careful one. She notes punctual excursions from one field to the other but no systematic collaboration: 'second language researchers have been rather slow in taking advantage of learner corpora and their associated computerised methodologies . . ., and LCR is not always fully informed by SLA research'. The present volume sets out to give an updated evaluation and showcases the continued efforts of the two communities to grow closer to each other, this volume being one of them.

3 LCR Meets SLA

The initiative for this volume dates back to a workshop the two editors organized in March 2017. The goal was to bring together researchers interested in doing SLA research through LCR. The call that was launched invited contributions that would:

(1) address SLA research questions with the help of learner corpus data and corpus linguistic techniques;
(2) test key constructs in SLA theory on the basis of learner corpus data;
(3) carry out a learner corpus study and compare results with findings from previous SLA studies that relied on more experimental techniques;
(4) adopt a mixed method approach that involves learner corpus data as one of the data types used;
(5) revisit previous LCR studies in the light of SLA theory.

The submissions we received were mostly of types (1) to (3). The present volume brings together the majority of the papers that were presented at the workshop. Each paper was reviewed by a specialist in SLA and a specialist in LCR. We know this was a challenge both for the reviewers and the authors. We wholeheartedly thank all of them for their efforts.

In the remainder of this introduction we give a brief description of the different research contributions. We leave the evaluation of the interaction between SLA and LCR to two eminent scholars, one from the field of LCR, the other from the field of SLA. Sylviane Granger and Florence Myles gracefully agreed to write commentary chapters. These conclude the volume.

4 Overview of Chapters

The origins of this volume make it clear that it is by no means intended as a survey of all current SLA-oriented work in LCR (see Tracy-Ventura & Paquot, in press). However, we believe the volume provides a fair impression of how the fields of LCR and SLA are currently interacting with each other. It showcases in an exemplary way how SLA theory can be used today to inform learner corpus analyses and how learner corpus findings can be used to inform SLA theory. This cross-fertilization has arguably started to take place with the broadening of learner data types collected in LCR. The first learner corpora consisted of written texts – typically argumentative essays – produced by intermediate to advanced English as a Foreign Language (EFL) learners in higher education. However, the chapters in this volume show that many different types of learner corpora are now being compiled, e.g. spoken learner corpora, corpora of foreign languages other than English, cross-sectional corpora representing various proficiency levels, and longitudinal learner corpora. Similarly, learner corpus researchers have always sought to describe learner data and complement them with text and learner variables such as L1 background, age, or time spent studying English at school. More recently, however, efforts have been made to widen the scope of recorded metadata and include variables that are key to the SLA research agenda (e.g. external measurement of proficiency, answers to a motivation test, language aptitude scores) (see Möller 2017). The chapters in this volume further bear witness to the ever more sophisticated ways researchers succeed in making learner corpora speak, from data extraction to statistical analysis. A final strength of current learner-corpus-based research highlighted by the volume is its inclusive character: all theoretical frameworks are welcome, data are shared, and bridges are built, e.g. to the neighbouring discipline of World Englishes.

We have refrained from organizing the volume into clearly delimited parts but found it practical for the purposes of this overview to highlight some common themes in the chapters that appear together.

4.1 Universal Tendencies and Cross-Linguistic Influence

The first three chapters focus on classical themes in SLA, namely the role of cross-linguistic influence, the role of universal tendencies, and the interaction between the two.

Tania Ionin and María Belén Díez-Bedmar bring together their SLA and LCR expertise to compare the L2 article acquisition of Spanish and Russian B1 and B2 learners of English. The empirical basis of their investigation consists of 200 texts from the *Cambridge Learner Corpus*. The results confirm the generalization that learners with a native article language (like Spanish) are quicker in picking up and applying relevant semantic insights when acquiring a second article language than learners with an article-less L1 (like Russian). The results, however, do not confirm the role specificity has played in uncovering universal tendencies in SLA research (Ionin et al. 2004; Ionin et al. 2009).

Valentin Werner, Robert Fuchs, and Sandra Götz investigate the role of cross-linguistic influence and universal mechanisms in the acquisition of the perfect/simple past alternation in English. Cantonese and German learner data are drawn from the LINDSEI corpus (*Louvain International Database of Spoken English Interlanguage*) and the ICLE corpus. Native comparison data come from the LOCNEC and LOCNESS corpora (*Louvain Corpus of Native English Conversation* and *Louvain Corpus of Native English Essays*). The authors follow the MuPDAR approach (Multifactorial Prediction and Deviation Analysis with Regressions) (Gries & Deshors 2014; Gries & Bernaisch 2016; Wulff and Gries, this volume): they first determine the way different factors interact in native speaker production and then see how these factors play out in learner production. The results show that there are quantitative differences between Cantonese and German learners, the latter being closer overall to native production. The authors, however, also find that it is difficult to pinpoint where qualitative differences would reside that can be attributed unambiguously to L1 influence. They conclude – citing Bardovi-Harlig – that cross-linguistic influence, if at play, is to be found 'in the details rather than in the larger picture'.

Lea Meriläinen approaches SLA and LCR from the adjacent domain of World Englishes. What makes World Englishes corpora different from most LCR corpora is that they lack metadata on individual speakers' L1s. The focus in this field has consequently been on universal tendencies rather than cross-linguistic influence, and detailed comparisons between linguistic systems have been less central in this field than in SLA or LCR. The author presents two case studies based on learner data from the ICLE corpus and the MEC corpus (*Corpus of Matriculation Examination*) and on native data from the LOCNESS corpus. The learners come from a number of different L1 backgrounds: Finnish, German, Swedish, Chinese, and Japanese. The case studies focus on embedded inversions ('I don't know what are you asking me') and preposition omission ('She went town'). Results tentatively show that embedded inversions and preposition omission are found in the production of learners of all backgrounds but are most frequent when learners have L1s that differ in the relevant respects from the L2.

4.2 Proficiency and Time

The issue of proficiency extends beyond research focusing on the interplay between cross-linguistic influence and universal tendencies. Pinning down what it means to become more proficient over time is one of the core issues of SLA research. One way of approaching proficiency is through the constructs of *complexity*, *accuracy*, and *fluency*, CAF for short (see e.g. Housen & Kuiken 2009 for a classic reference). The rationale behind these is that learners who become more proficient will start using more complex language, will become more accurate, and will become more fluent in their production. A variety of automated measures have been proposed to operationalize the constructs of complexity and fluency. This does not hold for accuracy, though. Its operationalizations typically require laborious hand-coding and – depending on the dimension of accuracy the researcher is interested in – have led to varying degrees of reliability. Charlene Polio and Hyung-Jo Yoon, building on previous work by Bestgen and Granger (2014), introduce a number of automated measures of accuracy drawn from usage-based theories of SLA. They explore whether the construct of accuracy can be measured by checking if the bi- and trigrams occurring in learner texts also occur in large corpora like COCA (*Corpus of Contemporary American English*) and by assessing how likely the words composing them are to occur together in this corpus. Polio and Yoon's learner data are taken from three corpora: the Michigan State University (MSU) corpus (descriptive essays), the genre corpus (argumentative essays), and Yoon's dissertation pilot data (narrative essays). Their results show that bi- and trigrams that do not occur in COCA are in general considered erroneous by human judges. They also find that their automated measures of accuracy typically pattern with classical accuracy measures – as desired – and not with complexity measures. Finally, their results show that up to half of the variance of hand-coded error counts is accounted for by their automated measures, a welcome result that warrants further exploration.

Magali Paquot, Hubert Naets, and Stefan Gries's contribution focuses on phraseological complexity and looks into the effects of proficiency and time spent on learning English on the sophistication of verb + object co-occurrences. Interestingly, they assess phraseological complexity in much the same way as Polio and Yoon assess accuracy, namely by checking how likely words making up word combinations found in learner texts are to be found together in a large reference corpus. There are two crucial differences, though. First, Paquot et al. look not at bi- and trigrams but at words in a syntactic dependency relation, namely verbs and their objects. Second, they make use of mean mutual information (MI) scores to examine the phraseological complexity of foreign language texts; this association measure has been shown to promote relatively less frequent and more semantically complex word pairs, thus tapping into the sophistication of word combinations (cf. Paquot 2019).The learner data Paquot et al. use are taken from the LONGDALE corpus (*Longitudinal Database of Learner English*). Two important assets of this corpus are that it comes with up to three measure points per learner – spread over the three years of their undergraduate degrees – and that each learner text comes with an Oxford Quick Placement Test score. The reference corpus is ENCOW14 AX, a large web corpus. Results show that phraseological complexity improves with proficiency and that institutional status (i.e. the year the students are in) does not hold any predictive power. Next to establishing phraseological complexity as a good way to probe higher levels of proficiency, the crucial point the chapter makes is that time and institutional training do not have an effect on the development of phraseological complexity per se; what matters more is foreign language proficiency and whether learners rate higher on an external test from one year to the next.

The issue of time is also central to the next two chapters. Nicole Tracy-Ventura, Amanda Huensch, and Rosamond Mitchell look into forces of retention and attrition of the effects of institutional training, with a focus on lexical diversity. Data are taken from the original LANGSNAP corpus (*Languages and Social Networks Abroad Project*) that looked into the effects of a nine-month stay abroad in France or Spain by English students (with data collection before, during, and up to a year after the stay). These data are supplemented with those from a follow-up study with data collection four years after the stay abroad. The results show that lexical diversity continues to improve post-instruction in oral but not in written tasks and that peak attainment and language exposure/use contribute significantly to predicting gains, with peak attainment explaining most variance. The results are relevant for the Dynamic Model of Multilingualism (Herdina & Jessner 2002) and the Neurolinguistic Theory of Bilingualism (Paradis 1993, 2004).

Marjolein Verspoor, Wander Lowie, and Martijn Wieling report on a longitudinal study of Dutch high school students learning English. What makes the learner corpus they use exceptional is the high density of the data collection, with one measurement per week for a period of 23 weeks. The authors find that the holistic scores of the last two learner texts are significantly higher than those of the first two, suggesting an increase in proficiency. They also find that syntactic development (operationalized as mean length of T-unit or MLTU) and lexical development (operationalized as Guiraud) show an upward trend at the group level with a clear but small decrease at the end. Crucially, however, when the authors zoom in on the syntactic and lexical development of individual learners, they find that no learner follows the same path or evolves in a linear fashion. The only generalization that does seem to hold across learners is that gains in lexical development precede gains in syntactic development. Verspoor et al. interpret these results from a Complex Dynamics Systems point of view in which individual trajectories take centre stage.

4.3 Corpus Analysis and Development

The remaining two chapters focus on corpus analysis and development. The first responds to Verspoor et al.'s call for attention for individual learners. Stefanie Wulff and Stefan Gries further develop the MuPDAR approach that we also found in the contribution by Werner et al. On the basis of a case study of the *s*- and *of*-genitive alternation, they show how the approach provides a comprehensive picture of native speaker behaviour and allows for a fine-grained analysis of the aspects of a target structure the learner commands or still has difficulties with. They show how results can be obtained not only at the group level but also at the individual level, a move that is both relevant from a theoretical perspective and is also shown to lead to a better analysis of the data.

Philippa Bell, Laura Collins, and Emma Marsden offer a comprehensive overview of design choices they are facing in the development of a learner corpus looking into L2 development in foreign language classes in primary and secondary education. Their goal is both applied and theoretical. On the applied side, the main question is how and what to teach to optimize acquisition. On the theoretical side, they are interested in finding out how language is acquired in limited-exposure contexts. The authors report on and discuss design choices they piloted. These include the language of the instruction of the tasks, the tasks themselves, and transcription/coding issues.

Acknowledgements

We would like to thank the authors and reviewers for all their hard work on the volume. Special thanks go to Lex Tavenier for his in-house editorial support as well as to Cambridge University Press for their long-term support for this volume. We also gratefully acknowledge the financial support of the F.R.S.-FNRS, NWO, and the department of Language, Culture and Communication at Utrecht University.

References

Bestgen, Y. & Granger, S. (2014). Quantifying the development of phraseological competence in L2 English writing: An automated approach. *Journal of Second Language Writing* 26, 28–41.

Bonilla, C. L. (2015). From number agreement to the subjunctive: Evidence for Processability Theory in L2 Spanish. *Second Language Research* 31(1), 53–74.

Callies, M. & Paquot, M. (2015). Learner Corpus Research: An interdisciplinary field on the move. *International Journal of Learner Corpus Research* 1(1), 1–6.

Granger, S. (1993). The International Corpus of Learner English. In J. Aarts, P. de Haan, & N, Oostdijk (eds.), *English Language Corpora: Design, Analysis and Exploitation*, 57–69. Amsterdam & Atlanta, GA: Rodopi.

(2008). *Learner Corpora*. In A. Lüdeling & M. Kytö (eds.), *Corpus Linguistics. An International Handbook*, 259–275. Berlin & New York, NY: Walter de Gruyter.

Granger, S., Gilquin G., & Meunier, F. (eds.) (2015). *The Cambridge Handbook of Learner Corpus Research*. Cambridge: Cambridge University Press.

Gries, S. Th. & Bernaisch, T. (2016). Exploring epicentres empirically: Focus on South Asian Englishes. *English World-Wide* 37(1), 1–25.

Gries, S. Th. & Deshors, S. (2014). Using regressions to explore deviations between corpus data and a standard/target: Two suggestions. *Corpora* 9(1), 109–136.

Herdina, P. & Jessner, U. (2002). *A Dynamic Model of Multilingualism: Changing the Psycholinguistic Perspective*. Clevedon: Multilingual Matters.

Housen, A. & Kuiken, F. (2009). Complexity, accuracy, and fluency in second language acquisition. *Applied Linguistics* 30(4), 461–473.

Ionin, T., Ko, H., & Wexler, K. (2004). Article semantics in L2 acquisition: The role of specificity. *Language Acquisition* 12(1), 3–69.

Ionin, T., Zubizarreta, M., & Philippov, V. (2009). Acquisition of article semantics by child and adult L2-English learners. *Bilingualism: Language and Cognition* 12(3), 337–361. https://doi.org/10.1017/S1366728909990149

MacWhinney, B. (2000). *The CHILDES Project: Tools for Analyzing Talk. 3rd Edition.* Mahwah, NJ: Lawrence Erlbaum Associates.

Möller, V. (2017). A statistical analysis of learner corpus data, experimental data and individual differences: Monofactorial vs. multifactorial approaches. In P. de Haan, S. van Vuuren, & R. de Vries (eds.), *Language, Learners and Levels: Progression and Variation*, 409–439. Louvain-la-Neuve: Presses universitaires de Louvain.

Myles, F. (2015). Second language acquisition theory and learner corpus research. In S. Granger, G. Gilquin, & F. Meunier (eds.). *The Cambridge Handbook of Learner Corpus Research*, 309–332. Cambridge: Cambridge University Press.

Paquot, M. (2019). The phraseological dimension in interlanguage complexity research. *Second Language Research* 35(1), 121–145. https://doi.org/10.1177/0267658317694221

Paradis, M. (1993). Linguistic, psycholinguistic, and neurolinguistic aspects of 'interference' in bilingual speakers: The Activation Threshold Hypothesis. *International Journal of Psycholinguistics*, 9(2), 133–145.

(2004). *A Neurolinguistic Theory of Bilingualism.* Amsterdam: John Benjamins.

Rankin, T. (2009). Verb second in advanced L2 English: A learner corpus study. In *Proceedings of the 10th Generative Approaches to Second Language Acquisition Conference*, 46–59. Somerville, MA: Cascadilla Proceedings Project.

Tracy-Ventura, N. & Myles, F. (2015). The importance of task variability in the design of learner corpora for SLA research. *International Journal of Learner Corpus Research* 1(1), 58–95.

Tracy-Ventura, N. & Paquot, M. (eds). (in press). *The Routledge Handbook of Second Language Acquisition and Corpora.* London: Routledge.

Article Use in Russian and Spanish Learner Writing at CEFR B1 and B2 Levels: Effects of Proficiency, Native Language, and Specificity

Tania Ionin and María Belén Díez-Bedmar

1 Introduction

Patterns of English article use among English language learners have, in the last three decades, been of great interest both to Learner Corpus Research (LCR) and to experimental approaches to Second Language Acquisition (SLA). Despite different methodologies, studies in both fields have addressed such issues as the role of proficiency and the role of the learners' first language (L1) and their effects on the L2 acquisition of articles, with a particular focus on differences between learners from L1s with vs. without articles (henceforth [+ART] vs. [−ART]). At the same time, there has not previously been much interaction between the different approaches to studying articles in learner language. The goal of this work is to bridge this gap by pursuing the following two objectives. First, this chapter seeks to provide an overview of prior work on English articles in both the LCR and SLA fields, with regard to the effects of the learners' L1 and their proficiency level. Second, this chapter reports on a learner corpus study that adopts a particular semantic framework from prior experimental work (Ionin 2003) and tests the predictions of this framework for learner corpora. After discussing the study results, we conclude that there are advantages and limitations to both corpus-based and experimental approaches, and argue that the study of articles in learner language benefits from a combination of both approaches.

2 Background and Study Goals

2.1 Prior Experimental Studies on Articles in Learner English

Early studies of the SLA of English articles (e.g., Huebner 1983; Master 1987) relied primarily on naturalistic or semi-naturalistic production data, but experimental studies on this topic go back to at least Thomas (1989) (see, among many others, Robertson 2000; Trenkic 2007, 2008; Ionin, Ko, & Wexler 2004; Ionin, Zubizarreta, & Bautista Maldonado 2008; Ionin, Zubizarreta, & Philippov 2009; Goad & White 2009; and the papers in García-Mayo & Hawkins 2009). It is well-established that L2-English learners both omit articles in obligatory contexts and misuse one article in place of the other; with regard to the latter, overuse of *the* instead of *a(n)* is particularly common (see, e.g., Thomas 1989; Ionin et al. 2004; Ionin et al. 2009). Studies that compare L2-English learners from [+ART] L1s, such as Spanish, and [−ART] L1s, such as Russian or Korean, furthermore find that errors of both article omission and article misuse are more common among learners from [−ART] L1s. This pattern of cross-linguistic influence has been found across a variety of elicited production methodologies: both untimed tasks, such as oral picture description (e.g., Thomas 1989) and highly controlled written elicited production (where participants fill in the blank or choose the target article, as in Hawkins et al. 2006 and Ionin et al. 2008); and tasks in which participants are placed under time pressure while orally describing a video (Trenkic & Pongpairoj 2013) or repeating a sentence (Chrabaszcz & Jiang 2014). While the majority of SLA studies on articles have used elicited production methodologies, a few studies have used acceptability/grammaticality judgment tasks to examine how learners rate sentences with correct, incorrect, and/or missing articles (e.g., Cho 2017) or have examined how articles are processed in real time, using self-paced reading (Kim & Lakshmanan 2009) or eye-tracking (Trenkic, Mirkovic, & Altmann 2013). To the best of our knowledge, judgment and processing studies of L2 articles have not examined effects of cross-linguistic influence by comparing learners from [+ART] and [−ART] L1s. Since in this chapter we are particularly concerned with the role of cross-linguistic influence, we will confine the rest of our discussion to studies of elicited production.

Whereas article omission by learners from [−ART] L1s is potentially attributable to cross-linguistic influence, there have been different explanations for article misuse in this population. Early SLA studies of article errors adopted the semantic wheel of Bickerton (1981) and the subsequent taxonomy of Huebner (1983), in which noun phrases (NPs) are classified based on two features: [+/− specific reference (+/−SR)] and [+/− assumed known to hearer (+/−HK)]. Studies conducted in this framework have disagreed on which feature combination(s) present the most difficulty to learners: e.g., Huebner (1983) and Master (1987) argue that L2-English learners associate *the* with the [+HK] feature, whereas Parrish (1987) and Thomas (1989) found that overuse of *the* by learners from [−ART] L1s occurs primarily with [+SR, −HK] indefinites, indicating that the [+SR] feature also matters. One problem with the Bickertonian framework, discussed by Ionin (2003), is that the [SR] feature is not clearly defined; it appears to correspond to the concept of *assertion of existence* (cf. Matthewson 1998), i.e., a [+SR] NP denotes a specific referent asserted to exist in the actual world.

Ionin (2003) (see also Ionin 2006; Ionin et al. 2004) proposes a different semantics of specificity than that assumed in the Bickertonian framework. For Ionin, specificity corresponds not to assertion of existence but rather to *speaker intent to refer* (a concept from the analysis of referential indefinites in Fodor & Sag 1982); this proposal is supported by cross-linguistic data showing that some languages encode specificity as speaker intent to refer in their determiner systems. On Ionin's proposal, L2-English learners from [−ART] L1s assume that the English definite article marks either definiteness (which requires both speaker and hearer knowledge) or specificity (which marks speaker intent to refer); until input informs learners that *the* marks definiteness rather than specificity, learners fluctuate between the two options. Ionin et al. (2004) tested this hypothesis by means of a written forced-choice elicitation task in which participants had to choose *the*, *a(n)*, or the zero article for the target noun. Consistent with the hypothesis, Ionin et al. (2004) found that learners overused *the* with specific indefinites such as (1) significantly more than with non-specific indefinites such as (2). Both contexts are indefinite in that the friend is new information not previously available to the hearer. At the same time, the speaker intends to refer to a specific individual in (1) but not in (2): only in the former is the identity of the friend important. Note that a particular friend is asserted to exist in both instances, and both instances would be classified as [+SR, −HK] in the Bickertonian framework, which would thus not be able to account for the greater overuse of *the* in (1) than in (2).

(1) *example of a specific indefinite from Ionin et al. (2004)*. Meeting on a street.
Roberta: Hi, William! It's nice to see you again. I didn't know you were in Boston.
William: I am here for a week. *I am visiting (a, the, –) friend from college – his name is Sam Bolton, and he lives in Cambridge now.*

(2) *example of a non-specific indefinite from Ionin et al. (2004)*
Chris: I need to find your roommate Jonathan right away.
Clara: He is not here – he went to New York.
Chris: Really? In what part of New York is he staying?

Clara: I don't really know. *He is staying with (a, the, –) friend – but I have no idea who that is.* Jonathan didn't leave me any phone number or address.

The association between overuse of *the* and specificity as speaker intent to refer has been found for L2-English learners from different [–ART] L1s, including Russian and Korean (Ionin et al. 2004), Japanese (Hawkins et al. 2006), and Mandarin Chinese (Trenkic 2008), though explanations of this finding have varied (in particular, Trenkic [2008] argues that this overuse is due to an explicit cognitive strategy rather than to a semantic universal; see Ionin et al. 2009 for a response and for a proposal that incorporates both semantic universals and strategies). In contrast, L2-English learners from a [+ART] L1, such as Spanish, are found not to be influenced by specificity, correctly using *the* with definites only (Ionin et al. 2008).

A limitation of this prior research is that it has generally relied on fairly explicit tasks, such as forced choice or fill-in-the-blank, which draw participants' attention to articles;[1] these tasks tend to find both correct article use and article misuse but not much article omission. In contrast, a more free-form written narration task used by Ionin et al. (2004) found both article omission and overuse of *the* in place of *a* for L1-Russian and L1-Korean L2-English learners.

As discussed in Section 1, this chapter examines whether the findings from experimental studies have parallels in learner corpus research. In the next subsection, we review existing findings with learner corpora that provide evidence for the role of cross-linguistic influence, consistent with experimental studies.

2.2 Prior Corpus-Based Studies on Articles in Learner English

Both competence and performance of article use have been analyzed using a variety of methods (e.g., Murphy 1997; Butler 2002; E.-H. Lee 2007; Sarker & Baek 2017). In the LCR literature, Computer-aided Error Analyses (CEAs) (Dagneaux, Denness, & Granger 1998), in which a general overview of the type and frequency of errors made by students at a certain level is provided, have revealed that the article

[1] It is of course possible to use more implicit experimental methods, such as online reaction-time measures, to examine article use. Kim & Lakshmanan (2009) did just this, using self-paced reading to examine the effects of specificity in processing; the results were largely inconclusive.

system is problematic for both [+ART] and [−ART] L1 learners of English (see, for instance, Izumi et al. 2003; Díez-Bedmar 2005, 2010b, 2011b; Kaszubski 2005; Prat Zagrebelsky 2005; Hasbún 2007; Chuang & Nesi 2008; MacDonald, García-Carbonell, & Carot-Siertta 2013; Abu-Melhim 2014; Crosthwaite 2016). On some occasions the Contrastive Interlanguage Analysis (CIA)[2] (Granger 1996, 2015) has been complemented with a corpus-based or literature-based Contrastive Analysis (CA) so that an Integrated Contrastive Model (Granger 1996; Gilquin 2000/2001) has also provided useful information (see, for instance, Díez-Bedmar & Papp 2008).[3]

[−ART] L1 learners of English show more problems in the use of the article system than [+ART] L1 learners of English, as can be seen in a number of CIAs which have analyzed learners' uses of articles in obligatory contexts and target-like uses (Pica 1983). These studies have looked at English article use by Spanish and Japanese learners (Trademan 2002), Finnish and Swedish learners (Jarvis 2002), and Spanish and Chinese learners (Díez-Bedmar & Papp 2008), the latter study also providing a comparison of the production of both learner groups with the native variety (L1 English) and contrastive analyses in an Integrated Contrastive Model (Granger 1996). These studies have found overuse of the zero article in generic contexts and underuse of the indefinite and zero articles in those contexts. Other CIAs have also compared the use of the article system by learners of English from [−ART] L1s, such as Mandarin Chinese, Korean, and Thai (Crosthwaite 2016).

Most studies to date provide information on those articles that pose more problems to learners of English, many of them leaving out the analysis of the zero article due to the difficulty of retrieving such instances from learner corpora automatically. Thus, the pseudo-longitudinal findings of J. Lee (2013) reveal that the indefinite article is the most problematic article in both oral and written narratives, although oral productions show more errors overall. Narita (2013) reports that the definite article poses more problems to learners because of its overuse as the level increases (from beginner to advanced), while the opposite happens with indefinite articles. However, these studies do not consider the zero article.

The learner-corpus-based analyses which have examined the tentative reasons behind learners' problems with the article system have

[2] In a CIA, two types of comparisons are possible. The first one involves the study of production by two learner groups. The second one consists of a comparison of learner language with a reference language variety.

[3] In an Integrated Contrastive Model two analyses are conducted, a CA and a CIA.

used the semantic-pragmatic features of speaker reference and hearer knowledge following the semantic wheel of Bickerton (1981) and the subsequent taxonomy of Huebner (1983), described in Section 2.1 (see, for instance, Leńko-Szymańska 2012 with Polish students; Díez-Bedmar & Papp 2008 with Chinese and Spanish students; Díez-Bedmar 2010b, 2015a, and Díez-Bedmar & Pérez-Paredes 2012 with Spanish students; Crosthwaite 2016 with Mandarin Chinese, Korean, and Thai students).

The studies on Spanish learners of English show that article errors are among the top five errors up to CEFR B2 level. In fact, statistically significant decreases in the mean rate of article errors are only found from CEFR B1+ onwards (Díez-Bedmar 2010a, 2015a). The most problematic aspects for Spanish learners are found in the use of the zero article in generic contexts (Díez-Bedmar & Papp 2008; Díez-Bedmar 2010b; Díez-Bedmar & Pérez Paredes 2012), as well as in non-referential contexts (Díez-Bedmar & Pérez Paredes 2012), as learners tend to incorrectly introduce the definite article in such contexts where the zero article would be correct. In fact, a comparison of learners' use of articles at various CEFR levels reveals that there is a statistically significant difference between B1 and B2 levels in the learners' accurate use of the zero article in non-referential contexts, this being one of the criterial features found between B1 and B2 levels. No changes are found, however, in the accurate use of the zero article in generic contexts (Díez-Bedmar 2015a).

The accuracy order in the acquisition of the article system by learners of English has also been a matter of analysis in LCR. As summarized by Díez-Bedmar (2015b), studies have yielded different results, probably because of the various tasks learners undertake and learners' proficiency levels. In all cases, even in the publication of Crosthwaite (2016) with pseudo-longitudinal data, the findings obtained contradicted Master's (1987) and Thomas's (1989) accuracy orders of article acquisition for [+ART] and [−ART] L1 language learners. Owing to the importance of analyzing the use of articles considering the context in which they are employed, Díez-Bedmar (2015a) included a cross-sectional analysis of the accuracy of use. The results obtained indicate that the definite article in referential definite contexts and the zero and indefinite articles in non-referential contexts show a higher accuracy of use than the zero article in referential indefinite contexts at A2 and B1 levels. At B2 level the difference found is that the accuracy of use of the indefinite article in non-referential contexts is not higher than that of the zero article in referential indefinite contexts.

2.3 Comparing the Methods

Both LCR and experimental approaches have their advantages as well as their limitations. Here, we discuss them in reference to the study of articles in L2 learners' productions.

On the one hand, in learner corpora, semi-authentic data produced by the learner are used, so the researcher has no control over the contexts in which learners use articles, which means that certain types of article uses never or rarely show up in the data (see, for instance, Díez-Bedmar 2015a). This is not a problem for experimental studies, where equal numbers of tokens per condition are elicited. However, a major disadvantage of many controlled studies is that learners are asked to explicitly focus on article use, and the researchers may not be obtaining information about the learners' underlying, implicit knowledge or their real use of the language in a communicative situation. Even if an experimental study uses a methodology that targets more implicit knowledge (e.g., through the use of time pressure or focus on meaning rather than form – see Ellis 2005), it still does not obtain information about authentic, naturalistic article uses, which is what we obtain with learner corpora. Another advantage of learner corpora over experimental research is that they provide us with a rich body of data that can be analyzed in various ways. In an annotated corpus, a hierarchical annotation system allows the researchers to retrieve information depending on the degree of granularity of the research questions. For example, as will be discussed below, in the present paper, we analyzed both broad categories of article use and narrow uses of singular specific and non-specific indefinites.

2.4 Study Goals

The goals of this study are twofold. First, in light of the prior learner corpus studies on articles discussed in Section 2.2, this study examines English article use in two L1 learner groups (Russian and Spanish) at different proficiency levels, B1 and B2 following the CEFR (Council of Europe 2001) classification. In particular, by comparing learners whose L1 has articles (Spanish) to those whose L1 lacks articles (Russian) at two proficiency levels in comparable subcorpora (regarding text-type written and writing conditions), this study examines what effect the L1 has on article use and omission in learner corpora. While a transfer-based comparison has been made before (e.g., Díez-Bedmar & Papp 2008 with a Chinese/Spanish learner groups comparison), the present study is the first one, to the best of our knowledge, that looks at English articles in an L1-Russian learner corpus and compares them to English articles in an L1-Spanish learner corpus. In addition to making a novel comparison in terms of populations, this study considers two proficiency levels, B1 and B2, thus conducting a cross-sectional analysis of article use by these two populations. Furthermore, this study follows previous work (Díez-Bedmar & Papp 2008; Díez-Bedmar 2010b; Díez-Bedmar & Pérez Paredes 2012; Díez-Bedmar 2015a) in examining use (and misuse) of the zero article alongside that of *the* and *a*. As discussed above, corpus studies often leave out the zero article because of the difficulty of extracting it automatically. The present study uses manual extraction in order to examine the zero article.

Second, this study looks at whether overuse of *the* in the learner corpora analyzed is governed by the factor of *specificity as speaker intent to refer*, as has been found for elicited production data, discussed in Section 2.1. As discussed in Section 2.2, prior learner corpus studies have used the Bickertonian framework; in this work, we instead adopt the view of specificity as speaker intent to refer (from Ionin 2003, 2006) described in Section 2.1 and ask whether it is supported by learner corpus data.

3 Methodology

3.1 The Learner Corpus

The cross-sectional corpus used for this study is a subsection of 200 written texts from the *Cambridge Learner Corpus* at CEFR B1 and B2 levels (see Table 1).[4] In order to allow a comparison by both L1 and proficiency level, we selected texts from four groups: L1-Russian B1 proficiency, L1-Russian B2 proficiency, L1-Spanish B1 proficiency, and L1-Spanish B2 proficiency, thus compiling four subcorpora for this study. Only texts from the descriptive/creative autobiographical genre were selected, as we hypothesized that this text type would be most conducive to eliciting article use in the context of specificity, given that participants may write about people, places, and objects of importance to them (though, as described below, this did not happen to the extent that we expected). The texts were timed and written under exam conditions, as they were part of the Cambridge English examinations.

[4] This corpus contains the production by students from all over the world who have taken any of the Cambridge English exams. Nowadays, the *Cambridge Learner Corpus*, together with the *Cambridge English Profile Corpus*, is part of the monitor corpus *Cambridge English Corpus*.

Table 1 Number of texts, number of words, mean, and standard deviation in the corpus (by level and L1 background)

Tag field	Number of texts	Number of words	Mean (words per text)	Standard deviation
B1 Russian	50 (40 B1 Russian, 10 B1 Ukrainian)	5,666	113.32	28.775
B1 Spanish	50	5,764	115.28	18.060
B2 Russian	50	10,251	205.02	39.935
B2 Spanish	50	9,475	189.50	37.260
Total	**200**	**31,156**		

Fifty texts per group (i.e., per L1/proficiency combination) were selected at random and manually extracted from the *Cambridge Learner Corpus* via Sketch Engine by the second author.[5] In the case of L1-Russian learners at B1 level, however, only 40 texts in the target genre were available; we therefore made the decision to include 10 additional texts from L1-Ukrainian learners of English, in order to have the same number of texts (50) per group. This decision was driven by the fact that Russian and Ukrainian are closely related East Slavic languages which do not differ with regard to the target phenomenon: both languages lack articles but have other types of determiners (e.g., demonstratives and quantifiers), and both have relatively free word order which is used to establish concepts such as old vs. new information, which are commonly marked by articles in English. Furthermore, most if not all speakers of Ukrainian are also fluent (and in many cases bilingual) in Russian (see, e.g., Yevhen & Tomasz 2017).[6] Henceforth, when we refer to the "B1 Russian" group, we are referring to the full set of 50 texts

[5] The learners' whole texts (as opposed to individual sentences) were compiled and manually annotated for two reasons. The first one was to follow the compilation criteria in learner corpora (Granger 2008). The second was the need to have the texts in full to analyze how article use was affected by specificity, which requires attention to context, as described below.

[6] An anonymous reviewer asks whether this means that the Ukrainian participants were in fact learners of English as an L3. Since no biographical information is provided in the *Cambridge Learner Corpus*, we are unable to answer this question; however, it is indeed possible that the Ukrainian speakers in our corpus were Ukrainian/Russian bilinguals learning English as an L3. Given that Russian and Ukrainian are virtually identical with regard to the phenomenon in question, we do not see that this bilingualism would make any difference. Furthermore, there is no reason to think that the Ukrainian speakers were the only group acquiring English as an L3 rather than as an L2: we have no way of

which includes 40 texts from Russian speakers and ten texts from Ukrainian speakers.

The corpus that was analyzed contained 31,156 words across the 200 texts, as shown in Table 1. Other than proficiency level, no further information is available for each learner taking the exam regarding their knowledge of other L2s or crucial aspects such as possible learning disorders (Díez-Bedmar 2011a). Unfortunately, no information is available on the language history of the learners (other than their proficiency level), since this information is not offered by *Cambridge Learner Corpus.*

3.2 Annotation System

Once the cross-sectional learner corpus for this study had been extracted from the *Cambridge Learner Corpus* and the texts cleaned (metadata removed, etc.), a native speaker of English underlined all the nouns in the text and checked every noun with regard to accuracy in the use of articles, other determiners (such as quantifiers, demonstratives, and numerals), and the number of the noun as singular vs. plural (given that number crucially interacts with article use – e.g., the zero article is OK with a plural but not with a singular count noun). For the purposes of the present chapter, we report only on correct and incorrect uses of articles (*the*, *a*, and the zero article) and leave aside all other determiners. All dubious or uncertain cases were referred to a second native speaker; the second native speaker's judgment was taken as definitive.

A taxonomy was then designed by both authors to account for up to five variables in the use of NPs by learners of English. Different versions of the taxonomy were piloted on a small subset of the texts until a final version of the taxonomy was determined that accounted for all uses of articles and nouns in the text. The corpus was then manually annotated by the first author using this taxonomy.

Each NP was tagged with a complex tag consisting of up to five fields, as illustrated in Table 2. The first field indicated whether the NP was entirely correct or contained an error (the error could be in the misuse or omission of a determiner, or in the misuse or omission of plural marking). The second field indicated the nature of the determiner that was used, such as definite (marked by def_), indefinite (marked by ind_), or no determiner (marked by bare_). A number of other options

knowing whether any of the L1 Russian or L1 Spanish students in the corpus had acquired another language prior to learning English.

Table 2 Tagging variables with examples of tags

Tag field	1	2	3	4	5
explanation	correct or not	category	article used/ should be	type and plurality	linguistic context
correct	c_	ind_, def_, bare_, and other categories (dem_, num_, poss_, wh_, etc.)	the_ , a_, zero_, this_, etc.	sg_, pl_, ms_, prsg_, etc.	e.g., pred_ (predicative), ws_ (wide scope), there_ (there-construction), etc.
incorrect	i_		the/a_, the/ zero_, a/zero_, zero/the_, etc.	sg/pl, pl/ ms, etc.	

were available for this field, including wh_ (for wh-determiners such as *which*), num_ (for numerals), and poss_ (for possessive pronouns). For the purpose of the present study, however, we focus exclusively on the tags def_, ind_, and bare_.

The third field indicated what determiner was actually used: the tag the_ indicates correct use of the definite article; the tag a_ indicates correct use of the indefinite article; the tag zero_ indicates correct lack of article.[7] If the determiner used was coded as incorrect, it was followed by a slash and the target article. Incorrect uses correspond to inappropriate uses of the article in place of another article: incorrect *the* corresponds to uses of *the* in place of *a* (the/a_) or zero (the/zero_), incorrect *a* corresponds to uses of *a* in place of *the* (a/the_) or zero (a/zero_), and incorrect zero corresponds to omission of *the* (zero/the_) or *a* (zero/a_).

The fourth field indicated the status of the noun as proper or common, and count or mass, and also indicated the use of plural marking; we will not discuss this field in this study, since our focus is on article use rather than on plurality. Finally, the fifth field provided detailed information about the linguistic context. For the bulk of our analysis, we do not consider field #5 at all, focusing only on fields #1 and #3 (i.e., focusing on the form of the article used as indefinite,

[7] We take no stand in this chapter as to whether the lack of an overt article, both grammatical (e.g., *I like books*) and ungrammatical (e.g., *I saw cat*), should be analyzed as the presence of a zero article or as the lack of an article (=article omission). Our terminology is intended to be purely descriptive, so that zero_ indicates that there is no overt determiner present.

definite, or zero, and examining whether this article was correct). We consider field #5 in the last part of our analysis, where we investigate specific vs. non-specific indefinites (see Section 3.4).

Examples of correct as well as incorrect uses of definite, indefinite, and zero articles are given in (3).

(3) a. Correct use of *the*: Chubby, arrogant and filthy wee **the [c_def_the_pl_post] words** that described him best. [576283_2, B2 Spanish]

b. Incorrect use of *the*: We met at **the [i_def_the/a_sg_noscope] rock concert** four years ago. [2669361_2, B1 Russian]

c. Correct use of *a*: I live in **a [c_ind_a_sg_noscope] small village** ... [2802271_2, B1 Spanish]

d. Incorrect use of a: I bought ***a* [i_ind_a/zero_pl_noscope] tickets** ... [574410, B1 Russian]

e. Correct use of zero: This wonderful resort attracts **[c_bare_zero_pl_gen] tourists** from the whole Europe ... [584751_2, B2 Russian]

f. Incorrect use of zero [=article omission]: He was **[i_bare_zero/a_sg_pred] very cruel man** ... [587676_2, B2 Russian]

For reasons of space, in (3) we provide only the extract that contains the sample article use. In the course of the annotating, however, attention was paid to the context surrounding the example. For example, out of context, (3b) looks like use of *the rock concert* could be correct; however, in light of the context (which made no prior mention of any rock concert, and brought up the concert out of the blue), the native speakers determined that *the* did not sound appropriate and that *a* was the better choice. For the fifth tag, the first author also relied on the context in order to make the determination of the linguistic properties of the NP in question. Section 3.4 discusses how this determination was made in the case of specific and non-specific indefinites.

3.3 Statistical Analyses

Inferential statistical analyses were run by the second author on the total number of words and total number of articles produced by both learner groups per level. The rest of the inferential statistical analyses in this study were conducted on normalized uses of articles per 100 words per text, as we were interested in analyzing the learners' selection of articles as a means to express semantic nuances in their texts per L1 background and level.

Since the data were non-normally distributed ($p < .001$ on the Kolmogorov–Smirnov test and Levene's test), non-parametric tests were run (Kruskal–Wallis and Mann–Whitney), with Bonferroni corrections for multiple comparisons. We report the effect sizes for each significant result (significance calculated at the alpha level of .05 with a Bonferroni correction for multiple comparisons where relevant), following the cut-off points in Cohen (1988) (where $r < .29$ is a small effect size, $.29 < r < .49$ is a medium effect size and $r > .5$ is a large effect size).

3.4 Operationalization of (Non-)Specificity

As discussed in Section 2.1, prior experimental research has found that L1-Russian L2-English learners (as well as L2-English learners from other article-less L1s) overuse *the* with specific indefinites significantly more than with non-specific indefinites. In contrast, L1-Spanish L2-English learners exhibit very little overuse of *the* with indefinites and do not show any effect of specificity. In order to examine whether the same patterns would hold up in semi-authentic learner writing, we coded indefinites with regard to specificity. We focus on singular indefinites only, and examine correct *a* uses (tag c_ind_a_sg_) and incorrect *the* overuses (tag i_def_the/a_sg_). Additionally, we restrict our attention to those contexts that can be classified as either +specific or −specific. The decision to restrict our attention to singular indefinites is driven by the fact that the experimental literature on specificity effects with indefinites in SLA also focuses almost exclusively on singulars (but see Ionin 2003 for evidence that specificity effects are also visible with plurals, although they are not as pronounced).

We operationalized (non-)specificity as follows, based on the discussion by Ionin (2003), where specificity is treated as *speaker intent to refer* (see Section 2.1). An indefinite was classified as non-specific if it occurred in the scope of another scope-bearing expression (4a), inside a *there*-construction (4b), or as the object of the verb *have* (4c). These are contexts that are in general known to be incompatible with specificity (e.g., specificity markers such as *a certain* are impossible with narrow scope and usually infelicitous in *there* and *have* constructions; see Ionin 2003 for more discussion).

(4) Types of non-specific indefinite uses:

a. the indefinite takes narrow scope under an operator: . . . you and we can organize a **[c_ind_a_sg_ns]** beautiful party. [2807330, B1 Russian]

b. the indefinite occurs inside a *there*-construction: . . . there is a **[c_ind_a_sg_there]** village with a small church . . . [762101, B2 Spanish]

c. the indefinite is an object of *have*: But I have a **[c_ind_a_sg_have]** special friend called Cristina. [2672640, B1 Spanish]

We operationalized an indefinite as specific if it takes scope over another scope-bearing element, as in (5a), where the writer has a specific place that she wants to tell the reader about. Indefinites were also classified as specific by exclusion, as in (5b), if they occurred in a sentence with no other scope-bearing elements, did not occur inside *there* or *have* constructions, and did not fit into any other annotated category (which included indefinites in predicate position, indefinites as object of certain prepositions, and generic uses of indefinites). There is no way to know for certain whether such indefinites are indeed specific or non-specific: in (5b), it is possible that the writer has as specific problem in mind that he or she wants to tell the reader about, but it is also possible that the writer does not know much, or anything, about the problem. All we know is that a context such as (5b) is in principle compatible with specificity.

(5) Types of specific indefinite uses:
  a. the indefinite takes wide scope over an operator: I want to tell you about a [**c_ind_a_sg_ws**] place I visited last week. [574410, B1 Russian]
  b. the indefinite occurs in a sentence with no other scope-bearing operators, and does not fit into other annotated categories of indefinites: Pat caused a [**c_ind_a_sg_noscope**] big, but stupid problem. [758017, B2 Spanish]

While only extracts are provided in (4) and (5), the determination of (non-)specificity required the first author to pay attention to context. For example in (4a), it was clear from the context that no specific party was being discussed, while in (5a), it was clear from the context that there is a particular place that the writer wants to tell the reader about.

We note that the view of specificity being tested here is different from the standard Bickertonian definition of 'specific reference' (see Section 2.1); in Bickerton's framework, only the NP type in (4a), where no referent is asserted to exist, would be classified as [−SR], while all the other types exemplified in (4) and (5) would be classified as [+SR].

4 Analysis and Results

As Table 1 shows, the two groups at the B2 level used about twice as many words as the two groups at the B1 level: i.e., the higher-level groups wrote longer narratives, which correspondingly gave rise to more contexts for article use, as shown in the means in both learner groups. In fact, the results of the Kruskal–Wallis test showed that there were statistically significant differences among the groups regarding the mean number of words per text and the mean number of articles used per text ($H(3) = 129.639$, $p < .001$; $H(3) = 118.677$, $p < .001$, respectively). Subsequent Mann–Whitney tests, followed by Bonferroni corrections, showed that the differences are statistically significant from B1 to B2 in both learner groups regarding the mean number of words per text and level ($U = 89.500$, $z = -8.001$, $p < .001$; $U = 90.500$, $z = -7.994$, $p < .001$, for Russian and Spanish learners, respectively; $r = .80$ in both learner groups) and the mean number of articles per text and level ($U = 64.000$, $z = -8.184$, $p < .001$; $U = 287.000$, $z = -6.646$; $p < .001$, for Russian and Spanish learners, respectively, $r = .82$ for Russian learners, $r = .66$ for Spanish ones).

In Table 3, we report the medians and interquartile ranges (IQRs) of the overall article uses, the overall number of correct and incorrect

Table 3 Medians and IQRs of correct and incorrect article uses, by level and L1 background

	B1 Russian	**B1 Spanish**	**B2 Russian**	**B2 Spanish**
Total uses	Mdn = 9.00 (IQR = 6)	Mdn = 10.00 (IQR = 6)	Mdn = 25.50 (IQR = 10)	Mdn = 20.50 (IQR = 13)
Total correct	Mdn = 8.50 (IQR = 5)	Mdn = 10.00 (IQR = 7)	Mdn = 23.50 (IQR = 10)	Mdn = 19.50 (IQR = 12)
Total incorrect	Mdn = 1.00 (IQR = 2)	Mdn = 0.00 (IQR = 1)	Mdn = 2.00 (IQR = 3)	Mdn = 6.00 (IQR = 5)
Correct *the*	Mdn = 2.00 (IQR = 2)	Mdn = 3.00 (IQR = 4)	Mdn = 8.00 (IQR = 8)	Mdn = 6.00 (IQR = 5)
Incorrect *the*	Mdn = 0.00 (IQR = 1)	Mdn = 0.00 (IQR = 0)	Mdn = 0.00 (IQR = 1)	Mdn = 0.00 (IQR = 1)
Correct *a*	Mdn = 1.50 (IQR = 3)	Mdn = 2.00 (IQR = 3)	Mdn = 5.00 (IQR = 5)	Mdn = 4.50 (IQR = 5)
Incorrect *a*	Mdn = 0.00 (IQR = 0)	Mdn = 0.00 (IQR = 0)	Mdn = 0.00 (IQR = 0)	Mdn = 0.00 (IQR = 0)
Correct *zero*	Mdn = 4.00 (IQR = 4)	Mdn = 4.00 (IQR = 4)	Mdn = 9.00 (IQR = 7)	Mdn = 8.00 (IQR = 7)
Incorrect *zero*	Mdn = 0.00 (IQR = 1)	Mdn = 0.00 (IQR = 0)	Mdn = 1.00 (IQR = 2)	Mdn = 0.00 (IQR = 0)

Table 4 Normalized data: medians and IQRs (article uses per 100 words, text and level)

	B1 Russian	B1 Spanish	B2 Russian	B2 Spanish
Total uses	Mdn = 8.89 (IQR = 7.90)	Mdn = 12.09 (IQR = 7.85)	Mdn = 52.27 (IQR = 33.27)	Mdn = 40.17 (IQR = 27.13)
Total correct	Mdn = 8.46 (IQR = 8.04)	Mdn = 11.22 (IQR = 8.76)	Mdn = 45.67 (IQR = 31.35)	Mdn = 38.31 (IQR = 27.36)
Total incorrect	Mdn = 0.97 (IQR = 1.90)	Mdn = 0.00 (IQR = 1.16)	Mdn = 4.18 (IQR = 5.91)	Mdn = 0.74 (IQR = 2.96)
Correct *the*	Mdn = 1.98 (IQR = 2.33)	Mdn = 3.43 (IQR = 3.95)	Mdn = 15.97 (IQR = 19.55)	Mdn = 11.78 (IQR = 10.67)
Incorrect *the*	Mdn = 0.00 (IQR = 0.96)	Mdn = 0.00 (IQR = 0.00)	Mdn = 0.00 (IQR = 2.59)	Mdn = 0.00 (IQR = 1.60)
Correct *a*	Mdn = 1.33 (IQR = 3.00)	Mdn = 2.46 (IQR = 3.62)	Mdn = 11.84 (IQR = 12.23)	Mdn = 8.18 (IQR = 10.09)
Incorrect *a*	Mdn = 0.00 (IQR = 0.00)	Mdn = 0.00 (IQR = 3.00)	Mdn = 0.00 (IQR = 0.00)	Mdn = 0.00 (IQR = 0.00)
Correct *zero*	Mdn = 4.26 (IQR = 5.57)	Mdn = 4.00 (IQR = 5.33)	Mdn = 16.72 (IQR = 15.44)	Mdn = 14.97 (IQR = 15.60)
Incorrect *zero*	Mdn = 0.00 (IQR = 1.15)	Mdn = 0.00 (IQR = 0.00)	Mdn = 1.95 (IQR = 4.60)	Mdn = 0.00 (IQR = 0.00)

uses, and the correct and incorrect uses for each article (*the*, *a*, and zero); in Table 4, we report the normalized data on article use per 100 words, as we wanted to analyze the learners' use of articles to express semantic nuances in texts.

4.1 Broad Categories of Article Use

In order to meet our first research goal, i.e., to examine the effects that both proficiency level and L1 background have on learners' article use, the second author ran a Kruskal–Wallis test on the normalized data for each category and applied the Bonferroni correction. The four groups were found to differ significantly on correct uses of *the*, *a*, and the zero article ($H(3) = 110.134$, $p < .001$; $H(3) = 82.692$, $p < .001$; $H(3) = 89.919$, $p < .001$, respectively), as well as on incorrect uses of *the* and the zero article ($H(3) = 18.189$, $p < .001$; $H(3) = 30.509$, $p < .001$, respectively).

In order to pin down the sources of group differences, follow-up Mann–Whitney tests with a Bonferroni correction were conducted, comparing the B1 and B2 levels within the Spanish group, the B1 and B2 levels within the Russian group, the two L1 groups at B1 level, and the two L1 groups at B2 level. Both level and L1 background were found to affect performance, but in somewhat different ways. We address each in turn.

4.1.1 EFFECTS OF PROFICIENCY LEVEL

As noted in the previous section, for both the Spanish and the Russian groups, the B2 group produced significantly more articles per 100 words, as well as significantly more words overall, than the B1 group. We now examine the different types of article uses in more detail.

The B2 Spanish group produced significantly more correct uses of all three article types, per 100 words, than the B1 Spanish group ($U = 312.000$, $z = -6.47$, $p < .001$, $r = .65$ for correct *the*; $U = 587.000$, $z = -4.571$, $p < .001$, $r = .46$ for correct *a*; $U = 288.000$, $z = -6.632$, $p < .001$, $r = .66$ for correct zero, the correct definite and the correct zero having large effect sizes, and the correct indefinite having a medium to large effect size), but there were no significant differences in the number of incorrect uses. Given that the median of correct article uses per 100 words is more than three times as high in B2 as in B1, the fact that the number of errors remains stable indirectly suggests that accuracy improves with proficiency for the Spanish group.

For the Russian group, the effect of level is somewhat different: as in the case of the Spanish group, the B2 Russian group produces significantly more correct uses per 100 words of all three article types than the B1 Russian group ($U = 100.000$, $z = -7.930$, $p < .001$, $r = .79$ for correct *the*; $U = 176.000$, $z = -7.417$, $p < .001$, $r = .74$ for correct *a*; $U = 274.000$, $z = -6.728$, $p < .001$, $r = .67$ for correct zero, with large effect sizes in all cases). Additionally, however, the B2 Russian group produces significantly more incorrect instances of the definite article ($U = 880.500$, $z = -2.941$, $p = .003$, $r = .29$) and the zero article ($U = 763.000$, $z = -2.605$, $p < .001$, $r = .36$) than the B1 group, although with low and medium effect sizes, respectively. This means that for the Russian group, as proficiency goes up, and more articles are produced per 100 words per text, article omission and misuse go up as well; this in turn indirectly suggests that, with regard to article errors, accuracy does not improve with proficiency.

4.1.2 EFFECTS OF L1 BACKGROUND

Turning to the effect of L1 background, we find that at the B1 level, the Spanish group produced significantly more instances of correct *the* (U = 852.500, z = -2.743, p = .006, r = .27) as well as correct *a* (U = 880.500, z = −2.554, p = .011, r = .25) than the Russian group, although with low effect sizes. The two B1 groups did not differ with regard to the zero article or with regard to incorrect uses. The fact that the Spanish group exhibited more correct uses per 100 words and text than the Russian group, while the two groups had comparable rates of incorrect uses, indicates an advantage for the Spanish group in the correct use of overt articles.

Interestingly, at the B2 level, the Russian and Spanish groups did not differ on any category, with a single exception: the Russian group exhibited significantly more uses (per 100 words and text) of incorrect zero article than did the Spanish group, with a medium effect size (U = 696.000, z = −4.284, p < .001, r = .43). Thus, while the two B2 groups are similar in their correct article uses, article omission (that is, use of the zero article) persists for the Russian group.

Overall, the broad results are consistent with the effects of L1 transfer from a language with overt articles (Spanish) vs. without (Russian). Correct uses of overt articles are more common for Spanish than for Russian speakers at lower proficiency (B1 level), while article omission is more common for Russian speakers than for Spanish speakers at higher proficiency (B2 level).

4.2 Specific Categories of Article Use: Specificity

As discussed earlier, the second goal of our study was to examine whether specificity *as speaker intent to refer* influences *the* overuse in semi-authentic learner writing, and whether this is specific to learners from an article-less L1. Based on prior experimental studies, we make two specific predictions, given in (6).

(6) Prediction 1: In learner writing, there is more overuse of *the* in place of *a* from L1-Russian than from L1-Spanish L2-English learners.
Prediction 2: Overuse of *the* in place of *a* from L1-Russian L2-English learners is greater with specific than with non-specific indefinites.

These predictions were tested by looking at all instances of correct *a* and incorrect *the* uses with singular indefinites, as described in detail in Section 3.4.

4.2.1 QUANTITATIVE RESULTS

The overall numbers of both correct and incorrect uses of overt articles with singular indefinites in the learner corpora were rather low, as shown in Table 5 for the raw numbers and Table 6 for the normalized uses per 100 words and text.

The Kruskal–Wallis test showed that, across all groups, there were statistically significant differences for the correct uses of overt articles with specific indefinites ($H(3) = 39.863$, $p < .001$) and non-specific

Table 5 Specific and non-specific indefinites: total number of uses, by level and L1 background

	c_ind_a_sg_ specific	*i_def_the/a_sg_ specific*	*c_ind_a_sg_ non_specific*	*i_def_the/a_sg_ non_specific*
B1 Russian	26	4	34	6
B1 Spanish	61	2	42	0
B2 Russian	103	9	59	7
B2 Spanish	82	1	60	0

Table 6 Specific and non-specific indefinites: medians and IQRs of correct and incorrect uses per 100 words and text, by level and L1 background

	c_ind_a_sg_ specific	*i_def_the/a_sg_ specific*	*c_ind_a_sg_ non_specific*	*i_def_the/a_sg_ non_specific*
B1 Russian	Mdn = 0.0000 (IQR = 1.12)	Mdn = 0.0000 (IQR = 0.00)	Mdn = 0.0000 (IQR = 1.31)	Mdn = 0.0000 (IQR = 0.00)
B1 Spanish	Mdn = 1.0900 (IQR = 2.18)	Mdn = 0.0000 (IQR = 0.00)	Mdn = 1.0150 (IQR = 1.25)	Mdn = 0.0000 (IQR = 0.00)
B2 Russian	Mdn = 3.5600 (IQR = 7.62)	Mdn = 0.0000 (IQR = 0.00)	Mdn = 1.7100 (IQR = 3.81)	Mdn = 0.0000 (IQR = 0.00)
B2 Spanish	Mdn = 2.0150 (IQR = 5.90)	Mdn = 0.0000 (IQR = 0.00)	Mdn = 1.8200 (IQR = 3.91)	Mdn = 0.0000 (IQR = 0.00)

indefinites ($H(3) = 14.199$, $p = .003$), as well as for the incorrect uses of *the* with non-specific indefinites ($H(3) = 11.845$, $p = .008$), but no significant difference with regard to incorrect uses of *the* with specific indefinites. Further Mann–Whitney tests were run to follow up the significant results. (Throughout this section, only significant effects are reported, owing to space limitations.)

For correct uses of *a* with specific indefinites, there were significantly more uses in the B1 Spanish group than the B1 Russian group ($U = 901.5000$, $z = -2.604$, $p = .009$, $r = .26$), with a small effect size, and also significantly more uses in the B2 Russian group than the B1 Russian group ($U = 519.000$, $z = -5.304$, $p < .001$, $r = .53$), with a large effect size. Furthermore, there were more uses by the B2 Spanish group than by their B1 counterparts ($U = 830.000$, $z = -2.954$, $p = .003$, r $= .29$), with a small to medium effect size. Thus, correct use of specific indefinites per 100 words increases from B1 to B2 levels in the case of both Russian and Spanish learners. For correct uses of *a* with non-specific indefinites, there was only one difference among the groups ($U = 874.500$, $z = -2.745$, $p = .006$, $r = .27$), found in the production by B1 and B2 Russian students, with a small effect size, with the B2 group showing more such correct uses per 100 words.

Turning to the incorrect use of *the* with specific indefinites, no statistical differences were found among groups, even though numerically the Russian groups showed a greater rate of misuse. In the case of incorrect use of *the* with non-specific indefinites, the Spanish learners made no errors at all. The only difference found is between the Russian and the Spanish B2 groups, with the Russian learners showing more incorrect uses of *the* with non-specific indefinites than their Spanish counterparts ($U = 1214.000$, $z = -2.416$, $p = .016$, $r = .25$), with a small effect size.

Thus, we see that the predictions in (6) are only partially supported. We first consider Prediction 1, on which more errors were expected from the Russian groups than the Spanish groups. Numerically, the Russian groups did indeed produce more overuse of *the* per 100 words and text than the Spanish groups at the same level of proficiency; however, most of these differences did not reach significance, with the single exception of *the* overuse with non-specific indefinites at the B2 level, with a small effect size, which suggests that the effect is weak. Furthermore, at the B1 level, the Spanish group produced significantly more correct uses of *a* with specific indefinites than the Russian group, although the small effect size again indicates that the L1 effect is weak. Thus, Prediction 1 was partially supported.

With regard to Prediction 2, there was no effect of specificity, for any group of learners, so this prediction was not supported.

4.2.2 QUALITATIVE RESULTS: THE ROLE OF CONTEXT

The inferential statistical analysis fails to fully support the predictions of *the* overuse, as noted above; this could well be due to the fact that the overall rate of *the* overuse in both groups is fairly small. We next asked what could lie behind the cases of *the* overuse in both [+specific] and [−specific] contexts that we do find: that is, did overuse of *the* in both types of contexts have the same characteristics? According to Ionin (2003, 2006), specific indefinites are often (though by no means always) accompanied by some indication that the speaker knows some important/noteworthy property of the referent. For example, if a speaker states *I read a really interesting and exciting book*, the object NP is more likely to be [+specific] than if the speaker simply states *I read a book*: in the former case, the adjectival modification suggests that the speaker intends to refer to a particular book of importance. Such additional information can be conveyed through adjectival modification, through relative clause modification, and/or about further mention of the referent later on in the discourse. In contrast, the prototypical non-specific indefinite is an NP with no modification and no further mention.

Looking in detail at each case of *the* overuse reported in Table 7, we examined whether it involved modification and/or further mention in the text. The numbers are too small to allow for statistical analysis, so we report only the descriptive results.

As shown in Table 7, overuse of *the* with the Spanish groups is virtually non-existent. In the case of the Russian groups, and especially the B2 Russian group, which has the highest number of occurrences, a possible trend can be discerned: namely, *the* overuse with specific indefinites tends to involve additional information provided about the referent, while *the* overuse with non-specific indefinites does not.

Table 7 Properties of the *overuse in place of* a: *number of instances involving additional information about the referent, via modification and/or further mention*

	i_def_the/a_sg_specific		*i_def_the/a_sg_non_specific*	
	additional information provided	no additional information provided	additional information provided	no additional information provided
B1 Russian	2	2	2	4
B1 Spanish	2	0	0	0
B2 Russian	6	3	1	6
B2 Spanish	0	1	0	0

Examples are given in (7): while additional information is provided via the italicized modifying clause of *island* in (7a) and a reference back to the party in the italicized second sentence in (7b), there is no additional information provided about the volleyball match in (7c) or the reason in (7d) or the café in (7e).

(7) Examples of *the* overuse with vs. without additional information:

a. non-specific indefinite use, additional information provided via modification: So, he decided that it would be a good idea to find himself on **the [i_def_the/a_sg_ns] island** *where he'd be alone.* [578828_2, B2 Russian]

b. specific indefinite use, additional information provided via later mention: We first met at **the [i_def_the/a_sg_noscope] party** five years ago. *It was a wonderful party.* [2670239_2, B2 Russian]

c. specific indefinite use, no additional information: We went to **the [i_def_the/a_sg_noscope] volleyball match** yesterday. [2670239_2, B2 Russian]

d. non-specific indefinite use, no additional information: We have never quarelled, because we didn't have **the [i_def_the/a_sg_ns] reason** to [2669712_2, B1 Russian]

e. non-specific indefinite use, no additional information: Also, we can go to **the [i_def_the/a_sg_ns] caffe** and have a meal there or first talk to each other [26700044_2, B1 Russian]

The results are suggestive of the following trend: when *the* is overused with specific indefinites, the reason is indeed specificity as speaker intent to refer, as evidenced by the fact that the referent is described in some detail, either via a modifier or via later mention, and is important to the discourse; but when *the* is overused with non-specific indefinites, there is some other reason, which has nothing to do with importance for the discourse. For example, in (7e), the NP use was coded as narrow scope (hence [−specific]) because the writer is inviting a friend to go to any café, not any specific one; however, it is possible that the writer is attempting a generic use of *the café*, analogous to native English speakers' use of *the doctor* (as in, *I need to go to the doctor*). While some of the overuses of *the* with non-specific indefinites might be explained in this way, the overuses of *the* with specific indefinites do appear to be cases of the speaker intending to draw attention to a specific, important individual or entity, consistent with the analysis by Ionin (2003, 2006).[8] However, the results in Table 7 must be treated with caution, given that the numbers are very low.

[8] A possible follow-up analysis could look at every single *correct* use of *a* with specific vs. with non-specific indefinites and code it for the presence vs. absence of additional

5 Discussion

At the broad level, our findings are consistent with the effects of L1 transfer, and furthermore show how transfer interacts with proficiency. For the [+ART] L2-English learners, previous results concerning criterial features between B1 and B2 (Díez-Bedmar 2015a) are confirmed: the rate of correct article uses increases with proficiency, but there is no corresponding growth in article errors. In general, the Spanish group made very few errors of article use, at either level. In contrast, for the [−ART] L2-English learners, errors of article omission persist at B2 as well as B1 levels, suggesting little change with proficiency.

Turning to the effects of specificity on article misuse, the corpus findings only partially support prior experimental findings. Numerically, overuse of *the* in place of *a* is largely restricted to [−ART] learners, consistent with prior literature; however, most comparisons between the [−ART] and [+ART] groups fail to reach significance. As for the [+ART] learners, the current findings are consistent with previous learner-corpus-based research with Spanish learners of English (Díez-Bedmar & Pérez-Paredes 2012; Díez-Bedmar 2015a), which found limited overuse of the definite article with specific and non-specific indefinites, as well as a significant decrease of such errors with non-specific indefinites as the learners' command of English increases. However, it is important to be cautious when comparing the current results to those of Díez-Bedmar and Pérez-Paredes (2012) and Díez-Bedmar (2015a), since the concept of *specificity* was operationalized differently in those studies (which adopted the four contexts of article use in the Bickerton 1981/Huebner 1983 framework) and in the current study (which adopts the view of specificity from Ionin 2003, 2006).

While the [+ART] learners made almost no errors of *the* overuse with specific and no errors with non-specific indefinites, and the [−ART] learners did make such errors, no effects of specificity with the [−ART] learners are observed in the present corpus. As discussed in Section 4.2.2, there are some indications that the errors of *the* overuse with [+specific] vs. with [−specific] indefinites have different

information. The prediction is that, in the Russian groups, additional information (in the form of modification or later mention) would be more common when *the* is overused with specific indefinites than when *a* is used correctly. However, given how low the number of *the* overuses actually is, and given that correct *a* uses are ten times more frequent than *the* overuses in the normalized data of the Russian groups, this analysis would not yield meaningful results.

sources (only the former actually involve an association of *the* with *speaker intent to refer*). However, given how very low the overall numbers of *the* overuses are, we cannot say anything definitive on this matter.[9]

One question is why the instances of *the* overuse were so rare overall. A possible explanation is that there simply were not enough instances in the data where the learners were writing about people or entities of great importance to them, i.e., the kinds of contexts that were found to elicit *the* overuse in experimental studies. By selecting texts from the descriptive/creative autobiographical genre, we had hoped to maximize the possibility that learners would be writing about individuals or objects of importance to them. However, many of the texts were letters describing what the participant would like to do in the future, or made-up stories in which no particular importance was attached to any one individual. Thus, the participants chose topics which were not conducive to many instances of specific indefinites.

One way to maximize the possibility of participants writing about specific individuals or entities of importance is to provide participants with corresponding prompts. This is precisely what Ionin et al. (2004) did in an elicited narration task, where participants were asked, e.g., to write about valuable objects that they had once had. Ionin et al. (2004) did indeed find more overuse of *the* when learners were writing about objects and individuals that were well-known and important to the writer. In the present study, we sought to determine whether semi-naturalistic learner data, not obtained in the course of an experiment, would yield the same results. While the overall pattern of *the* overuse with indefinites was partially replicated with the corpus data, the effects of specificity were rather difficult to detect.

6 Conclusion

The overall aim of this study was to bring together LCR and SLA approaches to the study of articles in learner language. We have examined learner corpus data for errors of article omission and overuse of *the* with specific indefinites. The overall findings largely support

[9] We note that analyzing results in the Bickertonian framework would have led to even less definitive findings: given that only indefinites in the scope of an operator are considered [−SR] in this framework, only indefinites of the type exemplified in (4) would have been categorized as [−SR], while those in (4b–c) would have been [+SR], along with the types in (5). Thus, the vast majority of the indefinites would have been considered *specific* ([+SR]), hence making it nearly impossible to examine the relationship between specificity and article use, given how rare overuse of *the* was in the corpus.

the conclusions of experimental studies, but we also found that in corpus data, when learners are free to write on a variety of topics, they do not appear to use *the* to convey specificity.

In light of the advantages and limitations of both approaches (discussed in Section 2.3), it is particularly important to triangulate, using both learner corpus and experimental methods to examine the same linguistic phenomena. When corpus and experimental findings converge, the results are particularly convincing.

References

Abu-Melhim, A.-R. (2014). The presence or absence of definiteness in the native language and its impact on ESL Learning. *English Language Teaching* 7(1), 50–56.

Bickerton, D. (1981). *Roots of Language.* Ann Arbor, MI: Karoma Press.

Butler, Y. (2002). Second language learners' theories on the use of English articles: An analysis of the metalinguistic knowledge used by Japanese students in acquiring the English article system. *Studies in Second Language Acquisition* 24(3), 451–480. https://doi.org/10.1017/S0272263102003042

Cho, J. (2017). The acquisition of different types of definite noun phrases in L2-English. *International Journal of Bilingualism* 21(3), 367–382.

Chrabaszcz, A. & Jiang, N. (2014). The role of native language in the use of the English nongeneric definite article by L2 learners: A cross-linguistic comparison. *Second Language Research* 30, 351–379.

Chuang, F.-Y. & Nesi, H. (2008). An analysis of formal errors in a corpus of L2 English produced by Chinese students. *Corpora* 1(2), 251–271. https://doi.org/10.3366/cor.2006.1.2.251

Cohen, J. (1988). *Statistical Power Analysis for the Behavioral Sciences, 2nd Edn.* Hillsdale, NJ: Lawrence Erlbaum.

Council of Europe (2001). *Common European Framework of Reference for Languages: Learning, Teaching, Assessment.* Cambridge: Cambridge University Press.

Crosthwaite, P. (2016). L2 English article use by L1 speakers of article-less languages: A learner corpus study. *International Journal of Learner Corpus Research* 2(1), 68–100.

Dagneaux, E., Denness, S., & Granger, S. (1998). Computer-aided error analysis. *System* 26(2), 163–174. https://doi.org/10.1016/S0346-251X(98)00001-3

Díez-Bedmar, M. B. (2005). Struggling with English at University level: Error patterns and problematic areas of first-year students' interlanguage. In P. Danielsson & M. Wagenmakers (eds.), *Proceedings of Corpus Linguistics 2005*, retrieved from www.corpus.bham.ac.uk/PCLC/ (accessed June 13, 2020).

(2010a). Analysis of the Written Expression in English in the University Entrance Examination at the University of Jaén. Unpublished Ph.D. dissertation, University of Jaén.

(2010b). From secondary school to university: The use of the English article system by Spanish learners. In B. Belles-Fortuno, M. C. Campoy, & L. Gea-Valor (eds.), *Exploring Corpus Linguistics in English Language Teaching*, 45–55. Castellón: Publicacions de la Universitat Jaume I.

(2011a). Detecting learning disorders in students' written production in the foreign language: Are learner corpora of any help? *Porta Linguarum* 15, 35–54.

(2011b). Spanish pre-university students' use of English: CEA results from the University Entrance Examination. *International Journal of English Studies* 11(2), 141–158.

(2015a). Article use and criterial features in Spanish EFL writing: A pilot study from CEFR A2 to B2 levels. In M. Callies & S. Götz (eds.), *Learner Corpora in Language Testing and Assessment*, 163–190. Amsterdam: John Benjamins.

(2015b). The use of learner corpora to describe, teach and assess EFL writing: Focus on the article system. In E. Castello, K. Ackerley, & F. Coccetta (eds.), *Studies in Learner Corpus Linguistics: Research and Applications for Foreign Language Teaching and Assessment*, 37–69. Bern: Peter Lang.

Díez-Bedmar, M. B. & Papp, Sz. (2008). The use of the English article system by Chinese and Spanish learners. In G. Gilquin, S. Papp, & M. B. Díez-Bedmar (eds.), *Linking Up Contrastive and Learner Corpus Research*, 147–175. Amsterdam: Rodopi.

Díez-Bedmar, M. B. & Pérez-Paredes, P. (2012). A cross-sectional analysis of the use of the English articles in Spanish learner writing. In Y. Tono, Y. Kawaguchi, & M. Minegishi (eds.), *Developmental and Crosslinguistic Perspectives in Learner Corpus Research*, 139–157. Amsterdam: John Benjamins.

Ellis, R. (2005). Measuring implicit and explicit knowledge of a second language: A psychometric study. *Studies in Second Language Acquisition* 27(2), 141–172. https://doi.org/10.1017/S0272263105050096

Fodor, J. & Sag, I. (1982). Referential and quantificational indefinites. *Linguistics and Philosophy* 5, 355–398.

García-Mayo, M. & Hawkins, R. (2009). *Second Language Acquisition of Articles: Empirical Findings and Theoretical Implications*. Amsterdam: John Benjamins.

Gilquin, G. (2000/2001). The integrated contrastive model: Spicing up your data. *Languages in Contrast* 3(1), 95–123.

Goad, H. & White, L. (2009). Prosodic transfer and the representation of determiners in Turkish–English interlanguage. In N. Snape, Y.-k. I. Leung, & M. Sharwood Smith (eds.), *Representational Deficits in SLA: Studies in Honor of Roger Hawkins*, 1–26. Amsterdam: John Benjamins.

Granger, S. (1996). From CA to CIA and back: An integrated contrastive approach to computerized bilingual and learner corpora. In K. Aijmer, B. Altenberg, & M. Johansson (eds.), *Languages in Contrast: Text-Based Cross-Linguistic Studies*, 37–51. Lund: Lund University Press.

(2008). Learner corpora. In A. Lüdeling & M. Kytö (eds.), *Corpus Linguistics. An International Handbook*, 259–275. Berlin and New York, NY: Mouton de Gruyter.

(2015). Contrastive interlanguage analysis: A reappraisal. *International Journal of Learner Corpus Research* 1(1), 7–24.

Hasbún, L. H. (2007). Fossilization and acquisition: A study of learner language. *Filología y Lingüística* 33(1), 113–129.

Hawkins, R., Saleh Al-Eid, I., Almahboob, P., Athanasopoulos, R., Chaengchenkit, J., Rezai, M., ... Velasco-Zárate, K. (2006). Accounting for English article interpretation by L2 speakers. In S. Foster-Cohen, M. M. Krajnovic, & J. M. Djigunović (eds.), *EuroSLA Yearbook* 6, 7–25. Amsterdam: John Benjamins.

Huebner, T. (1983). *A Longitudinal Analysis of the Acquisition of English*. Ann Arbor, MI: Karoma Press.

Ionin, T. (2003). Article Semantics in Second Language Acquisition. Unpublished Ph.D. thesis, Massachusetts Institute of Technology.

(2006). This is definitely specific: Specificity and definiteness in article systems. *Natural Language Semantics* 14(2), 175–234. https://doi.org/10.1007/s11050-005-5255-9

Ionin, T., Ko, H., & Wexler, K. (2004). Article semantics in L2 acquisition: The role of specificity. *Language Acquisition* 12(1), 3–69.

Ionin, T., Zubizarreta, M., & Bautista Maldonado, S. (2008). Sources of linguistic knowledge in the second language acquisition of English articles. *Lingua* 118(4), 554–576.

Ionin, T., Zubizarreta, M., & Philippov, V. (2009). Acquisition of article semantics by child and adult L2-English learners. *Bilingualism: Language and Cognition* 12(3), 337–361. https://doi.org/10.1017/S1366728909990149

Izumi, E., Uchimoto, K., Saiga, T., Supnithi, T., & Isahara, H. (2003). Automatic error detection in the Japanese learners' English spoken data. In *Proceedings of 41st Annual Meeting of the Association for Computational Linguistics, Sapporo (Japan)*, 145–148. East Stroudsburg, PA: Association for Computational Linguistics.

Jarvis, S. (2002). Topic continuity in L2 English article use. *Studies in Second Language Acquisition* 24(3), 387–418. https://doi.org/10.1017/S0272263102003029

Kaszubski, P. (2005). Typical errors of Polish advanced EFL learner writers, retrieved from http://ifa.amu.edu.pl/~kprzemek/concord2adv/errors/errors.htm (accessed June 13, 2020).

Kim, L. K. & Lakshmanan, U. (2009). The processing role of the article choice parameter: Evidence from L2 learners of English. In M. d. P. García-Mayo & R. Hawkins (eds.), *Second Language Acquisition of Articles: Empirical Findings and Theoretical Implications*, 87–113. Amsterdam: John Benjamins.

Lee, E.-H. (2007). English Article Usage in Online Graduate Forums by Non-Native EFL Teachers. Unpublished D.Phil. dissertation, Indiana University.

Lee, J. (2013). The effects of discourse types on the use of English articles by Korean learners of English: Oral vs. written narratives. *English Language Teaching* 6(8), 33–43.

Leńko-Szymańska, A. (2012). The role of conventionalized language in the acquisition and use of articles by EFL learners. In Y. Tono, Y. Kawaguchi, & M. Minegishi (eds.), *Developmental and Crosslinguistic Perspectives in Learner Corpus Research*, 83–103. Amsterdam: John Benjamins.

MacDonald, P., García-Carbonell, A., & Carot-Siertta, J. 2013. Computer learner corpora: Analyzing interlanguage errors in synchronous and asynchronous communication. *Language Learning and Technology* 17(2), 36–56.

Master, P. (1987). A Cross-Linguistic Interlanguage Analysis of the Acquisition of the English Article System. Unpublished Ph.D. dissertation, University of California Los Angeles.

Matthewson, L. (1998). *Determiner Systems and Quantificational Strategies: Evidence from Salish*. The Hague: Holland Academic Graphics.

Murphy, S. (1997). Knowledge and Production of English Articles by Advanced Second Language Learners. Unpublished Ph.D. dissertation, University of Texas at Austin.

Narita, M. (2013). The use of articles in Japanese EFL learners' essays. In S. Granger, G. Gilquin, & F. Meunier (eds.), *Twenty Years of Learner Corpus Research: Looking Back, Moving Ahead. Corpora and Language in Use - Proceedings 1*, 357–366. Louvain-la-Neuve: Presses universitaires de Louvain.

Parrish, B. (1987). A new look at methodologies in the study of article acquisition for learners of ESL. *Language Learning* 37, 361–383.

Pica, T. (1983). Methods of morpheme quantification: Their effect on the interpretation of second language data. *Studies in Second Language Acquisition* 6(1), 69–78. https://doi.org/10.1017/S0272263100000309

Prat Zagrebelsky, M. (2005). I computer learner corpora: una risorsa per la costruzione di attività di consapevolezza e di recupero per apprendetti di inglese come lengua straniera. In *Proceedings of the NAPLES Associazione Italiana Centri Linguistici Universitari (AICLU) Conference*. AICLU.

Robertson, D. (2000). Variability in the use of the English article system by Chinese learners of English. *Second Language Research* 16(2), 135–172. https://doi.org/10.1191/026765800672262975

Sarker, B. & Baek, S. (2017). Revisiting fluctuations in L2 article choice in L1-Korean L2-English learners. *Journal of Psycholinguistic Research* 46(2), 367–393. https://doi.org/10.1007/s10936-016-9440-4

Thomas, M. (1989). The acquisition of English articles by first- and second-language learners. *Applied Psycholinguistics* 10, 335–355.

Trademan, J. (2002). The Acquisition of the English Article System by Native Speakers of Spanish and Japanese: A Cross-Linguistic Comparison. Unpublished Ph.D. dissertation, University of New Mexico.

Trenkic, D. (2007). Variability in second language article production: Beyond the representational deficit vs. processing constraints debate. *Second Language Research* 23(3), 289–327. https://doi.org/10.1177/0267658307077643

(2008). The representation of English articles in second language grammars: Determiners or adjectives? *Bilingualism: Language and Cognition* 11(1), 1–18. https://doi.org/10.1017/S1366728907003185

Trenkic, D., Mirkovic, J., & Altmann, G. (2013). Real-time grammar processing by native and non-native speakers: Constructions unique to the second language. *Bilingualism: Language and Cognition* 16, 1–21.

Trenkic, D. & Pongpairoj, N. (2013). Referent salience affects second language article use. *Bilingualism: Language and Cognition* 16, 152–166.

Yevhen, M. & Tomasz, M. (2017). Language differentiation of Ukraine's population. *Journal of Nationalism, Memory & Language Politics* 11(2), 181–197. https://doi.org/10.1515/jnmlp-2017-0008

L1 Influence vs. Universal Mechanisms: An SLA-Driven Corpus Study on Temporal Expression

Valentin Werner, Robert Fuchs, and Sandra Götz*

1 Introduction

The acquisition of temporal expression (TE) has been labeled one of the "most intensively investigated" areas (Jarvis & Pavlenko 2008, 94; see also Fuchs & Werner 2018, 143) or, less prosaically speaking, "a very important piece of the puzzle of L2 acquisition" (Salaberry 2008, 2). At the same time, TE acquisition has been recognized as complex owing to the multitude of linguistic subsystems affected, and, accordingly, as a challenging area for learners, characterized by variation of expression and an overall gradual and slow emergence of a target-like system (Shirai 2009, 167; Vraicu 2015, 290).

Past marking through the Present Perfect (PP) and the Simple Past (SP) in L2 English seems to constitute a special area of interest. While the PP–SP alternation is characterized by pervasive variation in English in general (see e.g. Werner et al. 2016), both SLA and Learner Corpus Research (LCR) has found that in this domain an adequate form–function mapping only takes place at advanced proficiency stages (Housen 2002, 79; see also Deshors 2018). Further, the presence of both transfer (e.g. Collins 2002) and universal learning mechanisms (e.g. Bardovi-Harlig 2000; Housen 2002) has been claimed. Both claims are weighed against each other in the present contribution by way of a case study on German- and Cantonese-speaking learners of English. Conceptually, the current contribution can thus be categorized as top-down or "SLA-driven" (Myles 2015, 318); that is, it seeks to test transfer as a theoretical SLA notion (vs. universal principles) in the area of morphologically realized TE with an LCR approach.

More specifically, three facts complicate the picture for L2 learners. First, only a minority (c. 3 percent; Dahl & Velupillai 2013) of the world's

* We would like to thank Kathrin Kircili for her invaluable help with the data coding and Judith Szislo for validation of the figures. We would also like to thank Stefan Gries and Sandra Deshors for extensive statistical advice.

languages (and thus the learners' potential L1s) have a form comparable to the PP (i.e. a grammaticalized possessive). Even if the learners' L1 has a comparable "perfect" form, a second relevant typological aspect is that the English PP is not archetypic for the "perfect" category in its persistence in resultative contexts (Werner 2014, 14) and the resulting constraints on combinability with definite temporal adverbials (Werner 2014, 356). Third, in English the PP (*I have met her* [at least at one point in the past]) and SP (*I met her* [at one specific point in the past]) show semantic overlap in terms of both forms relating to anteriority, with the PP carrying an additional notion of current relevance of the event/situation expressed (Bybee et al. 1994, 54; Fuchs et al. 2016, 299).

1.1 Universal Principles, Transfer, and LCR

Research on TE acquisition has identified a universal sequence of how temporality is established linguistically in the course of increasing proficiency.[1] Commonly, a three- or four-stage model is proposed (see e.g. Bardovi-Harlig 1992, 299–300; Howard & Leclercq 2017, 8):

(i) pragmatic stage: simple chronological ordering and temporally scaffolded discourse;
(ii) lexical stage: use of temporal adverbials and conjunctions;
(iii) grammatical stage: subdividable into an early stage with unsystematic (i.e. non-target-like), and a later stage with systematic (i.e. target-like) use of verbal morphology.

Within the grammatical stage, the main focus of the present study, a form-oriented view recognizes a developmental hierarchy along the lines SP before PP (Bardovi-Harlig 2000, 169; Svalberg 2019).[2]

Another universal principle widely treated (and controversially discussed) in SLA research on TE is the Aspect Hypothesis (AH). Its central arguments pertain to the interaction of grammatical and lexical aspect, starting from the claim that "second language learners will initially be influenced by the inherent semantic aspect of verbs … in the acquisition of tense and aspect markers associated with or affixed to these verbs" (Andersen & Shirai 1994, 133). The relation of the AH to all issues involving tense and aspect provides a theoretical rationale

[1] For a general view of developmental sequences and their usefulness in the description of learner language, see Ellis (2015).

[2] In aspectual (and cross-linguistic) terms, this developmental hierarchy could alternatively be labeled "perfective before imperfective" (Howard & Leclercq 2017, 4). Note that – and terminology for historical reasons is admittedly confusing here – the SP (and crucially not the PP) is perfective.

why lexical aspect (*Aktionsart*) should be considered as a variable in all relevant studies. As regards universal principles more generally, it is also clear from the foregoing that they are strongly interrelated with linguistic categorizations and factors, which implies that a closer investigation of such factors is worthwhile.

Both the SLA (e.g. Jarvis & Pavlenko 2008, 214) and LCR communities (e.g. Rogatcheva 2012, 151) have drawn attention to the fact that L1 influence, despite its explanatory potential, has (unwarrantedly) been disregarded in relevant studies. More recently, however, there have been calls for new efforts to systematically explore transfer (alternatively referred to as "cross-linguistic influence" or "L1 influence/effects") across various learner L1 backgrounds to be able to discern general principles and processes from specific L1 effects (Shirai 2009, 183).

In the present study, we follow Jarvis's (2000, 2010) unified model for transfer research in SLA, based on the working definition that "L1 influence refers to any instance of learner data where a statistically significant correlation (or probability-based relation) is shown to exist between some feature of learners' IL [= interlanguage] performance and their L1 background" (Jarvis 2000, 252). To make a compelling case for or against transfer and to exclude, among other things, the influence of universal learning principles, Jarvis (2000, 259) suggests that at least two types of analyses are necessary,[3] namely tests for (i) homogeneity of learners with a common L1 background in their L2 production ("intra-L1-group homogeneity") as well as for (ii) heterogeneity of the L2 production by two (or more) learner groups with differing L1s ("inter-L1-group heterogeneity"). (i) is already largely determined at the data compilation stage, while the likelihood of (ii) can be assessed through a contrastive analysis (Jarvis 2010, 189) of the structures investigated (see Section 1.2).

However, what is also necessary is to exclude the influence of potentially confounding factors as far as possible (Jarvis 2000, 260). To this end, such external factors (e.g. age, personality, motivation, proficiency, educational background, type and amount of language exposure, task type, etc.; see also Paquot 2013) should be controlled in terms of holding them constant or them being "actively investigated" (Jarvis 2000, 260). Jarvis (2000, 261) concedes, though, that this is an idealization to a certain degree, as some factors (such as the learners' personalities) are hard or even impossible to trace.

[3] A third type, assessments of "intra-L1-group congruity between learners L1 and IL performance" is also listed but considered "unrealistic in many cases" (Jarvis 2000, 255).

We argue that the methodological guidelines set by Jarvis (2000, 2010) can be followed within the corpus-based Contrastive Interlanguage Analysis (CIA) framework (Granger 1996, 2015) employed in this study (see Gilquin 2008 for a related approach), where corpus data from two internally largely homogeneous learner groups are contrasted to each other, the only remaining major difference being L1 background (German vs. Cantonese). Cross-linguistic effects may be quite nuanced. For instance, forms across languages could be formally similar but functionally diverging (Vraicu 2015, 292; see Section 1.2). Yet, contexts of usage (i.e. cognitive and intralinguistic factors) have been largely ignored (but see Deshors 2018). This clearly suggests the necessity of looking beyond contrasts at a superficial level (e.g. considering mere raw or normalized frequencies), so that it may be "in the details rather than in the larger picture that first language influence is found" (Bardovi-Harlig 2000, 411).

1.2 The Learning Problem

To establish inter-L1-group heterogeneity, a contrastive analysis of the two L1s involved (German and Cantonese) for the area tested (PP use and its alternation with the SP) is a central prerequisite for any study of transfer to exclude parallel effects in the L2 (English) emerging from the different L1s (Jarvis 2010, 189).

Typologically, the English PP (HAVE + past participle) can be categorized as anterior, that is, it represents a temporally unspecified situation in the past (Bybee et al. 1994, 85). L1 German learners, for instance, may relate to the German *Perfekt* (HABEN/SEIN 'have'/'be' + past participle) when expressing the PP, as it is morphologically similar (and thus arguably morphologically transparent for German learners). The formal similarity between the two forms is "deceptive" (Rogatcheva 2012, 152), however. While both forms may be used as resultatives (König & Gast 2018, 92), the functional range of the German *Perfekt* is much wider than that of the PP, with the former being used in all contexts where the PP may appear (e.g. resultatives) but additionally as a narrative tense, that is, as a perfective describing a "single, unified, discrete situation" (Bybee et al. 1994, 83),[4] a function canonically covered by the SP in English. This implies that the definite temporal adverbial constraint, characteristic of the PP, does not apply in German, as illustrated in (1).

[4] A similar situation applies for the French *passé composé* (see e.g. Deshors 2018) and the Italian *passato prossimo*.

(1) *Er hat gestern ein Auto gekauft.*
He has yesterday a car bought.
'He bought a car yesterday.'

In sum, German learners will in all likelihood recognize the form (*Perfekt* = PP) but may struggle with functional/meaning differences (*Perfekt* vs. PP/SP) in the area of past time-reference.[5] Thus, the alternation between PP and SP is an area where transfer may become visible. As usage contexts differ, so may factors influencing the choice.

Against the background of the findings for German learner English, it will be relevant to explore whether learners with an L1 without a (formally and, to a restricted degree, semantically) PP-like structure struggle even more with the PP. If this is the case, it would strongly suggest PP acquisition is generally challenging but mediated by L1 influence. A comparison with German-speaking learner data will indirectly allow us to assess the effect of typological distance, which has been established as a crucial variable in transfer research (although some have questioned its relevance, especially when semantic aspects are investigated; see e.g. Ringbom 1987). As a test case, we will contrast data from Cantonese-speaking learners from Hong Kong and mainland China, since Cantonese lacks a grammaticalized structure morphologically similar to the PP or SP (Bayley 1994, 163; Bybee et al. 1994, 84; Dahl & Velupillai 2013; Matthews & Yip 2013, 204; see further Dahl & Velupillai 2013). However, it has both a perfective to report completed events in the past, realized by the particle *-jó* (see (2)), and an experiential to report events that have occurred at least once in the past, realized by the particle *-gwo* (see (3); examples adapted from Matthews & Yip 2013).

(2) *Gūngsī jaahn-jó msíu chin.*
Company earn-PFV not-little money
'The company made a good deal of money.'

(3) Ga dihnlóuh waaih-gwo géi chi.
CL computer break-EXP few time
'This computer (has) crashed a few times before.'

It emerges that, depending on the context, both particles may be "translated with either the English perfect or the past tense" (Matthews & Yip 2013, 206), so there is no clear form–function mapping that Cantonese-speaking learners could potentially exploit. Thus, they have to master not only the semantics of the PP (and its

[5] This pertains to what Jarvis (2010, 175–176) has termed "intralingual contrasts," which can be viewed as additional testing ground for cross-linguistic influence.

alternation with the SP, which is fairly strictly regulated in English) but also the (morphosyntactic) form.

In the literature we find some conflicting statements as to the implications of the "tenseless" nature of L1s with this property for learners of English. Hinkel (2004, 14) claims that the SP "is one of the easier English tenses to acquire" for these learner populations (including Cantonese speakers), suggestive of a reliance on the SP as default past marker. By contrast, both Hong (2007, 177) and Xu (2013, 5) emphasize the influence of typological distance (and resulting cross-linguistic effects), and report that L1 Cantonese speakers have an overall tendency to rely indiscriminately on either the base form or simple present as structurally least complex TA forms in all contexts where past marking would be expected. However, the latter investigation also recognizes that some learners may overuse the SP (Xu 2013, 70). These studies stay at a fairly general level, as they do not consider intralinguistic factors (i.e. usage contexts; see Section 2.2; see also Deshors 2018, 50).

In summary, for the two learner samples investigated, we see, above all, that neither of the L1s involved possesses a (morphosyntactic) structure *semantically* similar to the English PP. This implies that none of the learner populations studied may have an edge over the other in terms of simply having to "re-map" meanings or functions (or indeed the presence of a grammatical category, as described in Roberts & Liszka 2013, for instance) from the L1 to the L2 (see also Domínguez et al. 2017, 452). Yet, German learners may benefit from the typological proximity between German and English, as they can rely on a *formal* one-to-one mapping (i.e. overt morphological marking; Rothman & Slabakova 2018, 422) for the PP, which may facilitate positive transfer (Jarvis 2000, 297) or even lead to overuse (Jarvis 2000, 248; see Deshors 2018, 49), but is absent for the Cantonese learners.

1.3 Research Questions

The following issues are tackled:

(1) The PP as challenging structure: Which usage rates do learners show? How and where do they differ from native speaker usage?
(2) SLA principles: Is TE acquisition and the difference to native speaker usage (i) influenced by cross-linguistic effects, (ii) guided by universal principles and factors (irrespective of the learners' L1), or rather by an interaction of (i) and (ii)?
(3) Linguistic principles: Can PP/SP use be predicted by cognitive-linguistic variables, such as persistence, *Aktionsart* (lexical aspect), etc.?

This study also addresses further SLA and LCR desiderata by way of (i) providing an analysis of both spoken and written learner production, (ii) going beyond mere analysis of errors (negative transfer), the main focus of SLA transfer studies to date, and (iii) including learners from a non-European L1 background (Cantonese), which as yet are underrepresented in SLA research (Tenfjord et al. 2017, 1).

2 Data and Methodology

2.1 Corpora

The analysis of the spoken data relies on the German and the Chinese subcorpora of the *Louvain International Database of Spoken English Interlanguage* (LINDSEI; Gilquin et al. 2010) and the native-speaker counterpart *Louvain Corpus of Native English Conversation* (LOCNEC; De Cock 2004). The German and Chinese subcorpora of LINDSEI (LINDSEI-GE, Brand & Kämmerer 2006; and LINDSEI-CH) comprise 50 orthographically transcribed interviews held with English majors (third/fourth year of study). These interviews consist of three parts: talking about a set topic, a free informal interview, and a picture description task. For LINDSEI-CH, we used only data produced by speakers with L1 Cantonese (or other South Chinese dialects with perfective particles), as gathered from the learner profiles, and discarded the other (or unclear) data. The LOCNEC interviews resemble those in LINDSEI.

The analysis of the written data is based on the German and Chinese component of the *International Corpus of Learner English* (ICLE; Granger et al. 2009). GICLE and CHICLE consist of timed and untimed argumentative and literary essays written by students majoring in English (first to fifth year of study). For our analysis of CHICLE, the same exclusion criteria as for LINDSEI-CH were applied, and only data from learners who stated Cantonese as their first language were used. The majority of the learners included in the databases can be described as advanced (Granger 2003, 568), as they have all reached the final "key language learning stage in a typical instructed setting" (Domínguez et al. 2017, 441) after a comparable amount of instruction (Jarvis 2000, 294).[6]

[6] The proficiency of individual learners originally was not assessed in terms of CEFR levels, merely because the CEFR had not yet been implemented when the data were compiled (mostly mid-1990s). The categorization in terms of institutional status (English majors having passed an entrance exam) was complemented by later assessments of small random samples through human raters, who assigned high-intermediate (B2) to advanced (C1) levels to most of the material (cf. Gilquin et al. 2010, 10). Drawing on Granger et al. (2009, 12) for our data, we can assume a slightly lower average proficiency of the Cantonese-speaking learners, even though we have to be aware that the representativeness of the manual rating (20/300 essays for ICLE, 5/50 for LINDSEI) is restricted.

Table 8 Breakdown of native and non-native corpora

Corpus	Group	Mode	Level	*n* learners	Words
LOCNESS-GB	Native	Writing	School	90	55,049
	Native	Writing	University	90	92,254
LOCNESS-US	Native	Writing	University	232	168,400
LOCNEC	Native	Speech	University	50	118,000
					433,703
GICLE	German	Writing	University	437	234,000
LINDSEI-GE	German	Speech	University	50	86,100
					320,100
CHICLE	Cantonese	Writing	University	818	412,900
LINDSEI-CH	Cantonese	Speech	University	50	65,000
					477,900

The native control corpus is the *Louvain Corpus of Native English Essays* (LOCNESS), consisting of argumentative essays composed of British pupils' A-level essays, British university students' essays, and American university students' essays. All native data stem from speakers aged 17 or older.[7] Table 8 gives an overview of the corpora.

2.2 Data Extraction and Coding

All corpora were POS-tagged with the *CLAWS* tagger (C7 tagset; Garside & Smith 1997). *AntConc* (Anthony 2014) identified all tokens of the PP and SP through regular expressions (cf. Fuchs et al. 2016, 308), with less than 1 percent false positives. For the PP, they retrieved any form of HAVE + past participle (allowing for intervening complex forms and intervening adverbials and noun phrases); for the SP, they retrieved all past tense verbs. Table 9 shows the number of instances these queries yielded for the PP and the SP across corpora.

Next, we manually classified all c. 4,000 PP instances and – because of the high number of c. 20,000 across the corpora – a subset of 500 instances per subcorpus for the SP (totaling c. 3,000 instances) for several variables (see Table 10).[8] These were chosen as possibly being influential predictors for PP/SP use, as they (i) are directly related

[7] www.uclouvain.be/cps/ucl/doc/cecl/documents/LOCNESSdescriptionall.pdf

[8] All tokens were classified by an independent rater (research assistant, L1 German) first. Difficult cases were discussed and resolved in collaboration with the authors.

Table 9 Instances of PP and SP across corpora

Corpus	*n* PPs	*n* SPs
LOCNESS	706	2,319
LOCNEC	838	3,595
GICLE	731	5,075
LINDSEI-GE	272	3,559
CHICLE	1,064	3,029
LINDSEI-CH	143	1,799
TOTAL	3,754	19,376

to the verb phrase (e.g. *Aktionsart*), (ii) have been found to be important for the PP–SP alternation specifically (e.g. temporal adverbials), or (iii) are, as cognitive-linguistic variables, of a broader relevance for all kinds of linguistic production (e.g. persistence). With this, we aim at a comprehensive coverage of usage contexts and, as posited in Deshors (2018, 37), at going beyond the mere exploration of morphological overlap (or its absence) between the learners' L1 and the target. Note that overall semantic "readings" (such as "resultative," "extended-now," etc.) were not considered as a variable, owing to their highly subjective nature and the multiplicity of approaches attempting to establish comprehensive categorizations (see e.g. Werner 2014, 60–72 for discussion).

The analysis includes only full verb phrases (i.e. subject + finite verb). Instances excluded were repetitions, self-corrections (here, the corrected form was selected), irrealis forms (e.g. *If I were you*), possessive *got* (e.g. *I've got a bike*), and uses of *have* in the sense of eating or in the construction *have (got) to* (as in (4) and (5)), contracted forms if the contraction did not allow for a classification of the form, whenever the time-reference form was not identifiable due to an idiosyncratic/erroneous construction by the learner, and when PP or SP forms were part of direct speech, while the previous part of the sentence/utterance was not (as in (6)).

(4) *it's mainly fish erm you have for for the for lunch or dinner* (LINDSEI GE003)

(5) *you've got to register for the practical in the lab* (GICLE AU3097)

(6) *Above all there was never the jelous* [sic] *question* ***where have you been or what have you done*** *when I returned late* (GICLE AU1058)

Table 10 Independent variables

Variable	Category (and examples)	Literature
(VERB) SEMANTICS (in the sentence)	ACTIVITY (subject performs an act: *look, hunt, catch, play*) ASPECTUAL (*start, begin, continue, cease*) CAUSATIVE (*let, make, have, get, help*) COMMUNICATION (*answer, talk, shout*) EXISTENCE (*be, exist, live*) MENTAL (*believe, wonder, guess*) OCCURRENCE (*happen*)	Deshors (2017)[a]
AKTIONSART (lexical aspect)	ACCOMPLISHMENTVERBS (*build, draw [a circle], run [a mile]*) ACHIEVEMENTVERBS (*discover, reach [the top], cross [the river]*) ACTIVITYVERBS (*run, eat, fly*) STATIVEVERBS (*be, believe, belong, feel, imagine*)	Vendler (1967), Katz (2003), Deshors (2018)
TIMEADVERBIAL	DEFINITE (precise points in time: *two days ago, last year, tonight*) INDEFINITE (not precise relationships in time: *always, constantly, ever*) NOTIMEREFERENCE	Werner (2013, 2014), Götz et al. (2019)
MODE	active passive	
VERBCLASS	regular irregular	
NEGATION	true false	
PERSISTENCE[b]	simple past present perfect present modal other[c]	Szmrecsanyi (2005), Levey (2006), Jackson (2018)

[a] This broad typology is intended to cover all verbs.
[b] While "persistence" is the term used in corpus-based studies, experimental studies often refer to this "discourse-level effect" (Levey 2006, 139) as "structural priming," defined as "the phenomenon whereby speakers are more likely to repeat a structure they have recently heard or produced" (Jackson 2018, 539).
[c] Verb forms in the progressive aspect were subsumed under the non-progressive counterparts. We first worked with a more fine-grained categorization but were forced to reduce the number of variable levels to avoid data sparsity.

2.3 Statistical Analysis

To allow us to present a more detailed (and arguably more accurate) view of transfer, we follow calls for using statistical approaches developed outside a learner language paradigm (Osborne 2015, 353) that can account for multiple factors simultaneously and thus may help to reveal complex patterns in the data (Osborne 2015, 338–345; Wulff 2017, 750).

Comparable integrated approaches have not been absent from previous SLA research. A related attempt at testing predictions of SLA theories statistically is Bayley (1994), which recognized the influence of several structural and non-structural factors on verbal morphology in learner language and applied a variable rule analysis to sociolinguistic interview data. While this is a point to tie in, we submit that the statistical approach used in the present study is even more fitting for the type of "theory culling" envisaged by Bayley (1994, 169), as it considers more factors and also uses directly comparable native control material, so that valid baseline data (Jarvis 2010, 174) can be taken into consideration.

For the present analysis, we rely on the approach known as Multifactorial Prediction and Deviation Analysis with Regressions (MuPDAR), developed by Gries and Deshors (2014) and Gries and Bernaisch (2016). MuPDAR allows the researcher to assess resemblances and differences between native speakers ("target") and learners in linguistic choices (in our scenario, choice between PP and SP), and considers differences as to how individual factors influence this choice. As MuPDAR also takes account of how factors influence the choice in different learner populations (in our scenario, German and Cantonese), it enables us to conduct a fully-fledged CIA and, thus, to disentangle both cross-linguistic effects from general learner patterns as well as the specific factor(s) where the cross-linguistic effects are salient (see Gries & Deshors 2014, 111–112). The application of MuPDAR to learner data comprises three steps:

(1) Regression R_1 is based on the native data only and indicates which factors influence the linguistic choice in native usage.
(2) This regression model is then applied to the learner data to predict, for all instances, whether a native speaker would have made the same choice under similar circumstances.
(3) Finally, another regression, R_2, explores how the learners' choices differ from native usage and which linguistic variables can account for this difference.

In our analysis, we followed these steps, except for a modification of step (3). We were not able to construct a regression model R_2 that adequately represents the data and honors the model assumptions, specifically normally distributed residuals and low variance inflation factors. Instead, we opted for a related approach and used a Classification and Regression Tree (CART; Loh 2011), which considers one variable at a time and does not suffer from the above-mentioned problems of regression models.[9] CART iteratively splits the data into two groups using the independent variable that maximizes the difference between the two groups. This process is repeated until no further split is possible that exceeds a previously specified stop criterion. The statistical analysis was carried out in *R* (R Development Core Team 2017):[10]

(1) In regression R_1, a logistic model was fitted for the native data with the dependent variable TIMEREFERENCEFORM (PP vs. SP) and the independent variables described in Section 2.2. We selected the model with the smallest value for the Bayes Information Criterion (BIC; using the *glmulti* package; Calcagno 2015) and allowed for pairwise interactions between the independent variables.

(2) The model from regression R_1 is then applied to the learner data and predicts whether a native speaker would have made the same choice as the learner did in this linguistic context. The native choice is represented as a rational number ranging from 0 to 1 that quantifies the probability of a native speaker choosing the PP in this context. Put differently, values lower than 0.5 indicate a choice of SP and greater than 0.5 of PP. Moreover, a number close to 0 or 1 indicates that the linguistic context strongly favors SP or PP, respectively, in native usage. Conversely, a value close to 0.5 indicates that the choice between SP and PP is less clear-cut. This information is valuable in evaluating the learner error gravity. For example, if the predicted native PP probability is 0.52 in a particular context and the learner opted for the SP, the learner departed much less from native usage than if the PP probability were 0.92.

(3) Following Gries and Bernaisch (2016, 12–13), we define a variable VARIETYSPECIFICITY set to 0 in cases where the learner made the choice predicted for native usage. When the learner did not

[9] A related modification of MuPDAR, called MuPDARF, uses random forests to address this issue (see e.g. Heller et al. 2017).

[10] The *R* code used in the analysis and the data are available at osf.io/kgvd3/.

make the choice predicted for native usage, VarietySpecificity is set to the absolute of 0.5 minus the predicted PP probability. VarietySpecificity thus ranges from 0 to 0.5, with higher numbers representing more radical departures from native usage. This variable is then used as the dependent variable in the last step, which explores the linguistic contexts in which the learners departed from native usage. The independent variables in this analysis comprised all variables selected as significant by the analysis in step (1), the choice the learner made (LearnerChoice: PP or SP), and the learner's L1 (Chinese, German). This step was carried out with a conditional inference tree (the *ctree* function from the *party* package; Hothorn et al. 2017), which we illustrate for better readability in table format (see Table 11).[11]

While Gries and Bernaisch (2016) chose a logistic regression and used VarietySpecificity as a binary variable (native-like vs. non-native-like choice) to be able to choose a regression model fulfilling the model assumptions (Stefan Gries, pers. comm.), our use of CART allowed us to retain VarietySpecificity as a variable quantifying the gradual nature of non-native-like choices. In turn, this enabled us to identify those linguistic contexts where learners departed strongly from the native norm as opposed to contexts where their non-native usage was less problematic.

Finally, the variable LearnerChoice will allow us to explore in how far learners depart from the native norm in PP and SP choice, while the variable L1 will be relevant in the analysis in so far as the errors committed by Chinese and German speakers are similar or different, allowing us to assess the presence, extent, and specific factor(s) of transfer.

In addition to CART, we use a statistically more robust generalization of this method called random forests, and apply both methods to the same data in step (3). The CART analysis allows us to develop a fine-grained analysis of the linguistic contexts of native-like and non-native-like PP and SP use (e.g. that the PP should be avoided with definite time adverbials). The random forests approach, then, allows us to quantify how far each of the variables contributes to explaining where learners deviate from native usage (e.g. that TimeAdverbial is a more important factor than L1). Random forests is a statistically robust approach because it repeatedly samples a data subset and fits a

[11] We used this function with standard parameters except for mandating a minimal size of 30 tokens for each "stump"/terminal node of the analysis to avoid overfitting of the data.

conditional inference tree to it. This analysis was conducted with the *cforest* function from the *party* package.[12]

3 Results

3.1 Regression Model Accounting for Native Usage

In step (1), we fitted a regression model on the native data as indicated in Section 2.3. This model comprised the variables SEMANTICS, TIMEADVERBIAL, PERSISTENCE, and MODE, and no interactions. For reasons of space and in keeping with previous MuPDAR analyses (e.g. Gries & Deshors 2014), we do not explore the fixed-effects structure of this model in detail here but discuss the goodness-of-fit measures the model provides. With a C-index of 0.84, a Somers' D of 67.9, and a classification accuracy of 78.4 percent, the model accounts for the data relatively well.

3.2 Application of Native Regression Model to Learner Data

Step (2) consisted of the application of the native regression model to the learner data to predict which linguistic choice a native speaker would have made under similar circumstances. The results reveal that the prediction and the actual choice the learners made are identical in 72.4 percent of all cases on average, with a better classification accuracy in the German learner data (81.2 percent for PP, 74.1 percent for SP) than the Chinese learner data (77.8 percent for PP, 51.7 percent for SP). The remainder, 27.6 percent, is to be considered erroneous (i.e. non-target-like) usage, as in (7) or (8) below.

(7) [. . .] *the government* ***has spent*** *$908 million on consultants* ***in 1989*** *which is expensive* (CHICLE HK1050)

However, the error gravity is mediated by the variable VARIETYSPECIFICITY, which indicates how strongly the learners' choices depart from native usage. On this basis, we explore in Section 3.3 which linguistic variables account for the learners' departure from native usage (e.g. learners might follow native usage in the influence of verb SEMANTICS on the choice between PP and SP but not in the influence of TIMEADVERBIAL), providing a bird's-eye view of differences between learner and native usage. In Section 3.4 we

[12] We used standard parameters except for a minimal size of 30 tokens for each terminal node.

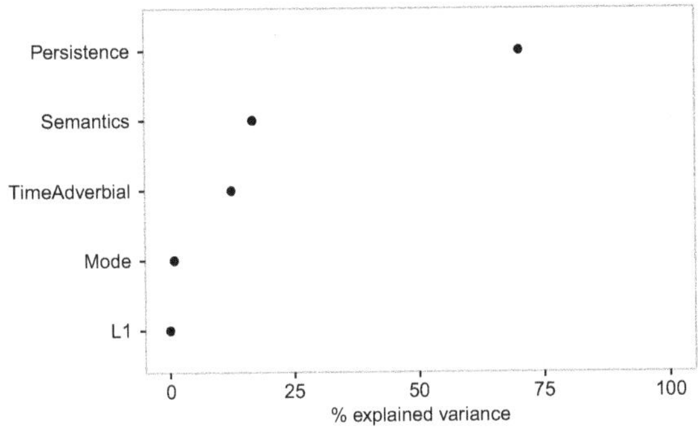

Figure 1 Importance of variables in explaining differences between native and non-native usage

proceed to a detailed analysis of how specifically learner and native choice differ.

3.3 Analysis of Divergence of Learner Choices from Native Usage: Analysis of Variable Importance

The random forests analysis (see Figure 1) reveals that PERSISTENCE is the most important variable when it comes to explaining differences between native and learner usage, accounting for 70.1 percent of the explained variance in the data, followed by SEMANTICS and TIMEADVERBIAL. MODE accounts only for a small and L1 for a negligible amount of the variance.

3.4 Analysis of Divergence of Learner Choices from Native Usage: Detailed Analysis

On the basis of the predicted probability of the native linguistic choice, the variable VARIETYSPECIFICITY was constructed and used as the dependent variable in the CART analysis. Table 11 shows its results. On a broader level, the selection of an intralinguistic variable by the CART analysis indicates that in this variable the learners' PP and SP choices differ from native usage. The variables selected are SEMANTICS, MODE, PERSISTENCE, and TIMEADVERBIAL. Below we discuss how and in which specific contexts the learners' choices depart from native usage. Conversely, variables not selected by the CART analysis do not contribute significantly to the linguistic conditioning of learner usage. Crucially, this is the case for the learners' first language (variable L1), indicating that German-speaking and

Table 11 Classification of VarietySpecificity *based on the CART analysis (Node = terminal node in CART analysis, n = number of cases in this terminal node, Mdn = median variety specificity of all cases in this terminal node)*

Var	Split	Var	Split	Var	Split	Var	Split
Tense	PP	**Persist-ence**	Modal, other, P, PP	**Time adv**	Indefinite, none	**Seman-tics**	Activity, aspectual, causative, existence, occurrence
							Communication, mental
					Definite		
			SP	**Time adv**	Indefinite		
					Definite, none	**Seman-tics**	Activity
							Causative, Communication, existence, mental, occurrence
	SP	**Persist-ence**	Modal, other, SP	**Persistence**	SP	**Time adv**	Definite, none
							Indefinite
					Modal, other	**Seman-tics**	Communication, existence, mental
							Activity, aspectual, causative, occurrence
			P, PP	**Semantics**	Communi-cation, existence, mental	**Seman-tics**	Mental
							Communication, existence
					Activity, Aspectual, causative, occurrence	**Time adv**	Definite
							Indefinite, none

Var	Split	Var	Split	Var	Split	n	Mdn	Node
Semantics	Activity, aspectual, causative, occurrence					1,269	0.00	45
	Existence	Persistence	P, PP			151	0.00	44
			Modal, other	Time adv	Indefinite	46	0.00	43
					None	33	0.12	42
Persistence	P, PP	Semantics	Communication			89	0.00	38
			Mental			40	0.02	37
	Modal, other					137	0.11	35
						57	0.43	32
						63	0.09	30
Mode	Spoken					39	0.17	29
	Written					69	0.26	28
						31	0.39	26
						793	0.00	22
Semantics	Aspectual, communication, existence, mental					35	0.00	21
	Activity, causative					34	0.02	20
						130	0.00	17
						164	0.12	16
						43	0.00	13
Mode	Written					85	0.10	12
	Spoken					81	0.20	11
						35	0.00	8
Mode	Written					126	0.29	7
	Spoken					112	0.36	6

Cantonese-speaking learners do not differ substantially in the intra-linguistic contexts in which their choices differ from native usage.[13] Further, AKTIONSART does not emerge among the important variables, which may be read as an indication that the predictions of the AH (cf. Section 1.1), which imply that learners are not fully able to replicate the influence of AKTIONSART on the PP–SP alternation in native usage, are not borne out in the present data.

We first discuss cases where the learners chose the PP and aggregate over splits with minor importance. For each case, we indicate the number of the terminal node in Table 11. Recall that a value of 0 on VARIETYSPECIFICITY indicates PP or SP usage classified as native-like. Conversely, a VARIETYSPECIFICITY score greater than 0 indicates a non-native-like construction with higher VARIETYSPECIFICITY scores indicating greater error gravity. Further, in Table 11, each split indicates a variable that partly explains how far learner usage departs from native usage. With each split, the data is separated into two groups, with variable levels indicated in the following column. The rightmost columns list the terminal nodes along with the median of VARIETYSPECIFICITY for all cases belonging to each terminal node. For example, node 6, the final terminal node, consists exclusively of cases with a relatively high VARIETYSPECIFICITY and thus a relatively greater degree of departure from native usage.

When preceded by a verb in the SP, the use of the PP usually resulted in an erroneous pattern, although the error gravity is mediated by other variables. That is, under most circumstances, a verb in the SP is expected to be followed by another SP (see the discussion of node 22 at the end of this section). However, there are a few exceptions to this general pattern. The learners' PP choice deviated least from the native predictions, and in a few cases was in fact native-like, when used together with an indefinite time adverbial (node 30, median VARIETYSPECIFICITY = 0.09). By contrast, with a definite or no time adverbial, PP use was more problematic in almost all cases (node 26, median VARIETYSPECIFICITY = 0.39), as in (8), where the definite time adverbial *in November* is used together with the PP. Activity verbs form an exception in this context, with lower error gravity in spoken (node 29, median VARIETYSPECIFICITY = 0.17) than in written language (node 28, median VARIETYSPECIFICITY = 0.26).

[13] This result is robust even if we adjust the analysis parameters. Removing the constraint of a minimal size of 30 tokens per terminal node yields a tree with 45 terminal nodes (as compared to 23 terminal nodes in the present analysis) but still does not involve the variable L1.

(8) *it was* ***in November*** *when we'****ve been*** *there* (GICLE AU3026)

So far, the analysis of PP occurrences revealed that its use is usually non-native-like when preceded by a verb in the SP. The situation is different with PPs preceded by any other time-reference form. Here, PP use is mainly erroneous when used together with a definite time adverbial (node 32, median VARIETYSPECIFICITY = 0.43). PP use can also be erroneous, with very moderate error gravity, in a few other specific contexts. This is the case when a communication or mental verb is preceded by a modal verb or miscellaneous time-reference form (node 35, median VARIETYSPECIFICITY = 0.11) or when existence verbs are preceded by a modal or miscellaneous time-reference form and used with an indefinite or no time adverbial (node 42/43, median VARIETYSPECIFICITY = 0.12 and 0.00, respectively), as in (9) with the indefinite time adverbial *always*. In all other cases, PP use is almost always native-like. This is especially the case for activity, aspectual, causative, and occurrence verbs, whose native-like use with the PP accounts for a substantial proportion of the data (34.7 percent, node 45, median VARIETYSPECIFICITY = 0.00).

(9) *Banning smoking in restaurants* ***has always been*** *a controversial topic in our society.* (CHICLE CNHK1600)

Having discussed occurrences where the learners used the PP, we now turn to those where the learners used the SP. When preceded by a verb in the present or PP and when using a verb belonging to the activity, aspectual, causative, or occurrence semantic classes in conjunction with an indefinite or no time adverbial, the learners' SP choice resulted in a non-native pattern, with greater error gravity in speech (node 6, median VARIETYSPECIFICITY = 0.36; see example (10)) than in writing (node 7, median VARIETYSPECIFICITY = 0.29). However, combined with a definite time adverbial, choosing the SP was almost always correct (node 8, median VARIETYSPECIFICITY = 0.00).

(10) *very unfortunately I seldom travel yeah the the farthest place I* ***traveled*** *is is er Guangzhou* (LINDSEI CH012)

By contrast, mental, existence, and communication verbs behave differently when primed by a preceding verb in the present or PP. SP use with communication and existence verbs tends to be incorrect, and error gravity is again higher in spoken (node 11, median VARIETYSPECIFICITY = 0.20) than in written language (node 12, median VarietySpecificity = 0.10), whereas SP use with mental verbs results in a pattern that is almost always correct in this context (node 13, median VarietySpecificity = 0.00).

Still discussing cases where learners chose the SP, we now consider persistence contexts (i.e. a preceding verb in the SP). Combined with a definite or no time adverbial, the SP was almost always the native-like choice in this context (node 22, median VarietySpecificity = 0.00), which accounts for a substantial proportion of our data (21.7 percent). Together with an indefinite time adverbial, choosing the SP has a higher but still very moderate chance of being incorrect (nodes 20 and 21, median VarietySpecificity = 0.02 and 0.00, respectively). Compare this to an SP being preceded by a modal verb or a miscellaneous time-reference form. This results in higher error likelihood and gravity, which is worse for activity, aspectual, causative, and occurrence verbs (node 16, median VarietySpecificity = 0.12) than for communication, existence, and mental verbs (node 17, median VarietySpecificity = 0.00).

4 Discussion

We set out to model PP and SP use in native and learner data and to test if/how learners from two different L1 backgrounds deviate from native usage in the same linguistic environment. In doing so, we went beyond a mere comparison of frequencies ("over-/underuse"), and applied a recently developed statistical method (see Gries & Deshors 2014) that uses a three-step procedure allowing us to factor in many variables and thus to test if, how, and in which linguistic environments advanced German and Chinese learners of English differ in PP/SP use from each other and from native speakers (see also Deshors 2018). In the first step, we were able to predict native speakers' use of either of the two time-reference forms quite well (factors: Semantics, TimeAdverbial, Persistence, Mode).

Regarding our first research question, pertaining to how and where learners differ from native speaker usage, the fine-grained coding scheme as well as the advanced analytical method (step (3)) allowed us to uncover the major deviances learners show from native speakers with an appropriate level of detail. We could uncover these areas in which advanced learners were already approximating native usage and almost always opted for a native-like choice (e.g. in cases of persistence, i.e. a preceding verb in the present or PP, and when using a verb belonging to the activity, aspectual, causative, or occurrence semantic classes in conjunction with a definite time adverbial), as well as those where they still show a high likelihood of deviations from the native speakers (e.g. when the context included an indefinite or no time adverbial, choosing the SP yields a non-native-like pattern, with a higher error gravity in spoken than in written language).

As far as our second research question is concerned, that is, whether TE acquisition and the difference to native speaker usage is influenced by transfer, guided by universal principles (irrespective of the learners' L1), or by an interaction of the two can only be answered in connection to our third research question, namely whether PP/SP use can be predicted by linguistic variables, such as persistence and *Aktionsart* (lexical aspect). While error rates differ between the two learner populations studied (Section 3.2), our findings suggest that universal principles (involving linguistic factors) rather than L1-specific ones are crucial in the acquisition of the PP–SP alternation, despite the typological differences between German and Cantonese. While lexical aspect did not emerge as an influential variable in the present analysis, in our models the variables with the most significant effect on the (native as well as non-native) speakers' use of a PP vs. an SP construction were indeed (cognitive-)linguistic ones: persistence, the semantics of the word class, the use of a time adverbial, and the mode in which the time-reference form is used.

Our study also revealed how variables and their subclasses sometimes conspire, allowing us to uncover the cases in which even advanced learners still show significant deviation from the native speakers (see Section 3.4). For time adverbials, our findings run counter to previous research, which indicated that the use of time adverbials would result in the learners' avoidance of "double marking" by morphological marking of the verb, especially when a "tenseless" L1 like Cantonese is involved (see Yang & Huang 2004). Previous research also revealed that native speakers use these at a baseline of c. 20 percent of all tensed verbs, whereas advanced learners make use of them in 25 percent of all cases (beginner/intermediate learners at even c. 40 percent) (Bardovi-Harlig 1992, 305–306). Since using time adverbials is one of the most important factors prompting learners to make a native-like choice, we recommend they should be emphasized in teaching (keeping in mind that actual native production largely does without them; Götz et al. 2019). Other variables, such as persistence, are hardly ever investigated in LCR; yet, they have proven to have a huge effect on speakers' performance (Szmrecsanyi 2005; Levey 2006). Consequently, future work should investigate this inherently complex factor (including similarity, cumulativity, etc.) as well, adding to the recently emerging body of relevant corpus-based studies (see e.g. Gries & Koostra 2016).

Overall, the findings of our analysis suggest that, when factors playing a part in native speaker data are taken as a baseline, cross-linguistic influence emerges in the larger picture (i.e. error rates; see Section 3.2) rather than in the details (i.e. linguistic conditioning of the errors; see Section 3.4). In other words, target-like use of a past-referring time-reference form (i.e. using it like a native speaker under the same contextual conditions) is mediated by L1 influence (German vs. Cantonese), while transfer is not traceable when the distributions of the usage contexts are compared across the learner samples (and with native baseline data).

Yet, it emerged that it is difficult to pinpoint one specific factor or factor group responsible for differences between learner groups with typologically diverse L1s. This result is striking in view of earlier claims to the contrary (cf. Bardovi-Harlig 2000, 411). Note also that the findings of the current study converge with statements that cross-linguistic effects (in our case, in the larger picture) persist to advanced learner stages (Jarvis & Pavlenko 2008, 95; see also Collins 2002). Taking this into account, the error rate difference between the two learner groups could, however, also be partly due to a generally lower proficiency of the Chinese learners compared to the German learners, further supporting the conclusion that transfer plays a limited role in the present analysis in the more detailed view. Unfortunately, however, overall proficiency scores for individual learners are unavailable for the ICLE data (see Section 2.2). As a further caveat, note that although we have explored aspects of transfer, there remain others, such as avoidance (SP for PP; Housen 2002, 95; Salaberry 2008, 13; Fuchs et al. 2016, 327), which will have to be tackled with different approaches in future studies.

5 Conclusion

Ending on a few general notes, we submit that our results are relevant for SLA more generally, as they draw attention to the importance of testing a broad range of intralinguistic factors in any transfer study to be able to map the type of statistical tendencies posited by Jarvis (2000), for instance. In sum, such an account views learner (as well as native) production from a multifactorial and probabilistic perspective (Wulff 2017, 747), which serves to increase the depth of how transfer research can be done (cf. Jarvis 2010, 189). In the spirit of Tenfjord et al. (2017, 9), we hope to have shown how an LCR approach can serve to inform transfer studies in SLA, and in the area of TE specifically. By illustrating that corpus data can be subject to a rigorous framework such as the one developed by Jarvis (2000, 2010), we also hope to have shown that SLA and LCR share a lot of common ground and that SLA-driven corpus-based analyses of learner language can address core SLA issues (Myles 2015, 312).

We further submit that in the future we need integrated approaches recognizing the mutual benefits of both paradigms to move forward toward a complete picture of learner language and its development. LCR will profit from taking account (i) of research on SLA principles and paradigms (such as transfer) in terms of establishing a theoretical basis against which corpus data can be empirically tested and (ii) of factors identified in experimental research exerting influence on learner development and usage. SLA, conversely, will profit from insights gathered through LCR, as it can offer a complementary large-scale quantitative perspective on qualitative or small-scale quantitative findings (both in terms of the number of speakers involved and of words produced; e.g. eight learners in Bardovi-Harlig 1992 versus hundreds of learners in the present study). The need for quantification has been recognized by SLA researchers and has been deemed particularly helpful for testing the predictions of universal SLA hypotheses (see e.g. Bayley 1994) like the ones tested for the area of morphologically realized TE in the present study. On a related note, corpus data usually come in large(r) quantities, and thus are seen as a welcome addition to the SLA toolkit for investigating all kinds of structures in natural production data for which specifically elicited material would otherwise have to be used (see also Meriläinen in this volume).

Similarly, this applies to the validation of generative SLA theories, where – to date – metalinguistic and experimental approaches dominate and corpus-based methodologies have not been used widely (Rothman & Slabakova 2018, 430, 436; see also Wulff 2017, 750). This does certainly not mean that experimentally or clinically elicited data are without value; rather, where possible, triangulating analyses of different data types (e.g. learner journal entries [Bardovi-Harlig 1992], transcribed personal narratives [Klein & Perdue 1997], acceptability judgments [Xu 2013], corpus material, etc.) will help us obtain a generalizable perspective on learner patterns and will contribute toward assessing the generalizability of results across analyses, in particular for studies on transfer (Osborne 2015, 351), but also in general (Myles 2015, 317–318).

To expand on the current findings in the aforementioned spirit, future research could take at least two avenues. First, results could be complemented by a bi-directional study (Odlin 1989, 156), that is, an investigation of uses of the German *Perfekt* and the imperfective–perfective distinction in Cantonese by L1 speakers of English, to obtain a complete cross-linguistic overview of the TE systems involved. Second, the perspective could be expanded to a longitudinal or cross-sectional analysis. Younger learners are as yet underrepresented in both SLA and LCR transfer studies (Osborne 2015, 352), and such a view would help to establish even more firmly the effects of typological distance as well as the differences between cross-linguistic and developmental effects at various stages (Odlin 1989, 155). On a related note, it emerged that *Aktionsart*, a factor that featured prominently in earlier work within the paradigm of the AH (see Section 1.1) did not emerge as an important variable in the present analysis. This can be motivated by the fact that the predictions of the AH appear to be largely relevant for learners at earlier stages rather than for advanced learners as represented in the current study (see, however, Salaberry 2008, 130–131; Deshors 2018, 48) and that its predictions are not specifically geared toward the description of the PP–SP alternation. Similarly, salience in terms of irregular vs. regular forms (see Section 2.2) did not emerge as an influential variable, but may feature more prominently in earlier learner production (Jarvis & Pavlenko 2008, 112; Howard & Leclercq 2017, 9). Therefore, future studies with a similar approach should take into consideration early-intermediate learners of English (e.g. at school).

References

Anthony, L. (2014). *AntConc (Version 3.4.3)*. Tokyo: Waseda University, retrieved from www.laurenceanthony.net/software/antconc (accessed June 13, 2020).

Andersen, R. & Shirai, Y. (1994). Discourse motivations for some cognitive acquisition principles. *Studies in Second Language Acquisition* 16(2), 133–156.

Bardovi-Harlig, K. (1992). The use of adverbials and natural order in the development of temporal expression. *International Review of Applied Linguistics in Language Teaching* 30(4), 299–320.

(2000). *Tense and Aspect in Second Language Acquisition: Form, Meaning and Use*. Oxford: Blackwell.

Bayley, R. (1994). Interlanguage variation and the quantitative paradigm: Past tense marking in Chinese-English. In E. Tarone, S. M. Gass, & A. D. Cohen (eds.) *Research Methodology in Second-Language Acquisition*, 157–181. Hillsdale, NJ: Erlbaum.

Brand, C. & Kämmerer, S. (2006). The Louvain International Database of Spoken English Interlanguage (LINDSEI): Compiling the German component. In S. Braun, K. Kohn, & J. Mukherjee (eds.) *Corpus Technology and Language Pedagogy: New Resources, New Tools, New Methods*, 127–140. Frankfurt: Lang.

Bybee, J., Perkins, R., & Pagliuca, W. (1994). *The Evolution of Grammar: Tense, Aspect, and Modality in the Languages of the World*. Chicago, IL: University of Chicago Press.

Calcagno, V. (2015). Glmulti: Model selection and multimodel inference made easy. R package 1.0.7, retrieved from rdrr.io/cran/glmulti/ (accessed June 13, 2020).

Collins, L. (2002). The roles of L1 influence and lexical aspect in the acquisition of temporal morphology. *Language Learning* 52(1), 43–94.

Dahl, Ö. & Velupillai, V. (2013). The perfect. In M. S. Dryer & M. Haspelmath (eds.), *The World Atlas of Language Structures Online*. Munich: Max Planck Digital Library, retrieved from wals.info/chapter/68 (accessed June 13, 2020).

De Cock, S. (2004). Preferred sequences of words in NS and NNS speech. *Belgian Journal of English Language and Literatures* 2, 225–246.

Deshors, S. (2017). Zooming in on verbs in the progressive: A collostructional and correspondence analysis. *Journal of English Linguistics* 45(3), 260–290.

(2018). Does the passé composé influence L2 learners' use of English past tenses? A semantic exploration of the present perfect in French–English interlanguage. *International Journal of Learner Corpus Research* 4(1), 23–53.

Domínguez, L., Arche, M., & Myles, F. (2017). Spanish imperfect revisited: Exploring L1 influence in the reassembly of imperfective features onto new L2 forms. *Second Language Research* 33(4), 431–457.

Ellis, R. (2015). Researching acquisition sequences: Idealization and de-idealization in SLA. *Language Learning* 65(1), 181–209.

Fuchs, R., Götz, S., & Werner, V. (2016). The present perfect in learner Englishes: A corpus-based case study on L1 German intermediate and advanced speech and writing. In V. Werner, E. Seoane, & C. Suárez-Gómez (eds.), *Re-assessing the Present Perfect*, 297–337. Berlin: Mouton de Gruyter.

Fuchs, R. & Werner, V. (2018). Tense and aspect in second language acquisition and learner corpus research. *International Journal of Learner Corpus Research* 4(2), 143–163.

Garside, R. & Smith, N. (1997). A hybrid grammatical tagger: CLAWS4. In R. Garside, G. Leech, & T. McEnery (eds.), *Corpus Annotation: Linguistic Information from Computer Text Corpora*, 102–121. London: Longman.

Gilquin, G. (2008). Combining contrastive and interlanguage analysis to apprehend transfer: Detection, explanation, evaluation. In G. Gilquin, S. Papp, & M. B. Díez-Bedmar (eds.), *Linking Up Contrastive and Learner Corpus Research*, 3–33. Amsterdam: Rodopi.

Gilquin, G., De Cock, S., & Granger, S. (2010). *The Louvain International Database of Spoken English Interlanguage*. Handbook and CD-ROM. Louvain-la-Neuve: Presses universitaires de Louvain.

Götz, S, Werner, S., & Fuchs, R. (2019). Temporal adverbials in the acquisition of past-time reference: A cross-sectional study of L1 German and Cantonese learners of English. In A. Abel, A. Glaznieks, V. Lyding, & L. Nicolas (eds.), *Widening the Scope of Learner Corpus Research*, 43–70. Louvain-la-Neuve: Presses universitaires de Louvain.

Granger, S. (1996). From CA to CIA and back: An integrated approach to computerized bilingual and learner corpora. In K. Aijmer, B. Altenberg, & M. Johansson (eds.), *Languages in Contrast: Text-Based Cross-Linguistic Studies*, 37–51. Lund: Lund University Press.

(2003). The International Corpus of Learner English: A new resource for foreign language learning and teaching and second language acquisition research. *TESOL Quarterly* 37(3), 538–546.

(2015). Contrastive interlanguage analysis: A reappraisal. *International Journal of Learner Corpus Research* 1(1), 7–24.

Granger, S., Dagneaux, E., Meunier, F., & Paquot, M. (2009). *The International Corpus of Learner English, Version 2*. Handbook and CD-ROM. Louvain-la-Neuve: Presses universitaires de Louvain.

Gries, S. Th. & Bernaisch, T. (2016). Exploring epicentres empirically: Focus on South Asian Englishes. *English World-Wide* 37(1), 1–25.

Gries, S. Th. & Deshors, S. (2014). Using regressions to explore deviations between corpus data and a standard/target: Two suggestions. *Corpora* 9(1), 109–136.

Gries, S. Th. & Koostra, G. J. (2016). Structural priming within and across languages: A corpus-based perspective. *Bilingualism: Language and Cognition* 20(2), 235–250.

Heller, B., Bernaisch, T., & Gries, S. Th. (2017). Empirical perspectives on two potential epicenters: The genitive alternation in Asian Englishes. *ICAME Journal* 41(1), 111–144.

Hinkel, E.. (2004). Tense, aspect and the passive voice in L1 and L2 academic texts. *Language Teaching Journal* 8(1), 5–29.

Hong, W. (2007). Lexical Aspect and L1 Influence on the Acquisition of English Verb Tense and Aspect among Hong Kong Secondary School Learners. Unpublished Ph.D. dissertation, Hong Kong Polytechnic University.

Hothorn, T., Hornik, K., Strobl, K. & Zeileis, A. (2017). Party: A laboratory for recursive partitioning. R Package 1.2-3, retrieved from cran.r-project.org/web/packages/party/index.html (accessed June 13, 2020).

Housen, A. (2002). A corpus-based study of the L2-acquisition of the English verb system. In S. Granger, J. Hung, & S. Petch-Tyson (eds.), *Computer Learner Corpora, Second Language Acquisition, and Foreign Language Teaching*, 77–116. Amsterdam: Benjamins.

Howard, M. & Leclercq, P. (2017). Tense, aspect and modality in second language acquisition: An overview. In M. Howard & P. Leclercq (eds.), *Tense-Aspect-Modality in a Second Language: Contemporary Perspectives*, 1–25. Amsterdam: Benjamins.

Jackson, C. (2018). Second language structural priming: A critical review and directions for future research. *Second Language Research* 34(4), 539–552.

Jarvis, S. (2000). Methodological rigor in the study of transfer: Identifying L1 influence in the interlanguage lexicon. *Language Learning* 50(2), 245–309.

(2010). Comparison-based and detection-based approaches to transfer research. *EuroSLA Yearbook* 10, 169–192.

Jarvis, S. & Pavlenko, A. (2008). *Crosslinguistic Influence in Language and Cognition*. New York, NY: Routledge.

Katz, G. (2003). On the stativity of the English perfect. In A. Alexiadou, M. Rathert, & A. von Stechow (eds.), *Perfect Explorations*, 205–234. Berlin: Mouton de Gruyter.

Klein, W. & Perdue, C. (1997). The basic variety (or: Couldn't natural languages be much simpler?). *Second Language Research* 13(4), 301–347.

König, E. & Gast, V. (2018). *Understanding English–German Contrasts*. Berlin: ESV.

Levey, S. (2006). Tense variation in preadolescent narratives. *Journal of English Linguistics* 34(2), 126–152.

Loh, W.-Y. (2011). Classification and regression trees. *Data Mining and Knowledge Discovery* 1, 14–23.

Matthews, S. & Yip, V. 2013. *Cantonese: A Comprehensive Grammar*. London: Routledge.

Myles, F. (2015). Second language acquisition theory and learner corpus research. In S. Granger, G. Gilquin, & F. Meunier (eds.), *The Cambridge Handbook of Learner Corpus Research*, 309–332. Cambridge: Cambridge University Press.

Odlin, T. (1989). *Language Transfer: Cross-Linguistic Influence in Language Learning*. Cambridge: Cambridge University Press.

Osborne, J. (2015). Transfer and learner corpus research. In S. Granger, G. Gilquin, & F. Meunier (eds.), *The Cambridge Handbook of Learner Corpus Research*, 333–356. Cambridge: Cambridge University Press.

Paquot, M. (2013). Lexical bundles and transfer effects. *International Journal of Corpus Linguistics* 18(3), 391–417.

R Development Core Team. (2017). *R: A Language and Environment for Statistical Computing*. Vienna: R Foundation for Statistical Computing, retrieved from www.r-project.org (accessed June 13, 2020).

Ringbom, H. (1987). *The Role of the First Language in Foreign Language Learning*. Clevedon: Multilingual Matters.

Roberts, L. & Liszka, S. A. (2013). Processing tense/aspect agreement violations online in the second language: A self-paced reading study with French and German L2 learners of English. *Second Language Research* 29(4), 413–439.

Rogatcheva, S. (2012). Perfect problems: A corpus-based comparison of the perfect in Bulgarian and German EFL writing. In S. Hoffmann, P. Rayson, & G. Leech (eds.), *English Corpus Linguistics: Looking Back, Moving Forward*, 149–163. Amsterdam: Rodopi.

Rothman, J. & Slabakova, R. (2018). The generative approach to SLA and its place in modern second language studies. *Studies in Second Language Acquisition* 40(2), 417–422.

Salaberry, R. (2008). *Marking Past Tense in Second Language Acquisition: A Theoretical Model*. London: Continuum.

Shirai, Y. (2009). Temporality in first and second language acquisition. In W. Klein & P. Li (eds.), *The Expression of Time*, 167–194. Berlin: Mouton de Gruyter.

Svalberg, A. (2019). Mapping tense form and meaning for L2 learning: From theory to practice. *International Review of Applied Linguistics in Language Teaching* 57(4), 417–445.

Szmrecsanyi, B. (2005). Language users as creatures of habit: A corpus-based analysis of persistence in spoken English. *Corpus Linguistics and Linguistic Theory* 1(1), 113–149.

Tenfjord, K., Jarvis, S., & Golden, A. (2017). Introduction. In A. Golden, S. Jarvis, & K. Tenfjord (eds.), *Crosslinguistic Influence and Distinctive Patterns of Language Learning: Findings and Insights from a Learner Corpus*, 1–11, Bristol: Multilingual Matters.

Vendler, Z. (1967). *Linguistics in Philosophy.* Ithaca, NY: Cornell University Press

Vraicu, A. (2015). The simple present and the expression of temporality in L1 English and L2 English oral narratives: When form meets discourse. In D. Ayoun (ed.), *The Acquisition of the Present*, 289–333. Amsterdam: Benjamins.

Werner, V. (2013). Temporal adverbials and the present perfect/past tense alternation. *English World-Wide* 34(2), 202–240.

(2014). *The Present Perfect in World Englishes: Charting Unity and Diversity.* Bamberg: University of Bamberg Press.

Werner, V., Seoane, E., & Suárez-Gómez, C. (eds.). (2016). *Re-assessing the Present Perfect.* Berlin: Mouton de Gruyter.

Wulff, S. (2017). What learner corpus research can contribute to multilingualism research. *International Journal of Bilingualism* 21(6), 734–753.

Xu, J. (2013). The Temporal (Re-)construal of Experience: How Native Speakers of English and Advanced Chinese Learners Select and Interpret Simple Past/Present Tenses. Unpublished Ph.D. dissertation, Macquarie University.

Yang, S. & Huang, Y. Y. (2004). The impact of the absence of grammatical tense in L1 on the acquisition of the tense-aspect system in L2. *International Review of Applied Linguistics in Language Teaching* 42(1), 49–70.

The Interplay between Universal Processes and Cross-Linguistic Influence in the Light of Learner Corpus Data: Examining Shared Features of Non-native Englishes

Lea Meriläinen

1 Introduction

One of the central aims of the compilation of large learner corpora representative of different L1 populations is the identification of L1-specific and universal features of learner language (e.g. Granger 2015, 12). This is an area where learner corpus research can inform the field of Second Language Acquisition (SLA) research, where the relative importance of cross-linguistic influence and universal processes of SLA has long been a controversial issue (for a review, see Ellis 2008, 361–366). In the early days of SLA research, universal processes and cross-linguistic influence were seen as opposing and mutually exclusive forces (e.g. Dulay & Burt 1974). More recent works, however, suggest that these two phenomena are often intertwined, which manifests itself in quantitative or qualitative differences behind superficially similar features (Jarvis & Pavlenko 2008, 192–193). Although this interaction between universal processes and cross-linguistic influence is often acknowledged in contemporary SLA literature, it has not been backed up by more extensive corpus evidence.

This study examines potential universal features of non-native English in learner corpus data and places them under closer scrutiny in order to identify possible L1-induced quantitative/qualitative variation. The focus is on two morphosyntactic features that have been found to commonly occur in different types of non-native Englishes (i.e. indigenized L2 varieties, English as a foreign language and English as a lingua franca by speakers of various L1 backgrounds): embedded inversion (i.e. inversion of subject–verb [SV] word order in indirect questions) and the omission of prepositions. These features will be closely examined in terms of their types and frequencies in learner corpus data.

This chapter starts with a discussion of cross-linguistic influence and universal processes in the fields of SLA (Section 2) and Learner Corpus Research (LCR) (Section 3). Sections 4.1 and 4.2 present evidence of the examined features in learner corpus data. The discussion and concluding sections relate these findings to earlier discussion concerning universal aspects of learner language both within SLA and LCR, consider the implications of the findings for future research and discuss the connections between research into learner English and L2 varieties of English.

2 Cross-Linguistic Influence and Universal Processes: SLA Perspectives

Cross-linguistic influence (CLI) and universal acquisitional processes are both acknowledged as important factors in the process of SLA. CLI (or language transfer) refers to "the influence of a person's knowledge of one language on that person's knowledge or use of another language" (Jarvis & Pavlenko 2008, 1), and it has been of a central concern in the field of SLA since the very beginning. The field has moved a long way from a behaviorist view of interference of prior linguistic knowledge towards a cognitive account of the phenomenon (for a review, see Ellis 2008, 349–403, Jarvis & Pavlenko 2008, 1–10), and recent years have seen significant theoretical and methodological advancements in the study of CLI. The seminal volume by Jarvis and Pavlenko (2008) provides an extensive synthesis of the different manifestations of CLI (e.g. underuse or avoidance, overuse or preference, differing paths or lengths of acquisition), factors that interact with it (e.g. L1–L2 similarity, developmental processes or L2 proficiency) and how it operates on different levels of language and cognition. The cognitive foundations of CLI are also explored by Jarvis et al. (2013), who point out connections between the degree of L1–L2 (non-) congruence and learner executive control, working memory capacity and patterns of conceptualization, as well as N. Ellis (e.g. 2006), who outlines CLI within usage-based theories of L2 acquisition as a factor that overshadows or blocks learner attention to linguistic features that lack a (direct) counterpart in L1 (i.e. L1 entrenchment). On the methodological plane, the guidelines proposed by Jarvis (2000) have helped to achieve empirical rigor as well as better reliability and comparability of findings in the study of CLI. According to this framework, in order to reliably identify CLI and rule out developmental and universal factors we need to examine three types of evidence: (a) intra-L1-group-homogeneity in learners' IL performance (i.e. learners with the same L1 behave in a similar manner), (b) inter-L1-group-heterogeneity in learners' IL performance (i.e. learners with a different L1 behave in a different manner), and (c) intra-L1-group congruity between learners' L1 and IL performance (i.e. the learners' use of the L2 corresponds to the use of a particular feature in their L1).

The notion of universal processes of SLA, on the other hand, has received less attention in recent SLA research than CLI. Jarvis and Pavlenko (2008, 192–193; see also Ellis 2008, 80–82, 548–549) discuss two types of acquisitional universals that explain similar types of non-target forms that learners from vastly different L1 backgrounds make: simplification and overgeneralization. Simplification is the omission of structures that are obligatory in the target language, such as auxiliary verbs, articles or bound morphemes (Ellis 2008, 81; Jarvis & Pavlenko 2008, 192). Overgeneralization is defined as "the overuse or overapplication of a structure to contexts where it is ungrammatical or unconventional in the target language" (Jarvis & Pavlenko 2008, 192), such as applying a regular past tense ending *-ed* to irregular verbs (e.g. *goed*; Ellis 2008, 471). The notions of simplification and overgeneralization have been present in theories of SLA ever since the Interlanguage Hypothesis (Selinker 1972), which entails the idea that L2 learners restructure the target language in a systematic manner, starting with a basic version and gradually complexifying the system. One of the first works to highlight the importance of universal processes in SLA is Dulay and Burt (1974), which proposed that L2 acquisition is guided by universal cognitive mechanisms similar to L1 acquisition and that the learner's L1 plays an insignificant role in the process. Universal characteristics have also been argued to exist in the acquisition orders of certain linguistic structures, such as grammatical morphemes (e.g. Dulay & Burt 1974; see also Luk & Shirai 2009) and relative clauses (Shirai & Ozeki 2007; for a review, see also Braidi 1999, 25–39 and Ellis 2008, 91–98). Furthermore, specific theories and hypotheses incorporate the idea of universal developmental characteristics of SLA, such as the Aspect Hypothesis (Andersen & Shirai 1996) and the Processability Theory (Pienemann 2005).

What is characteristic of the research originating from the 1970s and 1980s is the dichotomous view of acquisitional universals *as opposed to* CLI; for example, if a certain feature occurs in the target language production of several learner groups, this feature must originate from universal processes independent of the learners' L1. More recent works, however, provide evidence for the interrelatedness of these two phenomena. Jarvis and Odlin (2000) find that although both L1 Finnish and L1 Swedish learners manifest overgeneralization of English prepositions, the patterns they produce reflect the corresponding preposition or case inflection in their L1. Collins (2002) shows that the acquisition of tense/aspect markers by francophone learners of English, although largely conforming to the Aspect Hypothesis (Andersen & Shirai 1996), manifests simultaneous L1 effects. The idea of universal acquisition order has also been challenged in the case of morphemes (Luk & Shirai 2009) as well as relative clauses (Shirai & Ozeki 2007). The above findings are in line with Jarvis and Pavlenko (2008, 192–193; see also Ellis 2008, 394–396), who highlight CLI as a phenomenon that does not occur in isolation but interacts with and is modulated by a number of factors, universal processes being one of them. While this idea is now widely accepted in SLA literature, it is based on studies examining elicited data from a relatively small number of learners – a gap which learner corpora can help fill.

3 L1-Specific and Universal Aspects of Learner Language: LCR Perspectives

The differentiation between shared and L1-specific aspects of learner language is often mentioned as one of the central questions that large, multi-L1 learner corpora can help answer (Leech 1998, xv; Granger 2015, 12; Myles 2015, 382), but to date there has been no systematic treatment of the topic. The (reliable) separation between CLI-induced and shared aspects of learner language is known to be complicated because of the multitude of CLI effects and the many variables that influence their occurrence (see Osborne 2015, 410–411). The relevance of Jarvis's (2000) model for the identification of CLI in learner corpus data is recognized in a number of studies (Gilquin 2008; Paquot 2010, 2013; Murakami & Alexopoulou 2016). A similar contrastive design is also widely employed in LCR in the form of contrastive interlanguage analysis (CIA; Granger 1996, 2015), which entails corpus-based comparisons between learner varieties and native language varieties, with the aim of identifying features distinctive of learner language and of certain learner populations. Studies applying this framework have found evidence for L1-induced differences in the use of formulaic sequences (Paquot 2013; for a review, see Paquot & Granger 2012), different lexical phenomena (Gilquin 2008; Hasselgård & Johansson 2011), adverb placement (Osborne 2008) and article use (Díez-Bedmar & Papp 2008; Crosthwaite 2016). In the study of morpheme acquisition, Murakami and Alexopoulou (2016) present compelling corpus-based evidence for L1-induced differences in morpheme accuracy across different proficiency levels, thereby seriously challenging the universal order of acquisition of English morphemes.

Earlier research has also identified learner behavior that seems to be common for learners from different L1 backgrounds, such as overuse or underuse of certain trigrams (Aarts & Granger 1998, 140), high-frequency verbs (Ringbom 1998) or pragmatic expressions (Vyatkina & Cunningham 2015, 353). Gilquin et al. (2007; see also Paquot 2010) identify general areas of difficulty in the academic writing by learners from different L1 backgrounds: patterns of frequency different from native language (e.g. overuse of a limited set of words), lack of register awareness (i.e. use of spoken language features in writing), positioning of connectors (e.g. *however*, *though*), semantic misuse and (unidiomatic) phraseology. Recent studies also draw parallels between learner English, L2 varieties of English and English as a lingua franca, and identify processes that seem to give rise to commonly occurring patterns in learner corpora. Callies (2016) discusses several intralingual (i.e. L2 based) processes giving rise to lexical innovations in the area of derivational morphology, including (over-)regularization (e.g. *unmoral* for 'immoral'), simplification (e.g. *critize* for 'criticize') and analogy (e.g. *economical* for 'economic'). Schneider and Gilquin (2016) also find the process of analogy to be an explanatory factor behind innovative verb/adjective + preposition combinations, such as *discuss about* or *independent on* (instead of 'discuss something' or 'independent from').

A number of learner corpus studies also discuss simultaneous evidence for CLI and shared tendencies in learner language. Ringbom (1998) finds general overuse of high-frequency verbs by seven learner populations in the *International Corpus of Learner English* (ICLE), but also overuse or underuse phenomena that appear to be related to the structure of the learners' L1 (e.g. underuse of prepositions by L1 Finnish learners). Paquot (2010) identifies a number of general learner language characteristics based on ten L1 populations in the ICLE as well as specific expressions and patterns that are common to L1 French but not to other learner groups. Díez-Bedmar and Papp (2008) observe non-native use of English articles in both Chinese and Spanish learners' interlanguage, but L1 Chinese learners, whose L1 lacks articles, manifest more frequent use of zero article and overgeneralization of the definite article into inappropriate contexts. Rogatcheva (2014) finds that both German and Bulgarian learners underuse the English progressive in comparison to native control corpora but that some of their distinctive usage patterns can be traced back to their respective L1s.

As the above literature review has demonstrated, the idea of the co-occurrence of L1 influence and universal aspects of L2 learning and use is present in both SLA and LCR literature. Both fields also have a relatively similar understanding of the concept of CLI, but universals of SLA or learner language appear to be understood in slightly different ways. While in SLA the term is used to explain commonalities in the acquisition or (non-standard) use of specific linguistic features or subsystems caused by developmental or universal processes (Jarvis & Pavlenko 2008, 192–193), in LCR it is understood in much broader terms as general tendencies emerging from corpus-based investigations of learner language (e.g. Gilquin et al. 2007; Paquot 2010). Many learner corpus studies, in fact, prefer using terms such as "general interlanguage features" (Paquot 2010, 142–181) or "cross-linguistic invariants" (Granger 2015, 12). Ädel (2006, 151) defines universal learner strategies as "linguistic behaviour that is common to all learners, regardless of their L1 or L2." In a similar vein, Jantunen (2008) describes universals of learner language as certain common phenomena that occur regardless of the source or the target language, such as atypical frequencies, unconventionality or even CLI, which is a common tendency in learner language but realized in different ways depending on the source or the target language. This terminological difference reflects the differing objectives of these two fields. LCR is mostly descriptive in its orientation and has only quite recently began to engage with SLA theory (Myles 2015; Fuchs & Werner 2018). The focus of LCR has also often been on features that are easily searchable in corpora (e.g. lexical items, connectors, trigrams), which are more rarely studied in SLA. This study takes as its starting point the notion of universal processes of SLA (i.e. simplification and overgeneralization) and sets out to find evidence for these in learner corpus data.

4 Two Case Studies

This study focuses on two morphosyntactic features that are considered common in non-native Englishes, embedded inversion (Section 4.1) and the omission of prepositions (Section 4.2), and examines the roles of CLI and the processes of simplification or overgeneralization as potential explanatory factors behind them in learner English corpora. The motivation for the choice of these features stems from the extensive evidence found in the field of world Englishes (i.e. research into indigenized L2 varieties of English) for similar non-standard morphosyntactic features occurring across L2 varieties (e.g. Kortmann & Szmrecsanyi 2004; Kortmann et al. 2020), with embedded inversion and omission of prepositions among them. The assumed cause for the observed morphosyntactic similarities is the process of SLA at the initial stages of variety formation (e.g. Biewer 2011), which is why learner English can be expected to manifest similar features. Embedded inversion is seen as the result of overgeneralization of direct question word order into indirect questions, whereas omission of prepositions represents a form of simplification. These features will be closely examined in terms of their types and frequencies in data representing selected learner groups, based on structural (dis)similarities between the learners' L1 and English.

This study sets out to answer the following research questions:

(1) To what extent do learners from different L1 backgrounds produce similar patterns of embedded inversion and preposition omission?
(2) If such similar patterns are found, do they manifest quantitative or qualitative variation pointing towards the interplay between CLI and universal processes?

The data for these two case studies derive from the ICLE (Granger et al. 2009) and the Corpus of Matriculation Examination compositions by Finnish-speaking and Swedish-speaking students (MEC; Meriläinen 2010). The ICLE consists of argumentative essays by university undergraduates in the English language whose English proficiency ranges from upper intermediate to advanced (CEFR B2–C2; Granger et al. 2009, 11–12). Different L1 populations in the ICLE are known to vary in terms of their proficiency level, with Finnish and Swedish learners among the most advanced (CEFR C1–C2). The MEC therefore provides a point of comparison to the ICLE because it contains examination compositions by L1 Finnish and L1 Swedish Upper Secondary school students in Finland, who are at intermediate levels of proficiency (CEFR B1–B2; Meriläinen 2010, 45). L1 Finnish and Swedish learners are considered to represent ideal comparison groups in research into CLI because of their culturally and educationally similar backgrounds but typologically different L1s (e.g. Jarvis 2000; Jarvis & Odlin 2000; Meriläinen 2010). This study also includes other learner populations in the ICLE, which are selected on the basis of (non-)congruence between L1 and English. The American English component of the *Louvain Corpus of Native English Essays* (LOCNESS), consisting of argumentative essays by American students, is included for comparison.[1] The analysis focuses on frequencies of the examined features per corpus as an aggregated whole instead of looking at individual differences between learners, which makes this study exploratory in nature.

The methodological framework for this study is CIA (Granger 2015; see Section 3). Comparisons between different corpora adhere – as closely as possible with the present data – to the methodological

[1] See www.learnercorpusassociation.org/resources/tools/locness-corpus/.

principles proposed by Jarvis (2000; see Section 2) for the rigorous identification of CLI, which relies on the comparison of learner groups from different L1 backgrounds, and the comparison of the relevant structures in the learners' L1 and the L2 (see also Jarvis & Pavlenko 2008, 48–58; Meriläinen 2010, 57–62). As defined by Jarvis (2000, 252), "L1 influence refers to any instance of learner data where a statistically significant correlation (or probability-based relation) is shown to exist between some feature of learners' IL performance and their L1 background." In this study, statistically significant quantitative differences between learner groups in their usage of the examined features as well as qualitatively distinctive usage that can be traced back to the structure of the L1 are regarded as evidence for CLI. Quantitatively and qualitatively similar usage patterns across L1 populations, on the other hand, are considered to provide evidence for universal processes.

4.1 Embedded Inversion

4.1.1 EARLIER RESEARCH

Embedded inversion (i.e. the inversion of SV word order in subordinate interrogative clauses) is a widely attested phenomenon in L2 varieties of English (for a review, see Meriläinen & Paulasto 2017). Example (1) illustrates inverted word order in WH-questions and (2) in Yes/No-questions (from Kortmann et al. 2020):

(1) *I don't know what are you asking me* (cf. standard English 'I don't know what you are asking me')

(2) *She asked me do I know her name* (cf. standard English 'She asked me if/whether I know her name')

Embedded inversion is sometimes found in spoken language by native speakers, and it is described as a compromise between direct and indirect speech in that it preserves the word order of direct questions (cf. *What are you asking me? Do you know her name?*) but may contain a pronoun or tense shift typical of reported speech (Biber et al. 1999, 920–921). It is a phenomenon more typical of spoken language, but is also found in written genres (Kolbe & Sand 2010). Embedded inversion is more frequent in L2 varieties in comparison to British or American English (Kortmann et al. 2020; Meriläinen & Paulasto 2017), and it is often described as L2 speakers' overgeneralization of direct question word order into indirect questions (Sand 2008; Kolbe & Sand 2010). There are also commonalities across L2 varieties of English in that embedded inversion tends to be more common in WH-questions than in Yes/No-questions, with matrix verbs that introduce direct speech (e.g. *ask*) and in fixed chunks involving interrogative pronoun and the verb *be* (e.g. *what's*, *how's*; Kolbe & Sand 2010; Hilbert 2011; Gilquin 2015; Meriläinen & Paulasto 2017). However, qualitatively distinctive usage and higher frequencies of embedded inversion are widely documented in Irish English, which provides evidence for substrate influence from Irish (e.g. Hilbert 2011; Meriläinen & Paulasto 2017).

Earlier studies examining English usage by foreign language speakers show that embedded inversion is found in English as a lingua franca usage by speakers of various L1 backgrounds (Ranta 2013), and in learner English, albeit in smaller frequencies than in L2 varieties (Gilquin 2015; Meriläinen & Paulasto 2017). Gilquin (2015) shows that embedded inversion is often governed by similar linguistic principles in learner English and second or native language varieties. The structure of the learners' native language has also been found to be a factor behind frequencies of non-standard subordinate interrogative clauses in L1 Finnish and Swedish learners' written English (Meriläinen 2010, 111–115). All in all, embedded inversion provides a fruitful testing ground to examine the roles of CLI and universal processes in learner English.

4.1.2 DATA AND METHODS

This study examines the Finnish, German and Swedish components of the ICLE and Finnish-speaking and Swedish-speaking students' data in the MEC.[2] Finnish differs from English in that it has a similar word order in direct and indirect questions and no subordinating conjunction in Yes/No-questions, whereas in German and Swedish indirect questions are structurally similar to English. In order to reliably identify native language influence, learners of a bilingual background were excluded from the study by using the ICLE search interface selection criteria "language at home (first): Finnish/Swedish/German,"

[2] The data presented here form part of two earlier studies: a conference presentation by Gilquin and Meriläinen (2012), with minor adjustments made in the classification, and Meriläinen and Paulasto (2017), which focuses on the six most frequent matrix verbs (*ask*, *know*, *see*, *tell*, *understand*, *wonder*). The focus of these studies is different from the present one in that they compare learner data with a number of L1 and L2 English corpora in order to identify similarities and differences between them, whereas this study examines learner corpora more closely in order to find evidence for CLI and universals.

Table 12 Corpora examined for embedded inversion

Corpus	Word count
ICLE-FI	162,489
ICLE-GE	144,717
ICLE-SW	142,498
MEC-FI	96,789
MEC-SW	28,225
LOCNESS	149,574

"language at home (second): none" and "language at home (third): none." The examined corpora and their word counts are listed in Table 12.

Indirect questions were extracted from the corpora by searching for matrix verbs that earlier corpus-based investigations have shown to commonly precede *wh*-, *whether*- and *if*-clauses (Biber et al. 1999, 683–693). These include altogether 114 verbs, covering speech act verbs (N = 24; e.g. *ask*, *question*, *tell*), other communication verbs (N = 12; e.g. *indicate*), cognition verbs (N = 41; e.g. *assess*, *find out*), perception verbs (N = 10; e.g. *see*, *hear*), verbs of attitude and emotion (N = 22; e.g. *doubt*, *feel*) and aspectual verbs (N = 5, e.g. *end*) (see Appendix 1 for the full list of verbs). Although this method does not retrieve all instances of indirect questions, it should retrieve a sample large enough to see what the proportion of embedded inversion is out of indirect questions in general. Irrelevant instances were manually excluded: direct questions (indicated with spelling, such as quotation marks or a colon), *to*-infinitives, nominal relative clauses, exclamative clauses and clauses where a *wh*-pronoun is the subject (see also Ranta 2013, 105–124; Meriläinen & Paulasto 2017). After this, the ratio of correctly formed indirect questions and those containing SV inversion was calculated. In order to examine more closely the syntactic environment of embedded inversion, the results were grouped according to question type (WH-questions or Yes/No-questions), the matrix verb and the embedded verb.

4.1.3 RESULTS

Table 13 shows the raw frequencies and the relative frequencies per 100,000 words of standard-like indirect questions and those containing embedded inversion in the examined corpora. The final column

Table 13 Indirect questions and embedded inversions

	Indirect questions		Embedded inversions		Proportion of EI
Corpus	Raw freq.	Rel. freq. per 100,000 words	Raw freq.	Rel. freq. per 100,000 words	%
ICLE-FI	135	83	6	4	4.3
ICLE-GE	143	99	4	3	2.7
ICLE-SW	144	101	2	1	1.4
MEC-FI	122	126	45	46	26.9
MEC-SW[a]	45	159	3	11	6.3
LOCNESS	170	114	5	3	2.9

[a] The relative frequency for MEC-SW is an approximation, because this corpus is considerably smaller than the other examined corpora (see Table 12). For the sake of comparison, the relative frequencies were calculated per 100,000 words for all corpora.

gives the percentage of embedded inversion out of all indirect questions[3]. As can be seen in Table 13, the highest proportion of embedded inversion is found amongst intermediate-level L1 Finnish learners (MEC-FI; 26.9 percent), which differs significantly from the rest of the corpora ($p < .01$).[4] There are no significant differences between the other corpora. It is noteworthy that intermediate-level L1 Swedish learners (MEC-SW) produce low frequencies of embedded inversion, which shows that lower proficiency does not give rise to embedded inversion if the learners' L1 and L2 are structurally similar. In the case of L1 Finnish learners, L1–L2 non-congruence appears to give rise to embedded inversion at intermediate levels but more rarely at advanced levels of proficiency.[5]

When we examine the syntactic context for embedded inversion more closely, we find further differences between the learner groups.

[3] The instances of embedded inversion are evenly distributed across different learners so that the total 65 instances observed in the data derive from 55 students, with 46 students producing one instance, 8 students 2 instances and 1 student 3 instances of embedded inversion.

[4] The p-values refer to Fisher's Exact Test (with Bonferroni correction for multiple comparisons), which is the recommended test for statistical independence when dealing with low frequencies (e.g. Levshina 2015, 214). The results are considered significant at the $p < 0.05$ level.

[5] These results are in line with Gilquin (2015, 102), who finds proportions of embedded inversion to be low in spoken data by advanced L1 French, German and Swedish learners (0–2.2 percent).

Table 14 Embedded inversion in WH-questions and Yes/No-questions

Corpus	WH-questions	Yes/No-questions
ICLE-FI	5.8% (6/103)	0.0% (0/38)
ICLE-GE	3.7% (4/107)	0.0% (0/40)
ICLE-SW	1.8% (2/112)	0.0% (0/34)
MEC-FI	17.9% (22/123)	52.3% (23/44)
MEC-SW	6.1% (2/33)	6.7% (1/15)
LOCNESS	3.7% (5/134)	0.0% (0/41)

Table 14 gives the proportion of embedded inversion of all indirect questions for WH-questions and Yes/No-questions separately. The difference between MEC-FI and the other corpora is significant in Yes/No-questions ($p < .001$), and in WH-questions MEC-FI significantly differs from the ICLE subcorpora ($p < .001$) but not from MEC-SW. Finnish learners also stand out in producing high frequencies of embedded inversion in Yes/No-questions (52.3 percent of all indirect Yes/No-questions), while in the other corpora embedded inversion tends to be found in WH-questions only. The findings from the ICLE subcorpora, LOCNESS and MEC-SW are, thus, in line with earlier studies showing that embedded inversion is more commonly found in WH-questions, where the line between direct and indirect speech is more easily crossed than in Yes/No-questions, by L1 and L2 speakers alike (Kolbe & Sand 2010; Hilbert 2011; Meriläinen & Paulasto 2017). Intermediate-level Finnish learners, however, do not conform to this universal tendency but use embedded inversion more frequently in Yes/No-questions. This is possibly due to transfer from Finnish, which differs from English in having an SV word order with no subordinating conjunction in indirect Yes/No-questions (see Meriläinen 2010, 144–153).

A qualitative look into the matrix verbs with which embedded inversion occurs shows that in the ICLE subcorpora, LOCNESS and MEC-SW the most common verbs are *ask* ($n = 12$) and *wonder* ($n = 4$), which have been shown to commonly precede embedded inversion in L1 and L2 Englishes (Sand 2008; Kolbe & Sand 2010; Meriläinen & Paulasto 2017). In MEC-FI, however, we find a wider variety of matrix verbs, the most frequent ones being *know* ($n = 16$) and *think* ($n = 9$). The instances found in the ICLE subcorpora, LOCNESS and MEC-SW can also generally be explained with linguistic factors that have previously been found to govern the occurrence of embedded inversion: lengthy subjects and frequent chunks (Hilbert 2011; Gilquin

2015). In particular, the common occurrence of chunks with the verb *be* has been identified as one of the main factors giving rise to embedded inversion (Hilbert 2011). In the present data, it co-occurs with 10 out of the total 19 instances of embedded inversion found in the ICLE subcorpora, LOCNESS and MEC-SW, but only 12 out of the 45 embedded inversions found in MEC-FI. Examples (3) and (4) illustrate these typical patterns with a lengthy subject and the verb *be* found in all the other corpora, and examples (5) and (6) the types of patterns found in MEC-FI.

(3) *I intend to look into the future asking myself what are the long-term consequences of unemployment* (ICLE-SW)

(4) [. . .] *you might say and wonder what is the point of my unbiased observation* (ICLE-GE)

(5) *I don't even know could I forgive her if she were sorry!* (MEC-FI)

(6) *I can't know get I ever married, but I'm sure that time will show it to me* (MEC-FI)

All in all, the frequencies of embedded inversion are relatively low in the ICLE subcorpora, LOCNESS and MEC-SW (cf. the 21–25 percent of embedded inversion in WH-questions in the L2 varieties examined by Meriläinen & Paulasto 2017), and the observed instances largely adhere to the universal constraints of embedded inversion identified by earlier research: WH-questions, interrogative matrix verbs and chunks with the verb *be*. In MEC-FI, the majority of instances cannot be explained with a similar blending of direct and indirect questions but seem to arise from a different source, the learners' L1.

4.2 The Omission of Prepositions

4.2.1 EARLIER RESEARCH

The omission of standard English prepositions has been observed in several L2 varieties of English as well as in English-based pidgins and creoles (e.g. Mesthrie & Bhatt 2008, 73; Kortmann et al. 2020). Examples (7) and (8) illustrate two types of contexts where prepositions are frequently omitted: motion verbs and certain prepositional or phrasal verbs (from Kortmann et al. 2020).

(7) *She went Ø town* (cf. standard English 'She went to town')

(8) *It depend Ø what you are wearing* (cf. standard English 'It depends on what you are wearing')

Prepositions are sometimes left out in certain contexts in L1 varieties (e.g. days of the week, as in *I'll see you Monday*, Quirk et al. 1985, 693; as a part of complex prepositions, e.g. *go up (to)*, Cheshire et al. 1989), but in L2 varieties this is reported to occur more often and in a broader range of contexts. Preposition omission is often examined alongside other types of non-standard prepositional constructions, such as new verb–preposition combinations and redundant prepositions (e.g. *attached with*, *discuss about*; Mesthrie & Bhatt 2008, 73; Schneider 2012, 74). Nesselhauf (2009) observes competition between semantically similar expressions, one of which takes a prepositional complement and another a noun complement (e.g. *talk/speak about* vs. *discuss*), in L2 varieties and learner English alike.

In learner English, preposition omission is found to be particularly frequent if the learners' L1 does not have prepositions similar to English (e.g. Finnish: Jarvis & Odlin 2000; Meriläinen 2010; Japanese: Kaneko 2008; Chinese and Japanese: Schumann 1986). At the same time, learners from different L1 backgrounds are reported to omit prepositions, which Jarvis and Pavlenko (2008, 192) explain with universal simplification tendencies. While preposition omission is often mentioned as a prime example of simplification, it has been examined relatively little in SLA research and even less so in LCR, which has primarily focused on features that can be retrieved from corpus data more easily than zero items.

4.2.2 DATA AND METHODS

The data for this case study derive from the Chinese, Finnish, Japanese and Swedish components of the ICLE and the L1 Finnish and Swedish components of the MEC.[6] These learner groups were selected in order to compare learners whose L1 does not have prepositions similar to English (Chinese, Finnish and Japanese) and learners whose L1 is

[6] The data presented here has been included in a conference presentation by Meriläinen and Paulasto (2015) with the aim of comparing L1 and L2 varieties of English and learner Englishes, but the more detailed annotation and qualitative analysis of the results was done for the purposes of this study. The samples from the MEC are also included in Meriläinen (2010), but they have been reanalyzed for the present study. The annotation was done by the author for the examined learner corpora, but the criteria were established in collaboration and the results cross-checked by both authors of Meriläinen and Paulasto (2015).

structurally similar to English (Swedish). Swedish has a system of prepositions that shares many similarities with English, but Finnish has a complex system of case endings that largely correspond to the function of prepositions (e.g. Jarvis & Odlin 2000, 541–553, Meriläinen 2010, 163–175). Japanese uses postpositions or the combination of nouns and postpositions instead of prepositions (Cho 2010, 260–263). Chinese uses prepositions, postpositions, a combination of both and coverbs, which have features of verbs and prepositions (Huang 2010, 157–158). In order to examine possible quantitative and qualitative differences between learner groups, this study resorts to a manual analysis and annotation of corpus samples of c. 30,000 words. Samples from the corpora were selected at random by choosing an approximately equal number of essays from different universities represented in the subcorpora (for the composition of the ICLE subcorpora, see Granger et al. 2009). Learners of a bilingual background were excluded from the study by using the search criteria described in Section 4.1.2. Overview of the examined corpus samples and their word counts is given in Table 15 (see Appendix 2 for a full list of selected file names).

The following instances were excluded from the analysis: when the meaning or the structure of the sentence was unclear, where a preposition mentioned earlier in the sentence was ellipted and where a preposition can be left out in standard English (e.g. certain temporal expressions, such as *We stayed there (for) three months*; see Quirk et al. 1985, 692–695). The instances of preposition omission were classified into descriptive categories based on the syntactic function of the prepositional phrase (i.e. complement, adverbial or postmodifier; see Quirk et al. 1985, 657–658), which functions as a starting point for a closer qualitative examination.

4.2.3 RESULTS

Table 16 shows the raw frequencies and the relative frequencies per 10,000 words of instances of preposition omission found in the corpus samples.[7] There are significant quantitative differences between the learner groups. The highest relative frequency of preposition omission

[7] The instances of preposition omission (n = 194) were relatively evenly distributed in the analyzed samples in that 81 learners had produced 1 instance, 25 learners 2 instances, 10 learners 3 instances, 4 learners 4 instances, 2 learners 5 instances and 1 learner 7 instances. The learners producing 4–7 instances of preposition omission in the data were all from ICLE-JP and MEC-FI, where the frequencies of preposition omission were the highest.

Table 15 Corpora examined for preposition omission

Corpus	Word count
ICLE-CH	30,170
ICLE-FI	30,514
ICLE-JP	30,284
ICLE-SW	30,214
MEC-FI	35,207
MEC-SW	28,225
LOCNESS	30,220

Table 16 Frequencies of preposition omission

Corpus	Raw freq.	Rel. freq. per 10,000 words
ICLE-CH	33	11
ICLE-FI	13	4
ICLE-JP	58	19
ICLE-SW	4	1
MEC-FI	76	22
MEC-SW	5	2
LOCNESS	5	2

is found in MEC-FI (22), followed by ICLE-JP (19) and ICLE-CH (11). The Finnish-speaking learners in the MEC differ highly significantly from their Swedish-speaking peers (LL = 60.04, $p < .001$).[8] The difference between the ICLE subcorpora and the LOCNESS is also highly significant (LL = 91.6, $p < .001$). These findings suggest that learners' L1 is the primary factor giving rise to these differences, because the highest frequencies of preposition omission are found amongst learners whose L1 does not have prepositions similar to English (Chinese, Japanese and Finnish intermediate-level learners). Swedish-speaking learners, whose L1 is structurally similar to English, do not differ from native speakers at an advanced nor at an intermediate level. As discussed in Jarvis and Odlin (2000, 550), learners whose L1 uses postponed morphology (case endings in Finnish or

8 The p-values derive from the log-likelihood ratio test (see, e.g. Rayson 2003, 43–58). The significance thresholds for log-likelihood are LL 3.84 for $p < .05$, LL 6.63 for $p < .01$, LL 10.83 for $p < .001$ and LL 15.13 for $p < .0001$. The results are considered significant at the $p < 0.05$ level.

postpositions in Japanese and Chinese) may be less attuned to paying attention to preposed morphology. It is also notable that while there is a highly significant difference between MEC-FI and LOCNESS (LL = 64.38, $p < .001$), the difference between ICLE-FI and LOCNESS does not reach the level of statistical significance (LL = 3.6). This points to preposition omission being primarily a feature of less advanced learners. Slightly lower proficiency level of Japanese and Chinese learners may also explain why the frequencies of preposition omission are higher in ICLE-CH and ICLE-JP in comparison to ICLE-FI (see Granger et al. 2009, 11–12). Thus, besides the learners' L1, lower proficiency emerges as another factor that is likely to influence the frequency of preposition omission.

A closer look at the types of contexts preposition omission occurred in (i.e. complement, adverbial or postmodifier) reveals a very varied picture.[9] Among the instances where the omitted preposition functioned as a complement of a certain head word, there were 50 different head words, most of which occurred only once or twice. There were only five head words that occurred three times or more often in the whole data: *agree* (N = 4), *care* (N = 4), *decide* (N = 3), *talk* (N = 8) and *think* (N = 8). Earlier literature on non-native Englishes has generally drawn a more systematic picture of the contexts where preposition omission occurs (e.g. semantically similar and competing expressions such as *talk about* vs. *discuss*; see Section 4.2.1). In the present data, such recurrent contexts are rare. Competition between semantically similar expressions (cf. Nesselhauf 2009) or analogy (cf. Schneider & Gilquin 2016) could explain some of the instances of preposition omission (*talk about* vs. *discuss*, *think about* vs. *consider*; example (9)), but in many cases there does not appear to be a closely related expression that could give rise to a confusion or extension of analogy between a prepositional or a noun complement (example (10)).

(9) *Now we are talking Ø Finlans future* (MEC-FI)

(10) *Schools should hire teatchers who listen Ø students* (MEC-FI)

[9] Earlier literature has identified preposition omission in stranded contexts as a typical feature in L2 varieties and learner English alike (e.g. Kortmann et al. 2020; Kao 2001), but since stranded contexts were very infrequent in the examined corpus samples, they will not be included in the present analysis. Similarly, complex prepositions (cf. Cheshire et al. 1989) were so infrequent in the data that they do not lend themselves for further analysis.

Similarly, there was a wide array of the types of adverbial phrases in which preposition omission occurred, including adverbials of space (position, destination), time (position, duration), cause, means and post-modifying *of*-phrases. The only distinctive pattern that emerges from the data is the large number of space position adverbials in Finnish intermediate learners' data (21 out of the total 76 instances in MEC-FI). In fact, the most typical kind of preposition omission for Finnish learners is the omission of the preposition *in* in a space position adverbial (example (11)). Finnish learners' difficulty in expressing spatial relations with prepositions in English has been observed in earlier studies (Jarvis & Odlin 2000; Meriläinen 2010), which goes back to Finnish expressing spatial relations with case endings.

(11) *It is hard to be strange place with strange people* (MEC-FI)

What seems to be found in all the examined corpora is preposition omission in post-modifying *of*-phrases (28 out of the total 118 adverbials), which in many cases are on the borderline between standard and non-standard use (example (12)). These also constitute 4 out of the 5 instances of preposition omission in native speakers' data (LOCNESS). A possible reason for this may be found in the relatively low salience of the preposition *of*, which may factor behind its omission in both learner and native data.

(12) *Yoga is a relaxation technique typically practiced by what some Westerners would classify as "new age" type Ø* people (LOCNESS)

Although the present study into preposition omission in the selected learner corpora is very exploratory in nature and based on small sets of data, it allows the careful conclusion that preposition omission is influenced primarily by the learners' L1. The findings point to preposition omission being a feature of learners whose L1 does not have prepositions similar to English, and in particular learners of a lower proficiency level. We do not find much evidence for universal simplification tendencies independent of the learners' L1 background.

5 Discussion

This study has examined two different types of morphosyntactic features: embedded inversion and omission of prepositions in learner English corpora. The study examined corpus-based indications of (1) similar patterns across various L1 populations possibly induced by universal processes of SLA and (2) quantitative or qualitative variation in the use of these features indicative of simultaneous CLI effects. Overall, there is only meager evidence for similar features across the examined corpora. While some instances of embedded inversion and preposition omission were found in all the examined corpora, these features were significantly more common for learners with a non-congruent L1. A qualitative examination of the linguistic contexts of embedded inversion and preposition omission identified some similar patterns, namely embedded inversion in WH-questions with an interrogative matrix verb (confirming earlier findings based on L2 varieties of English) and preposition omission in post-modifying *of*-phrases. While these patterns could arise from overgeneralization or simplification tendencies (i.e. generalization of direct question word order into indirect questions or avoidance of phonetically less salient functional morphemes), these instances constitute a small proportion of the results. The quantitative and qualitative differences between the examined corpora provide strong evidence for CLI. The finding that CLI emerges as a more prominent explanatory factor behind the results is not surprising in light of the fact that there is a growing body of research in the field of SLA that challenges the idea of universal aspects of L2 acquisition and highlights CLI as a more significant factor (see Section 2).

Whether there is evidence for universals of learner language seems to depend on how the concept is defined. Many learner corpus studies understand it in a very broad sense, encompassing general tendencies or learner behavior such as overuse/underuse, lack of register differences or unidiomatic phraseological patterning (cf. Jantunen 2008; Paquot 2010; Gilquin et al. 2007). The existence of such tendencies is well established in LCR, but it must be noted that these tendencies do not exclude CLI. However, if we approach learner language universals at the level of specific linguistic features, as in the present study, there is no evidence for invariable universal aspects. It is important for future studies to be clear about how they define and what they regard as evidence for universal aspects of learner language.

The findings of this study also show that it is important to take the variable of proficiency into account in the investigation of CLI or universal learner language characteristics, as L1–L2 non-congruence combined with a lower level of proficiency resulted in higher frequencies and qualitatively distinctive use of the examined features. This suggests that there are also some developmental tendencies behind the acquisition of these structures. Proficiency is noted to be a fuzzy variable in the ICLE (Granger et al. 2009, 11–12), and care should be taken in drawing conclusions on CLI or universal characteristics of learner language based on this corpus. Corpora covering different proficiency levels by the same L1 populations could provide new insight into the relationship between CLI and L2 proficiency, which earlier SLA research has shown to be a complex and a non-linear one (for a review, see Jarvis 2000, 246–247; Jarvis & Pavlenko 2008, 201–203; Meriläinen 2010, 29–32).

Overall, the fields of SLA and LCR have accumulated more evidence for L1-induced than for universal aspects of learner language (see Sections 2 and 3), but it must be pointed out that there have been no large-scale, systematic attempts to chart such aspects. The meager evidence that exists this far should not be taken to indicate that there is not much to be found. The adjacent field of world Englishes has accumulated extensive empirical evidence for shared features of L2 varieties (see e.g. Kortmann & Szmrecsanyi 2004; Sand 2008; Hilbert 2011; Meriläinen & Paulasto 2017). Similar features are also found in the English usage by speakers of English as a lingua franca from various L1 backgrounds (e.g. Mauranen 2012; Ranta 2013). It is now well established that L2 varieties of English have many parallels to learner English (e.g. Mukherjee & Hundt eds. 2011; Gilquin 2015), and an increasing number of studies have found evidence for similar processes of SLA that operate behind them, such as simplification, overgeneralization, explicitation or analogy (Biewer 2011; Callies 2016; Schneider & Gilquin 2016). The debate about the relative importance of L1-induced and universal causes behind the observed shared features is also prominent in the field of world Englishes, with several studies showing that many features that appear similar on the surface may conceal distributional or functional variation indicative of influence from local substrate languages (e.g. Sharma 2009; Davydova et al. 2011). Unlike world Englishes corpora, which lack metadata on individual speakers' L1s, learner English corpora such as the ICLE enable reliable identification of L1 background and can therefore make an important contribution in this debate.

This study also has its limitations. It has examined only a relatively small number of learner populations and frequencies of the examined features per corpus (rather than individual differences between learners), and more research is needed to identify further commonalities between different learner groups. Furthermore, the focus of this study was on predetermined morphosyntactic features, the frequencies of which turned out to be quite low in the examined corpora. This approach does not allow for applying more elaborate multivariate statistical methods, which is an increasingly common practice in LCR (e.g. Gries & Deshors 2015). The results of this study therefore remain tentative. The study of features such as embedded inversion or preposition omission is, nevertheless, of interest to SLA, because they involve the processes of simplification and overgeneralization. Through the choice of such features, the present study has attempted to build connections between earlier SLA literature, research into world Englishes and LCR.

6 Conclusion

Universal acquisitional processes and CLI are two central concepts in SLA research, but the relationship between them has long been a mystery. Twenty years ago, Leech (1998, xv) considered it "odd" that SLA has failed to account for the proportion of L1-induced features of learner language as opposed to those features shared by all learners regardless of their L1, and emphasized the potential of learner corpora in resolving this issue. In the light of our current understanding of the complexity of CLI effects and their interaction with different variables, it may not always be possible to separate these two to begin with (see also Osborne 2015). As emphasized in more recent SLA literature, CLI and universals should not be treated as opposites (Jarvis & Pavlenko 2008, 192–193); rather, CLI may occur *within* general learner language tendencies such as overuse/underuse, unconventional or unidiomatic patterns, simplification or overgeneralization. Understanding this interaction is important in future research in order to make sound claims about universals of learner language.

It is also evident that research addressing universals of learner English or any learner language should take into account the findings from the fields of world Englishes and English as a lingua franca. This is also encouraged in the revised CIA of Granger (2015), which embraces the comparisons of learner language with other types of cross-lingual varieties, such as L2 varieties, lingua francas and translated language in order to uncover similarities between them and shed light on the cognitive processes that give rise to common tendencies across different forms of non-native English. The findings that have hitherto been obtained from such comparisons strongly encourage additional research in this direction, for it may provide key answers to the roles of CLI and universal tendencies in non-native language processing and use.

Acknowledgments

This research was supported by the Research Council for Culture and Society, Academy of Finland (Project no. 269385). I would like to thank the editors and two anonymous reviewers for their comments on earlier version of this chapter.

References

Aarts, J. & Granger, S. (1998). Tag sequences in learner corpora: A key to interlanguage grammar and discourse. In S. Granger (ed.), *Learner English on Computer*, 132–141. London: Longman.

Ädel, A. (2006). *Metadiscourse in L1 and L2 English*. Amsterdam: John Benjamins.

Andersen, R. & Shirai, Y. (1996). The primacy of aspect in first and second language acquisition: The pidgin-creole connection. In W. C, Ritchie & T. K. Bhatia (eds.), *Handbook of Second Language Acquisition*, 527–570. San Diego, CA: Academic Press.

Biber, D., Johansson, S., Leech, G., Conrad, S., & Finegan, E. (eds.) (1999). *Longman Grammar of Spoken and Written English*. London: Longman.

Biewer, C. (2011). Modal auxiliaries in second language varieties of English: A learner's perspective. In J. Mukherjee & M. Hundt (eds.), *Exploring Second-Language Varieties of English and Learner Englishes: Bridging a Paradigm Gap*, 7–33. Amsterdam: John Benjamins.

Braidi, S. (1999). *The Acquisition of Second Language Syntax*. London: Arnold.

Callies, M. (2016). Towards a process-oriented approach to comparing EFL and ESL varieties: A corpus-study of lexical innovations. *International Journal of Learner Corpus Research* 2(2), 229–251.

Cheshire, J., Edwards, V., & Whittle, P. (1989). Urban British dialect grammar: The question of dialect levelling. *English World-Wide* 10(2), 185–225.

Cho, K. (2010). Fostering the acquisition of English prepositions by Japanese learners with networks and prototypes. In S. De Knop, F. Boers, & A. De Rycker (eds.), *Fostering Language Teaching Efficiency through Cognitive Linguistics*, 259–275. Berlin: Mouton de Gruyter.

Collins, L. (2002). The roles of L1 influence and lexical aspect in the acquisition of temporal morphology. *Language Learning* 52(1), 43–94.

Crosthwaite, P. (2016). L2 English article use by L1 speakers of article-less languages: A learner corpus study. *International Journal of Learner Corpus Research* 2(1), 68–100.

Davydova, J., Hilbert, M., Pietsch, L., & Siemund, P. (2011). Comparing varieties of English: Problems and perspectives. In P. Siemund (ed.), *Linguistic Universals and Language Variation*, 291–323. Berlin: de Gruyter Mouton.

Díez-Bedmar, M. B. & Papp, S. (2008). The use of the English article system by Chinese and Spanish learners. In G. Gilquin, S. Papp, & M. B. Díez-Bedmar (eds.), *Linking Up Contrastive and Learner Corpus Research*, 147–175. Amsterdam: Rodopi.

Dulay, H. & Burt, M.K. (1974). Natural sequences in child second language acquisition. *Language Learning* 24(1), 37–53.

Ellis, N. (2006). Selective attention and transfer phenomena in SLA: Contingency, cue competition, salience, overshadowing, blocking and perceptual learning. *Applied Linguistics* 27(2), 164–194.

Ellis, R. (2008). *The Study of Second Language Acquisition, 2nd Edn*. Oxford: Oxford University Press.

Fuchs, R. & Werner, V. (2018). Tense and aspect in second language acquisition and learner corpus research. *International Journal of Learner Corpus Research* 4(2), 143–163.

Gilquin, G. (2008). Combining contrastive and interlanguage analysis to apprehend transfer: Detection, explanation, evaluation. In G. Gilquin, S. Papp, & M. B. Díez-Bedmar (eds.), *Linking Up Contrastive and Learner Corpus Research*, 3–33. Amsterdam: Rodopi.

(2015). At the interface of contact linguistics and second language acquisition research: New Englishes and learner Englishes compared. *English World-Wide* 36(1), 91–124.

Gilquin, G., Granger, S., & Paquot, M. (2007). Learner corpora: The missing link in EAP pedagogy. *Journal of English for Academic Purposes* 6(4), 319–335.

Gilquin, G. & Meriläinen, L. (2012). Combining learner English and World Englishes perspectives: The case of embedded inversion. Paper presented at the 22nd Annual Conference of the European Second Language Association (EuroSLA). Poznan, Poland September 6–8, 2012.

Granger, S. (1996). From CA to CIA and back: An integrated contrastive approach to computerized bilingual and learner corpora. In K. Aijmer, B. Altenberg, & M. Johansson (eds.), *Languages in Contrast: Text-Based Cross-Linguistic Studies*, 37–51. Lund: Lund University Press.

(2015). Contrastive interlanguage analysis: A reappraisal. *International Journal of Learner Corpus Research* 1(1), 7–24.

Granger, S., Dagneaux, E., Meunier, F., & Paquot, M. (2009). *The International Corpus of Learner English, Version 2*. Handbook and CD-Rom. Louvain-la-Neuve: Presses Universitaires de Louvain.

Gries, S. Th. & Deshors, S. (2015). EFL and/vs. ESL? A multi-level regression modeling perspective on bridging the paradigm gap. *International Journal of Learner Corpus Research* 1(1), 130–159.

Hasselgård, H. & Johansson, S. (2011). Learner corpora and contrastive interlanguage analysis. In F. Meunier, S. De Cock, G. Gilquin, & M. Paquot (eds.), *A Taste for Corpora: In Honour of Sylviane Granger*, 33–61. Amsterdam: John Benjamins.

Hilbert, M. (2011). Interrogative inversion as a learner phenomenon in English contact varieties: A case of angloversals? In J. Mukherjee & M. Hundt (eds.), *Exploring Second-Language Varieties of English and Learner Englishes: Bridging a Paradigm Gap*, 125–144. Amsterdam: John Benjamins.

Huang, L-S. (2010). The potential influence of L1 (Chinese) on L2 (English) communication. *ELT Journal* 64(2), 155–164.

Jantunen, J. (2008). Haasteita oppijankielen korpusanalyysille: Oppijankielen universaalit [Challenges for learner corpus research: Universals of learner language]. In P. Eslon (ed.), *Õppijakeele analüüs: võimalused, probleemid, vajadused*, 67–92. Tallinna ülikooli eesti filoloogia osakonna edetised 10. Tallinn: TLÜ Kirjastus.

Jarvis, S. (2000). Methodological rigor in the study of transfer: Identifying L1 influence in the interlanguage lexicon. *Language Learning* 50(2), 245–309.

Jarvis, S. & Odlin, T. (2000). Morphological type, spatial reference, and language transfer. *Studies in Second Language Acquisition* 22(4), 535–556.

Jarvis, S. & Pavlenko, A. (2008). *Crosslinguistic Influence in Language and Cognition*. New York, NY: Routledge.

Jarvis, S., O'Malley, M., Jing, L., Zhang, J., Hill, J., Chan, C., & Sevostyanova, N. (2013). Cognitive foundations of crosslinguistic influence. In J. W. Schwieter (ed.), *Innovative Research and Practices in Second Language Acquisition and Bilingualism*, 287–308. Amsterdam: John Benjamins.

Kaneko, T. (2008). Use of English prepositions by Japanese university students. *Gakuen* 810, 1–12.

Kao, R.-R. (2001). Where have the prepositions gone? A study of English prepositional verbs and input enhancement in instructed SLA. *International Review of Applied Linguistics in Language Teaching* 39(3), 195–215.

Kolbe, D. & Sand, A. (2010). Embedded inversion worldwide. *Linguaculture* 2(1), 25–42.

Kortmann, B., Lunkenheimer, K. & Ehret, K. (eds.) (2020). *The Electronic World Atlas of Varieties of English*. Zenodo, retrieved from http://ewave-atlas.org (accessed August 20, 2020).

Kortmann, B. & Szmrecsanyi, B. (2004). Global synopsis: Morphological and syntactic variation in English. In B. Kortmann, E. W. Schneider, K. Burridge, R. Mesthrie, & C. Upton (eds.), *A Handbook of Varieties of English. Volume 2: Morphology and Syntax*, 1142–1202. Berlin: Mouton de Gruyter.

Leech, G. (1998). Preface. In S. Granger (ed.), *Learner English on Computer*, xiv–xx. London: Longman.

Levshina, N. (2015). *How to Do Linguistics with R: Data Exploration and Statistical Analysis*. Amsterdam: John Benjamins.

Luk, Z. P-S. & Shirai, Y (2009). Is the acquisition order of grammatical morphemes impervious to L1 knowledge? Evidence from the acquisition of plural *-s*, articles, and possessive'*s*. *Language Learning* 59(4), 721–754.

Mauranen, A. (2012). *Exploring ELF: Academic English Shaped by Non-native Speakers*. Cambridge: Cambridge University Press.

Meriläinen, L. (2010). *Language Transfer in the Written English of Finnish Students*. Publications of the University of Eastern Finland. Dissertations in Education, Humanities, and Theology, no 9. Joensuu: University of Eastern Finland.

Meriläinen, L. & Paulasto, H. (2015). Preposition omission as an angloversal across Englishes? Paper presented at Changing English: Integrating cognitive, social and typological perspectives. Helsinki, June 8–10, 2015.

(2017). Embedded inversion as an angloversal: Evidence from Inner, Outer and Expanding Circle Englishes. In M. Filppula, J. Klemola, & D. Sharma (eds.), *The Oxford Handbook of World Englishes*, 676–696. Oxford: Oxford University Press.

Mesthrie, R. & Bhatt, R. (2008). *World Englishes: The Study of New Linguistic Varieties*. Cambridge: Cambridge University Press.

Mukherjee, J. & Hundt, M. (eds.). (2011). *Exploring Second-Language Varieties of English and Learner Englishes: Bridging a Paradigm Gap*. Amsterdam: John Benjamins.

Murakami, A. & Alexopoulou, T. (2016). L1 influence on the acquisition order of English grammatical morphemes: A learner corpus study. *Studies in Second Language Acquisition* 38(3), 365–401.

Myles, F. (2015). Second language acquisition theory and learner corpus research. In S. Granger, G. Gilquin, & F. Meunier (eds.), *The Cambridge Handbook of Learner Corpus Research*, 309–332. Cambridge: Cambridge University Press.

Nesselhauf, N. (2009). Co-selection phenomena across New Englishes: Parallels and differences to foreign (learner) varieties. *English World-Wide* 30(1), 1–26.

Osborne, J. (2008). Adverb placement in post-intermediate learner English: A contrastive study of learner corpora. In G. Gilquin, S. Papp, & M. B. Díez-Bedmar (eds.), *Linking Up Contrastive and Learner Corpus Research*, 127–146. Amsterdam: Rodopi.

(2015). Transfer and learner corpus research. In S. Granger, G. Gilquin, & F. Meunier (eds.), *The Cambridge Handbook of Learner Corpus Research*, 333–356. Cambridge: Cambridge University Press.

Paquot, M. (2010). *Academic Vocabulary in Learner Writing: From Extraction to Analysis*. London: Continuum.

(2013). Lexical bundles and L1 transfer effects. *International Journal of Learner Corpus Research* 18(3), 391–417.

Paquot, M. & Granger, S. (2012). Formulaic language in learner corpora. *Annual Review of Applied Linguistics* 32, 130–149.

Pienemann, M. (ed.) (2005). *Cross-Linguistic Aspects of Processability Theory*. Amsterdam: John Benjamins.

Quirk, R., Greenbaum, S., Leech, G., & Svartvik, J. (1985). *A Comprehensive Grammar of the English Language*. London: Longman.

Ranta, E. (2013). *Universals in a Universal Language? Exploring Verb-Syntactic Features in English as a Lingua Franca. Acta Electronica Universitatis Tamperensis* 1366, retrieved from https://tampub.uta.fi/handle/10024/94555 (accessed June 13, 2020).

Rayson, P. (2003). Matrix: A Statistical Method and Software Tool for Linguistic Analysis through Corpus Comparison. Unpublished Ph.D. dissertation, Lancaster University.

Ringbom, H. (1998). Vocabulary frequencies in advanced learner English: A cross-linguistic approach. In S. Granger (ed.), *Learner English on Computer*, 41–52. London: Longman.

Rogatcheva, S. (2014). Aspect in Learner Writing: A Corpus-Based Comparison of Advanced Bulgarian and German Learners' Written English. Unpublished Ph.D. dissertation, University of Giessen.

Sand, A. (2008). Angloversals? Concord and interrogatives in contact varieties of English. In T. Nevalainen, I. Taavitsainen, P. Pahta, & M. Korhonen (eds.), *The Dynamics of Linguistic Variation*, 183–202. Amsterdam: John Benjamins.

Sharma, D. (2009). Typological diversity in New Englishes. *English World-Wide* 30(2), 170–195.

Schneider, E. (2012). Exploring the interface between World Englishes and second language acquisition – and implications for English as a lingua franca. *Journal of English as a Lingua Franca* 1(1), 57–91.

Schneider, G. & Gilquin, G. (2016). Detecting innovations in a parsed corpus of learner English. *International Journal of Learner Corpus Research* 2(2), 177–204.

Schumann, J. (1986). Locative and directional expressions in basilang speech. *Language Learning* 36(3), 277–294.

Selinker, L. (1972). Interlanguage. *IRAL – International Review of Applied Linguistics in Language Teaching* 10(1–4), 209–232.

Shirai, Y. & Ozeki, H. (2007). Introduction. *Studies in Second Language Acquisition* 29(2), 155–167.

Vyatkina, N. & Cunningham, J. (2015). Learner corpora and pragmatics. In S. Granger, G. Gilquin, & F. Meunier (eds.), *The Cambridge Handbook of Learner Corpus Research*, 346–376. Cambridge: Cambridge University Press.

Appendix 1

List of Matrix Verbs Preceding Wh-, Whether- and If-Clauses

Semantic domain	Verbs
Speech act verbs (24)	*argue, ask, confess, contradict, criticize, debate, disclose, discuss, enquire, emphasize, explain, express, inquire, offer, point out, query, question, relate, repeat, report, say, sing, state, tell*
Other communication verbs (12)	*define, demonstrate, describe, dictate, indicate, prove, record, reveal, show, signify, teach, write*
Cognition verbs (41)	*anticipate, ascertain, assess, believe, calculate, consider, concentrate on, confirm, compare, decide, detect, determine, discover, establish, estimate, fathom, figure (out), find out, foresee, forget, gather, guess, imagine, investigate, judge, know, learn, ponder, plan, plot, predict, realize, recognize, reconsider, reflect (on), be reminded of / remind* NP *of, remember, study, think of / about, understand, wonder*
Perception verbs (10)	*hear, listen to, look (at), note, notice, observe, perceive, read, see, watch*
Verbs of attitude and emotion (22)	*accept, agree with, approve, beware of, brood over, care, condemn, condone, cope with, doubt, dread, endorse, feel, give a damn, hate, laugh at, like, loathe, love, matter, mind, respect*
Aspectual verbs (5)	*complete, end, finish, start, stop*

Based on Biber et al. (1999), 683–693

Appendix 2

List of Files in Samples from ICLE and LOCNESS

ICLE-Chinese (57 essays, 30,170 words)

CNHK1001, CNHK1002, CNHK1003, CNHK1004, CNHK1005, CNHK1006, CNHK1007, CNHK1008, CNHK1010, CNHK1011, CNHK1012, CNHK1013, CNHK1014, CNHK1015, CNHK1017, CNHK1018, CNHK1019, CNHK1020, CNHK1021, CNHK1022, CNHK1023, CNHK1024, CNHK1025, CNHK1026, CNHK1027, CNHK1028, CNHK1030, CNHK1031, CNHK1032, CNHK1033, CNHK1034, CNHK1035, CNHK1036, CNHK1037, CNHK1038, CNHK1039, CNHK1040, CNHK1041, CNHK1042, CNHK1043, CNHK1044, CNHK1045, CNUK1056, CNUK1090, CNUK1095, CNUK4002, CNUK4003, CNUK4006, CNUK4007, CNUK4009, CNUK4023, CNUK4024, CNUK4025, CNUK4027, CNUK4028, CNUK4029, CNUK4037

ICLE-Finnish (42 essays, 30,514 words)

FIHE1001, FIHE1002, FIHE1003, FIHE1005, FIHE1006, FIHE1007, FIHE1008, FIHE1009, FIHE1010, FIHE1011, FIHE1012, FIHE1013, FIHE1014, FIHE1015, FIJO1001, FIJO1002, FIJO1003, FIJO1004, FIJO1005, FIJO1006, FIJO1007, FIJO1008, FIJO1009, FIJO1010, FIJY1001, FIJY1002, FIJY1004, FIJY1006, FIJY1007, FIJY1008, FIJY1009, FIJY1010, FIJY1011, FIJY1012, FIJY1013, FIJY1014, FIJY1015, FIJY1016, FITU1002, FITU1003, FITU1004, FITU1005

ICLE-Japanese (53 essays, 30,284 words)

JPAI1001, JPAI1002, JPDO1001, JPFJ1001, JPHI1001, JPHI1002, JPHI1003, JPHI1004, JPHI1005, JPKO1001, JPKO1002, JPKO1003, JPKO1004, JPKO1005, JPKW1001, JPKW1002, JPKY1001, JPKY1002, JPMI1001, JPMI1002, JPMJ1001, JPMJ1002, JPMU1001, JPMU1002, JPNH1001, JPOK1001, JPRI1001, JPRI1002, JPSE1001, JPSH1001, JPSH1002, JPSH1003, JPSH1004, JPST1001, JPST1002, JPSW1001, JPSW1002, JPSW1003, JPSW1004, JPSW1005, JPTF1001, JPTF1002, JPTF1003, JPTF1004, JPTF1005, JPTK1001, JPTK1002, JPTM1001, JPTM1002, JPTM1003, JPTM1004, JPTM1005, JPWA0002

ICLE-Swedish (from Finland) (51 essays, 30,214 words)

FIAB1001, FIAB1002, FIAB1003, FIAB1005, FIAB1006, FIAB1007, FIAB1008, FIAB1009, FIAB1010, FIAB1011, FIAB1012, FIAB1013, FIAB1015, FIAB1016, FIAB1017, FIAB1018, FIAB1020, FIAB1021, FIAB1022, FIAB1023, FIAB1024, FIAB1028, FIAB1029, FIAB1030, FIAB1031, FIAB1032, FIAB1034, FIAB1035, FIAB1036, FIAB1037, FIAB1038, FIAB1039, FIAB1040, FIAB1041, FIAB1042, FIAB1043, FIAB1044, FIAB1045, FIAB1046, FIAB1047, FIAB1048, FIAB1049, FIAB1050, FIAB1051, FIAB1052, FIAB1053, FIAB1055, FIAB1056, FIHE1004, FIHE2001, FIHE2002

LOCNESS (40 essays 30,220 words)

USMRQ1001,	USMRQ1002,	USMRQ1003,	USMRQ1004,
USMRQ1005,	USMRQ1006,	USMRQ1007,	USMRQ1008,
USMRQ1009,	USMRQ1010,	USIND1001,	USIND1002,
USIND1003,	USIND1004,	USIND1005,	USIND1006,
USIND1007,	USIND1008,	USIND1009,	USIND1010,
USMICH1001,	USMICH1002,	USMICH1003,	USMICH1004,
USMICH1005,	USMICH1006,	USMICH1007,	USMICH1008,
USMICH1009,	USMICH1010,	USSCU1001,	USSCU1002,
USSCU1003,	USSCU1004,	USSCU1005,	USSCU1006,
USSCU2001,	USSCU2002,	USSCU2003,	USSCU2004

Exploring Multi-Word Combinations as Measures of Linguistic Accuracy in Second Language Writing

Charlene Polio and Hyung-Jo Yoon

1 Introduction

Most second language (L2) writing research assesses accuracy through measures that require identifying errors (e.g., error-free unit ratios or the number of different types of errors). These widely used measures are not without problems at both the theoretical and practical levels. In this chapter, we first address the theoretical problems by addressing how error has been defined and why we might want to rethink our conception of accuracy in relation to native-speaker norms. This is followed by a review of traditional measures of accuracy including their shortcomings. We then turn to what we call usage-based approaches to accuracy drawing on the work of corpus linguists who compare learner language to native-speaker language.

By looking at the construct of accuracy in a new light, we propose a series of n-gram-based measures that allow comparisons of learner language to an established reference corpus, in this case, the *Corpus of Contemporary American English* (COCA). These new automated measures are easier to use than traditional hand-coded measures and, perhaps, more theoretically motivated. Through a factor analysis and regression, we show that nondependency-based n-gram measures are a viable alternative, both practically and theoretically, to traditional accuracy measures.

2 Review of the Literature

2.1 Definitions of Accuracy and the Relationship to Native-Speaker Norms

Concerns beyond the reliability and practicality of assessing accuracy are rarely discussed in the cognitively oriented literature. Although most Second Language Acquisition (SLA) researchers would agree that SLA is contextually driven through available input, the relationship between accuracy and what might be considered an error in relation to the input has been given little attention. Socially oriented scholars have been more forthcoming in problematizing the notion of error in specific contexts (e.g., Friedman 2010; Canagarajah 2006). Since accuracy has been defined as "freedom from error" (Foster & Skehan 1996, 304) or "the ability to be free from errors while using language" (Wolfe-Quintero et al. 1998, 33), we need to define error. Lennon defined an error as "a linguistic form or combination of forms which, in the same context and under similar conditions of production, would, in all likelihood, not be produced by the speakers' native speaker counterparts" (1991, 182). This definition is reasonable but, of course, highlights issues of comparability such as what are to be considered the same or similar contexts and who is a native speaker.

Cook (1999) raised concerns about what he called the *native speaker model* and questioned whether it was appropriate to compare L2 users to native speakers. On the one hand, we agree that we need to consider why we would expect native-speaker-like accurate grammar use when most teachers and researchers do not see accent-free language use a goal. On the other hand, we believe that comparing learner language to a (mostly) native-speaker corpus is a better way to consider what might be accurate language as opposed to using researcher judgments, a method that has been criticized for decades (e.g., Hymes 1972) because judgments are socially situated.

Mukherjee (2005) nicely summarizes the debate about the concept of the native speaker and explains his usage-based definition of a native speaker, saying that it is an abstraction of all users who have a sense of what language is acceptable in specific settings and whose language is idiomatic within a speech community. Furthermore, he argues that this definition can be operationalized through corpus linguistics:

> The native speaker norm is a linguistic approximation to the way a given language should ideally be used in terms of lexicogrammatical correctness, context-dependent acceptability and frequency-based idiomaticity. The norm can be described by generalizing and abstracting from a vast amount of representative performance data (i.e., linguistic corpora).
>
> (2005, 15)

Granger (2015), in her review of contrastive interlanguage analysis, takes on the criticisms leveled at L1/L2 comparative analyses, namely that learner language must be studied as a system in its own right and that the L2 norm is not monolithic, the latter addressed by Mukherjee (2005). Granger cogently argues for including comparisons to a target, the L2, and in particular draws on R. Ellis and Barkhuizen, who stated that "learners are typically targeted on native-speaker norms and as such themselves perform 'cognitive comparisons' in the process of learning an L2" (2005, 360) and thus these norms are psycholinguistically valid.

2.2 Traditional Measures of Accuracy

Three studies have comprehensively reviewed measures of accuracy used in L2 writing research (Polio 1997; Polio & Shea 2014; Wolfe-Quintero et al. 1998). In the most recent study, Polio and Shea reviewed published research between 2000 and 2011 and found 35 studies that assessed linguistic accuracy in some way. They classified the measures as falling into the following categories: holistic scales, proportion of error-free units, number of errors per words, number of specific error types per words, and measures that take into account error severity (but see also the discussion of Laufer and Waldman [2011] in the next section). None used automated measures. Most of the studies that Polio and Shea reviewed did not justify the choice of an accuracy measure in terms of either practicality or theory. Exceptions include Hartshorn et al. (2010), who chose error-free T-units because Wolfe-Quintero et al. found it to be "the most effective" measure (1998, 90), a point also made by Larsen-Freeman (2006). Wolfe-Quintero et al. do state that error-free T-units and errors per T-unit are the best measures of accuracy, but we believe that such a conclusion is in need of reconsideration because of inconsistent results, lack of reliability, variation in study designs, and the very small number of studies conducted prior to 1998.

Evans et al. (2014) and Kuiken and Vedder (2008) argued for measures that take into account severity, something not captured by error counts. Both studies refer to comprehensibility as influencing severity, and Evans et al. suggest as an example that morphosyntactic errors might interfere less with comprehensibility than a word choice or word order error. This approach, however, is contested by Pallotti, who states that accuracy, "the degree of conformity to certain norms" (2009, 592), is distinct from the construct of comprehensibility. This mirrors concepts discussed in the pronunciation literature, namely accentedness versus comprehensibility (e.g., Derwing & Munro 2005). Note that the written severity measures are likely tapping into error type as well as comprehensibility.

Polio and Shea (2014) investigated 10 measures: two subscores from an analytic scale that assessed "language" and "vocabulary," which included reference to errors in the descriptors; percentage of error-free

T-units and percentage of error-free clauses; weighted error-free T-units, which took into account number of errors and comprehensibility of the unit; and normalized error counts (total errors, verb phrase errors, preposition errors, article errors, and lexical errors per number of words). With regard to reliability, they found over .80 interrater reliability on all measures except preposition, verb phrase, and lexical errors, with lexical error reliability being the lowest at .54. In an attempt to validate the measures, Polio and Shea applied all 10 of them to a longitudinal dataset of student writing to determine whether or not the measures could detect improvement. They found that students showed change only with regard to a decrease in preposition errors. The lack of improvement on the accuracy measures does not necessarily invalidate them – it could be that the measures were not appropriate to the proficiency levels or that students simply did not improve their accuracy – but their study did not suggest a best measure of accuracy. To sum up, although some studies using accuracy measures have found change over time (Polio et al. 1998) and differences across proficiency levels (Verspoor et al. 2012), no measure has been clearly validated, and all measures are extremely labor-intensive.

2.3 Usage-Based Approaches to Accuracy

The error-based measures discussed so far do not rely on any SLA theory and, in fact, may be in opposition to theories that see the lexicon and grammar as inseparable (e.g., Römer 2009) when lexical errors are coded as separate from morphosyntactic errors. Usage-based approaches may offer some guidance. Although usage-based approaches are broadly conceived, N. Ellis and Wulff (2015) identified the common tenet as being that learners learn from the input by inducing rules using general cognitive mechanisms. More specifically, they focus on the importance of constructions (e.g., as defined by Goldberg [2006], combinations of words), frequency, the process of form–meaning mapping, learning from exemplars, and the notion that language learning is a complex adaptive system. The emphasis on word combinations is also highlighted by N. Ellis et al., who presume that "every word has its own local grammar" (2016, 31) and that language is a series of different levels of word combinations or constructions. We return to some of these tenets of usage-based approaches in our description of our measures.

Most usage-based SLA research has not discussed the construct of accuracy, but we take as our starting point one notable exception. Wulff and Gries (2011) argued cogently for corpus-driven methods of assessing accuracy. They suggested a probabilistic view of accuracy involving "the selection of a construction in its preferred context within a particular target variety and genre" (2011, 70). This approach does not view accuracy as binary, but rather as a gradient, that is as the degree to which the use of words and phrases in a certain context resembles native speakers' selection. In their study, Wulff and Gries focused on datives and the gerund/infinitive constructions. For example, they examined which verbs were used in a ditransitive construction (*John gave the cashier the money*) versus in a prepositional dative (*John gave the money to the cashier*). Among native speakers, verbs likely used in the ditransitive construction involve direct contact between the agent and the recipient (*I told my son a story*), while those in the prepositional dative involve distance with the patient being moved along some path (*I passed the salt to my mother*). They found that the nonnative speakers' patterns matched the native speakers' choice to a large extent, with some glaring differences, such as with the verb *send*. Native speakers preferred the ditransitive construction, despite its indicating movement; nonnative speakers used the verb in the prepositional dative construction. The point here is that a sentence like *I sent a letter to my grandmother* would hardly be classified as erroneous, but it is a deviation from what native speakers do and what is common in the input.

Wulff and Gries (2011) focused on very specific constructions from a native-speaker corpus. While this study does not take that approach, we prescribe to their probabilistic view of accuracy. Other studies have examined combinations of words in learner corpora in comparison to native-speaker use as ways to assess L2 writing, without explicitly discussing accuracy. For example, Laufer and Waldman examined learner verb–noun collocations for the most frequent 220 nouns in their learner and native-speaker corpora. They labeled collocations as errors if they did not appear in the *British National Corpus* (BNC) and collocation dictionaries and were judged incorrect by a native speaker. Examples included *solve the disease* and *inflict arguments* (2011, 258). Focusing on the quantity of verb–noun collocation errors, Laufer and Waldman also found little difference among three levels of proficiency. This finding suggests that verb–noun combination errors may not be associated with overall language development. This study, like the Wulff and Gries study, was limited in its focus when comparing learner language to native-speaker production.

Bestgen and Granger (2014), however, conducted a broader analysis that did not focus on specific constructions. They piloted a measure of phraseological competence (CollGram) that assigned mutual information (MI) and t-scores to all bigrams in the Michigan State University (MSU) learner corpus, the same dataset used in Polio and

Shea (2014). They examined how these scores changed over one semester and how they correlated with essay scores (MI-score correlations were significant, but t-scores were not). They also included a novel measure: the proportion of bigrams not found in their reference corpus, COCA. Although they found no change over time for this measure, they found significant negative correlations between the essays' language scores and the proportion of absent bigrams.

Bestgen and Granger (2014) did not address accuracy per se, but of the 200 absent bigrams randomly chosen, 130 (67 percent) were ungrammatical (e.g., *everything are*) while some were creative or low-frequency constructions that simply did not appear in COCA (e.g., *brother-in-law graduated*). Although Polio and Shea (2014) found higher correlations between raters' scores and traditional error measures on the same data set, Bestgen and Granger (2014) noted that the bigram measures, despite their weaker correlations, were fully automatic. One caveat here is that Granger and Bestgen (2017) were not able to replicate their finding related to absent bigrams when using a more advanced set of essays and using the BNC as their comparison corpus. They explain that some collocations found in COCA are not found in the BNC because the BNC is smaller, and this would result in more absent bigrams; 80 percent of a random sample of absent bigrams in the replication study were considered correct as opposed to only 33 percent in the original study. Another explanation is that the writers made fewer morphological errors than in the original study, while many absent bigrams in the original study were morphological errors (e.g., *he beguns*). Nevertheless, their study suggests that looking at n-grams in comparison to a corpus may be a way to assess accuracy, or the absence of errors.

Some of the tenets of usage-based approaches suggest that the n-gram unit might be useful in assessing accuracy. If learners learn from input, it is important to compare their language to the input and not idealized research judgments. This is obviously difficult to do because of the various quantities and types of input that learners get, but as explained, the COCA corpus is likely a reasonable approximation. Certain n-gram-related measures might reflect learning, or lack thereof. Specifically, learners might create novel word combinations that are infrequent and may be detected by low MI scores or their absence in a reference corpus, while conversely, certain frequent exemplars or chunks of language would be reflected with high MI scores. In this way, accuracy can be measured more precisely than when using a binary scale. Of course, n-grams are not dependency-based and are constructions based only on adjacency. Using n-grams does not allow us to analyze a range of constructions such as dative versus prepositional phrases as in Wulff and Gries (2011). Nevertheless, they rely on the usage-based notion that language is a series of different levels of word combinations or constructions. In addition, the n-gram unit allows the detection of morphological errors such as subject–verb agreement, infelicitous article use, and derivational errors.

2.4 Summary of Accuracy Measures

Overall, no traditional measure of accuracy is fully satisfying. Practically, they are all extremely time-consuming to code for, particularly given that it is best to have two coders fully code all of the data. Also, it is not clear what level of language proficiency a coder needs to code reliably. While reliability can be obtained on some measures such as error-free T-units and number of errors (Polio 1997; Polio & Shea 2014), both of these measures result in the loss of information, particularly error-free T-units, which counts only T-units that are fully correct. Coding for specific error types is challenging because sentences can be fixed in a number of ways, and Polio and Shea noted poor reliability on verb phrase errors and lexical errors. Identification of verb phrase errors involves decisions on correct tense and aspect, which can be challenging to make because they often require fully understanding the writer's perspective. Getting two coders to agree on what is a lexical error is challenging because it is difficult to decide if an item is awkward or wrong or to determine exactly what is to be considered a collocation error.

Theoretically, measures of accuracy are not linked to any theory of SLA, and different theories view errors somewhat differently. For a full discussion, see Polio (2012), but as an example, processability theory (Pienemann & Lenzig 2015) would not necessarily see a reduction of morphological errors as development, but skill-acquisition theory (DeKeyser 2015) would. Thus, we argue for exploring corpus-based measures that we believe are supported by usage-based theories of SLA because they view language as a set of constructions or chunks. We believe that by comparing learner language to a corpus of real language use, mostly by native speakers, we can develop a more principled approach to accuracy.

3 Research Questions

The purpose of this paper is to propose some usage-based measures and attempt to validate them as automatic and theory-based measures of accuracy. We hope that this study encourages further attempts to validate the same or similar measures using other validation methods and learner populations. Our general research question is: Can usage-based measures derived from comparing structures from a learner corpus to a native-speaker corpus assess linguistic accuracy?

Our specific questions are:

(1) To what extent are bigrams and trigrams from student essays that are absent in a reference corpus indicators of errors?
(2) In a factor analysis, do the usage-based measures group with accuracy, complexity, or lexical measures?
(3) In a regression, can the usage-based measures predict holistic measures of accuracy and scores from traditional error counts?

4 Method

4.1 Learner and Reference Corpora

For this study, we examined 139 timed essays written by 139 English as a Second Language (ESL) students in the upper levels of an English language program, meaning that most participants were either taking university courses concurrently or would be eligible to do so at the end of the course, if they passed. The essays come from three corpora: the MSU corpus (58 descriptive essays; Connor-Linton & Polio 2014), the genre corpus (51 argumentative essays; Yoon & Polio 2017), and dissertation pilot data (30 narrative essays; Yoon 2017). They were all written under the same time constraint of 30 minutes with no sources. We intentionally chose essays of different types to ensure that our results were not specific to a particular genre. Because of the large number of essays required to conduct a factor analysis and the fact that the accuracy measures had to be hand-coded, we did not look at proficiency as a variable.

Taking into account the context of the learner essays, namely that they were written by ESL students enrolled in a US English program, we selected COCA as a reference corpus. COCA is a large, balanced corpus of American English that contains the five genres of speech, fiction, popular magazines, newspapers, and academic journals. This corpus included 533,788,932 words at the time of this study. The particular use of COCA was to assign frequency and MI scores for the items included in the final lists of learner bigrams and trigrams and to identify bigrams and trigrams from the students' essays that were absent in the comparison corpus. We do not have data on the individuals who produced the texts found in COCA, but we assume that COCA can be considered as an approximation of the *native speaker norm*, the term used by Mukherjee (2005), so we refer to COCA as a native-speaker corpus in contrast to a learner corpus.

4.2 Procedure and Corpus-Based Measures

To calculate the corpus-based measures, we pre-processed the learner essays to make them suitable for n-gram extraction. Specifically, we removed spelling errors when their correct forms were evident from the context. Then, we added part-of-speech (POS) tags to the data using TreeTagger (Schmid 1994), which is a probabilistic tagger relying on lexical information for tagging. This procedure of POS tagging enabled a clear distinction between contracted forms that appear the same but function differently (e.g., two possible full forms *would* and *had* from one contracted form *'d*) as well as the identification of proper nouns and numerals. We then replaced contracted forms with full forms (e.g., *I_PP'm_VBP* into *I_PP am_VBP*; *he_PP'd_MD* into *he_PP would_MD*; *we_PP'd_VHD* into *we_PP had_VHD*).

After the text cleaning, we extracted all bigrams and trigrams, together with their POS tags. Python code was used for n-gram extraction, and n-grams that contained a proper noun or a numeral were excluded. Also, all n-grams interrupted by a punctuation mark were excluded, because such n-grams are not considered word combinations (e.g., *hand we* would not be considered a bigram in the chunk of text *on the other hand, we*). In calculating bigram and trigram MI scores, we used the frequency information of single words, bigrams, and trigrams in COCA. In an attempt to include in the analysis most n-grams that might contribute to the general impression of linguistic accuracy, we did not set a particular occurrence threshold. For trigram MI scores, we used an alternative formula proposed by Wei and Li because this method was found to be less sensitive to n-gram length than other formulas (see Wei & Li [2013] for a detailed explanation).

We chose MI as the target association measure based on the finding of Bestgen and Granger (2014) that MI measures predicted L2 writing quality significantly, while the t-score measures did not. MI indicates a statistical association strength of word constituents, which is based on the frequency of an n-gram in relation to the frequency of each word. A positive MI score indicates a greater co-occurrence of word constituents than expected by chance from their individual frequencies (i.e., the words have a strong association with each other), while a negative MI score presents a weak association of word constituents. To illustrate, a strongly associated bigram *hot weather* has a frequency of 373 in COCA, and its MI is 6.67, while *environment problem*, a weakly associated bigram, occurred only twice in COCA and its MI score is −3.87. The bigram *unforgetfully beautiful* is morphologically erroneous and does not appear in COCA (i.e., it is an absent bigram).

Table 17 Summary of measures

General measure	Specific measure
Unit length	Mean length of sentence (MLS) Mean length of clause (MLC)
Clause-level complexity	Number of clauses per T-unit (C/T) Number of T-units per sentence (T/S)
Phrase-level complexity	Number of coordinate phrases per clause (CP/C) Number of complex nominals per clause (CN/C)
Lexical sophistication	Sophisticated word types per total types (T_s/T)
Accuracy	Number of syntactic errors per 100 words Number of morphological errors per 100 words Number of prepositional errors per 100 words
Corpus-based measures	Proportion of absent bigrams Proportion of absent trigrams Mean bigram MI scores Mean trigram MI scores
Holistic accuracy	Rubric score

We included two corpus-based measures used by Bestgen and Granger (2014): the proportion of absent bigrams (i.e., those that do not appear in COCA), and mean bigram MI scores. In addition, we included the proportion of absent trigrams and mean trigram MI scores, all of which are based on the data from COCA. Because the focus of this study is on the identification of textual features contributing to the general impression of linguistic accuracy as well as on their interaction with the quantity of linguistic errors, this study explores n-gram measures that take into account *all* n-grams (i.e., n-gram token measures). All the measures used in this study are shown in Table 17.

4.3 Complexity, Traditional Accuracy, Lexical, Fluency, and Holistic Measures

To conduct a factor analysis to determine which measures the corpus-based measures of accuracy grouped with, we calculated complexity, accuracy, lexical, and fluency (CALF) measures for the essays, also provided in Table 17. For syntactic and lexical complexity, we used Lu's Syntactic Complexity Analyzer (Lu 2010) and Lexical Complexity Analyzer (Lu 2012). To tap into the multidimensional aspects of linguistic complexity and, at the same time, avoid redundancy (Norris & Ortega 2009), we selected six syntactic complexity measures and one lexical sophistication measure that have been shown in some studies to be valid measures (e.g., Laufer & Nation 1995; Yang et al. 2015; Yoon & Polio 2017). Specifically, we included two unit-length measures (mean length of sentence and mean length of clause), two clause-level measures that tap into subordination and coordination (number of clauses per T-unit and number of T-units per sentence), and two phrase-level measures (number of coordinate phrases per clause and number of complex nominals per clause). Lexical sophistication can be defined as "the proportion of relatively unusual or advanced words in the learner's text" (Read 2000, 203), and the lexical sophistication measure employed in this study is sophisticated word types (the "beyond 2,000" words of the Lexical Frequency Profile; Laufer 1994) per total types. Of the five lexical sophistication measures that can be obtained from Lu's processing tool, we chose Laufer's measure because it was the only measure that involves both lexical and function words.

For accuracy, we examined the number of specific error types. The three error types targeted in the study are syntactic, morphological, and prepositional errors (details of the coding are given in Yoon & Polio 2017). Syntactic errors included incorrect word order, sentence fragments, run-on sentences, missing constituents, extra verbs or subjects, and incorrect relative clause use. Morphological errors involved incorrect word forms, agreement, plurals, articles, and double negatives. Prepositional errors included all incorrect uses of prepositions. Spelling errors were not targeted, because they were all removed during the text cleaning process. The MSU corpus and genre corpus did not initially use the same coding schemes, but we were able to convert the coding in the MSU corpus used by Yoon and Polio by collapsing categories from the MSU categories. Two native English-speaking coders completed the error coding of the dissertation pilot data. The data sets using the syntactic, morphological, and preposition scheme had over .80 interrater reliability for the three categories. Reliability for the MSU corpus is discussed in Polio and Shea (2014). Note that lexical errors were not included because of the difficulty in obtaining interrater reliability on lexical errors, as explained by Polio and Shea. We return to this point later.

Given the timed condition of essay writing, we used the total number of words as a fluency measure. Although problematic because of variation caused by planning time (Abdel Latif 2013), this quantity-based fluency measure has been found to detect L2 development and contribute validly to overall text quality (e.g., Grant & Ginther 2000; Knoch et al. 2014).

We also included a measure of holistic accuracy using a rubric (see Appendix) that focused on the quantity and quality (i.e., severity related to comprehensibility) of linguistic errors. This measure provides an alternate way to assess accuracy. It is not necessarily more valid, but it approaches a concept of accuracy based on human judgments. Its inclusion is mostly exploratory, and we are not arguing that a holistic assessment of accuracy is more appropriate. The score range of this rubric was from 1 to 7. Two expert raters participated in holistic accuracy rating. They were both Ph.D. students with experience of rating ESL essays. The interrater reliability of their accuracy scores was .68, which is low but not unexpected given that our sample was somewhat homogeneous and the scale was likely better at assessing a wider range of proficiency levels. We used their average scores, and for the 14 essays whose accuracy scores differed by more than 1, a third rater assigned third scores. Then, we used the average of the two closest scores. The mean accuracy score for the entire set of essays was 4.8 (minimum 3; maximum 6.5).

5 Results

5.1 Absent Bigrams and Trigrams

Our first research question explored the extent to which bigrams and trigrams from student essays that are absent in a reference corpus can be considered errors. We manually coded all of the bigrams that did not appear in the reference corpus as error or non-error. Each absent bigram was considered in context and counted as an error if the bigram was a clear morphological or syntactic error, a lexical error, an awkward collocation, or simply sounded slightly strange. In other words, we erred on the side of over-coding errors because we were exploring a new concept of accuracy that was related to what a native speaker might produce, and the assumption was that the corpus might be better at finding anomalies than two coders. There were a total of 802 absent bigrams after cleaning (e.g., exclusion of items that were absent because of missing punctuation; *style nobody* in *because of her teaching style nobody was quiet in class*). One of the authors coded all of the items, and a second coder coded 10 percent of the items. Interrater reliability on error/non-error categorization was 90 percent. Because of the large number of absent trigrams from the 139 essays (7,163), we randomly selected 29 essays (20 percent), and one person coded the 1,465 trigrams from those essays as was done for the bigrams.

Table 18 Examples of absent bigrams and trigrams coded as errors or non-errors

Bigrams	
Errors	**Non-errors**
be penalize	bank faced
during we	prohibit laptops
every facilities	issued electronically
make performance	soap they
feel relax	some roommates
obtain humor	squirrels stroll
she decorate	sumo team
books locate	visa quickly
book shelter	procedure simpler
flower become	lecture better
she decorate	demon grew

Trigrams	
Errors	**Non-errors**
the school locates	our field hockey
can use internet	realize how harmful
brainstorm style to	Korean people know
are tremendous innumerable	with helpful professors
expensive to found	a Taiwanese guy
the really people	college students prefer
they always traveling	though this meeting
helpful about develop	she would summarize

The results of this analysis indicated that 87 percent of the absent bigrams were somehow erroneous, and the remaining items (13 percent) were accurately used phrases or expressions that did not appear in the reference corpus by chance. As shown in Table 18, absent bigrams coded as erroneous contained various types of errors including verb form (*books locate*), word choice (*book shelter*; *obtain humor*), and agreement errors (*every facilities*; *flower become*; *she decorate*). On the other hand, most of the absent bigrams coded as non-erroneous were coincidentally absent (*bank faced*; *procedure simpler*; *prohibit laptops*; *lecture better*; *some roommates*; *visa quickly*). In other words, for each of these bigrams, acceptable sentences that contain them can be constructed (e.g., *He found the procedure simpler than before*), but there were also some expressions that might be considered creative (*demon grew*;

squirrels stroll). The coding of the absent trigrams revealed that 77 percent contained some type of error, and examples are given in Table 18.

5.2 Factor Analysis of Measures

Our second research question asked how corpus-based measures grouped with traditional linguistic measures that tap into syntactic complexity, lexical sophistication, accuracy, and fluency. To address this question, we used an exploratory factor analysis. Because no previous research had suggested that our measures were related to any of the CALF measures, we chose an exploratory instead of a confirmatory factor analysis. Prior to running the analysis, we checked for multicollinearity between the individual measures using Pearson's correlation coefficient (see Table 19). For any highly correlated measures ($r > .70$), we retained only one variable that showed the highest correlation with holistic accuracy scores, which is the major focus of this study. After this step, the mean length of clause was excluded because it was highly correlated with complex nominals per clause ($r = .79$). Also, the proportion of absent trigrams was excluded due to its high correlations with bigram MI ($r = -.73$) and the proportion of absent bigrams ($r = .69$). As a result, 10 traditional CALF measures and three corpus-based measures remained for the factor analysis.

The analysis with the remaining measures informed us that the assumptions for factor analysis were satisfactory (KMO: .52; Bartlett's test: $\chi^2(78) = 689.8$, $p < .001$; Determinant: .006). With an eigenvalue of 1 as the minimum threshold, we extracted four factors explaining 64.7 percent of the variance. Table 20 shows the pattern matrix of the four factors. Following Pett et al.'s (2003) suggestion, we viewed factor loadings greater than .40 as significant (boldface in the table).

The results showed that the unit length and clause-level complexity measures (mean length of sentence, clauses per T-unit, and T-units per sentence) loaded together on Factor 2, while the two phrase-level complexity measures loaded on Factor 3 (coordinate phrases per clause and complex nominals per clause). The lexical sophistication measure grouped together with the fluency measure (Factor 4), and we did not explore the reason for this. The most notable finding from this factor analysis is that the corpus-based measures (proportion of absent bigrams, bigram MI, and trigram MI) grouped together with the error-count measures (number of syntactic errors, morphological errors, and prepositional errors), explaining 24.8 percent of the total variance (Factor 1). This finding suggests that these measures may be assessing accuracy, but other alternatives are discussed below.

Table 19 Correlations between individual measures

	Holistic	MLS	MLC	C/T	T/S	CP/C	CN/C	T_s/T	Synt E	Morp E	Prep E	Total W	Abs Bi	Abs Tri	Bi MI	Tri MI
Holistic	1															
MLS	.08	1														
MLC	.11	.48**	1													
C/T	.03	.60**	−.23**	1												
T/S	−.03	.56**	−.02	.16	1											
CP/C	−.04	.26**	.71**	−.22**	−.07	1										
CN/C	.18*	.37**	.79**	−.15	−.03	.51**	1									
T_s/T	.19*	−.12	.21*	−.28**	−.13	.28**	.23**	1								
Synt E	−.54**	−.01	−.10	.04	.10	.04	−.15	.07	1							
Morp E	−.58**	−.11	.05	−.14	−.08	.11	−.01	−.11	.34**	1						
Prep E	−.40**	−.14	−.08	−.11	−.01	.03	−.13	.08	.27**	.38**	1					
Total W	.22*	−.05	−.11	.01	.03	−.07	−.14	.25**	−.12	−.21*	−.01	1				
Abs Bi	−.33**	−.01	.17*	−.05	−.18	.15	.17	.21*	.36**	.49**	.16	−.07	1			
Abs Tri	−.44**	.04	.23**	−.11	−.06	.34**	.14	.15	.40**	.62**	.27**	−.16	.69**	1		
Bi MI	.50**	−.12	−.26**	.06	−.02	−.36**	−.10	.02	−.48**	−.58**	−.24**	.19*	−.42**	−.73**	1	
Tri MI	.42**	−.13	−.29**	.12	−.13	−.35**	−.25**	−.13	−.38**	−.42**	−.35**	.05	−.31**	−.41**	.65**	1

Note. * = significant at .05; ** = significant at .01

Table 20 Pattern matrix of the factor loadings

	Factor			
Measure	1	2	3	4
Syntactic complexity				
MLS	−.02	**.88**	.40	−.07
C/T	−.06	**.70**	−.20	−.18
T/S	.08	**.76**	−.04	.16
CP/C	.15	−.01	**.79**	.07
CN/C	−.10	.04	**.88**	−.05
Lexical sophistication				
T_s/T	.05	−.23	.36	**.69**
Accuracy				
Syntactic E	**.73**	.14	−.19	.05
Morphological E	**.75**	−.17	−.05	−.30
Prepositional E	**.60**	−.07	−.25	.21
Fluency				
Total words	−.11	−.11	−.15	**.79**
Corpus-based				
Abs. bigram prop.	**.58**	−.14	.17	−.05
Bigram MI	**−.79**	−.09	−.21	−.18
Trigram MI	**−.72**	−.15	−.29	−.12
Eigenvalues	3.22	2.08	1.86	1.25
% of variance	24.77	16.03	14.30	9.59

Note. Extraction method: principal component analysis; Rotation method: direct oblimin with Kaiser normalization

5.3 Predictions of Other Accuracy Measures

The third research question involved how the corpus-based measures predict traditional error counts and holistic accuracy scores. To answer this question, we conducted two hierarchical regression analyses: the first analysis with the total number of errors per 100 words as the outcome variable, and the second with holistic accuracy scores as the outcome. In this analysis, we used as predictor variables the three corpus-based measures that were included in the factor analysis (proportion of absent bigrams, bigram MI, and trigram MI). Table 21 presents the result of the regression analysis showing the relationship between the corpus-based measures and error counts.

The results show that 47.6 percent of the variance in error counts was accounted for by the three corpus-based measures. Of particular

Table 21 Hierarchical regression analysis to predict error counts

Entry	Predictor added	*r*	R^2	R^2 *change*	*B*	*SE*	Beta
1	Bigram MI	.624	.390	.390	−5.32	1.14	−.404
2	Absent bigram proportion	.681	.463	.073	0.80	0.19	.292
3	Trigram MI	.690	.476	.013	−1.63	0.90	−.150

Note. Estimated constant term = 21.96; *B* = unstandardized beta; *SE* = standard error; Beta = standardized beta

Table 22 Hierarchical regression analysis to predict holistic accuracy scores

Entry	Predictor added	*r*	R^2	R^2 *change*	*B*	*SE*	Beta
1	Bigram MI	.503	.253	.253	0.88	0.25	.355
2	Trigram MI	.516	.266	.013	0.29	0.20	.142
3	Absent bigram proportion	.529	.280	.014	−0.07	0.04	−.131

Note. Estimated constant term = 2.82; *B* = unstandardized beta; *SE* = standard error; Beta = standardized beta

note here is that bigram MI scores are inversely proportional to error counts, explaining 39 percent of the variance in error counts. In other words, the low association strength of the bigrams used in learner texts is indicative of the number of errors existing in the texts.

In predicting the holistic impression of linguistic accuracy in learner texts, the three corpus-based measures were found to explain 28 percent of the variance in holistic accuracy scores (see Table 22). Similar to the previous analysis, this result also showed that bigram MI functions as the most important measure in the prediction of holistic accuracy (25.3 percent of the variance explained).

With more than a quarter of the variance explained by the three corpus-based measures, we can interpret this finding as evidence showing the potential of the measures as alternative accuracy measures. However, we further analyzed the predictive power of traditional error counts and found that, as shown in Table 23, the error-count measures outperformed the corpus-based measures in predicting holistic accuracy scores (48.5 percent explained). We explain these results in the discussion section.

Because the proportions of absent bi- and trigrams were not as strong predictors as we expected, we compared the correlation of the

Table 23 Hierarchical regression analysis for traditional error counts' prediction of holistic accuracy scores

Entry	Predictor added	*r*	R^2	R^2 *change*	*B*	*SE*	Beta
1	Morphological errors	.580	.336	.336	−0.10	0.02	−.400
2	Syntactic errors	.683	.466	.130	−0.22	0.04	−.358
3	Prepositional errors	.697	.485	.019	−0.13	0.06	−.153

Note. Estimated constant term = 6.26; *B* = unstandardized beta; *SE* = standard error; Beta = standardized beta

holistic measure of accuracy and the proportion of absent bigrams ($r = .29$, $n = 139$, $p = .00$) and the holistic measure of accuracy and the proportion of absent bigrams with the non-errors removed ($r = .33$, $n = 139$, $p = .00$). Given the small difference and the extra work of manually removing non-erroneous bigrams, we did not use the corrected proportions in any further analysis.

6 Discussion

6.1 Summary and Interpretation of Results

The aim of our study was to determine if what we are calling usage-based measures, derived from comparing structures from a learner corpus to a native-speaker corpus, can assess linguistic accuracy or if they represent some other construct. More specifically, we asked three research questions:

(1) To what extent are bigrams and trigrams from student essays that are absent in a reference corpus indicators of errors?
(2) In a factor analysis, do the usage-based measures group with accuracy, complexity, or lexical measures?
(3) In a regression, can the usage-based measures predict holistic measures of accuracy and scores from traditional error counts?

We first chose to look at the proportion of absent bigrams with the idea that if they did not show up in a large corpus such as COCA, they might offer a way to automatically assess accuracy based on how language is actually used as opposed to coders' judgments. We found that with our learner corpus, and COCA as the comparison corpus, 87 percent of the absent bigrams and 77 percent of absent trigrams were judged erroneous. This suggests that such a quick approach to assessing accuracy is promising. We need to acknowledge, however, several caveats. First, our results had a higher error rate than found in Bestgen and Granger (2014) and Granger and

Bestgen (2017). It is clear then that a search for absent n-grams is likely dependent on the learner sample, in that more advanced writers will likely use more creative constructions, as well as on the comparison corpus. A corpus of the size of COCA might overestimate the number of errors since it may still be too small to serve as a model for analyses of word combinations in learner writing (cf. Paquot & Naets 2017). We also do not know how many errors the absent n-gram identification missed, though that issue is somewhat addressed by the regression analysis that showed nearly half of the variance in the error counts could be accounted for by n-gram measures. To provide more conclusive evidence, future research can explore how the errors identified in the learner text match the absent n-grams, that is, we can examine how many errors were missed by the absent n-gram analyses.

One positive aspect of the absent n-gram measures is that we believe it taps into lexical errors and awkward word combinations that native-speaker judgments cannot reliably assess. As stated earlier, we erred on the side of calling odd-sounding combinations errors because we saw this an aspect of accuracy that automated measures can consider. Note that the inclusion of such so-called awkward combinations could be another reason that our results differed from those of Bestgen and Granger (2014), who may have been more conservative about what they were labeling as errors. Finally, the number of absent bigrams was actually not among the strongest predictors of accuracy, suggesting a more gradable and less crude measure is needed. A related approach that we did not attempt might be to set a threshold level instead of focusing on absent n-grams. For example, one could calculate the proportion of bigrams that appear fewer than three times in COCA. This might catch more errors or awkward phrases, given that COCA contains n-grams that might include typos, slips of the tongue, or idiosyncratic examples.

To answer the second research question, we conducted an exploratory factor analysis to see how the usage-based measures grouped with the CALF measures. As shown in Table 20, they did indeed group with the traditional accuracy measures of syntactic, morphological, and prepositional errors and not with lexical or complexity measures. This is the most convincing evidence that the usage-based measures are related to accuracy. Interpreting the results of an exploratory factor analysis is not straightforward, but based on our arguments made earlier that our usage-based measures assessed accuracy, and given that the measures did not group with or correlate with vocabulary, fluency, or complexity, we feel somewhat confident in our claims. Of course, these findings do not preclude other

Figure 2 Results of regression analyses

explanations such as some other latent variable that includes the accuracy and usage-based measures.

Finally, we also conducted three regressions, but these results are somewhat more difficult to interpret. Figure 2 illustrates the results of these regressions.

If we use the usage-based measures to predict accuracy based on the holistic scores, we find only 28 percent of the variance accounted for, but if we use the number of errors as the outcome, the usage-based measures predict 47.6 percent of the variance. Ultimately, neither outcome variable is considered a definitive measure of accuracy. The error counts did not include lexical errors, but the fact that automated measures could account for 47.6 percent of the variance of the hand-coded error counts is very promising. Had lexical errors been coded, the automated measures would likely have accounted for even more of the variance. As for the holistic measure, the results are harder to interpret, because raters can be influenced by a variety of factors that are not part of the construct under investigation.

6.2 Future Validation Research

Validation research is not straightforward, and this is evidenced by the large number of studies that have appeared since the publication of

Wolfe-Quintero et al. (1998), particularly in the areas of syntactic and lexical complexity, though less so accuracy. This is partially because of the variety of methods that can be used to validate a measure. Some studies examine change or development, but most studies, including ours, do not have a full range of proficiency levels, and what might show change or development at a lower level might not show change at a higher level. Other studies might compare measures to raters' judgments, but as we noted, raters can be influenced by a variety of factors not related to the construct being studied.

To further validate our usage-based measures, more studies, particularly with a wider range of populations, that include laborious hand-coding may be necessary, because at present error counts seem to be the most widely agreed-on measures. Another approach is to compare a set of essays before and after the errors have been corrected. Although such an approach sets a very low bar, our first attempt using this approach showed that the usage-based measures increased strongly once essay errors had been corrected (Polio & Yoon 2018).

A confirmatory factor analysis on a different set of data is the next obvious step. This would strengthen our argument that the measures are tapping into accuracy by testing specific and alternate models. In addition, with a larger data set, we could include other usage-based variables to investigate. For example, as mentioned earlier, instead of the proportion of absent bigrams or trigrams, thresholds could be set. Another approach could be to include combinations of specific structures as was done by Laufer and Waldman (2011). They included only verb–noun combinations, but it is possible to include a larger range of collocations including adjective–noun or verb–adverb combinations as opposed to only adjacent combinations.

Finally, we have not addressed the fact that accuracy may be multidimensional. Multidimensionality has been demonstrated for the construct of complexity (e.g., Norris & Ortega 2009) but not so much for accuracy. Despite the fact that our MI and absent n-gram measures grouped with syntactic, morphological, and preposition errors, our measures might be more associated with specific types of errors including lexical errors. Furthermore, we do not know how these measures are related to Paquot's (2017) conceptualization of phraseological sophistication. She investigated dependency-based strength of association measures in relation to how they distinguished Common European Framework of References for Languages (CEFR) levels. While our measures were not dependency-based, it might be that high-association measures indicate phraseological sophistication while low ones indicate inaccuracy.

7 Conclusion

The goal of this study was to propose possible measures of accuracy that were related to usage-based theories of SLA. Specifically, we explored measures that were not based on coder judgments and that did not separate grammar and lexis. Through the use of MI scores, we were able to assess accuracy on a scale related to native-speaker usage and not on a binary scale (i.e., right or wrong). We have shown that the usage-based measures not only group with the accuracy-based measures but are also able to predict hand-coded error counts. We believe that further investigation and validation of these measures is warranted.

References

Abdel Latif, M. (2013). What do we mean by writing fluency and how can it be validly measured? *Applied Linguistics* 34(1), 99–105.

Bestgen, Y. & Granger, S. (2014). Quantifying the development of phraseological competence in L2 English writing: An automated approach. *Journal of Second Language Writing* 26, 28–41.

Canagarajah, A. (2006). The place of world Englishes in composition: Pluralization continued. *College Composition and Communication* 57, 586–619.

Connor-Linton, J. & Polio, C. (2014). Comparing perspectives on L2 writing: Multiple analyses of a common corpus: Introduction. *Journal of Second Language Writing* 23, 1–9.

Cook, V. (1999). Going beyond the native speaker in language teaching. *TESOL Quarterly* 33(2), 185–209.

DeKeyser, R. (2015). Skill acquisition theory. In B. VanPatten & J. Williams (eds.), *Theories in Second Language Acquisition: An Introduction*, 94–112. New York, NY: Routledge.

Derwing, T. & Munro, M. (2005). Second language accent and pronunciation teaching: A research-based approach. *TESOL Quarterly* 39(3), 379–397.

Ellis, R. & Barkhuizen, G. (2005). *Analyzing Learner Language*. Oxford: Oxford University Press.

Ellis, N., Römer, U., & O'Donnell, M. (2016). Constructions and usage-based approaches to language acquisition. *Language Learning* 66(S1), 23–44.

Ellis, N. & Wulff, S. (2015). Usage-based approaches to SLA. In B. VanPatten & J. Williams (eds.), *Theories in Second Language Acquisition: An Introduction*, 75–93. Mahwah, NJ: Erlbaum.

Evans, N., Hartshorn, K., Cox, T., & Martin de Jel, T. (2014). Measuring written linguistic accuracy with weighted clause ratios: A question of validity. *Journal of Second Language Writing* 24, 33–50.

Foster, P. & Skehan, P. (1996). The influence of planning on performance in task-based learning. *Studies in Second Language Acquisition* 18(3), 299–324.

Friedman, D. (2010). Speaking correctly: Error correction as a language socialization practice in a Ukrainian classroom. *Applied Linguistics* 31(3), 346–367.

Goldberg, A. E. (2006). *Constructions at Work: The Nature of Generalization in Language*. Oxford: Oxford University Press.

Granger, S. (2015). Contrastive interlanguage analysis: A reappraisal. *International Journal of Learner Corpus Research* 1(1), 7–24.

Granger, S. & Bestgen, Y. (2017). Using collgrams to assess L2 phraseological development: A replication study. In P. de Haan, S. van Vuuren, & R. de Vries (eds.), *Language, Learners and Levels: Progression and Variation*, 385–408. Louvain-la-Neuve: Presses universitaires de Louvain.

Grant, L. & Ginther, A. (2000). Using computer-tagged linguistic features to describe L2 writing differences. *Journal of Second Language Writing* 9(2), 123–145.

Hartshorn, K., Evan, N., Merrill, P., Sudweeks, R., Strong-Krause, D., & Anderson, N. (2010). Effects of dynamic corrective feedback on ESL writing accuracy. *TESOL Quarterly* 44(1), 84–109.

Hymes, D. (1972). On communicative competence. In J. B. Pride & J. Holmes (eds.), *Sociolinguistics*, 269–293. Harmondsworth: Penguin.

Knoch, U., Rouhshad, A., & Storch, N. (2014). Does the writing of undergraduate ESL students develop after one year of study in an English-medium university? *Assessing Writing* 21, 1–17.

Kuiken, F. & Vedder, I. (2008). Cognitive task complexity and written output in Italian and French as a foreign language. *Journal of Second Language Writing* 17(1), 48–60.

Larsen-Freeman, D. (2006). The emergence of complexity, fluency, and accuracy in the oral and written production of five Chinese learners of English. *Applied Linguistics* 27(4), 590–619.

Laufer, B. (1994). The lexical profile of second language writing: Does it change over time? *RELC Journal* 25(2), 21–33.

Laufer, B. & Nation, P. (1995). Vocabulary size and use: Lexical richness in L2 written production. *Applied Linguistics* 16(3), 307–332.

Laufer, B. & Waldman, T. (2011). Verb–noun collocations in second language writing: A corpus analysis of learners' English. *Language Learning* 61(2), 647–672.

Lennon, P. (1991). Error: Some problems of definition, identification, and distinction. *Applied Linguistics* 12(2), 180–196.

Lu, X. (2010). Automatic measurement of syntactic complexity in child language acquisition. *International Journal of Corpus Linguistics* 14(1), 3–28.

(2012). The relationship of lexical richness to the quality of ESL learners' oral narratives. *The Modern Language Journal* 96(2), 190–208.

Mukherjee, J. (2005). The native speaker is alive and kicking: Linguistic and language-pedagogical perspectives. *Anglistik* 16(2), 7–23.

Norris, J. & Ortega, L. (2009). Towards an organic approach to investigating CAF in instructed SLA: The case of complexity. *Applied Linguistics* 30(4), 555–578.

Pallotti, G. (2009). CAF: Defining, refining and differentiating constructs. *Applied Linguistics* 30(4), 590–601.
Paquot, M. (2017). The phraseological dimension in interlanguage complexity research. *Second Language Research* 35(1), 1–25.
Paquot, M. & Naets, H. (2017). The role of the reference corpus in studies of EFL learners' use of statistical collocations. Paper presented at ICAME38. Prague, May 24–28, 2017.
Pett, M., Lackey N., & Sullivan J. (2003). *Making Sense of Factor Analysis: The Use of Factor Analysis for Instrument Development in Health Care Research*. California: SAGE Publications Inc.
Pienemann, M. & Lenzig, A. (2015). Processability theory. In B. VanPatten & J. Williams (eds.), *Theories in Second Language Acquisition: An Introduction*, 159–179. New York, NY: Routledge.
Polio, C. (1997). Measures of linguistic accuracy in second language writing research. *Language Learning* 47(1), 101–143.
(2012). The relevance of second language acquisition theory to the written error correction debate. *Journal of Second Language Writing* 21(4), 375–389.
Polio, C., Fleck, C., & Leder, N. (1998). "If I only had more time": ESL learners' changes in linguistic accuracy on essay revisions. *Journal of Second Language Writing* 7(1), 43–68.
Polio, C. & Shea, M. (2014). An investigation into current measures of linguistic accuracy in second language writing research. *Journal of Second Language Writing* 26, 10–27.
Polio, C. & Yoon, H.-J. (2018). The reliability and validity of automated tools for examining variation in syntactic complexity across genres. *International Journal of Applied Linguistics* 28(1), 165–188.
Read, J. (2000). *Assessing Vocabulary.* Cambridge: Cambridge University Press.
Römer, U. (2009). The inseparability of lexis and grammar: Corpus linguistic perspectives. *Annual Review of Cognitive Linguistics* 7(1), 140–162.
Schmid, H. (1994). Probabilistic part-of-speech tagging using decision trees. Paper presented at the International Conference on New Methods in Language Processing. Manchester, UK.
Verspoor, M., Schmid, M. S., & Xu, X. (2012). A dynamic usage based perspective on L2 writing. *Journal of Second Language Writing* 21(3), 239–263.
Wei, N. & Li, J. (2013). A new computing method for extracting contiguous phraseological sequences from academic text corpora. *International Journal of Corpus Linguistics* 18(4), 506–535.
Wolfe-Quintero, K., Inagaki, S., & Kim, H.-Y. (1998). *Second Language Development in Writing: Measures of Fluency, Accuracy, and Complexity*. Honolulu, HI: University of Hawaii Press.
Wulff, S. & Gries, S. Th. (2011). Corpus-driven methods for assessing accuracy in learner production. In P. Robinson (ed.), *Second Language Task Complexity: Researching the Cognition Hypothesis of Language Learning and Performance*, 61–87. Amsterdam: John Benjamins.

Yang, W., Lu, X., & Weigle, S. (2015). Different topics, different discourse: Relationships among writing topic, measures of syntactic complexity, and judgments of writing quality. *Journal of Second Language Writing* 28, 53–67.

Yoon, H. (2017). Investigating the interactions among genre, task complexity, and proficiency in L2 writing: A comprehensive text analysis and study of learner perceptions. Unpublished Ph.D. dissertation, Michigan State University.

Yoon, H. & Polio, C. (2017). ESL students' linguistic development in two written genres. *TESOL Quarterly* 51(2), 275–301.

Appendix

Rubric for Holistic Accuracy

Score	Quantity	Quality
7	Very few errors of vocabulary, punctuation, and grammar	None that interfere with meaning
6	Some errors of vocabulary, punctuation, and grammar	None that interfere with meaning
5	Several errors of vocabulary, punctuation, and grammar	Generally do not interfere with meaning
4	Several errors of vocabulary, punctuation, and grammar	Occasionally interfere with meaning
3	Many errors of vocabulary, punctuation, and grammar	Frequently interfere with meaning
2	Many errors of vocabulary, punctuation, and grammar	Meaning is severely impacted but can be understood with reader effort
1	A great many errors of vocabulary, punctuation, and grammar	Severely impacted meaning despite reader effort

Using Syntactic Co-occurrences to Trace Phraseological Complexity Development in Learner Writing: Verb + Object Structures in LONGDALE

Magali Paquot, Hubert Naets, and Stefan Th. Gries*

1 Introduction

Many recent studies of word combinations in learner writing have relied on the use of statistical collocations to assess English as a Foreign Language (EFL) learners' phraseological competence.[1] Statistical collocations are word combinations such as *severe* + *weather*, *take* + *time*, and *ride* + *horse* that "co-occur more often than their respective frequencies and the length of text in which they appear would predict" (Jones & Sinclair 1974, 19). In learner corpus research (LCR), statistical collocations have typically been identified by means of association measures such as the pointwise mutual information (MI) score and the t-score (Gablasova et al. 2017).[2] The two statistical measures have often been used in tandem on the ground that MI will rank best word combinations made up of low-frequency words (e.g. *substantiating evidence*, *corroborative evidence*) while t-score will give

* Figures 5 and 6 in this chapter are available in color in the supplementary online materials of the volume. You can find them at https://www.cambridge.org/gb/academic/subjects/languages-linguistics/applied-linguistics-and-second-language-acquisition/learner-corpus-research-meets-second-language-acquisition?format=PB.

[1] This chapter is based on a paper first presented by the first two authors at the 3rd Learner Corpus Research Conference, the Netherlands, September 11–13, 2015.

[2] Note that there is also an extensive body of research that has approached word combinations in the form of constructions, most particularly verb-argument constructions, in learner language (e.g. Gries & Wulff 2005; Ellis et al. 2016; Kyle & Crossley 2017). In this particular strand of research, and as noted by one reviewer, other (directional) association measures such as Delta P have been used and promoted to investigate the degree of attraction of a lemma to a slot in one particular construction or the preference of a lemma for one particular construction over another. In this study, we did not use Delta P because we wanted to situate our work against previous research on collocations in learner writing, which is nearly exclusively based on t- and MI-scores.

prominence to word combinations composed of high-frequency words (e.g. *further evidence*, *empirical evidence*) (Durrant & Schmitt 2009).[3] The following procedure has often been adopted to assess collocations in a learner corpus. First, word pairs or co-occurrences are extracted from a large reference corpus such as the *British National Corpus* (BNC) and association measures are computed for each of them. Second, co-occurrences are extracted from learner corpora and the corresponding BNC-derived association measures are assigned to learners' production. Third, for each learner text, a mean MI score and/or t-score is computed (e.g. Bestgen & Granger 2014; Paquot 2019) or co-occurrences are categorized into collocational bands (see Granger & Bestgen 2014 for more details on this specific procedure).

This approach has generated a wealth of interesting results that stress the value of a frequency-based approach to phraseology (cf. Granger & Paquot 2008) to assess foreign language proficiency and trace foreign language development. Durrant and Schmitt (2009), for example, showed that, compared to native writers, L2 writers of English tend to overuse high-frequency noun/adjective + noun pairs identified by high t-scores (e.g. *good example*, *long way*, *hard work*) but underuse less common, strongly associated collocations as identified by high MI scores (e.g. *densely populated*, *bated breath*, *preconceived notions*). In a study that investigated the full range of contiguous word pairs instead of being restricted to modifier + noun sequences, Granger and Bestgen (2014) demonstrated that the same difference can be observed between intermediate and advanced EFL learners in a subset of learner texts from the *International Corpus of Learner English* (ICLE; Granger et al. 2009): advanced learners have a lower proportion of high-frequency collocations (t-score) and a higher proportion of lower-frequency collocations (MI score).

Bestgen and Granger also reported a significant decrease in the use of collocations made up of high-frequency words (average t-score values) from time 1 to time 3 (a six-month difference) in the *Michigan State University Corpus of Second Language Writing*, but no effect of time on average MI scores was found, which the authors argued can be explained by "the low frequency of the bigrams in the learners' input coupled with the short period in time covered" (2014, 37). However, mean MI scores of the bigrams used by L2 writers were shown to be positively correlated with the quality of the essays, while there was a negative correlation between the quality of the texts and the proportion

[3] This "dichotomous description" of collocation use, however, has also recently been criticized as "too general to be useful in [Language Learning Research]" (Gablasova et al. 2017, 163).

of bigrams that were absent in the reference corpus, most of which were shown to be erroneous. In a recently published follow-up study, Bestgen and Granger (2018) investigated the development of collocational strength in bigrams (types and tokens) in a set of essays produced by French-speaking learners of English and collected at a two-year interval within the framework of the *Longitudinal Database of Learner English* project (LONGDALE; see Section 2). Among the many results, the analyses based on tokens revealed a significant increase of bigrams with low t-score (Cohen's d = 0.36) and a significant decrease of bigrams with high t-score in the second set of essays (Cohen's d = 0.28). By contrast, only the category of high MI bigrams (types and tokens) showed a significant increase with time, with medium to large effect sizes (Cohen's d of 0.68 and 0.78, respectively).[4]

All the studies above rely on a positional or surface model of co-occurrence, where words are said to co-occur when they appear within a close distance from each other, measured in number of intervening words (cf. Evert 2005, 18–19; Evert 2008). More precisely, the above studies all set a minimal collocational span and investigated statistical co-occurrences as bigrams, i.e. contiguous sequences of two words. A significant advantage of positional co-occurrences and bigrams for L2 research (and more particularly for research with applied perspectives in language teaching and assessment, cf. Bestgen 2017) is that they can be extracted easily and quickly from corpora and their frequencies can be measured reliably with fully automatic techniques. The downside, however, is that positional co-occurrences are blind to syntactic relations such as subject + verb, verb + object, predicative adjectives, verb + particle or the pattern N *of* N in English. Some of these relations, however, have been shown to be particularly problematic for EFL learners, even at an intermediate to advanced level (e.g. Nesselhauf 2005, or Laufer & Waldman 2011, on verb + noun combinations).

As a consequence, in a study that aimed to put forward and operationalize the construct of phraseological complexity (see below for more information), Paquot (2019) adopted a relational or syntactic model of co-occurrences to investigate EFL learners' use of adjective modifiers, adverb modifiers, and verb + noun structures at the B2, C1, and C2 proficiency levels of the Common European Framework of References for Languages (CEFR; Council of Europe 2001) in the

[4] Unfortunately, as the method used in Bestgen and Granger (2018) is not the same as that used in Bestgen and Granger (2014), it is not straightforward to compare the six-month vs. two-year interval longitudinal studies and interpret the different results for MI-based bigrams.

Varieties of English for Specific Purposes dAtabase (VESPA) learner corpus (Paquot et al. 2013).[5] The corpus was part-of-speech (POS) tagged and parsed with the Stanford CoreNLP, and collocational strength was determined with MI on the basis of *amod*, *advmod*, and *dobj* Stanford-typed dependencies (cf. Section 2.2). Pairwise comparisons between groups revealed the following:

- Adjective + noun dependencies showed a significant difference in mean MI scores between the B2 and C2 levels, but differences were not large enough to distinguish between adjacent levels such as B2–C1 and C1–C2.
- Adverbial modifiers (i.e. adverb + adverb, adverb + adjective, adverb + verb) singled out upper intermediate (i.e. B2) learner writing from the more advanced (i.e. C1 and C2) learner productions.
- Verb + direct object structures were the best discriminators of the most advanced (C2) level: mean MI scores on *dobj* dependencies set C2 texts apart from B2 and C1 texts.
- No statistically significant difference was found between learner groups when their texts were analyzed with traditional measures of syntactic or lexical complexity.

In a follow-up study, Paquot (2018) made use of mixed-effects modeling to assess the influence of syntactic, lexical, and phraseological complexity on human raters' overall judgment of writing quality in the VESPA corpus. After stepwise model selection, the final model only included two mean-based phraseological measures, i.e. mean MI score for *dobj* dependencies and mean MI score for *amod* dependencies, as fixed effects (marginal $R^2 = 0.25$), thus demonstrating that the higher the average MI scores for *dobj* and *amod* dependencies in a student's paper, the better it was assessed on the CEFR scale.

From the above, it can be argued that studies of syntactic co-occurrences in learner language can usefully complement the body of research based on a positional model of co-occurrence, most particularly by shedding light on how collocational strength of specific structures such as verb + direct object relations can be used to describe L2 performance and assess L2 proficiency. No study so far, however, has examined whether syntactic co-occurrences can also serve to trace phraseological development in a longitudinal learner corpus. Theoretically, Paquot (2019) has argued that L2 complexity

5 https://uclouvain.be/en/research-institutes/ilc/cecl/vespa.html

research needs to broaden its scope on the ground that traditional measures of syntactic and lexical complexity fail to account for the fact that words naturally combine to form conventional patterns of meaning and use (cf. Sinclair 1991; Hanks 2013). This is particularly relevant since complexity is regarded as one of the "major variables in applied linguistic research" (Housen & Kuiken 2009): measures of linguistic complexity are widely used to describe L2 performance, assess L2 proficiency, and trace L2 development (Housen et al. 2012; Norris & Ortega 2009; Wolfe-Quintero et al. 1998). Following Ortega (2003, 492), the author offers the following working definition of phraseological complexity: "the range of phraseological units that surface in language production and the degree of sophistication of such phraseological units" (Paquot 2019, 4). Thus, a learner text with a wide range of (target-like) phraseological units and a high proportion of sophisticated units will be said to be more phraseologically complex than one where the same few basic word combinations are often repeated.

The main objective of the present work is therefore to investigate phraseological complexity development in French EFL learner writing from the LONGDALE. The focus is placed on verb + object structures, as they have typically not been investigated in studies that adopted a surface model of statistical co-occurrence but, as mentioned above, are otherwise considered a major stumbling block for EFL learners. Building on the current state of the art, the study addresses the following research questions:

RQ1: To what extent can syntactic co-occurrences, and verb + direct object structures more particularly, be used to trace the development of phraseological complexity in a longitudinal corpus of EFL learner writing?

RQ2: What are the effects of proficiency vs. time spent learning English on phraseological complexity in learner writing development?

2 Data and Analysis

To answer the research questions, the study replicates the methods used to extract and analyze syntactic co-occurrences from the VESPA in Paquot (2018, 2019) on the LONGDALE corpus described in Section 2.1. Section 2.2 summarizes the different methodological steps required for that purpose and Section 2.3 reports the results of the statistical evaluation, which are discussed in Section 3. The final section closes with concluding remarks.

Table 24 Number of texts in LONGDALE sample used for this study

	Number of texts (with OQPT scores)
Y1 (2008 or 2010)	184
Y2 (2009 or 2011)	109
Y3 (2010 or 2012)	124
Total	**417**

2.1 Data

The learner data come from LONGDALE, a learner corpus compilation initiative that was launched in 2008 by the Centre for English Corpus Linguistics (UCLouvain) with the aim of collecting learner productions over a minimum period of three years, with data collections organized at least once a year (cf. Meunier 2016).[6] The subset used for this study consists of 417 argumentative essays written by two cohorts of French-speaking undergraduate students (total = 237) of English language and literature at UCLouvain, Belgium followed from 2008 to 2010 and from 2010 to 2012, respectively (Table 24).

The students wrote their essays in a computer lab using Notepad, with no access to reference tools. During the allotted time (90 minutes), students were requested to fill in a learner profile questionnaire, take a short vocabulary placement test (see below), and write an essay of about 500 words. In Year 1 (Y1), students had to choose one topic among the following: "In our modern world, dominated by science, technology and industrialization, there is no longer a place for learning and imagination," "Violent films are harmful and should be banned," "Money is the root of all evil," and "Lying is immoral and should always be condemned." They could choose a topic in Y2 too (with four different prompts for Cohort 1, see Table 25) but were given the same topic in Y3 as the one they had selected in Y1 to ensure maximum comparability (Gentil & Meunier 2018, 276). As reported in Bestgen and Granger (2018, 282–283), "[a]ll the students proved to have enough time to write their essay. Although the exercise was compulsory, it was not part of a formal exam. However, the students did take it seriously, as they were promised individual feedback on the quality of their text."

[6] See also https://uclouvain.be/en/research-institutes/ilc/cecl/longdale.html.

Table 25 Prompts used in the LONGDALE sample

Code	Topic	Y1	Y2	Y3
modern	In our modern world, dominated by science, technology and industrialization, there is no longer a place for learning and imagination.	71	19	42
violence	Violent films are harmful and should be banned.	58	15	35
lying	Lying is immoral and should always be condemned.	28	16	22
money	Money is the root of all evil.	27	18	25
mothers	Mothers should stay home with their children.	0	15	0
media	The media pay too much attention to the personal lives of famous people.	0	13	0
judging	One should never judge a person by external appearances.	0	7	0
self	Self-confidence is the most important factor for success.	0	6	0

Each learner text comes with results from the Oxford Quick Placement Test (OQPT), one of several language tests used in the LONGDALE project to provide a measure of proficiency that is independent of learners' productions. The OQPT comprises 60 questions measuring knowledge of vocabulary and grammar; it has often been used as an indicator of general proficiency both in higher education (e.g. Meurant 2009)[7] and L2 research (see e.g. Hawkins et al. 2012).

Following Meunier and Littré (2013), OQPT scores were also converted into Common European Framework of Reference for Languages (CEFR) bands (Council of Europe 2001, 114), according to the following key: A1 (0–17), A2 (18–29), B1 (30–39), B2 (40–47), C1 (48–54), and C2 (55–60) for ease of interpretability. In this study, we used both OQPT scores and CEFR scores in separate models (cf. Section 2.3): we wanted to be able to compare our results with previous CEFR-based research while at the same time benefiting from the use of a potentially statistically more powerful numeric variable in the form of OQPT scores.

Crucially, learners at Y1 display a broad range of proficiency levels, from A2 to C2, with 79 percent at B1/B2, which makes it all the more important to investigate the role of proficiency vs. longitudinal development (RQ2) in LONGDALE.

[7] See also for example www.universiteitleiden.nl/en/language-centre/about-atc/information-for/prospective-students/english-language-assessment-for-ma-students.

Table 26 Number of EFL learners in LONGDALE sample

Trajectory	Number of students
Y1	86
Y1–Y2	17
Y1–Y2–Y3	66
Y1–Y3	15
Y2	10
Y2–Y3	16
Y3	27
Total	**237**

As discussed by Meunier and Littré (2013), attrition is one of the major challenges in dealing with longitudinal data, and the LONGDALE is no exception: Table 26 describes trajectories found in the learner corpus and shows, among other things, that 86 first-year students dropped out after the first year and 17 more did not provide data at Y3. Conversely, Table 26 also shows that 26 participants joined the study after the first year (Y1). Several methods have been used to deal with drop-in and drop-out phenomena in the LONGDALE. The first method is to use a sample of carefully selected learner texts, as done for example by Bestgen and Granger (2018), who selected a subset of LONGDALE texts produced by the same learners at Year 1 and Year 3. The drawback of such an approach, however, is that corpus size can quickly drop dramatically. Consequently, we opted for mixed-effects modeling, as the technique makes it possible to explore the effects of different variables while dealing with unbalanced or missing data (cf. Field et al. 2012; Cunnings & Finlayson 2015; Gries 2015). Such an approach has been used, for example, by Meunier and Littré (2013) in their study of the development of accuracy in tense and aspect usage.

2.2 Data Preparation: Co-occurrence Extraction and Analysis

To investigate verb + direct object structures, we first made use of Ucto[8] and the TreeTagger (Schmid 1994) to tokenize, lemmatize, and POS tag each LONGDALE text; we then used the MaltParser (Nivre

[8] https://languagemachines.github.io/ucto/

et al. 2007) to parse all learner texts (engmalt.linear-1.7.mco model).[9] The next steps consisted in extracting from each LONGDALE text all the verb + noun pairs of words found in *dobj* Stanford-typed dependency relations in the form of lemmas and simplified POS tags. As illustrated in (1), a Stanford-typed dependency is a binary grammatical relation between a governor and a dependent (cf. de Marneffe & Manning 2013).

(1) *dobj* direct object
He won the lottery. *dobj*(win + VV, lottery + NN)

For each dependency, the total frequency of each individual word in each pair was recorded as well as their combined frequency.

Unlike in previous similar research (e.g. Durrant & Schmitt 2009; Granger & Bestgen 2014; Bestgen & Granger 2018), the study will only report on what MI scores have to reveal about EFL learners' use of statistical collocations, on the following grounds:

- T-scores have repeatedly been criticized for not having "a very transparent mathematical grounding" (Gablasova et al. 2017; cf. also Evert 2005, 82–83); they are also strongly dependent on corpus size (Gablasova et al. 2017, 169).
- In several studies, t-scores have been shown to be largely uninformative about EFL learners' use of syntactic collocations and regression modeling unable to explain much of its variance on the basis of fixed effects such as learner proficiency, topic, or time (e.g. Paquot & Naets 2015a, 2015b).
- By promoting the relatively less frequent and more semantically complex word pairs in learner productions, MI can be used as a measure of the "sophistication" of word combinations (Paquot 2019).

Bestgen and Granger (2018) made use of the BNC, a 100 million-word collection of samples of written and spoken language from a wide range of sources designed to represent British English from the late twentieth century, to compute association measures and assign those values to word pairs extracted from LONGDALE texts. For the purposes of this study, however, we opted for the larger (9,578,828,861 tokens) and more recent Web corpus ENCOW14 (sentence shuffle AX version; Schäfer 2015).[10] As shown by Paquot and Naets (2017),

9 www.maltparser.org/mco/english_parser/engmalt.html
10 http://corporafromtheweb.org/encow14/

ENCOW14 will probably be a better choice when EFL learners' argumentative essays are investigated for at least the following two reasons:[11]

- ENCOW14 includes many co-occurrences that are perfectly idiomatic in English (e.g. *consult* + *dictionary*, *disprove* + *hypothesis*, *win* + *election*) but appear with too low frequency (fewer than five occurrences) in the BNC to be assigned an association score (e.g. Bestgen & Granger 2018, 284).
- Low frequencies, unreliable frequencies, or lack of appearance in the BNC can be attributed to too small a corpus size for collocation extraction and corpus age (Paquot & Naets 2017; cf. Brezina & Gablasova 2015 for a related discussion). If a larger and more representative corpus of today's English is used, the percentage of learners' co-occurrences used to compute indices of collocational strength also increases, thus improving the validity of such measures: focusing on verb + noun co-occurrences in the ICLE, Paquot and Naets (2017) showed that, on average, 33 percent of co-occurrences in each learner text were not used to compute a mean MI score when the BNC was used as a reference corpus; by contrast, only 6 percent were discarded when the ENCOW14 was used.

The ENCOW14 AX version also has the advantage of being distributed with Stanford-typed dependencies.

A list of *dobj* dependency-based pairs of words with frequency information was then used as input to the Ngram Statistics Package (NSP),[12] and an MI score was calculated for each word pair that appears with a frequency of at least five occurrences in ENCOW14.[13] Each word pair in the LONGDALE learner texts was

[11] In Paquot and Naets (2017), we also advocate the use of more than one reference corpus to assess learners' use of co-occurrences (see also Gablasova et al. 2017 for similar ideas).

[12] http://www.d.umn.edu/~tpederse/nsp.html

[13] Note that differences in proficiency level as represented in the LONGDALE learner texts have a small but not significant effect on the percentage of relational co-occurrences used to compute mean MI scores per text: a mean percentage of 87 percent of verb + object relations (tokens) are used to compute mean MI scores at A2, compared to 93 percent at C2. This is because the less proficient the learners, the more non-attested co-occurrences they use (from a mean of 2.7 unattested co-occurrences at B2 to 1.5 at C1). Spelling mistakes are also more frequent in the lower proficiency texts. In this study, we do not analyze these "absent" co-occurrences (but see Bestgen & Granger 2014 for a study that makes use of this specific category to describe learners' collocational competence). In terms of frequency, mean MI scores are computed on a mean of 15.95 verb + object relations (sd = 4.99) at A2 (mean text length = 606, sd = 158), while they are computed on a mean of 18.56 verb + object relations (sd = 5.4) at C1 (mean text length = 633, sd = 89).

Table 27 Corpus preprocessing workflow

	Tools	Corpus
1. Tokenization	Ucto	LONGDALE
2. Lemmatization	TreeTagger	LONGDALE
3. POS tagging		
4. Parsing	MaltParser (engmalt. linear-1.7.mco model)	LONGDALE
5. Extraction of dependencies	In-house Perl programs	ENCOW14 + LONGDALE
6. Simplify POS tags		
7. Compute corpus-based frequencies		
8. Compute MI scores for each pair of words in a dependency	In-house Perl program (using Ngram Statistics Package)	ENCOW14
9. Assign MI scores computed on the basis of the ENCOW14 to each pair of words in a dependency in each learner text	In-house Perl program	LONGDALE
10. Compute mean MI scores for each learner text	R	LONGDALE

then looked up in the list of dependencies extracted from the ENCOW14 to determine its MI score in a reference corpus of contemporary general English. If a word pair was not found or appeared fewer than five times in ENCOW14, it was removed from further analysis. The last step involved computing a mean MI score for each learner text on the basis of all the different word pairs found in the *dobj* dependencies (i.e. types). Mean association measures were calculated with R (R Core Team 2019). Table 27 summarizes the different steps of the corpus pre-processing workflow; the workflow applied to LONGDALE texts aimed at replicating as accurately as possible the way ENCOW14 was processed by its compilers.

The analysis of relational co-occurrences requires accurate automatic syntactic analysis. To verify the quality of our dataset, we carried out a precision and recall study of *dobj* dependencies in 50 learner texts from the LONGDALE. While precision proved reasonably good (88.8 percent), the 76.9 percent recall rate obtained mainly stems from two major issues, i.e. POS tagging errors and erroneous dependency attachments (e.g. *people* is parsed as the subject of *judging* in "many employers reject qualified people judging them on their appearance").

2.3 Statistical Evaluation

To answer our research questions, we made use of mixed-effects modeling to assess the influence of time (YEAR) on mean MI scores for *dobj* dependencies and investigate how it compares with the effect of proficiency, while taking into account any random variation observed across the participants (LEARNER). Proficiency effects were explored in terms of OQPT scores (OQPT) and CEFR levels (CEFR). We also included topic (TOPIC) as a fixed effect in our models because previous research has identified topic influence as an important explanatory factor for the presence or absence of specific word combinations in various text types and genres (e.g. Cortes 2004; Paquot 2014, 2017). All statistical analyses were performed with R (R Core Team 2019) and the *lme4*, *effects*, and *MuMIn* packages.

We began our analysis with an exploration of the main variables involved in the study. These exploratory steps led to some minor changes that were required or at least useful for the subsequent regression modeling. Specifically, we studied all predictors and the response univariately and in a pairwise fashion both numerically (with summary statistics) and visually (with histograms) to check for outliers, data sparsity issues, potential curvature, etc. As a result:

- We had to conflate several levels of the predictor TOPIC to avoid massive data sparsity for all essay topics only written about by students in Y2. Therefore, the essays on "judging," "media," "mothers," and "self" were conflated into a group labeled *other year 2*. In the absence of specific a priori hypotheses about the differences between topics, we then ordered the factor levels by their descriptive mean MI scores and defined orthogonal contrasts for sequential-differences testing.
- We had to conflate levels of the predictor CEFR given the quite small frequencies of the levels A2 and C2, which were combined with B1 (to a factor level A2/B1) and C1 (to a factor level C1/C2), respectively. Given the ordinal nature of this predictor (from A2/B1 to B2 to C), CEFR was also set to utilize orthogonal sequential-differences contrasts.
- The variable YEAR was set to utilize orthogonal sequential-differences contrasts.
- The numeric predictor OQPT was centered to facilitate the interpretation of the coefficients in our regression models, i.e. from every value of OQPT we subtracted OQPT's overall mean of 43.1175.

In order to then determine the degrees to which the response variable MI is correlated with the predictors, we undertook a model selection and comparison approach using linear mixed-effects modeling, which was conducted in several steps. First, we fitted a linear mixed-effects model with MI as the response variable, an overall intercept and the predictor TOPIC as fixed effects, and varying intercepts for participants; following Barr et al. (2013), we considered the possibility of a more comprehensive random-effects structure, but the nature of our data ruled that out: none of the speakers provided more than three data points (so the amount of repeated-measurements structure is minimal) and slightly more than 50 percent of the speakers provided more than one data point. (Some might argue that a mixed-effects model would not be required for these data, a point to which we will return briefly below.)

To determine which variable among YEAR, OQPT, and CEFR is the most useful predictor and answer RQ2, we followed the logic of Gries (2018); applied to this case, it means one needs to check which of these three predictors is most powerful and (i) whether Occam's razor then permits *adding* one or more of the others to the regression model already involving the most powerful predictor, or (ii) whether model comparison shows that in fact one or more of the other predictors (and potentially their interactions) can *replace* the most powerful predictor. Thus, we inspected the initial model involving only TOPIC and checked which predictor – OQPT, CEFR, or YEAR – would improve this model most (using both LR-tests and *AICc*-values, i.e. *p*-values using the traditional 0.05 threshold, and *AIC*-values corrected for smaller sample sizes). Both diagnostics showed that OQPT improved the model most, and OQPT was therefore added to the model. Following the above logic, we then tested both adding to and replacing OQPT. Model comparisons using *AICc* revealed that the model with TOPIC and OQPT ($AICc = 792.27$) was superior to:

- a model with YEAR instead of OQPT ($AICc = 819.39$);
- a model with CEFR instead of OQPT ($AICc = 805.6$);
- a model with YEAR and CEFR and their interaction instead of OQPT ($AICc = 811.14$).

In other words, the (preliminarily) final model contained only TOPIC and OQPT as predictors. However, an analysis of the coefficients for the predictor TOPIC showed that the five levels of the variable TOPIC were not justifiable from the perspective of Occam's razor; specifically, the only successive-differences contrasts that reached standard levels of significance ($p = 0.0454$) indicated a split between two kinds of topics: *money/modern/other* on the one hand vs. *violence/lying* on the other. We therefore created a binary version of TOPIC, i.e. one that only maintained these two levels and, to arrive at the most parsimonious model as well as determine that the results were not

Table 28 Summary results of the final regression model

	b / estimate	*se*	*df*	$t_{Satterthwaite}$	*p*
Intercept	1.529	0.041	241.7	37.224	<<<0.001
$TOPIC_{group1 \rightarrow group2}$	0.351	0.063	351	5.609	<<<0.001
$OQPT_{0 \rightarrow 1\ etc.}$	0.027	0.004	382.1	6.882	<<<0.001
Varying intercepts	PARTICIPANT	Residual			
	0.03	0.3			

affected in any way by the (lack of significant) differences between different topics, ran the above modeling process again.

As it turns out, the overall results were not affected by the simplification of the TOPIC variable: again, the final model involved just two predictors, TOPIC (now in its binary form) and OQPT (centered). The final statistics of this model are presented summarily in Table 28.

This model came with only a moderate amount of variance explanation, which, however, is unsurprising given the high degree of variability of such data and the small number of predictors involved: $R^2_{marginal}$ (the *R*-squared value quantifying the summed effect of all fixed-effects predictors) is 0.16, whereas $R^2_{conditional}$ (the *R*-squared value quantifying the summed effect of both fixed and random effects) is 0.22. This indicates that the fixed effects account for more variability than the random ones, which is a positive sign – the data are not just mostly speaker-specific variable – but it also indicates that including the random-effects structure was useful. Model diagnostics, in particular of the residuals, revealed no problematic aspects of the final model and suggested no curved relationship between MI and OQPT; neither did a test of a polynomial to the second degree of OQPT.

The nature of the fixed effects is relatively straightforward and shown in the two figures below. Figure 3 shows the predicted mean MI scores on the *y*-axis as a function of the predictor TOPIC on the *x*-axis. The effect is indicated with points (the size of which is proportional to the number of data points per group) and their 95 percent confidence intervals; the grey points represent the actually observed values by the speakers. As is obvious from Table 28, the average predicted MI for the essays on *money*, *modern*, and *other* is 1.53 and significantly lower than the average predicted MI of 1.88 for the essays on *violence* and *lying*.

The effect of OQPT is shown in Figure 4: again, the MI scores are on the *y*-axis and the predictor is on the *x*-axis (which, for ease of interpretation, we de-centered). The regression line indicates the

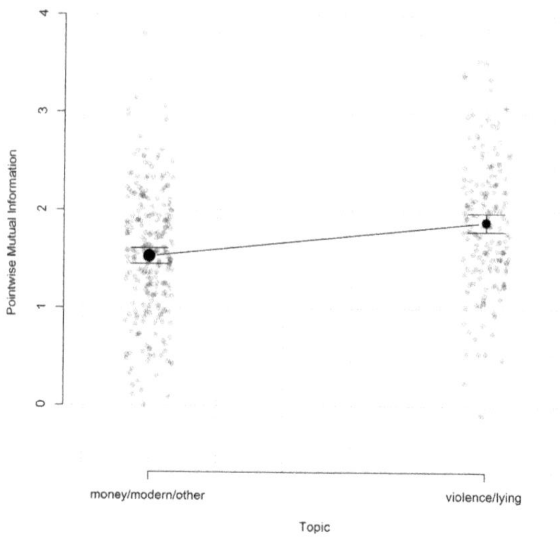

Figure 3 The main effect of Topic

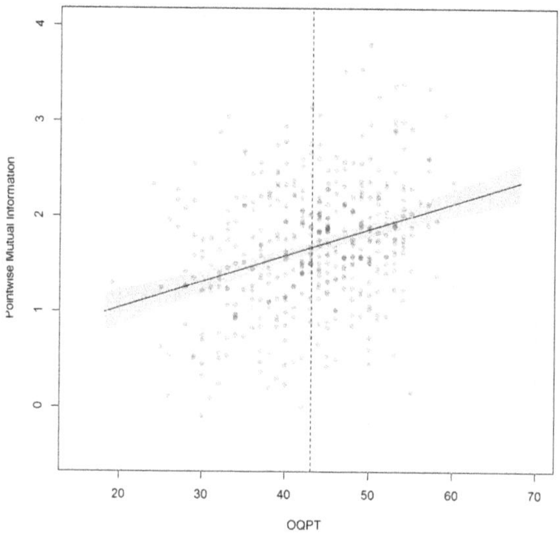

Figure 4 The main effect of OQPT

positive effect of OQPT on the mean MI scores (with a 95 percent confidence band) – the higher OQPT, the higher the mean MI scores – and the observed values are shown as grey points; the vertical line represents the mean of OQPT.

3 Discussion

Figure 5 represents the changes in average MI scores for *dobj* dependencies from Y1 to Y2 to Y3, with different colors representing different learner overall trajectories. As is clear, not all learners behave in the same way, and there is much variation in developmental trajectories at the individual level. As presented above, however, a mixed-model approach shows that, despite the apparent mess in data structure, there are also general patterns. First, the model reveals a significant effect of the prompt, with essays on "Violent films are harmful and should be banned" and "Lying is immoral and should always be condemned" featuring a higher MI mean value than the other essays. The effects are more subtle than just the typical reuse of word combinations primed by the prompt as documented in the literature (cf. for example, Ohlrogge 2009). For example, only 23.8 percent (436/1,835 tokens) of the *dobj* dependencies used in essays on

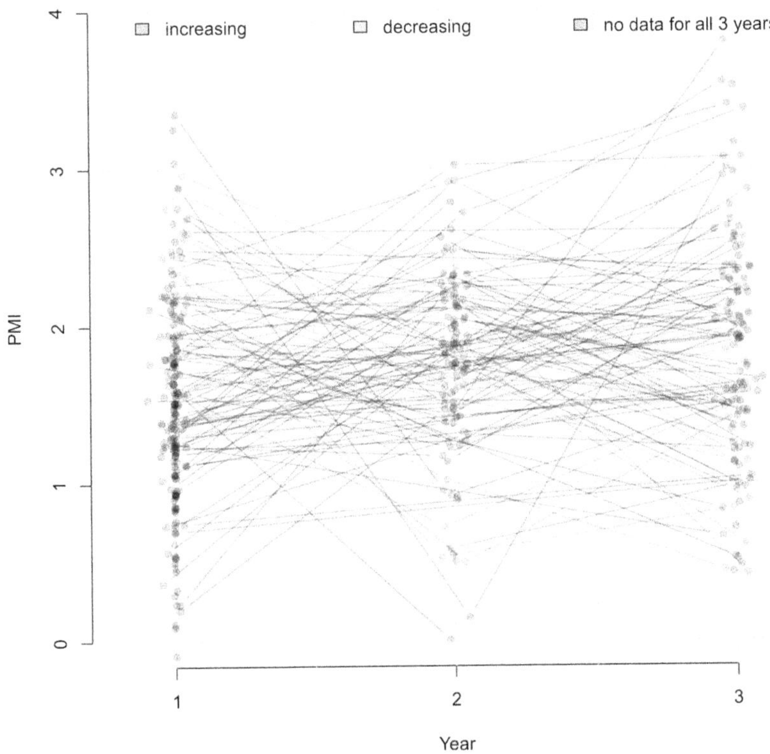

Figure 5 Average MI scores for dobj *dependencies per year*

"Money is the root of all evil" have a MI score above 3, which is a threshold often used in the literature for collocational status (e.g. Durrant & Schmitt 2009; Granger & Bestgen 2014). Examples of collocations that appear at least twice in the learner essays include *win + lottery, wear + clothes, play + role, cause + damage, pay + attention, break + rule, waste + money, spend + time, feed + family, donate + money, win + war, earn + money, reach + goal, spend + money, cause + problem, make + difference, bring + happiness, buy + house, imagine + world, buy + car,* and *make + profit*. Many other combinations of high-frequency words, including combinations with *money*, the theme of the prompt, have very low (if not negative) MI scores: *have + money, use + money, bring + money, receive + money, have + house, have + salary, buy + thing, have + value, give + food,* and *have + job*. By contrast, more than 30 percent (412/1,312 tokens) of the *dobj* dependencies used in EFL learner essays on "Lying is immoral and should always be condemned" have a MI score above 3, with examples as varied as *mow + lawn, commit + crime, answer + question, serve + purpose, solve + problem, play + role, achieve + goal, cross + line, cause + damage, witness + murder, pay + attention, break + law, ask + question, hurt + feeling, keep + secret, break + vase, spend + time, cause + trouble, save + life, make + mistake, tell + story, reveal + truth, discover + truth, hide + truth, tell + truth, tell + lie, make + difference, change + world, organize + party, give + chance, deny + fact, protect + child,* and *give + example*. From the examples above, it seems that to answer the "money" prompt, EFL learners only need to mobilize a limited set of related semantic domains that are made up of highly frequent words (frequently used nouns such as *money, food, family, job, time, war, house,* and *car*, and verbs such as *have, buy, use, give, win, play,* and *pay* belong to the 400 most frequent words in the *Corpus of Contemporary American English* (COCA).[14] By contrast, the "lying" prompt mobilizes more semantic domains and less frequent words (e.g. *lawn, lie, truth, goal, murder, secret, trouble, commit, serve, solve, achieve*), which can be explained by the variety of lying examples and anecdotes that are found in such essays as exemplified below:

- *First, there are the "kind" lies. Those that cannot hurt people, like a man saying to his wife that he* ***mew*** *the* ***lawn*** *when he did not.* (UCL0211_Y1)
- *Those lies can be used out of laziness, for instance with a husband who did not* ***mow*** *the* ***lawn*** *and prune the bushes as he had*

[14] www.wordfrequency.info/free.asp?s=y

promised to his beloved wife while he was having a day off. (UCL0211_Y3)

- *On the other hand, some people lie because they have to escape from a situation, from a person. For instance, they* ***committed*** *a* ***crime*** *and do not want to be sent to jail.* (UCL0256_Y1)

To provide a first partial answer to RQ1, our results thus suggest that statistical co-occurrences, and verb + object relations more particularly, will only be useful to trace phraseological complexity development in longitudinal learner data if and only if topic/prompt is controlled for, or used as a predictor.

The second, and last, significant predictor in our final model is OQPT, i.e. a continuous numeric variable that represents scores on the OQPT. As shown in Figure 4, the higher the OQPT score of a learner, the higher their MI mean score. OQPT selection in the final model instead of the predictor YEAR answers RQ2: learner proficiency, as assessed by an independent measure (i.e. a standardized test), is a better predictor of phraseological complexity in each learner writing sample than the actual time when the essay was written (at the start of the curriculum, after one year or after two years of English instruction at university). This may be explained by two different factors:

(1) As shown in Figure 6, not all learners start with the same proficiency at Y1 (i.e. first year of a Bachelor program in English language and literature) as represented in the LONGDALE.[15] Quite the contrary, learners range from A2 to C2.

(2) The foreign language proficiency of each learner develops at a different pace. Table 29 illustrates the variety of individual trajectories in the LONGDALE.

Our results thus suggest that the time spent learning English will not have an effect on collocation strength per se. What matters more is foreign language proficiency (cf. Bestgen & Granger 2014) and whether learners improve from one year to the next: if the general foreign language proficiency of a learner does not improve from one data point collection time to the next, there is no reason to expect more phraseological complexity in their written productions.

That OQPT gets selected in the final model instead of the CEFR predictor is interesting but perhaps not particularly surprising. Since its publication in 2001, the CEFR has become the most widespread

[15] In Figure 6 and Table 29, we report CEFR levels instead of OQPT results for ease of interpretability.

Table 29 Language proficiency development: Individual trajectories in LONGDALE

	Year 1	Year 2	Year 3
UCL0005	C2	C1	NA
UCL0006	B2	C1	C1
UCL0008	B1	NA	B2
UCL0009	B2	NA	C1
UCL0012	NA	C1	C1
UCL0015	C1	C1	C2
UCL0021	B1	B2	B2

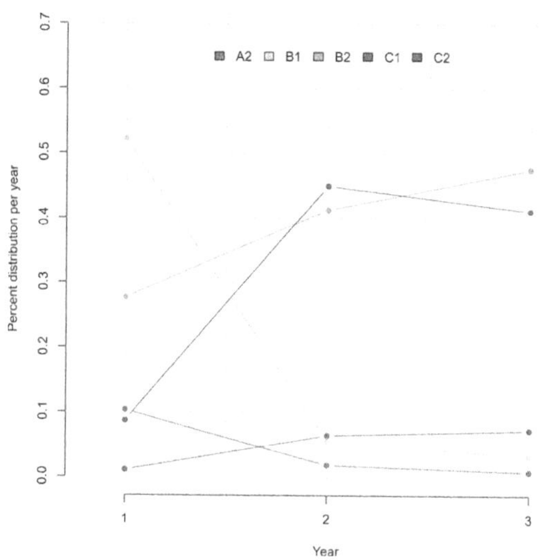

Figure 6 Percentage of A2 to C2 texts per year

reference tool in foreign language education and assessment across Europe, and learner corpus researchers have consequently seen a range of advantages in using a proficiency scale that is familiar to teachers, raters, and researchers in recent corpus compilation projects such as the KIAP or the MERLIN corpora (Carlsen 2012; Abel et al. 2014) as well as in post-hoc assessment of samples of learner texts from well-established learner corpora such as the ICLE (e.g. Thewissen 2013).[16]

[16] See Wisniewski (2017), however, for a discussion on why learner corpora should be linked only very carefully to the CEFR levels.

The use of (well-defined) proficiency categories also offers many advantages in Second Language Research (SLR), including ease of interpretation (i.e. learner groups at different proficiency levels can easily be compared) and enhanced comparability across studies, which in turn should ideally lead to more generalizability of the results and more practical outcomes. However, from a methodological/statistical perspective, our final model shows that the numeric predictor OQPT is more informative than its derived categorical predictor CEFR: it explains more variance in EFL learners' use of statistically assessed *dobj* dependencies in the LONGDALE. Our results thus support Ortega's call for more SLR study designs where proficiency is treated as an interval scale (i.e. individual proficiency scores), and not as a categorical variable as has most often been done in the field:

> SLA researchers have most often chosen to treat proficiency as a categorical variable and then have assessed mean differences in complexity values across proficiency groupings. Yet, this practice of converting interval variables (i.e. individual proficiency scores of some kind) into categorical ones (i.e. participants grouped by nominal proficiency levels) has always been criticized by statisticians because it discards much useful information. More specifically, it does away with the variance of continuous scores and leads to unreliability and increased likelihood of Type II errors (e.g. Skidmore and Thomson 2010), that is, the problem of failing to detect a difference, relationship, or effect that is in fact present because of some psychometric methodological problem, such as lack of power or (in the case at hand) lack of variance in the observations.
>
> (Ortega 2012, 131)

4 Conclusion

At EuroSLA2015, the first two authors reported on a monofactorial study that investigated the effect of time on mean MI scores in the LONGDALE; they used a mixed-effects modeling approach and showed that, on average, mean MI score per learner text increased significantly at a rate of 0.14 for every one unit increment in time (i.e. every year) (Paquot & Naets 2015b). However, the model performed badly, with the fixed effect explaining only 3 percent of the variance, and the random effects accounting for an additional 14 percent, i.e. between-speaker variability accounting for nearly five times as much as the fixed effect. In the new model presented in this study, the explained fixed-effects variance is five times as high (0.16) as in Paquot and Naets's (2015b) model, and what the between-speaker variability adds is only 7 percent. In other words, the fixed effects do five times as much as in the old model (which is good), while the random effects do only half as much as in the old model (which is also good). To obtain such better results, we re-examined the same dataset as used in Paquot and Naets's (2015b) study, this time, however, adopting a multifactorial design that includes two predictors that have already been shown to have an effect on EFL learners' use of word combinations of various types, i.e. proficiency level and essay prompt/topic. By doing so, we followed Gries (2018)'s recommendation to approach even a monofactorial hypothesis (here, time has an effect on phraseological complexity development in EFL learner writing) with a multifactorial design "to determine either (a) whether it adds anything to what we already know about the phenomenon (by statistically controlling for what we already know) or (b) whether it replaces (parts of) what we already know about the phenomenon" (Gries 2018, 296). We were able to determine that the time dimension does not add anything to or modify what we already know about EFL learners' use of statistical co-occurrences (as represented in the LONGDALE). Thus, the significant effect of time reported by Paquot and Naets (2015b) needs to be taken with a grain of salt, given how an overall better degree of variance explanation is in fact obtained by the (correlated, but more fine-grained) predictor of proficiency as well as that of topic/prompt.

Our findings have other important implications for LCR in general and longitudinal studies more particularly. First, they call for a more systematic control of topic/prompt in phraseological studies of learner language samples than has been done so far, including in the authors' own work. Second, they point to the need to account (statistically) for individual variation and individual trajectories in longitudinal corpora: not only do learners not start with the same initial proficiency level in English in the LONGDALE (as they would also be expected not to in other longitudinal learner corpora)[17] but their foreign language proficiency also develops in different ways. This also means that foreign language development over time in the LONGDALE should ideally be investigated in tandem with the development of proficiency as measured by means of the OQPT. The availability of independent proficiency scores in LONGDALE is certainly an invaluable strength of the longitudinal corpus.

[17] The diversity of proficiency levels represented in Year 1 in the LONGDALE also provides empirical support to repeated calls that we (this is an inclusive "we!") should exercise more caution in the use and analysis of learner language samples for which the foreign language proficiency of learners is operationalized by institutional status (cf. Tono 2003; Thomas 2006; Carlsen 2012).

The study also comes with limitations that we would like to address in future research. First, although we improved the study design as compared with Paquot and Naets (2015b) and examined the effects of four predictors (topic, time, and proficiency as operationalized by CEFR and OQPT) on the development of phraseological complexity in EFL learner writing, the explained variance is still limited. We would like to investigate whether other learner variables (e.g. time spent in an English-speaking environment) and text/linguistic variables (e.g. lexical diversity, lexical dispersion, lexical sophistication) could increase the amount of explained variance in our dataset. Examining the potential effects of traditional measures of lexical and syntactic complexity, for example, would also make it possible to explore how the various dimensions of linguistic complexity interact with time and/or proficiency (cf. Paquot 2019). Second, we would like to use other association measures than MI, more particularly Delta P or the log odds ratio to explore collocation strength and phraseological complexity in learner language: both keep frequency and effect size separate, and the first is also directional. Last but not least, we are very much aware that a mean MI is a very crude measure of a learner's phraseological competence, and we are currently investigating how to use more information from each learner text.

Acknowledgments

We would like to thank Professor F. Meunier (Centre for English Corpus Linguistics, UCLouvain) for granting us access to a set of French learners' essays from the LONGDALE.

References

Abel, A., Nicolas, L., Wisniewski, K., Boyd, A., & Hana, J. (2014). A trilingual learner corpus illustrating European reference levels. *Ricognizioni. Rivista di Lingue e Letterature e Culture Moderne* 2(1), 111–126, https://doi.org/10.13135/2384-8987/702

Barr, D. J., Levy, R., Scheepers, C., & Tily, H. (2013). Random effects structure for confirmatory hypothesis testing: Keep it maximal. *Journal of Memory and Language* 68(3), 255–278.

Bestgen, Y. (2017). Beyond single-word measures: L2 writing assessment, lexical richness and formulaic competence. *System* 69, 65–78.

Bestgen, Y. & Granger, S. (2014). Quantifying the development of phraseological competence in L2 English writing: An automated approach. *Journal of Second Language Writing* 26, 28–41.

(2018). Tracking L2 writers' phraseological development using collgrams: Evidence from a longitudinal EFL corpus. In S. Hoffmann, A. Sand,

S. Arndt-Lappe, & L. M. Dillman (eds). *Corpora and Lexis*, 277–301. Leiden & Boston: Brill Rodopi.

Brezina, V. & Gablasova, D. (2015). Is there a core general vocabulary? Introducing the New General Service List. *Applied Linguistics* 36(1), 1–22.

Carlsen, C. (2012). Proficiency level – a fuzzy variable in computer learner corpora. *Applied Linguistics* 33(2), 161–183.

Council of Europe. (2001). *Common European Framework of Reference for Languages: Learning, Teaching, Assessment*. Cambridge: Cambridge University Press.

Cunnings, I. & Finlayson, I. (2015). Mixed effects modelling and longitudinal data analysis. In L. Plonsky (ed.) *Advancing Quantitative Methods in Second Language Research*, 159–181. Abingdon: Routledge.

Cortes, V. (2004). Lexical bundles in published and student disciplinary writing: Examples from history and biology. *English for Specific Purposes* 23(4), 397–423.

De Marneffe, M.-C. & Manning, C. (2013). Stanford Typed Dependencies Manual, retrieved from http://nlp.stanford.edu/software/dependencies_manual.pdf (accessed June 13, 2020).

Durrant, P. & Schmitt, N. (2009). To what extent do native and non-native writers make use of collocations? *IRAL – International Review of Applied Linguistics in Language Teaching* 47(2), 157–177.

Ellis, N. C., Römer, U., & O'Donnell, M. B. (2016). *Usage-Based Approaches to Language Acquisition and Processing: Cognitive and Corpus Investigations of Construction Grammar*. Language Learning Monograph Series. Chichester: Wiley-Blackwell.

Evert, S. (2005). The Statistics of Word Cooccurrences: Word Pairs and Collocations. Unpublished Ph.D. thesis, Institut für maschinelle Sprachverarbeitung, University of Stuttgart, retrieved from www.collocations.de/phd.html (accessed June 13, 2020).

(2008). Corpora and collocations. In A. Lüdeling & M. Kytö (eds.), *Corpus Linguistics: An International Handbook*, 1212–1248. Berlin: Mouton de Gruyter.

Field, A., Miles, J., & Field, Z. (2012). *Discovering Statistics with R*. Los Angeles, CA: SAGE Publications Ltd.

Gablasova, D., Brezina, V., & McEnery, T. (2017). Collocations in corpus-based language learning research: Identifying, comparing, and interpreting the evidence. *Language Learning* 67(S1), 155–179.

Gentil, G. & Meunier, F. (2018). A systemic functional linguistic approach to usage-based research and instruction. The case of nominalization in L2 academic writing. In A. E. Tyler, L. Ortega, M. Uno, & H. I. Park (eds.), *Usage-Inspired L2 Instruction. Researched Pedagogy*, 267–289. Amsterdam and Philadelphia: Benjamins.

Granger, S. & Bestgen, Y. (2014). The use of collocations by intermediate vs. advanced non-native writers: A bigram-based study. *International Review of Applied Linguistics in Language Teaching* 52(3), 229–252.

Granger, S., Dagneaux, E., Meunier, F., & Paquot, M. (2009). *The International Corpus of Learner English, Version 2.* Handbook and CD-ROM. Louvain-la-Neuve: Presses universitaires de Louvain.

Granger, S. & Paquot, M. (2008). Disentangling the phraseological web. In S. Granger & F. Meunier (eds), *Phraseology: An Interdisciplinary Perspective*, 27–49. Amsterdam & Philadelphia: Benjamins.

Gries, S. Th. (2015). The most under-used statistical method in corpus linguistics: Multi-level (and mixed-effects) models. *Corpora* 10(1), 95–125.

(2018). On over- and underuse in learner corpus research and multifactoriality in corpus linguistics more generally. *Journal of Second Language Studies* 1 (2), 277–309.

Gries, S. Th. & Wulff, S. (2005). Do foreign language learners also have constructions? Evidence from priming, sorting, and corpora. *Annual Review of Cognitive Linguistics* 3, 182–200.

Hanks, P. (2013). *Lexical Analysis: Norms and Exploitations.* Cambridge, MA: MIT Press.

Hawkins, R., Althobaiti, M., & Ma, Y. (2012). Eliminating grammatical function assignment from hierarchical models of speech production: Evidence from the conceptual accessibility of referents. *Applied Psycholinguistics* 35(4), 1–31.

Housen A. & Kuiken, F. (2009) Complexity, accuracy, and fluency in second language acquisition. *Applied Linguistics* 30(4), 461–73.

Housen A., Kuiken F., & Vedder, I. (2012) (eds.), *Dimensions of L2 Performance and Proficiency: Complexity, Accuracy and Fluency in SLA.* Amsterdam: Benjamins.

Jones, S. & Sinclair, J. McH. (1974). English lexical collocations. *Cahiers De Lexicologie* 24, 15–61.

Kyle, K. & Crossley, S. A. (2017). Assessing syntactic sophistication in L2 writing: A usage-based approach. *Language Testing* 34(4), 513–535.

Laufer, B. & Waldman, T. (2011). Verb–noun collocations in second language writing: A corpus analysis of learners' English. *Language Learning* 61(2), 647–672.

Meunier, F. (2016). Introduction to the LONGDALE project. In E. Castello, K. Ackerley, & F. Coccetta (eds.), *Studies in Learner Corpus Linguistics: Research and Applications for Foreign Language Teaching and Assessment*, 123–126. Bern: Peter Lang.

Meunier, F. & Littré, D. (2013). Tracking learners' progress. Adopting a dual 'corpus cum experimental data' approach. *The Modern Language Journal* 97(1), 61–76.

Meurant, R. (2009). Computer-based Internet-hosted assessment of L2 literacy: Computerizing and administering of the Oxford Quick Placement Test in ExamView and Moodle. In D. Ślęzak, W. I. Grosky, N. Pissinou, T. K. Shih, T. Kim, & B. H. Kang (eds.), *Multimedia, Computer Graphics and Broadcasting. MulGraB 2009. Communications in Computer and Information Science, Vol. 60*, 84–91. Berlin & Heidelberg: Springer.

Nesselhauf, N. (2005). *Collocations in a Learner Corpus.* Amsterdam & Philadelphia: John Benjamins.

Nivre, J., Hall, J., Nilsson, J., Chanev, A., Eryigit, G., Kübler, S., Marinov, S., & Marsi, E. (2007). MaltParser: A language-independent system for data-driven dependency parsing. *Natural Language Engineering* 13(2), 95–135.

Norris, J. M. & Ortega, L. (2009). Towards an organic approach to investigating CAF in instructed SLA: The case of complexity. *Applied Linguistics* 30(4), 555–578.

Ohlrogge, A. (2009). Formulaic expressions in intermediate EFL writing assessment. In R. Corrigan, A. Moravcsik, H. Ouali, & K. M. Wheatley (eds.), *Formulaic Language: Vol. 2. Acquisition, Loss, Psychological Reality, and Functional Explanations*, 387–404. Amsterdam: John Benjamins.

Ortega, L. (2003). Syntactic complexity measures and their relationship to L2 proficiency: A research synthesis of college-level L2 writing. *Applied Linguistics* 24(4), 492–518.

(2012). Interlanguage complexity: A construct in search of theoretical renewal. In B. Kortmann & B. Szmrecsanyi (eds.), *Linguistic Complexity: Second Language Acquisition, Indigenization, Contact*, 127–155. Berlin & Boston: Mouton de Gruyter.

Paquot, M. (2014). Cross-linguistic influence and formulaic language: Recurrent word sequences in French learner writing. In L. Roberts, I. Vedder, & J. Hulstijn (eds.), *EuroSLA Yearbook*, 216–237. Amsterdam and Philadelphia, PA: John Benjamins.

(2017). L1 frequency in foreign language acquisition: Recurrent word combinations in French and Spanish EFL learner writing. *Second Language Research* 33(1), 13–32.

(2018). Phraseological competence: A useful toolbox to delimitate CEFR levels in higher education? Insights from a study of EFL learners' use of statistical collocations. *Language Assessment Quarterly* 15(1), 29–43. DOI: https://doi.org/10.1080/15434303.2017.1405421 10.1080/15434303.2017.1405421

(2019). The phraseological dimension in interlanguage complexity research. *Second Language Research* 35(1), 121–145. https://doi.org/10.1177/0267658317694221

Paquot, M., Hasselgård, H., & Oksefjell Ebeling, S. (2013). Writer/reader visibility in learner writing across genres: A comparison of the French and Norwegian components of the ICLE and VESPA learner corpora. In S. Granger, G. Gilquin, & F. Meunier (eds.), *Twenty Years of Learner Corpus Research: Looking Back, Moving Ahead. Corpora and Language in Use – Proceedings 1*, 377–387. Louvain-la-Neuve: Presses universitaires de Louvain.

Paquot, M. & Naets, H. (2015a). Adopting a relational model of co-occurrences to trace phraseological development. Paper presented at the 3rd Learner Corpus Research Conference. Netherlands, September 11–13 2015.

(2015b). Using relational co-occurrences to trace phraseological development in a longitudinal corpus. Paper presented at the 25th EuroSLA conference. Aix-en-Provence, August 27–29, 2015.

(2017). The role of the reference corpus in studies of EFL learners' use of statistical collocations. Paper presented at ICAME38. Prague, May 24–28, 2017.

R Core Team. (2019). *R: A Language and Environment for Statistical Computing*. R Foundation for Statistical Computing, Vienna, retrieved from www.R-project.org (accessed June 13, 2020).

Schäfer, R. (2015). Processing and querying large Web corpora with the COW14 architecture. In P. Bański, H. Biber, E. Breiteneder, M. Kupietz, H. Lüngen, & W. Andreas (eds.), *Proceedings of the 3rd Workshop on Challenges in the Management of Large Corpora (CMLC-3)*, 28–34. Mannheim: Institut für Deutsche Sprache.

Schmid, H. (1994). Probabilistic part-of-speech tagging using decision trees. Paper presented at the International Conference on New Methods in Language Processing. Manchester, UK.

Sinclair, J. M. (1991). *Corpus, Concordance, Collocation*. Oxford: Oxford University Press.

Thewissen, J. (2013). Capturing L2 accuracy developmental patterns: Insights from an error-tagged EFL learner corpus. *The Modern Language Journal*, 97(S1), 77–101.

Thomas, M. (2006). Research synthesis and historiography: The case of assessment of second language proficiency. In J. Norris and L. Ortega (eds.), *Synthesizing Research on Language Learning and Teaching*. Amsterdam: John Benjamins.

Tono, Y. (2003). Learner corpora: Design, development and applications. In P. Rayson, A. Wilson, T. McEnery, A. Hardie, & S. Khoja (eds.), *Proceedings of the Corpus Linguistics 2001 Conference*. UCREL Technical Paper Number 13, 800–809. Lancaster, Lancaster University.

Wisniewski, K. (2017). Empirical learner language and the levels of the Common European Framework of Reference. *Language Learning* 67(S1), 232–253.

Wolfe-Quintero, K., Inagaki, S., & Kim, H.-Y. (1998). *Second Language Development in Writing: Measures of Fluency, Accuracy, and Complexity*. Honolulu, HI: University of Hawaii Press.

Understanding the Long-Term Evolution of L2 Lexical Diversity: The Contribution of a Longitudinal Learner Corpus

Nicole Tracy-Ventura, Amanda Huensch, and Rosamond Mitchell

1 Introduction

1.1 Goals of the Study

The central goal of Second Language Acquisition (SLA) research is understanding the learner's underlying L2 knowledge system, its development, and what impacts upon both. To address these questions, most SLA research adopts cross-sectional designs comparing groups from different proficiency levels, or relatively short-term experimental designs. From a practicality point of view, this is reasonable, but for some questions of central concern for SLA research, taking a longitudinal perspective is necessary.

Compared to SLA, learner corpus research (LCR) has more traditionally involved the collection and analysis of large datasets of second language production. Large amounts of data from numerous participants help to improve generalizability of findings, and computerized tools make analysis of such data more feasible (Granger et al. 2015). Work in LCR is well ahead in this regard, as is work in L1 acquisition, and many sophisticated computerized tools are used in these fields. In the spirit of "open science" (Marsden et al. 2015), electronic learner corpora also ease the process of data sharing. Where learner corpora are publicly available, other researchers can exploit them, thus broadening the impact of the data collected which is particularly important for scarce longitudinal data (MacWhinney 2017; Meunier 2015). As evidenced by this volume, and other recent publications (e.g., Granger 2009; Hasko 2013; Myles 2015), there is now a growing interest in ways that SLA can benefit from the work being done in LCR and vice versa.

In this chapter we describe our work on the long-term evolution of L2 lexical diversity in a group of French and Spanish L2 university learners for whom we have been building a learner corpus since a first wave of data collection in May 2011. Our longitudinal learner corpus includes over 700,000 words (including data from L1 speakers), 88 percent of which is spoken data primarily from an oral interview. Metadata have been collected, the files are formatted using the Codes for the Human Analysis of Transcripts (CHAT: MacWhinney 2000) and have also been morpho-syntactically tagged. All of the files (audio, transcripts, and tagged files) are shared publicly on our website, and available on talkbank.org. Our newest data were collected in June 2016 and are allowing us to investigate the evolution of our participants' L2 skills four years after returning from a year abroad and three years after graduating from university.

Language proficiency is a dynamic phenomenon, subject to attrition as well as development. Understanding how second language proficiency evolves over time, and how both development and attrition relate to phases of increased and decreased input and interaction, should be of central concern to the field of SLA, increasing our understanding of the contribution of L2 use to the creation and stabilization of the underlying L2 knowledge system. However, there are few longitudinal studies which have collected information both on L2 proficiency and L2 use, and which have spanned more than one to two years. Research which has focused on the long-term evolution of bilingual speakers' language skills tends to center on first language attrition (L1: see Schmid 2011). In contrast, foreign language attrition, and variables that influence it, has received very little attention (Bardovi-Harlig & Stringer 2010; Schmid & Mehotcheva 2012; Weltens 1989). Longitudinal methods are needed to address questions of foreign language attrition as well as development and long-term retention.

In this article, we demonstrate how we are using our longitudinal corpus to investigate the possible outcomes of attrition, development, or retention in lexical diversity among advanced instructed FL learners three years after formal instruction has ended. Using data on L2 use collected systematically at the same time as the L2 production data, we explore the relations between evolving patterns of contact with L2 and these different potential proficiency outcomes.

Corpus-based methods are particularly suited for the analysis of L2 lexis. Compared to controlled and psycholinguistic tests of vocabulary knowledge, learner corpora provide more authentic samples of language, demonstrating what learners are capable of producing in real time. In previous research on L1 attrition of lexical diversity, interview data distinguished better between monolingual speakers and bilingual attriters than data elicited from more controlled tasks (Schmid & Jarvis 2014), suggesting that corpus data can contribute helpfully to the study of lexical maintenance and attrition. And of course, corpus-based methods make it possible to conduct lexical analyses of large amounts of data with automatic or semi-automatic tools.

1.2 Long-Term Evolution of Foreign Language Proficiency

As discussed above, there are three potential outcomes in the long-term evolution of foreign language proficiency: attrition, retention, or development. Although much research has focused on instructed language learning, little is known about what happens to language abilities once learners are no longer engaged in formal instruction. Interest in L2 attrition is evident from a number of early SLA studies (e.g., Bahrick 1984a, 1984b; Weltens 1989; Weltens et al. 1989), but this line of research has not yet developed into a serious research agenda. One potential reason for this is the difficulty of establishing the highest proficiency level attained among FL learners (Schmid & Mehotcheva 2012), or what Bardovi-Harlig and Stringer (2010) refer to as 'peak attainment'. In L1 attrition research participants who did not move out of the L1 context until aged 13–15 or over are assumed to have a fully developed L1 (and previous research has shown that under these conditions the L1 largely resists attrition: Schmid 2011). In contrast, no such assumption can be made for instructed FL learners, who are known to vary in the proficiency level attained, even given similar amounts of FL instruction or exposure. Therefore, it is extremely important to empirically establish the actual proficiency level attained, in order to study meaningfully the nature of retention and/or attrition during subsequent changing conditions of L2 use. Clearly, longitudinal research designs are required to address these issues.

Studies of all types of attrition (L1, L2) have also shown considerable individual variation. To explain this individual variation, researchers have appealed to a range of non-linguistic factors, including age at onset of (potential) attrition, level of proficiency, length of exposure, attitudes and motivation, and current contact with the language. The influence of these interacting factors has proved difficult to disentangle however. Thus, research on L1 attrition suggests that (in)frequency of use alone does not explain attrition, but rather it depends on context of use. For example, Schmid and Dusseldorp (2010) found that when an L1 is used for professional purposes, those speakers experience less attrition than those who do not use their L1 in more formal contexts. Research on FL attrition (Murtagh 2003; Weltens 1989; Xu 2010) has provided some indication that exposure post-instruction is not a strong predictor of attrition/retention, and that this is true for both extent of exposure and length of exposure.

Instead, the limited research suggests that proficiency level attained might better predict the amount of attrition/retention (Mehotcheva 2010; Murtagh 2003; Xu 2010). It has also been shown that in FL settings attrition is non-linear; initial attrition can be rapid but subsequently stabilizes (Weltens 1989).

A study of special relevance here is that of Mehotcheva (2010), who researched a population of mixed L2/FL learners similar to that under consideration in this study. She examined the FL Spanish attrition of L1 Dutch and L1 German university students, between 12 and 72 months following a period of study abroad (SA) in Spain. She had two groups of participants, one longitudinal ($n = 5$), where data were collected twice over a one-year period post-SA. The other participants contributed to a cross-sectional study. Here, four different groups were examined, at varying lengths of time post-SA. Data came from a variety of measures, including a sociolinguistic interview (which included questions about linguistic history and use, including during SA), a C-test, and a picture-naming test (designed to investigate lexical access). Analysis of the longitudinal data demonstrated that the participants experienced attrition, particularly reduced access to lexical items. Specifically, they used more foreign words, pseudowords and disfluency markers, and a lexical diversity measure (*D* scores in the interview) declined over the one-year period. Analysis of the cross-sectional data demonstrated that higher initial proficiency (measured via self-assessment) was a significant predictor of language retention. Little influence was found for attitude and motivation, disuse, language contact, or length of exposure during the post-SA and instructional period.

Other longitudinal studies focusing on the benefits of SA have in general found that linguistic gains abroad are retained over the following year, during which participants continued to receive formal instruction (Howard 2009; Huensch & Tracy-Ventura 2017; Llanes 2012; Regan 2005). For example, Llanes (2012) included a measure of lexical complexity, Guiraud's Index of Lexical Richness (number of types divided by the square root of the total number of tokens) and found that her participants retained the gains they made during SA in both oral and written language.

Several studies focusing on L1 attrition (Schmid & Dusseldorp 2010; Schmid & Jarvis 2014; Yilmaz & Schmid 2012) have investigated the difference in lexical diversity between L1 attriters and monolingual controls on tasks such as narrative retells and interviews. Such studies have also examined extralinguistic factors which correlate with levels of lexical diversity in these tasks and other measures as well (e.g., lexical access, disfluency) but with inconsistent results. For example, findings from Schmid and Dusseldorp (2010) suggested a relationship between length of emigration and lower lexical diversity scores. However, Schmid and Jarvis (2014) did not find any significant relationships between the extralinguistic variables they studied and lexical diversity scores. Results of their study did suggest that data elicited in interviews better predicted speakers as controls or attriters than data from more controlled tasks.

Schmid and Mehotcheva (2012) provide a useful overview of theoretical frameworks which have been employed in conceptualizations of FL attrition and are applicable to long-term retention as well. Some psycholinguistic theorists appeal to frequency/recency of exposure and use of FL. Thus for example, the Dynamic Model of Multilingualism proposed by Herdina and Jessner (2002) assumes that language proficiency is always in a state of dynamic change, with positive/negative growth taking place in different parts of the language system, depending on the extent and nature of active language use, and ongoing competition between different linguistic systems. The Neurolinguistic Theory of Bilingualism and associated Activation Threshold Hypothesis (ATH) advanced by Paradis (1993, 2004) argues somewhat similarly, that bilingualism comprises a "system of systems" where active use of part of the system (e.g., a particular language) lowers the neurolinguistic activation threshold for that part and inhibits other competing systems or subsystems. The practical effect is that the most commonly used system(s) are the most accessible, and attrition "is a result of lack of long term stimulation" (Paradis 2007, 125). However Paradis also allows that motivation as well as an advanced level of proficiency may have a protective effect. Given that different parts of the system may attrite at different rates, Paradis (2007) predicts that the lexicon is more susceptible to attrition than grammar, which is more strongly sustained by procedural memory.

To conclude this brief review, it is clear that while different theoretical frameworks have been proposed, there is limited empirical research on long-term FL retention/attrition which might help to choose among these. There is some evidence that lexical attrition occurs, but how it might differ in oral vs. written data from the same learners is not known. There is a suggestion that proficiency is a predictor of language retention, but other non-linguistic factors such as motivation or language contact have perhaps surprisingly not been shown to be predictors. Given the expense and effort of educational investment in FL learning, a fuller understanding of the long-term evolution of FL proficiency and the conditions which will promote retention is needed. This study aims to make a preliminary contribution to addressing these questions, using a longitudinal learner corpus of French and Spanish which is complemented with extensive data on participants' overall proficiency and patterns of FL exposure and use. In our previous research (Huensch et al. 2019) we focused on the attrition/retention/development of oral fluency and proficiency, and found that both language contact/use and peak proficiency attained were important variables in the retention of fluency and proficiency three years after formal instruction ended. The current study expands on this work by utilizing a corpus-based approach to investigate the attrition/retention/development of FL lexis, and its relation with (a) lexical proficiency attained at the end of SA and (b) post-SA FL exposure. The current study investigates the following research questions:

(1) To what extent does lexical diversity, operationalized as *D* (Malvern & Richards 2002) and the Moving Average Type–Token Ratio (MATTR), change four years after residence abroad, in speech and writing?
(2) To what extent can post-SA language exposure and peak lexical diversity attainment explain changes in lexical diversity of learners four years after residence abroad?

2 Methods

2.1 Participants

Participants in the current study are part of the Languages and Social Networks Abroad Project (LANGSNAP: Mitchell et al. 2017), an ongoing longitudinal study that began in 2011. LANGSNAP began as a project examining the social and individual factors that influenced language learning during residence abroad/SA. Over nearly two years, data were collected six times from 56 British university French and Spanish degree students: once at the end of Year 2 of their four-year degree (May 2011), three times during a nine-month stay abroad program during Year 3 (October 2011, February 2012, May 2012), and twice after return to their home university during Year 4 (October 2012, February 2013). In May 2016 a follow-up study was initiated to continue the project and examine the long-term evolution of their FL proficiency and patterns of FL use.

All of the original LANGSNAP participants ($n = 56$) were invited to participate in the current study. Contact was made primarily through a private project Facebook group, and 33 participants contributed once again: 15 Spanish L2 participants and 18 French L2 participants. Table 30 provides background data about the participants included in

Table 30 Age and years studying L2 of the 33 LANGSNAP 3.0 participants

	Spanish L2	French L2
Participants	15 (12 females)	18 (17 females)
Mean age	25.5	24.7
Years studying L2 at pretest	6.1	10.5

the current study. At the time of data collection, 12/15 of the Spanish participants were living in the UK, with the others living in Canada and Spain. Of the French participants, 12/18 were living in the UK, with the others living in Australia, Belgium, Finland, France, and Thailand.

2.2 Procedure

Participants living in the UK in 2016 were met by a member of the research team at a time and location convenient for them. Those living abroad were visited when feasible ($n = 3$) and if not, all tasks were completed online, including the oral tasks via Skype. Each data collection session lasted approximately 1.5 hours, and task sequencing was randomized.

2.3 Learner Corpus

Three communicative tasks produced the learner corpus analyzed in this study. For continuity, we selected from among the tasks that were used in the original LANGSNAP study (see Table 31), and administered an oral interview, an oral picture-based narrative, and a written argumentative essay (for more details see Tracy-Ventura et al. 2016). For both the oral picture-based narrative and the written argumentative essay, we used prompts which the participants had last completed four years earlier: the Cat Story (oral narrative) and a prompt on 'Gay marriage and adoption' (argumentative essay). Where tasks are used repeatedly, there could conceivably be some risk of priming (e.g., later performances might be more fluent than earlier ones), or a ceiling effect. However, we believed that the long gaps between task administrations reduced the priming risk. For the investigation of lexical development more particularly, it is known that the specific task prompt can influence measures of lexical diversity (see Tracy-Ventura et al. 2016; Kyle in press). In designing this

Table 31 Project timeline

Data collection wave	Location	Oral tasks	Written task (argumentative essay)
Pre-sojourn: May 2011	Home university	Oral interview Cat Story	Gay Marriage & Adoption
In-sojourn 1: Oct 2011	Abroad	Oral interview Sisters Story	Legalization of Marijuana
In-sojourn 2: Feb 2012	Abroad	Oral interview Brothers Story	Taxes on Junk Food
In-sojourn 3: May 2012	Abroad	Oral interview Cat Story	Gay Marriage & Adoption
Post-sojourn 1: Oct 2012	Home university	Oral interview Sisters Story	Legalization of Marijuana
Post-sojourn 2: Feb 2013	Home university	Oral interview Brothers Story	Taxes on Junk Food
Post-sojourn 3: June 2016	Varied	Oral interview Cat Story	Gay Marriage & Adoption

study, this was seen as a positive reason to compare data from collection waves which used the same prompts. In the current study, those waves are pre-sojourn, in-sojourn 3, and post-sojourn 3 (see Table 31).[1]

The semi-structured oral interview was administered by a member of the research team; the pre-established questions were designed to elicit information about participants' experiences since their last interview in February 2013. In particular, they were asked about what they had been doing since graduation (e.g., jobs, traveling), their current leisure activities, who they currently live with and spend time with, any plans for the future, and if they could do their degree over again, whether they would study languages.

The Cat Story was a picture-based story retell task, borrowed from Domínguez et al. (2013). The story depicts the experiences of a little

[1] A reviewer pointed out that it is important to demonstrate that any changes between in-sojourn 3 and post-sojourn 3 were not the result of gains made during the final year of instruction. A comparison of *D* scores between in-sojourn 3 and post-sojourns 1 and 2 indicated that in-sojourn 3 was the peak score for the interview and writing tasks. Post-sojourn 1 scores were higher than in-sojourn 3 scores for the narrative task, but that was likely due to task effects (see Tracy-Ventura et al. 2016). The same pattern of results was true for MATTR. In-sojourn 3 is the most appropriate choice of data collection wave for the current study because it represents the peak *D* and MATTR scores for the interview and because it used the same narrative task as post-sojourn 3 (Cat Story).

Table 32 LANGSNAP corpus word counts by task

	Oral narrative	Oral interview	Argumentative essay	Total
French				
L2 Learners 2011–2013 (*n* = 29)	65,905	222,014	36,339	324,258
L2 Learners in 2016 (*n* = 18)	6,365	16,957	3,094	26, 416
Spanish				
L2 Learners 2011–2013 (*n* = 27)	53,497	214,364	36,059	303,920
L2 Learners in 2016 (*n* = 15)	4,480	15,994	3,140	23,614
Total	130,247	469,329	78,632	678, 208

girl and her cat one day when the cat got lost. Participants were given a few minutes to look over the pictures and ask the researchers any questions they had about the story before beginning their retell, with support from the pictures. For those completing the task online, the pictures were made available via a link; all interviews and story retells were audio-recorded, via Skype where necessary.

The written argumentative essay was based on the prompt 'Do you believe that gay people have the right to get married and have children?' This prompt was borrowed from Lozano and Mendikoetxea (2013) and administered through a specially written computer program. Having seen the prompt, participants had three minutes of planning time and 15 minutes of writing time, with a target of 200 words. While writing, they could still see the prompt and a word counter. Buttons allowed for easy insertion of accented letters. If they finished early, they could click on a submit button. After 15 minutes, the program automatically closed and they were not allowed to write any more.

The total word counts for the LANGSNAP corpus are provided in Table 32 and are separated by task. These counts include the data from the original project which ran from 2011 to 2013, plus the new data (LANGSNAP 3.0).[2] As shown in this table, most data is oral, with the oral narrative and the oral interview together comprising 88 percent of the corpus.

[2] Data were also collected from L1-speaking controls. Those word counts are not included here. The L1 data are also freely available.

2.4 Other Materials

Participants also filled out a background questionnaire modeled after Mehotcheva (2010: see https://languageattrition.org/). This questionnaire collected information about language use and activities (e.g., work, travel, lifestyle) since participants' graduation. For example, participants answered questions related to L2 use at work, or partners with whom they spoke their L2. Questions also focused on whether they had pursued further L2 instruction, how confident they were speaking the L2, whether they planned to live abroad again, etc. In addition, they completed a reflective interview in English (see the Appendix) which asked questions about their perceived L2 abilities, their current professional/academic activities, the languages used in their current social networks, etc. Finally, participants completed the Language Engagement Questionnaire (LEQ, available on IRIS, see McManus et al. 2014) first designed for in-sojourn data collection waves in LANGSNAP, which asked them to first select any languages they used on a regular basis and then indicate how frequently they used each language for a variety of activities (e.g., watch movies, write emails, engage in small talk).

2.5 Analysis

The oral and written data were transcribed following CHAT conventions for use with CLAN (MacWhinney 2000). All transcripts were checked at least three times for accuracy by different members of the research team. Two CLAN commands provided the measures of lexical diversity used in the current study: VOCD and MATTR. VOCD is the command that generates a *D* score, a measure that has been used in previous research on L1 (e.g., Schmid & Jarvis 2014) and FL attrition (e.g., Mehotcheva 2010). We also chose to run our analyses using MATTR, which has been found to be less sensitive to text length (Fergadiotis et al. 2015) and is therefore a potentially more valid measure of lexical diversity.

To run VOCD, a minimum of 50 tokens is needed. The way that *D* is calculated is through a procedure that

> takes the average TTR from 100 random samples of 35 words drawn from a text, then 100 random samples of 36 words, then 37 words, all the way to 50 words. It plots the average TTR values for each sample size on a curve, and then uses a formula with a single parameter to find the best fit between the formula-generated curve and the observed TTR curve.
>
> (Castañeda-Jiménez & Jarvis 2014, 504)

MATTR (Covington & McFall 2010) on the other hand,

> calculates the lexical diversity of a sample using the Moving Average Type–Token Ratio (MATTR). This index is based on a moving window that computes TTRs for each successive window of fixed length (N). Initially, a window length is selected (e.g., 10 words) and the TTR for words 1–10 is estimated. Then, the TTR is estimated for words 2–11, then 3–12, and so on to the end of the text. For the final score, the estimated TTRs are averaged.
> (MacWhinney 2000, 95)

For this study we used a window length of 75 words, the shortest text length (Covington 2007).

Language exposure was analyzed based on participants' responses on the background questionnaire, the LEQ, and what they reported in their English and L2 interviews. Based on data from these four sources, each participant was coded as either having 'intense' or 'limited' exposure depending on the consistency and intensity of the L2 contact since graduation. Initial coding was based on five categories in which intensity and frequency were coded separately (e.g., neither intense/consistent; intense & sporadic; intense & consistent; limited & sporadic; limited & consistent). However, this coding proved complex because of participants' diverging experiences. Thus, a decision was made to limit the coding to either intense or limited. For example, participants in the limited category ($n = 20$) were living in their home countries and on the LEQ either reported practically no engagement with the L2 or, in seven cases, did not even list the L2 as a language used. On the other hand, nine participants had lived abroad again in a French- or Spanish-speaking country for an extended period of time (i.e., 9–12 months), or were still living abroad, and were coded as intense. Other participants coded as intense ($n = 4$) used their L2 with significant others or extensively at work. It should be noted, however, that even participants coded as intense made little use of L2 in writing.

To investigate research question (1), two separate three-way mixed repeated measures ANOVAs were conducted to understand the effects of language, time, and task on lexical diversity. For both tests, language (French, Spanish) was the between-subjects variable, and time (pre-sojourn, in-sojourn 3, post-sojourn 3) and task (interview, narrative, writing) were the within-subjects variables. Language was included as a variable because the data come from a smaller number of participants ($n = 33$) compared to the original project ($n = 56$). Analysis of the 2011–2013 data suggested that the two groups were similar (e.g., evidence of development while abroad and potential attrition after return home – see Mitchell et al. 2017). We felt it was important to replicate the analysis with this 2016 subset to examine whether the results would mirror those of the earlier data. For one test *D* was the dependent variable and for the other MATTR was the dependent variable. The data were within acceptable ranges concerning the assumptions of ANOVA tests (e.g., normally distributed, lacking extreme values) except that the assumption of sphericity was violated; thus, a Greenhouse–Geisser correction was applied. Alpha was set at 0.05. For posthoc comparisons, effect sizes are reported using *d* and interpreted using Plonsky and Oswald (2014)'s field-specific recommendations for within-groups: small effect (d = 0.60), medium effect (d = 1.00), and large effect (d = 1.40), and between-groups: small effect (d = 0.40), medium effect (d = 0.70), and large effect (d = 1.00).

3 Results

Research question (1) investigated to what extent lexical diversity, operationalized as *D* and MATTR, changed in speech and writing four years after residence abroad. First, descriptive statistics with the mean and standard deviations for tokens and types are provided in Table 33 for each task, data collection wave, and L2 group. As shown, the interview had the highest average number of words, while the written argumentative essay had the lowest average number of words.

Table 34 provides the means and standard deviations for all *D* scores separated by language group for each task and each time point. Results of the three-way mixed ANOVA with *D* scores demonstrated that there was no three-way interaction between language, time, and task, $F(2.94, 79.38) = 1.08$, $p = 0.361$, partial $\eta^2 = 0.04$. There was, however, a two-way interaction between time and task, $F(2.94, 79.38) = 7.40$, $p < 0.001$, partial $\eta^2 = 0.22$, but no two-way interaction between time and language, $F(1.89, 51.05) = 2.03$, $p = 0.144$, partial $\eta^2 = 0.07$, or task and language, $F(1.39, 37.43) = 0.65$, $p = 0.475$, partial $\eta^2 = 0.02$. A main effect of time, $F(1.89, 51.05) = 19.08$, $p < 0.001$, partial $\eta^2 = 0.41$, and a main effect of task, $F(1.39, 37.43) = 74.58$, $p < 0.001$, partial $\eta^2 = 0.73$, were also found.

Given the significant interaction between time and task, a one-way repeated measures ANOVA with time as the within-subjects variable was conducted for each task (with the language groups combined). Results for the interview task indicated a significant effect of time, $F(1.85, 55.44) = 42.56$, $p < 0.001$, partial $\eta^2 = 0.59$. Posthoc analyses demonstrated significant differences between all three time points: pre-sojourn–in-sojourn 3 ($p < 0.001$, $d = 1.12$),

Table 33 Descriptive statistics of types and tokens over time

	French			Spanish		
	Pre-sojourn	In-sojourn 3	Post-sojourn 3	Pre-sojourn	In-sojourn 3	Post-sojourn 3
Interview						
Tokens	1,353.82 (412.73)	1,277.06 (454.59)	942.06 (221.56)	1,104.47 (248.86)	1,653.20 (548.73)	1,066.27 (355.02)
Types	311.78 (75.30)	323.82 (79.28)	301.72 (49.72)	285.53 (53.78)	413.73 (98.53)	332.07 (81.19)
Narrative						
Tokens	438.33 (134.42)	393.59 (162.70)	374.41 (124.91)	292.27 (70.79)	302.36 (99.89)	320.00 (114.43)
Types	140.39 (32.13)	140.53 (38.97)	148.06 (37.74)	108.67 (17.50)	127.29 (28.47)	133.86 (38.98)
Writing						
Tokens	218.22 (27.24)	224.53 (30.59)	174.94 (43.04)	191.00 (28.76)	226.93 (30.80)	209.33 (39.88)
Types	110.89 (14.61)	117.59 (15.13)	102.50 (23.33)	105.47 (13.66)	124.00 (13.67)	116.73 (21.84)

Table 34 Descriptive statistics for D *scores over time*

	French			Spanish		
	Pre-sojourn	In-sojourn 3	Post-sojourn 3	Pre-sojourn	In-sojourn 3	Post-sojourn 3
Interview	60.16 (18.26)	77.46 (12.43)	88.70 (11.13)	67.84 (8.03)	79.64 (10.51)	84.59 (7.78)
Narrative	46.38 (8.97)	46.63 (11.18)	58.00 (9.04)	45.73 (7.24)	54.92 (8.75)	55.76 (9.23)
Writing	78.89 (20.34)	84.39 (17.00)	85.87 (25.10)	77.55 (18.11)	83.13 (15.94)	78.40 (14.81)

pre-sojourn–post-sojourn 3 ($p < 0.001$, $d = 1.92$), and in-sojourn 3–post-sojourn 3 ($p = 0.001$, $d = 0.86$).

Effect sizes of a small and medium effect between in-sojourn 3–post-sojourn 3 and pre-sojourn–in-sojourn 3, respectively, suggest that *D* scores increased throughout the testing period, with the largest effect occurring across the entire testing period between pre-sojourn and post-sojourn 3.

Similarly, results for the narrative task indicated a significant effect of time, $F(1.90, 53.08) = 18.51$, $p < 0.001$, partial $\eta^2 = 0.40$. Posthoc analyses demonstrated significant differences between pre-sojourn–post-sojourn 3 ($p = 0.001$, $d = 1.27$) and in-sojourn 3–post-sojourn 3 ($p = 0.008$, $d = 0.67$), but not pre-sojourn–in-sojourn 3 ($p = 0.060$, $d = 0.45$). These results suggest that when the scores of both groups are analyzed together, increases in *D* scores during SA were minimal (marginal significance and negligible effect), but that they improved between returning home from SA and three years after graduation (small effect) and throughout the testing period (medium effect). Unlike results from the oral tasks, results for the writing task did not indicate a significant effect of time, $F(1.87, 56.03) = 1.37$, $p = 0.263$, partial $\eta^2 = 0.04$.

Table 35 provides the means and standard deviations of the MATTR scores separated by language group for each task and each time point. Results of the three-way mixed ANOVA with MATTR scores demonstrated similar results. There was no statistically significant three-way interaction between language, time, and task, $F(3.48, 93.89) = 2.04$, $p = 0.104$, partial $\eta^2 = 0.07$. There were significant two-way interactions: one between time and task, $F(3.48, 93.89) = 6.97$, $p < 0.001$, partial $\eta^2 = 0.21$; and one between time and language, $F(1.90, 51.26) = 6.51$, $p = 0.003$, partial $\eta^2 = 0.19$. Thus, one-way repeated measures ANOVAs with time as the within-subjects variable were conducted for each task (with the language groups combined). Results for the interview task indicated a significant effect of time, $F(1.91, 57.40) = 44.79$, $p < 0.001$, partial $\eta^2 = 0.60$. Posthoc analyses demonstrated significant differences between all three time points: pre-sojourn–in-sojourn 3 ($p < 0.001$, $d = 1.15$), pre-sojourn–post-sojourn 3 ($p < 0.001$, $d = 1.94$), and in-sojourn 3–post-sojourn 3 ($p = 0.001$, $d = 0.99$). These results suggest that similar to the results for *D*, MATTR scores increased between each of the testing periods on the interview task, with the largest effect occurring across the entire testing period. Similarly, results for the narrative task indicated a significant effect of time, $F(1.63, 45.68) = 17.63$, $p < 0.001$, partial $\eta^2 = 0.39$. Posthoc analyses again demonstrated significant differences between all three time points: pre-sojourn–in-sojourn 3 ($p = 0.048$, $d = 0.58$), pre-sojourn–post-sojourn 3 ($p < 0.000$, $d = 1.23$), and in-sojourn 3–post-sojourn 3 ($p = 0.016$, $d = 0.62$). Like the narrative results for *D*, increases in MATTR scores were minimal during SA (marginal significance and negligible effect) but improved throughout the testing period (medium effect). These results suggest that when both language groups are analyzed together, the group means continue to improve at post-sojourn 3 in both oral tasks. Similar to the results for *D*, results for the writing task did not indicate a significant effect of time, $F(1.97, 59.15) = 1.60$, $p = 0.212$, partial $\eta^2 = 0.05$. In sum, these results suggest that there are no major differences between language groups, but rather the main difference appears to be between the oral and written tasks. Therefore, other variables likely explain the continued improvement of the group as a whole at post-sojourn 3, and two variables in particular are examined in research question (2).

Research question (2) investigates to what extent variables such as language exposure (since the last data collection wave in February 2013) and lexical diversity attained at the end of SA could predict changes in lexical diversity from in-sojourn 3 to post-sojourn 3. This analysis is restricted to the tasks that show significant changes over time (narrative and interview), and only results from the MATTR score regression analyses are reported.[3] Therefore, a standard multiple regression was conducted with the dependent variable of change in MATTR between in-sojourn 3 and post-sojourn 3. The two independent variables were peak attainment at the end of residence abroad (MATTR value at in-sojourn 3) and 'language exposure' (a nominal, dichotomous variable coded as 0 = 'limited' and 1 = 'intense'). Due to the small sample size, only two independent or explanatory variables could be included. The data were within acceptable ranges concerning the assumptions of a regression test.

Results of the multiple regression are displayed in Table 36. For the MATTR scores on the narrative, results indicated a statistically significant model, with an R^2 value of 0.58. Both language exposure ($p = 0.008$) and the MATTR score at in-sojourn 3 ($p < 0.001$) contributed significantly to the model. These results suggest that the two explanatory variables predict 58 percent of the variance in the change scores, with the MATTR score at in-sojourn 3 explaining the most variance (it has the higher score in the β column and a lower p value).

[3] Results from the regression analyses conducted with *D* scores patterned the same as those for MATTR scores. We chose to only report MATTR score results in this chapter both for space considerations and because of the finding that MATTR is less sensitive to text length (Fergadiotis et al. 2015) and thus a potentially more reliable measure of lexical diversity than *D*.

Table 35 Descriptive statistics for MATTR scores over time

	French			Spanish		
	Pre-sojourn	In-sojourn 3	Post-sojourn 3	Pre-sojourn	In-sojourn 3	Post-sojourn 3
Interview	0.65 (0.04)	0.68 (0.02)	0.71 (0.02)	0.64 (0.03)	0.69 (0.03)	0.70 (0.02)
Narrative	0.62 (0.03)	0.61 (0.04)	0.66 (0.03)	0.59 (0.05)	0.64 (0.03)	0.64 (0.03)
Writing	0.72 (0.04)	0.73 (0.04)	0.74 (0.05)	0.72 (0.04)	0.74 (0.04)	0.73 (0.03)

Table 36 Regression results

		B	SE_b	β	F	p	R^2
Narrative change	Intercept	0.472	0.078		$F(2,28) = 19.96$	0.000	0.58
	Exposure	0.027	0.009	0.355		0.008	
	MATTR S3⁺	–0.732	0.123	–0.736		0.000	
Interview change	Intercept	0.776	0.106		$F(2,30) = 25.28$	0.000	0.62
	Exposure	0.021	0.008	0.342		0.009	
	MATTR S3⁺	–1.116	0.157	–0.870		0.000	

Note. The degrees of freedom change between the two tasks because we have missing data points in the narratives. +S3 = in-sojourn 3

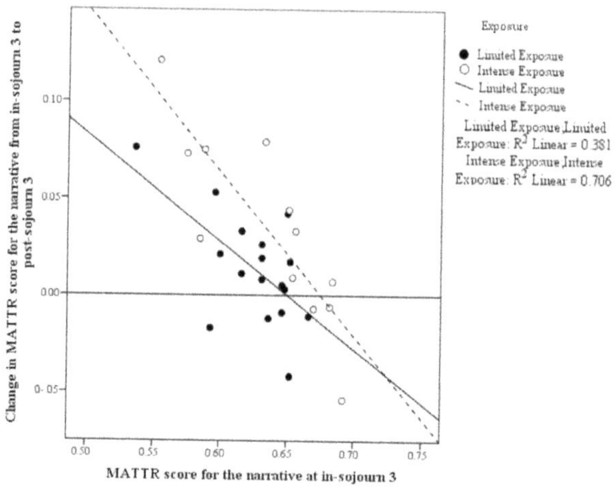

Figure 7 Scatterplot of Narrative regression results

According to Plonsky and Ghanbar (2018), this is considered a large effect. Figure 7 is a scatterplot which displays the results for each participant. Those participants who were categorized as limited exposure are represented by the black dots and those categorized as intense exposure are represented by the white dots. As shown in Figure 7, those participants who had lower MATTR scores at in-sojourn 3, tended to make the most gains.

Results of the regression testing MATTR scores on the interview also indicated a statistically significant model with an R^2 value of 0.62. Again, both variables contributed significantly to the model: language exposure ($p = 0.009$) and MATTR score at in-sojourn 3 ($p < 0.001$), with MATTR scores at in-sojourn 3 explaining the most variance. The scatterplot displaying these results is shown in Figure 8. There was less variation in MATTR scores at in-sojourn 3 in the interview than the narrative; however, the overall results are the same and suggest that changes in MATTR scores at post-sojourn 3 can be predicted by both MATTR scores at in-sojourn 3 and exposure post-instruction.

4 Discussion

The purpose of this study was to investigate the long-term evolution of lexical diversity post-SA and post-formal language instruction in two groups of participants, one L2 French and one L2 Spanish. Since graduating with their BA in French and Spanish, a majority of the participants were working in the UK in jobs that required little to no

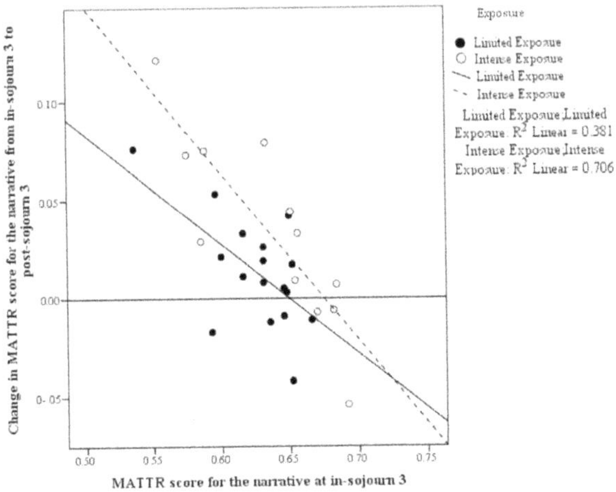

Figure 8 Scatterplot of Interview regression results

use of their L2s, and also reported limited use of the L2 in informal social settings. Another group was living abroad again and/or was maintaining social relations with one or more speakers of their L2, and used that language often in their everyday lives. These differences in L2 use allowed us to investigate the claims of previous researchers, regarding the relationship between L2 use and L2 vocabulary retention/development/attrition, for example the claim of Paradis (2007) that lexical knowledge is the most sensitive to attrition compared to grammar or phonetics, and that frequency of use is linearly related. Using a longitudinal learner corpus that was carefully designed to include oral and written data from the same participants, collected multiple times from 2011 to 2016, and formatted and annotated for semi-automatic analysis, we were able to compare participants' vocabulary use over several years and examine how factors such as ongoing language exposure/use and lexical diversity scores at the end of a year abroad predict retention four years later.

Research question one examined to what extent lexical diversity, operationalized as *D* and MATTR, changed four years after residence abroad. Two-way interactions between time and task were found for both the *D* and MATTR scores, and posthoc tests revealed that there were differences over time in the oral tasks but not the written tasks. In particular, the participants showed linear progress over time that continued at post-sojourn 3 during the 2016 data collection wave in both the oral narrative and interview tasks. The fact that lexical diversity did not change significantly over time in writing but did in speaking could be due to higher pretest scores in the writing task compared to the oral tasks, i.e., the existence of a ceiling effect for that particular task. However, participants also did not report much formal L2 writing from 2013 to 2016 (e.g., only three participants reported writing emails several times a week or more in the L2). Increases in oral lexical diversity over time could be explained by increased automaticity in lexical access that is improved in online speech production with continued practice/use.

The result that the group as a whole showed continued improvement at post-sojourn 3 (three years after formal instruction had ended) in the oral tasks was surprising and helped to motivate exploration of extralinguistic factors that could help explain this development. This was the focus of research question (2), which we investigated using a multiple regression. Due to the low number of participants ($n = 33$), it was only possible to include two predictor variables in the multiple regression: post-SA language exposure/use and peak lexical diversity attainment, variables that have been the focus of previous research on FL attrition (Bardovi-Harlig & Stringer 2010; Schmid & Mehotcheva 2012). Recall that research on L1 attrition has not found L1 use to be a significant predictor, except when it is used for professional purposes (Schmid & Dusseldorp 2010). That is, those people who use it for professional purposes have less L1 attrition than those who do not. In the current study we ran two multiple regressions, one using the MATTR scores in the narrative and another with the scores in the interview. In contrast to the L1 attrition research and the limited research on FL attrition (Mehotcheva 2010), in the current study language exposure/use was a significant predictor of change over time, as were MATTR scores at in-sojourn 3. The latter explained more of the variance, which suggests that higher MATTR scores at the end of their year abroad may initially help protect participants from attrition even with limited exposure after formal instruction. Neisser (1984) claimed that there may be a general critical threshold at which, once learners reach that level, their linguistic knowledge becomes permanent and immune to decay. As we continue this project into the future, we will be able to further test this claim.

The fact that L2 exposure/use post-instruction emerged as a significant predictor in the regression provides support for Paradis' (2004) Activation Threshold Hypothesis. Previous research on FL attrition has not found exposure to be a significant predictor. However, several methodological issues could help explain conflicting results. For example, Mehotcheva (2010) had only five participants in her longitudinal group, and in her cross-sectional data proficiency was assessed based on self-report. Additional longitudinal research is needed to corroborate these findings. Our research investigating oral fluency with these same participants (Huensch et al. 2019) also found exposure/use and peak attainment to be significant predictors of change three years after formal instruction.

We have only just begun to explore the variables that predict attrition/maintenance/development of the LANGSNAP participants' L2 French and Spanish abilities. Much future work remains. In particular, we plan to examine individual participants in more depth, providing case studies of those participants who demonstrated evidence of the most extreme development and attrition. Additionally, we plan to extend our analysis to include other aspects of lexical complexity, such as lexical sophistication, as well as accuracy and syntactic complexity. Lastly, in the future we will examine the role that individual differences, such as motivation and attitudes, play in FL retention and attrition.

Several limitations of the current study should be acknowledged. One issue is task familiarity. This was the third time that these participants orally retold the Cat Story and wrote an argumentative essay in response to the prompt about gay marriage and adoption. However, four years had passed since the last time they completed these tasks, which likely helped to address this concern. Additionally, performance on the writing task may have been limited by a ceiling effect; the more open-ended oral tasks were not affected in this way, however. Another potential limitation is the dichotomous operationalization of language exposure that was used. It is possible that if we were able to further differentiate the participants, then the results for language exposure/use may explain more of the variance in change scores.

These limitations notwithstanding, the current study takes us one small step closer to understanding variables that influence the long-term evolution of FL proficiency. By building a longitudinal learner corpus that includes the collection of metadata, is formatted using agreed-upon conventions, and is shared publicly, we aim to provide a resource that will support further investigations drawing on SLA theory, and encourage other researchers to conduct additional studies using these data.

Acknowledgments

LANGSNAP was funded by the ESRC (award number RES-062-23-2996). LANGSNAP 3.0 was funded by a *Language Learning* Small Research Grant, USF World Faculty Mobility Grant, and a USF New Researcher Grant. We are grateful to our LANGSNAP colleagues, the participants, and various research assistants for their contribution to this study.

References

Bahrick, H. (1984a). Fifty years of second language attrition: Implications for programmatic research. *The Modern Language Journal* 68(2), 105–118.

(1984b). Semantic memory content in permastore: Fifty years of memory for Spanish learned in school. *Journal of Experimental Psychology: General* 113(3), 1–29.

Bardovi-Harlig, K. & Stringer, D. (2010). Variables in second language attrition: Advancing the state of the art. *Studies in Second Language Acquisition* 32 (1), 1–45.

Castañeda-Jiménez, G. & Jarvis, S. (2014). Exploring lexical diversity in second language Spanish. In K. L. Geeslin (ed.), *The Handbook of Spanish Second Language Acquisition*, 498–513. Oxford: Wiley-Blackwell.

Covington, M. (2007). MATTR User Manual, retrieved from https://athenaeum.libs.uga.edu/handle/10724/19840 (accessed June 13, 2020).

Covington, M. & McFall, J. (2010). Cutting the Gordian knot: The moving-average type–token ratio (MATTR). *Journal of Quantitative Linguistics* 17(2), 94–100.

Domínguez, L., Tracy-Ventura, N., Arche, M., Mitchell, R., & Myles, F. (2013). The role of dynamic contrasts in the L2 acquisition of Spanish past tense morphology. *Bilingualism: Language and Cognition* 16(3), 558–577.

Fergadiotis, G., Wright, H., & Green, S. (2015). Psychometric evaluation of lexical diversity indices: Assessing length effects. *Journal of Speech, Language, and Hearing Research* 58(3), 840–852.

Granger, S. (2009). The contribution of learner corpora to second language acquisition and foreign language teaching: A critical evaluation. In K. Aijmer (ed.), *Corpora and Language Teaching*, 13–32. Amsterdam: John Benjamins.

Granger, S., Gilquin, G., & Meunier, F. (2015). Introduction: Learner corpus research – past, present, and future. In S. Granger, G. Gilquin, & F. Meunier (eds.), *The Cambridge Handbook of Learner Corpus Research*, 1–5. Cambridge: Cambridge University Press.

Hasko, V. (2013). Capturing the dynamics of second language development via learner corpus research: A very long engagement. *The Modern Language Journal* 97(S1), 1–10.

Herdina, P. & Jessner, U. (2002). *A Dynamic Model of Multilingualism: Changing the Psycholinguistic Perspective.* Clevedon: Multilingual Matters.

Howard, M. (2009). Short- versus long-term effects of naturalistic exposure on the advanced learner's L2 development: A case-study. In E. Labeau & F. Myles (eds.), *The Advanced Learner Variety: The Case of French*, 93–123. Oxford: Peter Lang.

Huensch, A. & Tracy-Ventura, N. (2017). L2 utterance fluency development before, during, and after residence abroad: A multidimensional investigation. *The Modern Language Journal* 101(2), 275–293.

Huensch, A., Tracy-Ventura, N., Bridges, J., & Cuesta-Medina, J. (2019). Variables affecting the maintenance of L2 fluency post-study abroad in the short and long term. *Study Abroad Research in Second Language Acquisition and International Education* 4(1), 96–125.

Kyle, K. (in press). Lexis. In N. Tracy-Ventura & M. Paquot (eds.), *Handbook of Second Language Acquisition and Corpora*. New York, NY: Routledge.

Llanes, À. (2012). The short- and long-term effects of a short study abroad experience: The case of children. *System* 40(2), 179–190.

Lozano, C. & Mendikoetxea, A. (2013). Learner corpora and second language acquisition: The design and collection of CEDEL2. In A. Díaz-Negrillo, N. Ballier, & P. Thompson (eds.), *Automatic Treatment and Analysis of Learner Corpus Data*, 65–100. Amsterdam: John Benjamins.

MacWhinney, B. (2000). *The CHILDES Project: Tools for Analyzing Talk*. (3rd edn.) Mahwah, NJ: Lawrence Erlbaum.

(2017). A shared platform for studying second language acquisition. *Language Learning* 67(S1), 254–275.

Malvern, D. & Richards, B. (2002). Investigation accommodation in language proficiency interviews using a new measure of lexical diversity. *Language Testing* 19(1), 85–104.

Marsden, E., Mackey, A., & Plonsky, L. (2015). The IRIS repository: Advancing research practice and methodology. In A. Mackey & E. Marsden (eds.), *Advancing Methodology and Practice: The IRIS Repository of Instruments for Research into Second Languages*, 1–21. New York, NY: Routledge.

McManus, K., Mitchell, R., & Tracy-Ventura, N. (2014). Understanding insertion and integration in a study abroad context: The case of English-speaking sojourners in France. *Revue Française de Linguistique Appliquée* 19(2), 97–116.

Mehotcheva, T. (2010). After the Fiesta Is Over: Foreign Language Attrition of Spanish in Dutch and German Erasmus Students. Unpublished Ph.D. dissertation, University of Groningen.

Meunier, F. (2015). Developmental patterns in learner corpora. In S. Granger, G. Gilquin, & F, Meunier (eds.), *The Cambridge Handbook of Learner Corpus Research*, 379–400. Cambridge: Cambridge University Press.

Mitchell, R., Tracy-Ventura, N., & McManus, K. (2017). *Anglophone Students Abroad: Identity, Social Relationships, and Language Learning*. New York, NY: Routledge.

Murtagh, L. (2003). Retention and Attrition of Irish as a Second Language. A Longitudinal Study of General and Communicative Proficiency in Irish among Second Level School Leavers and the Influence of Instructional Background, Language Use and Attitude/Motivation Variables. Unpublished Ph.D. dissertation, Rijksuniversiteit Groningen.

Myles, F. (2015). Second language acquisition theory and learner corpus research. In S. Granger, G. Gilquin, & F. Meunier (eds.), *The Cambridge Handbook of Learner Corpus Research*, 309–332. Cambridge: Cambridge University Press.

Neisser, U. (1984). Interpreting Harry Bahrick's discovery: What confers immunity against forgetting? *Journal of Experimental Psychology: General* 113(1), 32–35.

Paradis, M. (1993). Linguistic, psycholinguistic, and neurolinguistic aspects of 'interference' in bilingual speakers: The activation threshold hypothesis. *International Journal of Psycholinguistics* 9(2), 133–145.

(2004). *A Neurolinguistic Theory of Bilingualism.* Amsterdam: John Benjamins.

(2007). L1 attrition features predicted by a neurolinguistic theory of bilingualism. In B. Köpke, M. S. Schmid, M. Keijzer, & S. Dostert (eds.), *Language Attrition: Theoretical Perspectives*, 121–133. Amsterdam: John Benjamins.

Plonsky, L. & Ghanbar, H. (2018). Multiple regression in L2 research: A methodological synthesis and guide to interpreting R^2 values. *The Modern Language Journal* 102(4), 713–731.

Plonsky, L. & Oswald, F. (2014). How big is "big"? Interpreting effect sizes in L2 research. *Language Learning* 64(4), 878–912.

Regan, V. (2005). From community back to classroom: What variation analysis can tell us about context of acquisition. In J.-M. Dewaele, (ed.), *Focus on French as a Foreign Language: Multidisciplinary Approaches*, 191–209. Clevedon: Multilingual Matters.

Schmid, M. (2011). *Language Attrition.* Cambridge: Cambridge University Press.

Schmid, M. & Dusseldorp, E. (2010). Quantitative analyses in a multivariate study of language attrition: The impact of extralinguistic factors. *Second Language Research* 26(1), 125–160.

Schmid, M. & Jarvis, S. (2014). Lexical access and lexical diversity in first language attrition. *Bilingualism: Language and Cognition* 17(4), 729–748.

Schmid, M. & Mehotcheva, T. (2012). Foreign language attrition. *Dutch Journal of Applied Linguistics* 1(1), 102–124.

Tracy-Ventura, N., Mitchell, R., & McManus, K. (2016). The LANGSNAP longitudinal learner corpus: Design and use. In M. A. Ramos (ed.), *Spanish Learner Corpus Research: State of the Art*, 117–142. Amsterdam: John Benjamins.

Weltens, B. (1989). *The Attrition of French as a Foreign Language.* Dordrecht/Providence: Foris Publications.

Weltens, B., Van Els, T., & Schils, E. (1989). The long-term retention of French by Dutch students. *Studies in Second Language Acquisition* 11(2), 205–216.

Xu, X. (2010). English Language Attrition and Retention in Chinese and Dutch University Students. Unpublished Ph.D. dissertation, University of Groningen.

Yilmaz, G. & Schmid, M. (2012). L1 accessibility among Turkish-Dutch bilinguals. *The Mental Lexicon* 7(3), 249–274.

Appendix

Reflective Interview Questions

(1) After graduating from X University, have you had any significant travel experiences abroad, i.e., lived in a country other than the UK for more than a month? Have you returned to the place where you did your year abroad? Have you spent time in other countries where you used your foreign language(s)?
(2) How do you think your language abilities in French/Spanish compare now to when you returned from your year abroad and when you finished university? Better, worse, the same? Any other languages to compare?
(3) In what ways do you use your various languages now? Tell me about your YA language (French/ Spanish) first. Are there any other languages that you use regularly? What motivates you to continue to use that/these language(s)?
(4) Have you kept in touch with any people you met abroad? Who? (Other Erasmus or locals) How have you done so? What language (s) do you use with each other?
(5) Are there important people in your life with whom you use French/Spanish? Remember when you were abroad we asked about your top 5? Are there any people in your current top 5 who are French/Spanish users?
(6) Do you think your study abroad experience has benefitted you professionally? What about socially? Personally? Culturally? If so, how? If not, why not?

L2 Developmental Measures from a Dynamic Perspective

Marjolijn Verspoor, Wander Lowie, and Martijn Wieling

1 Introduction

One of the challenges for research into Second Language Acquisition (SLA) is to measure language proficiency in an objective, consistent, and reliable way. Traditionally, the focus of the measurements has been on the accuracy of use in different language domains, and proficiency has been determined by the number of errors in receptive language tests (reading and listening), errors in language production (writing and speaking), and vocabulary knowledge and use. Although this is still common practice in language testing, researchers since the 1970s have emphasized that accuracy is only half the story and that evaluation of the quality of second language (L2) use is at least equally important. Since the 1970s, there has been a quest to find the best "yardstick" (Larsen-Freeman 1978) to measure the quality of L2 use objectively. Since observations of language use are crucial in finding this ideal yardstick, SLA research has benefited considerably from corpus-based research in trying to establish measures that can help trace L2 development and help determine objective proficiency measures. For instance, many examples are available of studies that used techniques to measure syntactic complexity in second language writing automatically from learner corpora (Lu 2010; Vyatkina 2012).

Recently, studies from a complex dynamic systems theory (CDST) perspective – which starts from the assumption that development is nonlinear – have questioned whether a stable "yardstick" is what we should be after. A CDST perspective to second language development (De Bot et al. 2007; Larsen-Freeman & Cameron 2008) holds that different components or *subsystems* of language may need to develop before others, and various subsystems may interact differently with each other over time. In other words, it may be possible that L2 beginners will improve on the lexicon first, then sentence constructions, and then perhaps the lexicon again.

From a CDST perspective, the only way to see such dynamic development is to conduct longitudinal, individual case studies with enough data points in which various subsystems of the linguistic system are plotted and traced. The most important reason for the necessity of longitudinal studies is that the results from group studies cannot be individualized to the personal development of the members of that group. Although generalizations from group studies are valid for measurements at one moment in time, this type of generalization is problematic for measurements over time, as the dynamic change of variables cannot be assumed to be identical for different individuals. This has been referred to as the "ergodicity problem" (see Lowie & Verspoor 2019). Consequently, if we are interested in the process of development, we will have to make use of individual case studies. And although a wide variety of (relatively small) learner corpora is available and most of these include longitudinal data of second language use (see, for instance, the LONGDALE Corpus as introduced in Meunier 2016), these corpora do not include dense data of individual language use over time as required by CDST analyses. The exploration of the process of second language development is therefore based on a limited number of studies using small learner corpora.

So far, studies tracing individuals based on small and specific data sets reveal that learners show variability (intra-individual changes over time) in each of the subsystems studied and also show numerous interactions over time between different subsystems (cf. Verspoor et al. 2008). In a few small group studies, some general trends concerning the interaction between lexical and syntactic variables have been established through computer simulation (cf. Lowie et al. 2011). In an attempt to explore such developmental patterns in a cross-sectional study, Verspoor et al. (2012) worked with holistically scored texts (ranging from 1 to 5) to represent phases in the developmental process from absolute beginner to intermediate. Each text was coded for a great number of variables (or yardsticks) representing subsystems of the language, and indeed it was found that in different phases the subsystems developed differently, suggesting that development is non-linear and difficult to predict. To confirm the findings from the cross-sectional study of Verspoor et al. (2012), the current paper will use a longitudinal corpus with dense measurements to trace the development of 22 similar learners in a similar high school context over one academic year with up to 23 data points per learner. The current study indeed confirms that there is nonlinear growth in all variables, as each learner shows a great amount of intra-learner variability, and that there is an abundant amount of inter-learner variation, as no individual learner develops in exactly the same manner. However, using a generalized additive model (GAM) – an approach that is ideal for analyzing nonlinear change over time in iterated learning experiments – we can detect a general trend that shows clear nonlinear patterns for lexical and syntactic measures, suggesting that the fixed yardstick metaphor may be best replaced with one of "a bundle of twigs."

2 Finding an Index of Development

The field of applied linguistics – especially the field of second or foreign language development – has long benefited from corpus research in a quest to find the best predictors of language development. As early as the 1970s, both Hakuta (1976) and Larsen-Freeman (1978) called for a suitable SLA Index of Development. Based on predictors in L1 writing development, Hunt (1970) suggested the use of the T-unit. In subsequent studies such as Larsen-Freeman and Strom (1977) and Larsen-Freeman (1978), it was indeed found that in English as an L2, the average length of error-free T-units differs among developmental levels at the group level. In a comprehensive study 15 years later, Wolfe-Quintero et al. (1998) also found the best fluency measures to be T-unit length, error-free T-unit length, and clause length. However, these measures only represent a grand sweep of development at the group level, which is not necessarily the same for all the individuals in the group, as many factors may differentially affect the characteristics of writing products of L2 learners. For example, Wolfe-Quintero et al. (1998) and Ortega (2003) pointed out that variation in writing products across learners may occur when writers are compared across different tasks, in addition to the fact that learners from different first languages may have different problems with the L2. Moreover, individual differences, especially language aptitude, are known to have a strong effect on L2 development (Sparks et al. 2008). Recently, a large number of L2 developmental studies have also been discussed in terms of the dimensions of complexity, accuracy, and fluency (CAF), each of which can be operationalized with a variety of measures. In spite of the appealing subdivision in dimensions of language proficiency, Norris and Ortega warned against a universal CAF yardstick, because "it is illusory to think that what we are measuring in CAF is some kind of universal construct that can be applied across all possible learners and contexts" (2009, 575). In line with a CDST perspective, they claimed that especially complexification is variable and that such variability represents a fruitful side of development.

One of the main tenets of a CDST perspective is that variability (intra-individual change over time) is functional and inherent in the developmental process. The learner needs to select the best option from the many different forms he or she is trying out, so at certain times in the developmental process, more variability means more learning (Verspoor & Van Dijk 2012). Basically, to develop in language and learn something new, learners will have to try out different forms to begin with and only after sufficient iteration will they eventually settle for one form or the other. However, because of a lack of attentional resources, a form that may seemingly have been settled may become unstable again when the learning starts to concentrate on another new type of form. This process leads to variability and sometimes developmental peaks in many different subsystems of language. As development is an individually owned process and no individual develops in exactly the same manner (cf. Chan et al. 2015), variation (inter-individual differences at one point of time) is to be expected.

One excellent example of this variable, wave-like process with developmental peaks is the development of negative constructions in a 13-year-old Spanish learner of L2 English, originally reported on by Cancino et al. (1978) and later analyzed from a CDST perspective by Verspoor et al. (2008). This learner had been in the US for less than three months when his language development was traced for 10 months using data from elicitation interviews and free response data. As replicated in Figure 9 below, Cancino et al. (1978) plotted all verb phrases containing a negative construction to see if the L2 learner showed patterns from four developmental phases similar to L1 learners of English, starting with phase one with *No-V* constructions (*No singing song*), to the second phase with *Don't V* constructions (*I don't hear; He don't swim*), to the third phase with *Aux-negative* constructions (*You can't tell her*), and finally ending with adult-like forms in phase four with *Analyzed do* constructions (*One night I didn't even have the light*).

There are several nonlinear patterns noticeable in Jorge's development of these constructions. First of all, even at the very beginning he uses all four constructions, but not many of the two advanced phases. He uses the *No* and *Don't* constructions equally at first, but then there is a peak of *No* constructions at data point 3, which disappear quickly around data point 7, but remain at a very low level until data point 12. The *Don't* constructions are partially target forms that are overgeneralized here and show a developmental peak at data point 7. To evaluate the significance of this peak, we ran a Monte Carlo analysis, which calculates the chance of finding an instance in time (like a peak) by comparing the actual data to 5,000 permutations of randomized

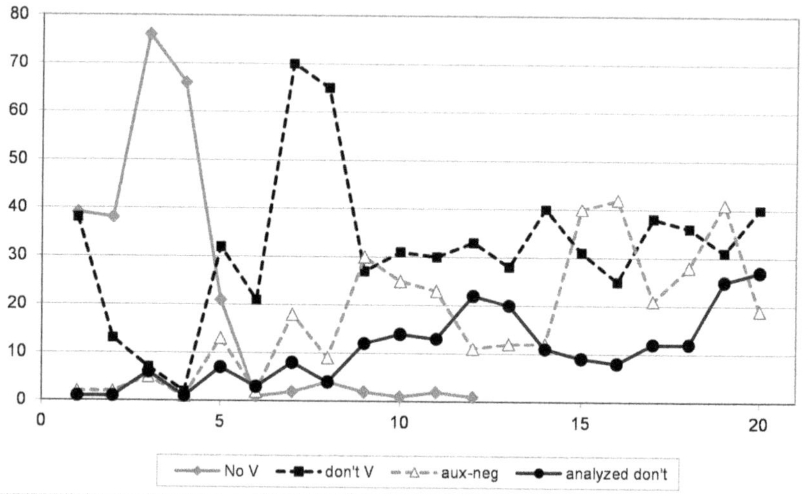

Figure 9 Jorge's (13-year-old Spanish learner of L2 English) development of negative constructions (with permission, Verspoor et al., 2011)
Note. The graph shows the percentage of correct use (y-*axis) over time in biweekly recordings* (x-*axis).*

sequences of the measurements observed. In these data, the chance of finding this peak in a random order turned out to be less than 5 percent. The *Aux-negative* constructions begin to develop more around data point 9 and by the end of the chart, there is a good mix of constructions that seem to be used in a target-like manner: the *No* constructions and the relative overuse of *Don't* constructions have disappeared from his repertoire. This example shows that this L2 learner had a developmental pattern very similar to L1 learners of English, but more importantly it demonstrates that such a longitudinal analysis also shows how intricate, variable, and jumpy the actual process is, with overlapping phases. This type of analysis can only be done on individuals, as group trajectories would average out all the peaks and dips (which learners have at different times). This also shows the relevance of multiple dense measurements in learner corpora.

Over the past 10 years there have been various longitudinal studies in the same vein, examining the writing development of one to 10 participants over the course of 10 months–13 years, and from absolute beginners to advanced learners. The findings can be summarized as follows: every study so far has shown variability in almost every variable traced, and especially beginners, like Jorge in the example given, seem to show peaks of overuse in various target or non-target-like constructions (Spoelman & Verspoor 2010; Verspoor et al. 2008). The studies have shown that there is a great degree of variability in each learner in almost every measure from broad to specific (Verspoor et al. 2017). We can also see that lexicon and syntax may compete even at advanced stages (Caspi & Lowie 2013; Penris & Verspoor 2017), and that similar learners, even identical twins in a similar context, will take different developmental paths (Chan et al. 2015; Tilma 2014; Vyatkina 2012). The strong point of these longitudinal studies is that they show in detail how each individual develops over time and how variables interact over time within the same individual. However, they do not lend themselves to generalizations about general trends at the group level.

While developmental findings of individual cases cannot be generalized to groups of learners, the results from group studies cannot be individualized, as they cannot reveal the nonlinear and variable paths that individual learners tend to follow. For example, as Verspoor et al. (2011) and Larsen-Freeman (2006) found, when the trajectories of learners are averaged out, the resulting line does not look like any one individual learner, as the insightful peaks and dips are smoothed away and even the direction of development may vary within the group. Verspoor et al. (2012) wanted to explore whether such variability and nonlinear behavior could also be detected in a cross-sectional study in which they controlled for inter-learner variation caused by known predictors, such as L1, age, aptitude, and task. Their corpus consisted of 437 writing samples from a homogeneous group: Dutch learners of English as a foreign language between the ages of 11 and 14 with similar scholastic aptitude scores. Each text received a holistic rating for the quality of their writing, resulting in groups of texts at five levels from beginner to intermediate. Each of these texts was coded for 64 CAF measures. The authors found several good predictors to discriminate consistently between proficiency levels, most of which had already been recognized in the literature. Noticeable about these measures was that they were all rather "broad" in that they averaged over a large number of instances (Guiraud index), they were clustered (all dependent clauses combined, all chunks combined,[1] all errors combined), or they were very frequently occurring constructions in the language (simple present versus other tenses). In other words, these measures were likely to show significant differences between all levels –

[1] "Chunks" are also commonly referred to as "formulaic sequences" or Conventional Ways of Saying Things (CWOSTs). Here we mean any type of fixed word combinations.

and therefore suggest linear growth – because they involved frequently occurring phenomena.

The data confirmed the working hypothesis that groups of learners move from the simplest and most frequent constructions to more complex and less frequent ones. For example, beginners, who rely on their L1 to a great extent, used mostly simple sentences in mainly the simple present tense. As the proficiency level increased, the language became somewhat more complex with an increase in all complexity, lexical, and accuracy variables. At the higher proficiency levels, all measures had improved with more complex and more accurate constructions at all levels. The total number of dependent clauses, total number of chunks, number of present or past finite tenses, and the type–token ratio of words occurring in the text were the strongest discriminators.

In addition to these rather linear trends in broad measures, there was also clear nonlinear development from one level to the next. At different proficiency levels, there were signs of overuse of different forms. At the lowest level, all simple constructions were overused, but at the third level, the present perfect and progressive showed a significant rise in the chart, accompanied by a peak in verb use errors. In addition, some (groups of) variables showed a significant difference between two consecutive levels once only, suggesting that particular aspects of the language were focused on at particular proficiency levels. Between levels 1 and 2, there was a significant difference in six variables (schematic chunks, fixed chunks, particles, most frequent words, lexical errors, and mechanical errors), which were mainly lexical in nature. Between levels 2 and 3, there was a change in seven variables (decrease in simple sentences and increase in complex sentences, adverbial clauses, non-finite clauses, partially schematic chunks, particular complement constructions, and spelling), which were mainly syntactic in character. Between levels 3 and 4, there was a mixture of changes: some syntactic measures (finite relative clauses), some lexical measures (fixed phrases), and some accuracy measures (verb use errors). Between levels 4 and 5, mainly lexical changes took place (particles, compounds, and fixed phrases) and very few syntactic changes were found.

To summarize, the cross-sectional data suggested that absolute beginners (between levels 1 and 2) are especially engaged in learning words. Then the learners seem to focus more on syntactic complexity (between levels 2 and 3), which continues between levels 3 and 4, but is then mixed with lexical measures. After changes in syntactic constructions, there is a focus again on lexical matters (between levels 4 and 5). Assuming that L2 learners go through these levels consecutively, albeit with some variability, Verspoor et al. (2012) suggested that it would be very useful to follow similar learners over time to check whether these patterns indeed occur longitudinally as suggested by this cross-sectional study.

The aim of the current paper is therefore to examine whether findings in L2 development based on this cross-sectional study can hold for individual learners over time. In other words, can findings from the group be generalized to the individual and vice versa? From a CDST perspective, we expect intra-learner variability and inter-learner variation, as each learner will follow his own developmental path, so the findings of one learner cannot be generalized to the group, nor can the findings of the group be generalized to the individual. However, as Molenaar and Campbell (2009) have pointed out, generalization to the wider population is possible if we find similar developmental paths in highly similar individuals. In line with these observations, we would expect to find some of the hypothesized general developmental findings from the cross-sectional study to apply to most of the individual learners in the current study.

To do so, learners similar to those in Verspoor et al.'s (2012) cross-sectional study are traced over the course of one academic year to see if their general proficiency develops from lower to higher levels, if learners show similar patterns of development in that they show variability in all measures and show developmental jumps in some (even if these jumps will occur at different points in time for different learners), and whether the group as a whole shows nonlinear patterns in lexical and syntactic development in the sense that one may develop before the other.

3 A Longitudinal Case Study

In this longitudinal multiple case study, we traced the development in L2 writing of 22 Dutch learners of English over 23 weeks. These learners were similar to those in the cross-sectional (CS) study by Verspoor et al. (2012) (from now on referred to as the CS study). They were 12 to 13 years old, they had similar levels of scholastic aptitude as measured by scores on a standardized scholastic aptitude test (CITO scores), and they were in a similar school setting (bilingual education). The one difference between the current longitudinal and the CS study is that in the current study, the writing tasks covered different topics, since it would be impossible to ask these young learners to write about the same topic every week as can be done in a CS study. As in the CS study, all learner data were first anonymized and then rated by a team of trained judges on proficiency levels from

1 to 5. Then each sample was analyzed on a number of syntactic and lexical variables.

For both the CS study and this longitudinal study, independent scoring sessions took place. With a team of eight experts the weakest and strongest writings were determined in the particular data set and given scores from 1 to 5. The cross-sectional data set contained texts by absolute beginners, who had not had any exposure to English before starting high school, and students at the beginning of the third year, who had had bilingual education for two years. The scores given in both the CS set and the current study ranged from 0 to 5. The least proficient (some English) received a 1 and the most proficient a 5. As these two data sets were rated independently from each other, the scores may be in a similar range but are not the same in an absolute sense.

3.1 Participants

The participants in our study were 22 Dutch learners of English who started secondary school shortly before the onset of data collection. These learners attended the same school in a small town in the north of the Netherlands and were of approximately the same age (12 or 13). The learners had enrolled in an English–Dutch bilingual stream, in which at least 50 percent of all classes (from History to Mathematics) were taught through English in a Content Language Integrated Learning (CLIL) setting. To be allowed into the bilingual stream, students were interviewed and selected on motivation and scholastic aptitude. This school setting and the pervasiveness of English in the Dutch environment affords rather massive exposure to English during the period of observation. The learners varied somewhat in the number of English classes they had had prior to starting high school. Lowie and Verspoor (2019) show in a regression analysis that in this homogeneous group neither motivation nor aptitude were predictors in proficiency gains.

3.2 Materials, Procedure, and Analyses

For the purpose of our study, students were asked to produce a short piece of writing on a topic decided on by the teacher every week, which yielded 23 longitudinal samples for each individual. Writing was done digitally on a school computer. The topics related to their experiences at school and in daily life, from “My first month at school” to “Christmas carols” and “The May break.” The data collection for this project still continues, but the data reported here were gathered between November 2015 and May 2016. Due to incidental absences, most learners had missed two or three writing sessions, leading to a total of 388 writing samples.

The following texts are examples written by Student 22 at the beginning and end of the data collection session.

Student 22, week 3: I like the first week at school the most, because I like playing games and we playing games in the building. First we doing team sports in the Gym building. I like the American Football the most. . . .

Student 22, week 22: Vlieland is a wonderful island with friendly inhabitants. Our hotel was at the coast and we came from the harbour to the hotel by a TukTuk (A kind of car). The hotel was nice and there were seagulls everywhere. When we came back to the mainland, I almost fell of the boat (Oops . . .). This was at the end of the holiday.

The holistic grading procedure of these writing samples was the same as in the CS study. First the students' writing samples were anonymized and fully randomized for student and sequence of writing. Ten experienced raters were trained until agreement was reached on the holistic scoring of a subset of samples from the data on a five-point scale, with 1 representing the weakest and 5 the strongest piece of writing in terms of overall proficiency (Note, however, that these ratings are based on the relative weak and strong samples within the corpus, so the current numbers 1–5 do not exactly match those in the CS). The focus was on the complexity and the fluency of the writing samples. After the training session, in which the team of raters created their own benchmarks, the remainder of the 388 samples was rated by three raters independently. All samples with more than one point difference among the raters were reassessed by two other raters. After this procedure the rater reliability was assessed by calculating an Intraclass Correlation Coefficient (ICC) on absolute agreement (two-way mixed model). The resulting ICC was 0.78, which indicates a good reliability. Then the holistic score for each text was calculated as the average of three ratings. Lowie and Verspoor (2018) checked for a possible effect of topic on the writing quality of the same data set by calculating average ratings for all topics. This evaluation showed a gradual increase of the scores on the topics over time (ranging from an average rating of around 2.1 for the early writings to 2.9 for the later writings). After correcting for the increasing trend, none of the scores for the topics seemed to deviate from the expected score and there was no reason to delete any of the topics from the data set. Average text length for the topics was 95 words and varied between 82 and 125 average words per text, with a gradual increase toward the later samples. In addition to the global ratings, the writing samples were analyzed on a number of syntactic and lexical complexity measures using TAASSC (Tool for the Automatic Analysis of Syntactic Sophistication and Complexity) (Kyle 2016; Lu 2010).

To allow for a comparison to the CS study, syntactic development in this study was operationalized as the mean length of T-unit (MLTU) and lexical development as Guiraud. These measures have shown to be robust developmental measures in both cross-sectional studies and longitudinal studies (cf. Bulté 2013). MLTU is a global measurement of syntactic complexity, and Guiraud is a measure of lexical richness corrected for text length that is a reliable measurement of the learner's productive lexicon (van Hout & Vermeer 2007).

3.3 Analyses

Regression analyses were run to test whether students had improved significantly in writing proficiency over time and which analytical measures correlated significantly with gains in proficiency.

To test for developmental peaks, each measure for each learner was tested using the model described by Verspoor et al. (2011) but using an R-script calculating permutations. Basically, the model uses 5,000 randomized iterations to test whether the maximal distance between the lowest and the highest score is random or not. If the chance of finding the same distance is less than 5 percent, the peak is considered significant, meaning it is not a random effect and therefore suggests a developmental peak.

To see if general patterns existed among the 22 learners, we used GAM (Wood 2006, 2017) as our analysis method. This approach is an application of linear mixed effects regression but allows for the analysis of potentially nonlinear patterns over time. The GAM analysis is very suitable to analyze individual (nonlinear) patterns of iterative development in time series, as each next step in development is predicted on the basis of the previous step, and no linear development is assumed (Winter & Wieling 2016). Since the models created with GAM analyses do not include easily interpretable coefficients, the best way to interpret the model fit is through visualization.

4 Results

4.1 Proficiency Gains

Lowie and Verspoor (2019) carried out a group analysis of the mean rating of the first two samples and the last two samples in the writing

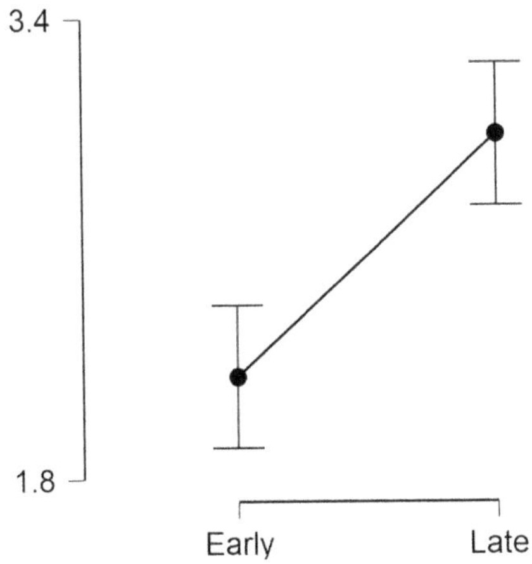

Figure 10 Average holistic rating (five-point scale) of first two (Early) and last two (Late) measurements of the writing samples of the 22 learners
(With permission, Lowie & Verspoor 2018)

corpus (Figure 10). This analysis showed that the group of learners had significantly higher average holistic scores at the end (Wilcoxon signed rank = 20.50; $p < 0.01$; Effect size (matched rank biserial correlation): $r = 0.84$). In other words, the group significantly improved in writing ability. As far as the complexity measures are concerned, a regression analysis indicated that only two lexical measures, *mean length of words* and *Guiraud* were significant predictors for the overall ratings.

4.2 MLTU

Figure 11 shows the individual patterns of the 22 learners' MLTU per text over time. The final graph shows the general trend by means of a GAM. Visual inspection reveals that no learner shows identical development; some learners show peaks early on (Learner 4), some in the middle (Learner 8), some toward the end (Learner 21), and some show no real single peaks at all (Learner 13). For each learner, all peaks were tested for significance over time using Monte Carlo simulations with 5,000 iterations. The analyses showed that for MLTU the peak showed a significant trend for Learner 12 (Mean = 7.7; Variance = 7.1. 342 out of 5,000 iterations yielded values equal to or larger than the critical value 11.45417; $p = 0.07$) and for Learner 17 (Mean = 6.2; Variance = 2.1. 258 iterations $\geq$ 8.6875: 258; $p = 0.05$). The individual plots have been scaled per individual by applying a

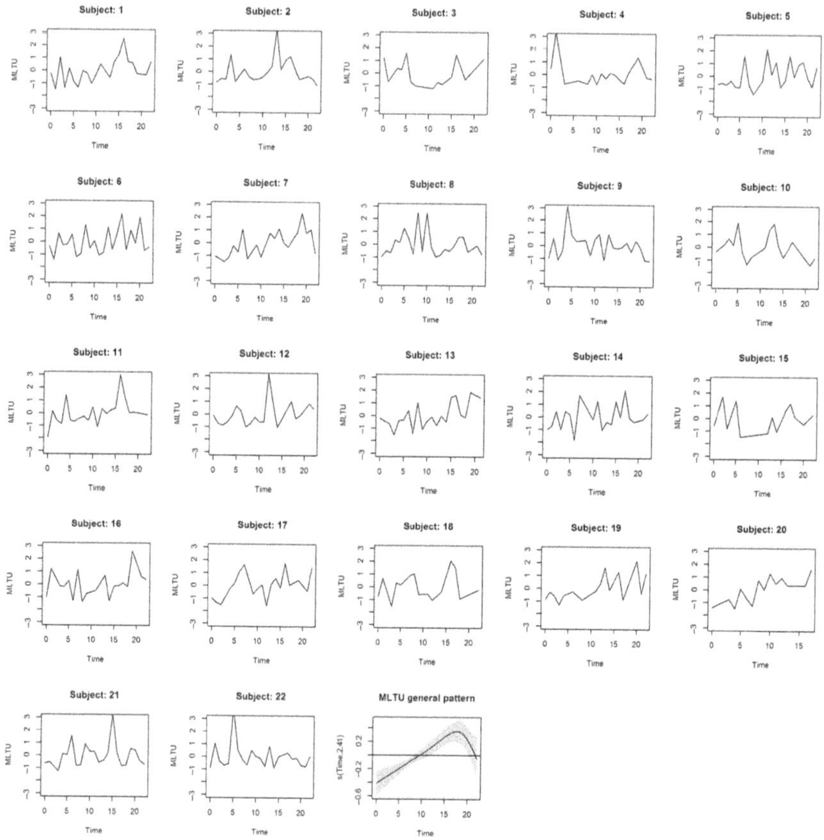

Figure 11 MLTU for individual learners over time in weeks (x-axis), scaled per individual by z-transformation
Note. The final graph shows a general MLTU pattern (GAM) for the group trend.

z-transformation. The GAM plot (last picture) shows a general trend for the group, taking individual variation into account by including individual scores as a random factor. These data show an upward trend, with a sharp decrease at the very end. The GAM analysis shows that the MLTU pattern deviates significantly from 0 ($p < 0.001$).

4.3 *Guiraud*

Figure 12 shows the individual patterns of the 22 learners' Guiraud per text over time, scaled per individual by using z-transformations. The final graph shows the general trend as the outcome of the GAM

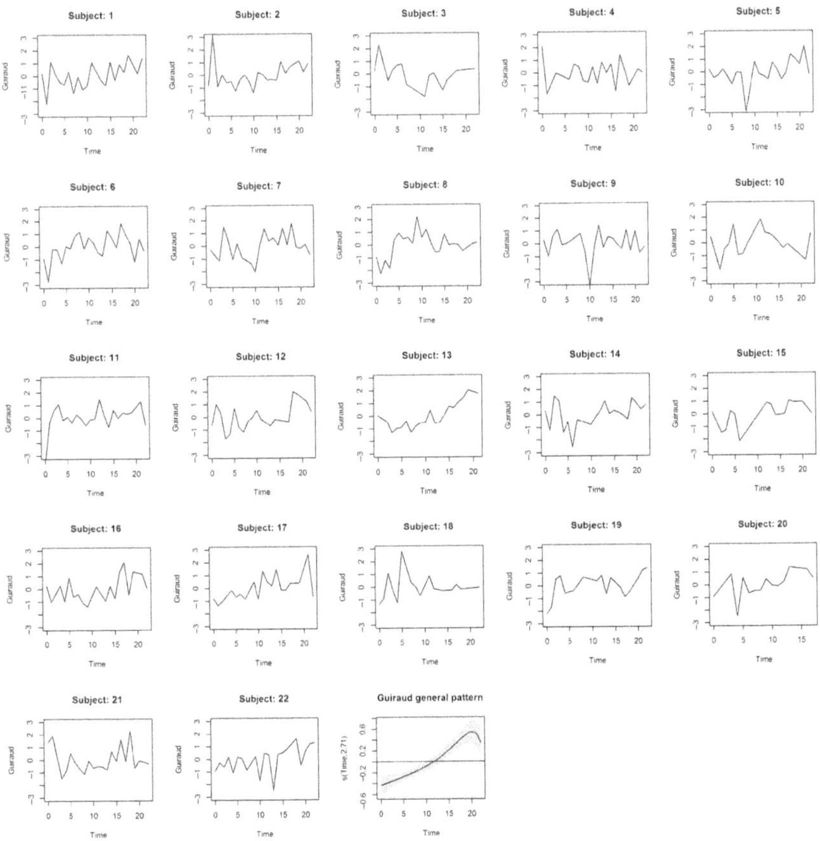

Figure 12 Development of Guiraud for individual learners over time in weeks (x-axis), scaled per individual with z-transformations (y-axis)
Note. The final graph shows the overall development for Guiraud resulting from a GAM analysis.

analysis. Much like the MLTU graphs, visual inspection of the Guiraud patterns seems to indicate that no learner develops in the same way. However, Monte Carlo analyses (simulations with 5,000 iterations) showed that none of the peaks reached significance. The GAM plot shows a general upward trend for the group, with a decrease at the very end.

4.4 MLTU versus Guiraud

Figure 13 compares the overall development of MLTU (on the left) and the Guiraud (in the middle) based on GAMs, as already shown in

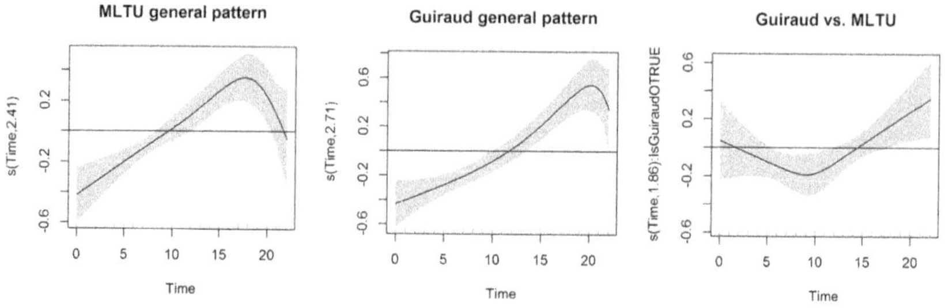

Figure 13 General effects over time in weeks for the MLTU measure (left; p < 0.001), the Guiraud measure (middle; p < 0.001), and their difference (right; p = 0.02)
Note. The measures were standardized for each subject using z-transformations for comparability of variables (y-axis).

Figures 11 and 12. Both analyses show a comparable pattern with an increase at first, which reduces at the end. The comparison between the MLTU and Guiraud (on the right) shows that especially between week 5 and week 15 the Guiraud scores are lower than those for MLTU, while toward the end Guiraud is higher than MLTU. This difference turned out to be significant ($p = 0.02$).

5 Discussion

In our continuing quest to find a common yardstick in L2 developmental studies that can make use of objective corpus research tools, freely available as in Kyle (2016) and Lu (2010), we compared the findings of a cross-sectional study (Verspoor et al. 2012) with those in a longitudinal multiple case study to explore whether group trends can be found in all the data with extensive variation among learners. The learners in the CS study and the current multiple case longitudinal study were very similar in L1, age, aptitude, and learning context. The topics of the writing tasks differed in the longitudinal study, and there is no doubt that the topics affected the individual learners differentially over time, but analyses showed that the average holistic ratings, once the incline over time had been corrected for, were rather similar. Inferential statistics showed that the learners progressed significantly over time, not only as assessed by holistic scores, but also in terms of syntactic complexity (MLTU) and lexical richness (Guiraud). Therefore, the first research question, i.e. whether the learners' general proficiency level would increase, can be answered positively: the group's writing samples were of a significantly higher level at the end. The observation that the quality of writing increased for all learners in this context is not surprising with this selective group of learners who had at least 15 hours of English exposure at school per week.

The second question about variability can also be answered somewhat positively. Like the learners in all studies from a CDST perspective, the learners in this study all showed variability in all measures (holistic, MLTU, and Guiraud), but only three (near) significant developmental peaks were found, all for the MLTU and none for the Guiraud. Visual inspection of the individual graphs did not show any obvious patterns that the learners in this study had in common.

However, in the current study, we also wanted to see if we could detect common nonlinear patterns for the measures in the group. The question was whether the lexicon and syntax develop synchronously or whether one develops before the other, as shown by Caspi (2010) and suggested by Verspoor et al. (2012). Using GAM analyses – which include iterative learning and variability in its algorithms – we were indeed able to detect nonlinear patterns in syntactic development (MLTU) and lexical development (Guiraud). For our purposes, the significantly different developmental patterns for syntax and lexicon are especially important. Figure 13, in which the values were transformed into z-scores per individual, suggests that the MLTU has higher values before Guiraud does. This finding does seem to confirm the findings in the CS study in that between levels 2 and 4 (approximately the comparable levels between the two datasets), there was a change in mainly syntactic variables after which lexical changes would take place, pointing to different growth patterns for different components or subsystems in the language. The regression analysis also showed that measures at the lexical level (Guiraud and mean length of word) were the only predictors for proficiency gains expressed in holistic scores. This suggests that at different phases in language development the subsystems may show different developmental patterns. These patterns vary among individuals, which is shown by the dispersion displayed by the bandwidth in Figure 13. The bandwidth is rather large at the initial stages, then tends to reduce over time, but dramatically increases toward the end of the data collection. The learners' development first converges, but then diverges again. This means that our metaphor for an index of development may indeed need to change from the static yardstick to the dynamic idea of a bundle of interacting twigs.

The current study also shows that as useful as cross-sectional studies can be to find general patterns in development, it is not until we look at individuals over time that we can see the real intricacies of the actual process, and that it may be less predictable and more chaotic than we might have been able to imagine.

An important implication of this finding is that we need more studies that allow us to track the process of development, i.e. longitudinal case studies with dense measurements over a long period of time. Both the density of the measurements and the duration of the period of observation depend on the expected amount of change, which may occur at different time scales for different learners and for different variables. This means that for some variables (or aspects of language development) we may have to measure over the period of a lifespan while for others we may have to focus on milliseconds (Plat et al. 2018). To quantify development, we should no longer aim to use one optimal yardstick for all learners and all timescales, but rather use a bundle of twigs. The corpus tools for efficient longitudinal analyses of learner language are available for the written modality (Kyle 2016). However, process-based research into second language development is dependent on learner corpora that consist of longitudinal data of individual learners and that are measured with the density and the duration that is relevant for the focus of the study. Currently, hardly any corpora exist that would allow for CDST analyses. The study of the process of second language development would therefore strongly benefit from the availability of additional corpora, starting from collections of written data that can be extended to corpora of spoken language.

References

Bulté, B. (2013). The Development of Complexity in Second Language Acquisition: A Dynamic Systems Approach. Unpublished Ph.D. Dissertation, University of Brussels.

Cancino, H., Rosansky, E., & Schumann, J. (1978). The acquisition of English negatives and interrogatives by native Spanish speakers. In E. M. Hatch (ed.), *Second Language Acquisition: A Book of Readings*, 207–230. Rowley, MA: Newbury House.

Caspi, T. (2010). *A Dynamic Perspective on Second Language Development*. Groningen: University of Groningen.

Caspi, T. & Lowie, W. M. (2013). The dynamics of L2 vocabulary development: A case study of receptive and productive knowledge. *Revista Brasiliera de Linguistica* 13(2), 437–462.

Chan, H., Verspoor, M., & Vahtrick, L. (2015). Dynamic development in speaking versus writing in identical twins. *Language Learning* 65(2), 298–325.

De Bot, K., Lowie, W. M., & Verspoor, M. H. (2007). A dynamic systems theory approach to second language acquisition. *Bilingualism: Language and Cognition* 10(1), 7–21. https://doi.org/10.1017/S1366728906002732

Hakuta, K. (1976). A case study of a Japanese child learning English as a second language. *Language Learning* 26(2), 321–351.

Hunt, K. W. (1970). Do sentences in the second language grow like those in the first? *TESOL Quarterly* 4(3), 195–202.

Kyle, K. (2016). Measuring Syntactic Development in L2 Writing: Fine Grained Indices of Syntactic Complexity and Usage-Based Indices of Syntactic Sophistication. Unpublished Ph.D. dissertation, Georgia State University.

Larsen-Freeman, D. (1978). An ESL index of development. *TESOL Quarterly* 12 (4), 439–448.

(2006). The emergence of complexity, fluency, and accuracy in the oral and written production of five Chinese learners of English. *Applied Linguistics* 27(4), 590–619.

Larsen-Freeman, D. & Cameron, L. (2008). *Complex Systems and Applied Linguistics*. Oxford: Oxford University Press.

Larsen-Freeman, D. & Strom, V. (1977). The construction of a second language acquisition index of development. *Language Learning* 27(1), 123–134.

Lowie, W. M. & Verspoor, M. H. (2019). Individual differences and the ergodicity problem. *Language Learning* 69(S1), 184–206.

Lowie, W. M., Caspi, T., Van Geert, P., & Steenbeek, H. (2011). Modeling development and change. In M. H. Verspoor, K. De Bot, & W. Lowie (eds.), *A Dynamic Approach to Second Language Development: Methods and Techniques*, 22–122. Amsterdam & Philadelphia: Benjamins.

Lu, X. (2010). Automatic analysis of syntactic complexity in second language writing. *International Journal of Corpus Linguistics* 15(4), 474–496. https://doi.org/10.1075/ijcl.15.4.02lu

Meunier, F. (2016). Introduction to the LONGDALE Project. In E. Castello, K. Ackerley, & F. Coccetta (eds.), *Studies in Learner Corpus Linguistics. Research and Applications for Foreign Language Teaching and Assessment*, 123–126. Berlin: Peter Lang.

Molenaar, P. C. M. & Campbell, C. G. (2009). The new person-specific paradigm in psychology. *Current Directions in Psychological Science* 18(2), 112–117.

Norris, J. M. & Ortega, L. (2009). Towards an organic approach to investigating CAF in instructed SLA: The case of complexity. *Applied Linguistics* 30(4), 555–578.

Ortega, L. (2003). Syntactic complexity measures and their relationship to L2 proficiency: A research synthesis of college-level L2 writing. *Applied Linguistics* 24(4), 492–518.

Penris, W. & Verspoor, M. (2017). Academic writing development: A complex, dynamic process. In S. Pfenniger & J. Navracsics (eds.), *Future Research Directions for Applied Linguistics*, 215–242. Bristol: Multilingual Matters.

Plat, R., Lowie, W., & de Bot, K. (2018). Word naming in the L1 and L2: A dynamic perspective on automatization and the degree of semantic involvement in naming. *Frontiers in Psychology* 8(2256). https://doi.org/10.3389/fpsyg.2017.02256

Sparks, R. L., Patton, J., Ganschow, L., Humbach, N., & Javorsky, J. (2008). Early first-language reading and spelling skills predict later second-language reading and spelling skills. *Journal of Educational Psychology* 100(1), 162–174.

Spoelman, M. & Verspoor, M. (2010). Dynamic patterns in development of accuracy and complexity: A longitudinal case study in the acquisition of Finnish. *Applied Linguistics* 31(4), 532–553.

Tilma, C. (2014). The Dynamics of Foreign versus Second Language Development in Finnish Writing Unpublished Ph.D. dissertation, Rijksuniversiteit Groningen/University of Jÿvaskyla.

Van Hout, R. & Vermeer, A. (2007). Comparing measures of lexical richness. In H. Daller, J. Milton, & J. Treffers-Daller (eds.), *Modelling and Assessing Vocabulary Knowledge*, 93–115. Cambridge: Cambridge University Press. https://doi.org/10.1017/CBO9780511667268

Verspoor, M. & Van Dijk, M. (2012). Variability in a dynamic systems theory approach to second language acquisition. In C. Chapel (ed.), *The Wiley-Blackwell Encyclopedia of Applied Linguistics*. Hoboken, NJ: Blackwell Publishing.

Verspoor, M., De Bot, K., & Lowie, W. (eds.) (2011). *A Dynamic Approach to Second Language Development: Methods and Techniques (Vol. 29)*. Amsterdam & Philadelphia: John Benjamins Publishing.

Verspoor, M., Lowie, W., Chan, H. P., & Vahtrick, L. (2017). Linguistic complexity in second language development: Variability and variation at advanced stages. *Recherches en didactique des langues et des cultures. Les cahiers de l'Acedle* 14(1). https://doi.org/10.4000/rdlc.1450

Verspoor, M., Lowie, W., & Van Dijk, M. (2008). Variability in second language development from a dynamic systems perspective. *The Modern Language Journal*, 92(2), 214–231.

Verspoor, M., Schmid, M. S., & Xu, X. (2012). A dynamic usage based perspective on L2 writing. *Journal of Second Language Writing* 21(3), 239–263.

Vyatkina, N. (2012). The development of second language writing complexity in groups and individuals: A longitudinal learner corpus study. *The Modern Language Journal* 96(4), 576–598.

Winter, B. & Wieling, M. (2016). How to analyze linguistic change using mixed models, Growth Curve Analysis and Generalized Additive Modeling. *Journal of Language Evolution* 1(1), 7–18.

Wolfe-Quintero, K., Inagaki, S., & Kim, H.-Y. (1998). *Second Language Development in Writing: Measures of Fluency, Accuracy, and Complexity*. Honolulu, HI: University of Hawaii Press.

Wood, S. (2006) *Generalized Additive Models: An Introduction with R*. Boca Raton, FL: CRC Press

(2017). *Generalized Additive Models: An Introduction with R, 2nd Edition*. Boca Raton, FL: CRC press.

Exploring Individual Variation in Learner Corpus Research: Methodological Suggestions

Stefanie Wulff and Stefan Th. Gries*

1 Introduction

In this chapter, we would like to make a case for corpus-based analyses of individual differences and variation in Second Language Acquisition (SLA), and specifically advocate for one corpus-based method, MuPDAR(F) (explained in detail below). After a compact overview of how individual differences and variation are defined in (non-corpus-linguistic) SLA in the rest of Section 1, we turn to corpus-based approaches to investigating learner language, presenting an argument in favor of MuPDAR(F)-type approaches to explore individual variation in Section 2. In Section 3, we present the results of a MuPDAR(F) analysis of the genitive variation in learner and native speaker data. In Section 4, we discuss the implications and desiderata for future corpus-based analyses of learner language as well as future corpus compilation projects.

1.1 Individual Differences and Variation in SLA Research

One of the first – and few to date – comprehensive discussions of individual differences in SLA research is offered by Dörnyei (2005) (see also Skehan 1986). He makes a case for including personality, aptitude, and motivation as key properties that differentiate individual learners, and he points to other research in SLA that also includes learning styles and learning strategies. Ultimately, "the concept of 'individual differences' is rather loose, containing certain core variables and many optional ones" (Dörnyei 2005, 7).

* Figures 15, 16, 17, 18, 19, 20 and 21 in this chapter are available in color in the supplementary online materials of the volume. You can find them at https://www.cambridge.org/gb/academic/subjects/languages-linguistics/applied-linguistics-and-second-language-acquisition/learner-corpus-research-meets-second-language-acquisition?format=PB.

A closer survey of SLA research confirms Dörnyei's position regarding the wide scope of how individual differences are defined. This aligns well with two by now established observations in SLA research that are shaping theory and methodology alike:

(i) SLA must be understood as an inherently complex process in which a multitude of factors, often in interaction with each other, drive and mold the acquisition process and determine ultimate attainment (VanPatten & Williams 2015).
(ii) Several of these factors are complex concepts themselves. For example, we can break down the concept of motivation minimally into intrinsic and extrinsic motivation, and many more complex definitions have been suggested (see Woodrow 2016 for a recent overview); similarly, the Modern Language Aptitude test defines aptitude as a combination of grammatical sensitivity, phonological decoding ability, memory capacity, and inductive learning ability (Carroll & Sapon 1959) and again, other definitions abound (see Singleton 2017).

Individual differences combine with other (both language-internal and language-external) factors such as the quality and quantity of the input received, the differences in form–function mappings between the first and the second language, the setting in which the learning takes place (for example either in an immersive or instructional context), or the specifics of the task at hand (timed vs. self-paced tasks, graded vs. non-graded assignments, etc.).

The interplay of individual differences with all these other factors inevitably gives rise to considerable variation in learner performance across comprehension, processing, and production. In fact, given this multi-layered complexity of SLA both in terms of "what goes in" as well as "what goes out," rather than being an alternative hypothesis to be justified, the existence of individual variation must be considered the null hypothesis. In fact, since a majority of the cognitive and even language-external factors not only characterize each L2 learner in different ways but native speakers just the same, there is a growing consensus that native speakers do not present a monolithic group. Instead, native speakers display significant amounts of individual variation as well, blurring, at times, the boundaries between native speakers and learners (and consequently rendering native speakers a questionable target norm, at least with regard to performance measures; see Hopp 2010; Street 2017).

A review of the empirical literature of the past decade or so indicates that both individual differences and individual variation are receiving increasing attention. Cognitive predispositions such as executive function and working memory (Wen et al. 2015), declarative vs. procedural memory (e.g., Hamrick 2015; Morgan-Short et al. 2014), aptitude (e.g., Granena 2013, 2016), and even resting qEEG (Prat et al. 2016) are among the most extensively studied individual differences. A good number of studies examine differences in personality types, learning styles, and learning strategies (e.g., Grey et al. 2015). A second large strand of research considers individual variation that emerges from the external circumstances and environment of the learners, such as the amount of input they receive (e.g., Unsworth 2016), the quality of the input (e.g., Rothman & Guijarro-Fuentes 2010), and the specific learning context (e.g., Collentine & Freed 2004; Grey et al. 2015). Additionally, and in accord with the line of reasoning outlined above, a growing number of studies also considers the relative impact of internal and external factors in combination (e.g., Chondrogianni & Marinis 2011; Courtney et al. 2017; Li 2013; Sun et al. 2016).

Corpus-based research, however, to date constitutes only a small portion of all studies in this area (see Möller 2017 for a recent exception). There might be several (inter-related) reasons for this. Firstly, corpus data are of limited use in the investigation of comprehension and processing-related individual variation, and much better suited to investigate individual variation in production. Secondly, the majority of learner corpora available to date do not include a wide array of metadata for the learners who contributed to the corpus. Speaker information usually includes information about the speakers' L1, age, and gender, as well as some information about their globally measured L2 proficiency; cognitive measures such as measures of executive control, working memory capacity, etc. are harder to come by. A third reason for the rare application of corpus data might be a commonplace misconception among non-corpus linguists that corpora only contain massive pools of data collapsed over anonymized speakers, with no option to tie data points to the individual speaker who produced them.

While we acknowledge that most corpora would benefit from adding more comprehensive batteries of metadata about the speakers captured in the corpus to allow meaningful discussion of individual differences, we would like to argue here that at least with regard to individual variation in production, corpus-linguistic methods offer a variety of advantages. For one, most corpora are designed such that data points can be traced back to individual speakers and whatever information is available about them. Furthermore, corpus linguistics is particularly well-equipped to deal with multifactorial phenomena. While corpus data are admittedly noisier/messier than experimental data, their ecological validity is higher and proper statistical control can help deal with the noise in instructive ways. In the following, we outline a corpus-linguistic approach that we believe to be particularly well-suited for the analysis of L2 production data and make some suggestions for how it can be employed to examine individual variation, specifically (see Gries 2018 for more detailed discussion than can be provided here).

1.2 The MuPDAR(F) Approach

One of the most recent methodological additions to both learner corpus research and indigenized-variety research is an approach called MuPDAR(F) (for multifactorial prediction and deviation analysis using regression/random forests) (Gries & Adelman 2014; Gries & Deshors 2014). This method is conceptually based on missing-data imputation: for every linguistic choice of a learner (or speaker of the target variety), one imputes what the native speaker (or speaker of the historical source variety) would have chosen given identical contextual conditions. While in the case study to be discussed below, we opted to compare the learners' choices with native speaker data, it is important to point out that MuPDAR does not require the reference data to be from native speakers – it is entirely up to the researcher to decide what a meaningful group for comparison should be.

MuPDAR(F) involves the following three steps:

- fitting a regression/random forest $R(F)_1$ that predicts the choices that speakers of the source/reference level (typically, native speakers of the reference variety) make with regard to the phenomenon in question;
- applying the results of $R(F)_1$ to the other/target speakers in the data (typically, learners or speakers of institutionalized second-language varieties) to predict for each of their data points what the native speaker of the source/reference variety would have done in their place;
- fitting a regression/random forest $R(F)_2$ that explores how the other speakers' choices differ from those of the speakers of the source/reference variety: predictors that are significant in this regression are ones that help understand where the target variety speakers make choices that are not those of the source/reference variety.

This approach can be useful because it focuses primarily on probabilistic differences that result in different speaker choices. In other words, it identifies not whether a learner is predicted to choose a modal verb with a probability of 25 percent while the native speaker is predicted to choose that modal verb with a probability of 20 percent – rather, it focuses on cases where the individual discrete choices of each target speaker represented in the data differ from what we can predict a reference speaker will do.

In this chapter, we apply the MuPDAR approach to the genitive alternation – *of* vs. *s*-genitives – in data from British English native speakers and Chinese and German second language learners of English. Section 2 explains our data, their annotation, and their statistical analysis. Section 3 discusses the results of our analysis; heeding the point made above that individual differences can manifest at different levels of granularity, we separately present (i) results that apply to all speakers, (ii) results that distinguish between speakers from different L1 backgrounds, and (iii) results that distinguish individual speakers. Section 4 concludes with some implications of these results for both future analysis of this kind of data and learner corpus compilation.

2 Methods

As mentioned above, this chapter is concerned with native speaker and learners' use of the genitive alternation as exemplified in (1).

(1)	a.	the squirrel's nuts	*s*-genitive: possessor'*s* possessed
	b.	the nuts of the squirrel	*of*-genitive: possessed *of* possessor

In this section, we discuss the data and their annotation for (in)dependent variables (Section 2.1) followed by a precise description of the statistical methods we used (Section 2.2).

2.1 Data

We retrieved examples of *of*- and *s*-genitives from three different corpora. For the learners, we retrieved all *of*- and *s*-genitives from the Chinese and the German sections of the *International Corpus of Learner English* (ICLE), version 2 (see Granger et al. 2009 for details on the content of the corpus). Given the large overall number of matches, we decided to randomly sample 1,000 attestations of each variant from the full concordances; manual checking of these 2,000 hits led to 10 (involving plurals) being discarded from the Chinese data. For the native speakers, we randomly sampled *of*- and *s*-genitives from all files of the British component of the *International Corpus of English* (ICE-GB), which resulted in examples being taken from 303 of the 500 files, which arguably constitutes a good representation of the target variety of the learners; from those, four examples had to be discarded. The overall distribution of the data is represented in Table 37.

The matches were then manually annotated for a large number of variables; many of these have been argued to play a role in previous work (Gries & Wulff 2013), and some others we added because they

Table 37 Composition of the data set

	of-genitive	*s*-genitive	Total
L1 Chinese	872	118	990
L1 German	817	183	1,000
L1 English	892	104	996
Total	2,581	405	2,986

turned out to be significant predictors in our own pilot studies. The following is the list of predictors that we included in our analysis:

- GENITIVE: *of* vs. *s*;
- number of possessor (POSSORNUMBER) and possessed (POSSEDNUMBER): *singular* vs. *regular plural* (with *s*) vs. *irregular plural* (e.g., *children* or *women*);
- animacy of possessor (POSSORANIM) and possessed (POSSEDANIM): inanimate vs. animate (but not human) vs. human;
- syntactic modification of possessor (POSSORBRANCH) and possessed (POSSEDBRANCH): *none* vs. *pre-modified* (e.g., *the natural environment*) vs. *post-modified* (e.g., *their right of choice of smoking*), where the underlined of is the genitive analyzed and *right* is post-modified by *of choice* vs. *pre- and post-modified* (e.g., *the richest source of protein of all veggies*);
- complexity of possessor (POSSORCOMPL) and possessed (POSSEDCOMPL): *simple* (e.g., non-modified nouns) vs. *intermediate* (nouns with adjectival or PP modification) vs. *complex* (nouns with clausal modification);
- difference in length between possessor and possessed (LENGTHDIFF): the difference between the number of characters of possessor minus possessed;
- avoidance of adjacent identical surface forms (HORRORAEQUI): all genitives were annotated with regard to whether they contained additional genitives: *none* (e.g., *the parts of the Saudi desert*) vs. *of* (e.g., *the part of the map of Kent*) vs. *s* (*my neighbour's dung heap's odours*);
- rhythmic alternation (RHYTHALTDIFF): every phrase with a genitive and its other-genitive counterpart was coded for its sequence of stressed and unstressed syllables (*people's personalities* = suuusuu; and *personalities of people* = uusuuusu). From these, we computed a value whose absolute size increases with the number of stress clashes (sequences of stressed syllables) and stress lapses (sequences of

unstressed syllables) and where positive and negative values indicate the criterion of rhythmic alternation would 'recommend' an *of*- and an *s*-genitive respectively; in addition, the higher the absolute value, the stronger that preference (see Wulff & Gries 2015 for details on how that value is calculated);

- segment alternation (SEGALTDIFF): every phrase with a genitive and its other-genitive counterpart was coded for its two transitions from the end of one noun phrase (NP) to the genitive marker and the genitive marker to the beginning of the next NP such that a transition from consonant (C) to vowel (V) or from V to C was scored as 0, a C_1C_2 transition (where $C_1 \neq C_2$) was scored as 1, and a C_1C_1 transition was scored as 2 (*Isobel_'s_grief* = 1+1 and *grief_of_Isobel* = 0+0, i.e., the difference is 2). We then changed the sign of these differences such that positive and negative values indicate the criterion of ideal syllable structure would 'recommend' an *of*- and an *s*-genitive respectively, and the higher the absolute value of the difference, the stronger that preference;
- first language (L1): the L1 of the speakers: *English* vs. *Chinese* vs. *German*.

These data were then used for the three-step MuPDAR approach.

2.2 Statistical Evaluation

In order to prepare the above data for a MuPDAR analysis, we did some initial data exploration. This included tabulating and plotting the data to determine whether variables needed to be transformed or variable levels needed to be conflated to avoid data sparsity, etc. As a result of this exploration,

- the variables POSSORANIM and POSSEDANIM were recoded to only two levels: *animate* (conflating *animate* and *human*) and *inanimate*;
- the variables POSSORBRANCH and POSSEDBRANCH were recoded to only three levels: *none*, *pre-modified* and *post-modified* (with or without additional pre-modification).

In addition, the numeric predictors LENGTHDIFF, RHYTHALTDIFF, and SEGALTDIFF were not just included as coded above but as orthogonal polynomials to the second degree, in order to allow for curvature in their effect on genitive choices (in the first model) or native-like choices (in the second model).

For the first step of the MuPDAR protocol, we decided against a mixed-effects regression model and chose a random forest (as in

Deshors & Gries 2016). Random forests are well-known for being very good at detecting predictive structure in a data set while at the same time avoiding overfitting. This is crucial to MuPDAR(F), because the second step involves imputing the choices that native speakers would have made. Thus, in this first step, the predictors were all the above; the response variable was GENITIVE; and we fitted 3,500 trees where, at each step, four variables were eligible to be used for the next split (this is the default setting for classification trees in randomForest:: randomForest; see Liaw & Wiener 2015).

We then explored whether the random forest yielded a better-than-chance prediction accuracy for the native speaker training data – if that was not the case, the imputation that MuPDAR(F) requires would not be feasible. (As will be shown below, we obtained an excellent prediction accuracy.) We then applied the random forest to the learner data to get native speaker predictions for each learner choice, and then compared whether the learner had made the native-like choice or not, which was captured in a variable NATIVELIKE (*no* vs. *yes*). In addition, we computed a variable called DEVIATION, which represents how much the learner choice differs from the imputed native speaker choice: values of 0 indicate the learner made a native-like choice (i.e., NATIVELIKE is *yes*), values between 0 and −0.5 and between 0 and +0.5 indicate the learner used an *of*-genitive and an *s*-genitive respectively when the native speaker would have used the respective other variant, with higher absolute values representing higher degrees of "nonnative-likeness."

In a final step, we conducted a model selection process using generalized linear mixed-effects modeling to determine what predicts whether learners make native-like choices or not. The response variable was NATIVELIKE and the predictors were all of the above variables (now applied to the learner data) as well as, of course, L1. To identify the best model, we employed the following stepwise model-checking procedure. Our first model involved no predictors at all but just an overall intercept, which was allowed to vary for each speaker/corpus file. Then, we performed a bidirectional model selection process such that we checked at every step (i) what would improve the model best, the deletion or addition of which main effect or pairwise interaction (using *AIC* provided in the *R* output as the model selection criterion), (ii) whether said deletion or addition would raise overall multicollinearity *VIF*-values above 10, and (iii) whether said deletion or addition would introduce overdispersion problems. We discuss the results in the following section.

3 Results

3.1 Results of RF_1 and Its Application to the Learner Data

The result of the random forests analysis to the native speaker yielded extraordinarily high prediction accuracies. The out-of-bag prediction accuracy reached 98.1 percent and a corresponding C-value of 0.99. Given these results, we applied the random forest model to the learner data, which resulted in an expectedly lower, but still very good prediction accuracy (88 percent) and a good C-value of 0.82 (which exceeds the usual threshold value of 0.8). Also, examining the variable importance measures we obtained, we found those variables that previous studies have shown to be most important also turned out to be important in our analysis, including, among others, PossorAnim, PossorNumber, or LengthDiff. From those predictions, we then added the two columns of Nativelike and Deviation to the learner data for subsequent analysis with R_2 and visualization.

3.2 Results of R_2

The model selection process as described above yielded a highly significant final model (LR-statistic = 221.36, $df = 21$, $p \approx 0$) with high R^2-values (in particular compared to some previous MuPDAR analyses): $R^2_m = 0.721$, $R^2_c = 0.75$. This final model achieved a classification accuracy of 90 percent, which, according to exact binomial tests, is significantly better than the baselines of the more frequent level of the Nativelike variable and proportional random sampling of the levels of Nativelike; the C-value for this model is 0.892. In the following sections, we discuss some of the results of R_2: for reasons of space, we only present a selection of instructive results in Sections 3.2.1 (results pertaining to all learners) and 3.2.2 (results distinguishing between learners of different L1s), before we turn to results pertaining to individual variation in Section 3.2.3.

3.2.1 RESULTS AT THE LEVEL OF ALL SPEAKERS

The first result is a main effect, namely that of LengthDiff, which is represented in Figure 14 (with two panels). In (nearly all of) the following graphs, the *x*-axis represents one predictor (i.e., here LengthDiff) while the *y*-axis represents the predicted probability of learners making the native-like choice; the left panel covers the complete range of LengthDiff values, whereas the right panel shows the same effect but zooms in to the central 90 percent of the

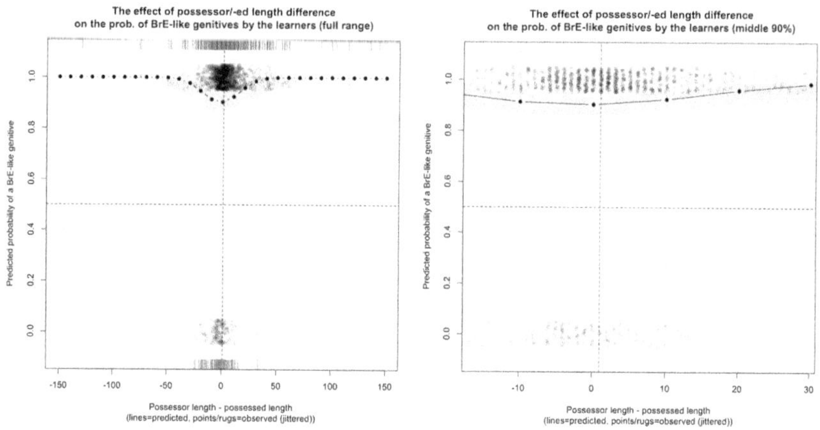

Figure 14 The effect of LENGTHDIFF ($p < 0.001$)

values. The black points connected by a line are the regression line representing the model's predictions (with a grey-shaded 95 percent confidence band), and the jittered points around $y = 0$ and $y = 1$ represent the non-native-like and native-like choices, respectively (at x-coordinates representing the observed length differences); these are also represented by the rugs at the bottom and the top x-axis. The horizontal dashed line marks the predicted probability of 50 percent (i.e., the one where the prediction would flip), and the vertical dashed line marks the median LENGTHDIFF value.

The result is relatively straightforward: while the native-like choices very strongly outnumber the non-native-like ones (see the large number of jittered grey points around $y = 1$ compared to the much smaller number around $y = 0$), the learners are least native-like when the length differences between possessor and possessed are small, i.e., when LENGTHDIFF makes no strong 'recommendation' for a constructional choice that is compatible with short-before-long. This is evident from two observations: (i) the noticeable dip of the regression line (in particular in the left panel) around LENGTHDIFF $= x = 0$ and (ii) the fact that the grey dots around $y = 0$ representing non-native-like choices are not attested at all with larger absolute length differences, i.e., they do not exhibit the same wide spread as the grey dots around $y = 1$ do.

Figure 15 represents the interaction of POSSEDNUMBER and POSSORANIM. The former variable is represented on the x-axis, the latter with different colors (as per the legend). The points' sizes are proportional to the frequencies with which the relevant combinations

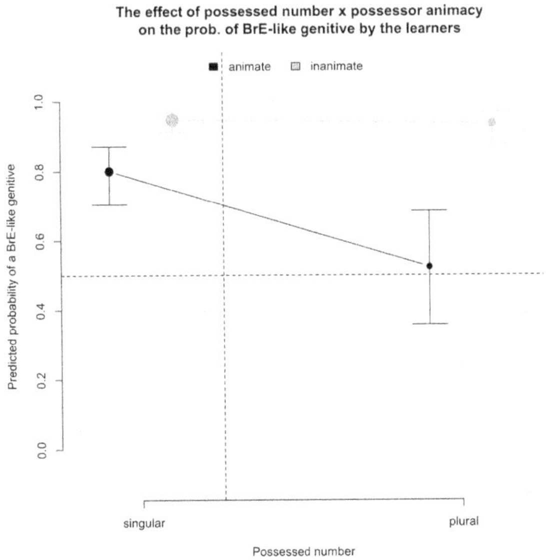

Figure 15 The effect of POSSEDNUMBER × POSSORANIM ($p < 0.037$)

are attested in the data; in this case that means that inanimate singular possessors were the most frequent of the four combinations, whereas animate plural possessors were the least frequent. The error bars around the points are 95 percent confidence intervals, and the vertical dashed line represents the relative frequency of the variable levels on the *x*-axis, indicating here that there are many more singular than plural possesseds in our data.

The plot shows that when the possessor is inanimate (light grey points/line), then the learners make very native-like choices regardless of POSSEDNUMBER, which, upon checking the native speaker data, turn out to be predominantly *of*-genitives. However, when the possessor is animate, then the learner choices become much less native-like, especially with plural possesseds.

While space does not permit revisiting individual examples to see where this effect arises, the effect perfectly highlights the shortcomings of a simpler over-/underuse approach: if one computes the percentages of *of*- and *s*-genitives for animate possessors and plural possesseds for the native speakers and learners, we yield Table 38.

As Table 38 shows, the overall relative frequencies of genitives for animate possessors and plural possesseds are virtually identical. In a traditional over-/underuse account, we would conclude that, with animate possessors and plural possesseds, learners behave native-like –

Table 38 Observed frequencies of genitives for animate possessors with plural possesseds

	PossedNumber: *plural*, PossorAnim: *animate*		
	of-genitive (%)	*s*-genitive (%)	Total (%)
native speakers	29 (65.9)	15 (34.1)	44 (100)
learners	57 (66.3)	29 (33.7)	86 (100)
Total	**86 (66.2)**	**44 (33.8)**	**130 (100)**

after all, the percentages of the genitives are nearly exactly the same. However, the more fine-grained resolution of multifactorial regression approaches in general and MuPDAR(F) in particular shows this to be false: with animate possessors and plural possessed, learners often make non-native-choices (as shown in Figure 15) by erroneously overusing *s*-genitives (which became obvious when we inspected the original data). (1)–(3) are a few examples from the data.

(1) ... the smokers simply have no right to endanger other**s'** lives [Chinese learner]

(2) Employee**s'** savings are maximized by private mpf service providers ... [Chinese learner]

(3) Teachers must set a good example and show their pupils that it is essential to see a person'**s** good qualities. [German learner]

The next effect – SegAltDiff × PossorNumber – is shown in Figure 16: SegAltDiff is on the *x*-axis, PossorNumber is symbolized by the two colors, which are used for predicted points, lines, confidence bands, and dots; again the left panel shows the whole range of SegAltDiff values while the right one shows the medial 90 percent.

With singular possessors, learners make more native-like choices, and they do so regardless of SegAltDiff. However, with plural possessors, where plural *s* often leads to an avoidance of *s*-genitives by native speakers, the learners perform more native-like by also avoiding the *s*-genitive. To fully understand this effect, it is important to focus on the right panel specifically, the one that covers the central 90 percent of the data, to see how (i) the black line is nearly consistently above the grey one and (ii) there are extremely few black points around $y = 0$, indicating that while the polynomial effect of

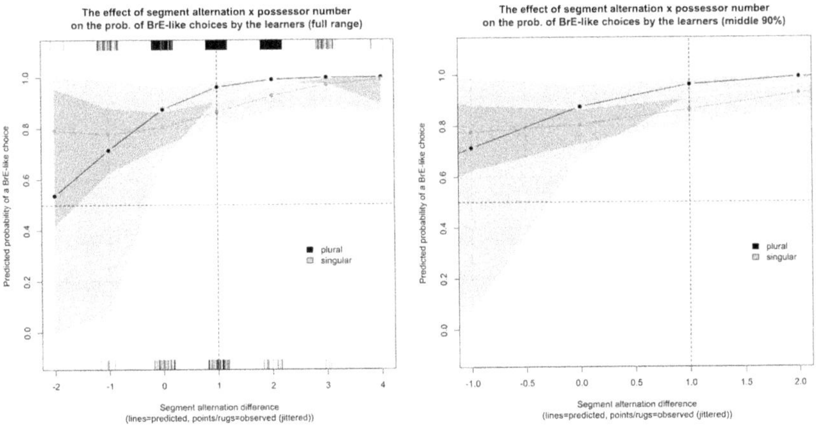

Figure 16 The effect of SegAltDiff × PossorNumber ($p < 0.123$)

SegAltDiff in the regression curves down a bit in both panels on the left side, there are actually hardly any data points for such low SegAltDiff values. A comparison with the native speaker data accordingly confirms what the bottom parts of Figure 16 already imply: the learners make most non-native-like choices when the possessor is singular and SegAltDiff makes no strong recommendation; (4)–(6) are a few examples from the data.

(4) The opening hour **of** the internet cyber café is 24 hours. [Chinese learner]

(5) . . . the consideration of the actual need **of** our society should be in a prior position. [Chinese learner]

(6) . . . use one car so that you use the full capacity **of** the car. [German learner]

In the next section, we turn to effects that distinguish between the learner groups.

3.2.2 RESULTS AT THE LEVEL OF SPEAKERS OF A CERTAIN L1

The first result pointing to differences between the Chinese and the German learners is L1 × PossorComplexity as represented in Figure 17. When the possessor involves at least some degree of complexity, both learner groups make more native-like choices. However, when the possessor is simple, the Chinese learners become much less native-like than (i) they are when it is complex or (ii) the Germans. In

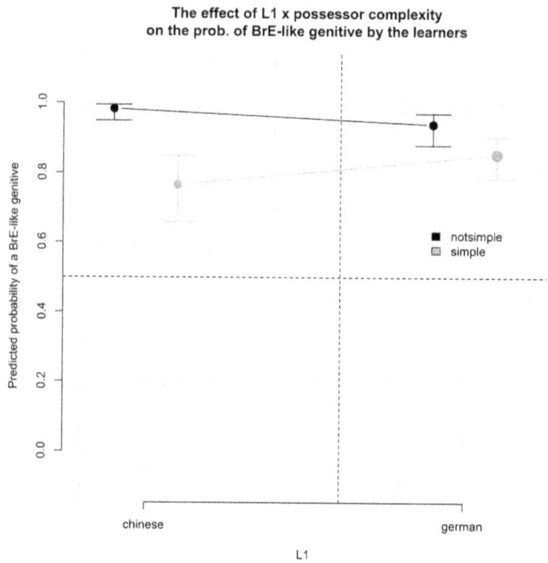

Figure 17 The effect of L1 × PossorComplexity ($p < 0.002$)

other words, PossorComplexity affects the Chinese learners more, and an exploration of the data reveals that with simple possessors, they underuse the *s*-genitive. (7) and (8) are examples from the Chinese learner data.

(7) . . . the recycling industry is mainly driven by the awareness and the choice **of** consumers. [Chinese learner]

(8) They claim that public construction increases the expensing **of** the government [Chinese learner]

Finally, let us consider Figure 18, which reveals that the German learners' performance is not affected by whether the possessed is singular or plural, but the Chinese learners' performance is: with singular possesseds, they are less native-like than with plural ones because, as drilling down into the data shows, they underuse *s*-genitives. Let us now zoom in even more and begin to address the issue of individual variation.

3.2.3 RESULTS AT THE LEVEL OF INDIVIDUAL SPEAKERS

How does the MuPDAR(F) approach inform individual variation? There are again multiple levels of resolution that are available. The

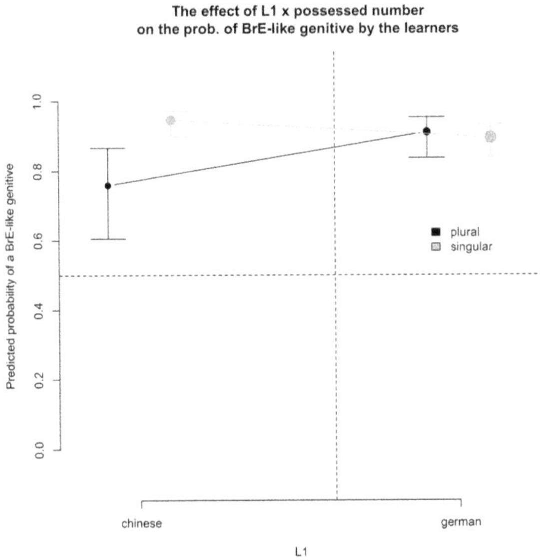

Figure 18 The effect of L1 × PossedNumber ($p < 0.001$)

present approach is not unlike error annotation: consider applying the results from the random forest to the learner data an annotator who checks for each learner choice whether it is native-like or not, and so we can determine the error rates for each learner. Those can be plotted for a bird's eye view of the data and then be used to go back to each relevant learner's data for post hoc exploration. Figure 19 is such a plot with genitive frequency on the *x*-axis and percentage of non-native-like uses on the *y*-axis; the circles and plusses are Chinese and German learners, respectively, and the grey and black dashed lines represent means for both axes. That means the learners at the top of the plot struggle with genitives most and might merit further exploration.

A more fine-grained resolution would be to also take the severity of the non-nativeness and its directionality into consideration, which we captured in the variable Deviation. Such a plot makes it possible to see which learner errs in which direction and how much, as in Figure 20. All speakers below $y = 0$ have more problems with overusing *of*, all speakers above $y = 0$ have more problems with overusing *s*.

Any of these types of results obtained for speakers could also be correlated with other information we have on the speakers, such as the kinds of individual differences discussed a lot in SLA research and surveyed above in Section 1.1. This can be done in various ways, but the two most obvious would be the following:

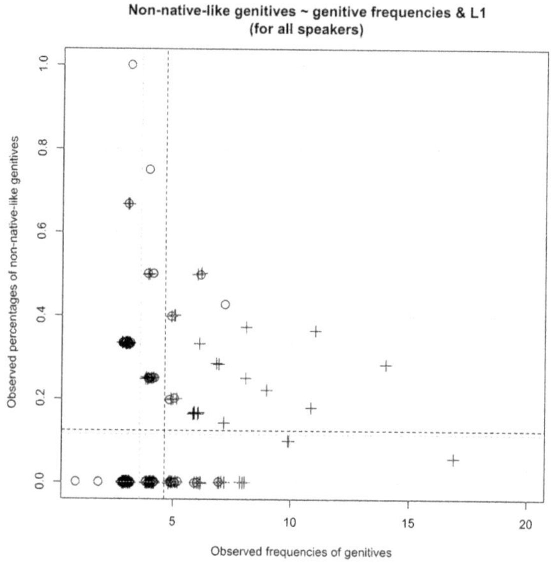

Figure 19 *Percentages of non-native-like uses against genitive frequencies*

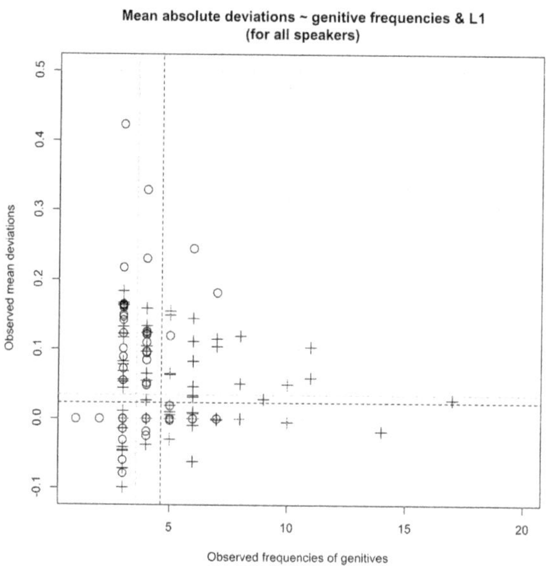

Figure 20 DEVIATION*-values against genitive frequencies*

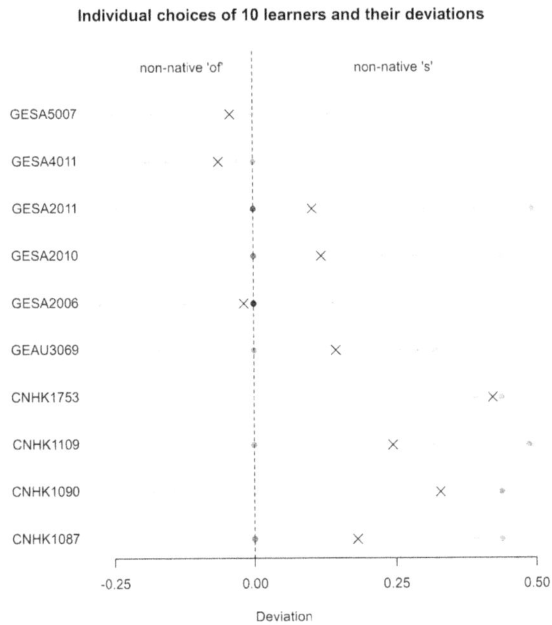

Figure 21 DEVIATION*-values of 10 speakers*

- speaker-specific information such as working memory, executive function, age of arrival, etc. can become a priori predictors in either a traditional multifactorial regression or a MuPDAR kind of analysis to see, for instance, how they correlate with learners making more or less native-like choices;
- such information can be explored a posteriori by correlating it after the fact with regression or MuPDAR results – if interesting correlations emerge, those can be interpreted tentatively and entered into subsequent statistical analyses of new data sets.

Finally, it is possible to drill down even deeper and check individual decisions of individual speakers. Figure 21 shows the individual deviation-values for 10 speakers of their genitive choices (with dots) and their means (with ×). We can immediately see that some learners' values show they have problems with non-native *of*-genitives whereas for others, it is non-native *s*-genitives that are problematic.

We could now examine those individual instances more deeply. In an attempt to at least very briefly demonstrate the degree to which the present approach can inform research on individual variation we did a cursory inspection of the three German and the three Chinese learners with the highest error rates (as determined from the results visualized in Figure 21), which turned out to be revealing because most of the non-native-like uses of the Chinese learners involved one and the same possessor – the proper name *Hong Kong* – whereas there was no obvious pattern discernible in the German learner data; we will return to this finding and what we believe it implies below.

4 Discussion and Concluding Remarks

The above analysis has some important implications for the analysis of learner corpus data and design. In particular, our data show two things. First, there is quite some degree of individual variation in learner corpus data. That is less trivial than it sounds because even a cursory survey of learner corpus studies will reveal that most studies of the types discussed in Section 1.2 do not include individual variation systematically. In our data, the fact that we used a mixed-effects regression model in R_2 of MuPDAR(F) makes quite a difference when it comes to accounting for what the learners are choosing, which becomes very obvious if one compares that regression's results to one that does not involve random effects: not only is the classification accuracy of the final fixed-effects regression model not significantly better than the baseline of always guessing the more frequent outcome, we also find that the interrater agreement between the mixed-effects and the fixed-effects regression model is somewhat strong, but not as high as one would wish for ($\kappa = 0.78$). Obviously, a lot of information is lost when the individual learners' differences are not included.

That being said, other ways of including both individual and group variation should also become (more) standardly used in learner corpus research. For instance, for corpora for which proficiency information (or any other text/speaker-specific information) is easily available, then, if proficiency is expected to make a difference for the phenomenon in question, it could be added as a predictor in $R(F)_2$ just like any other coded characteristic of the data. If proficiency information is not easily available or only considered post hoc, then it can be explored in heuristic ways based on text characteristics such as lexical diversity, average dispersion values of words, etc. For instance, as we discussed in the previous section, the Chinese speakers with the highest rates of non-native-like choices made many of those with one and the same lexical item, *Hong Kong*. A more general analysis of the learners' essays shows that the Chinese essays are characterized by a much higher degree of lexical repetitiveness (as measured by Yule's *K*):

- we computed a Yule's *K*-value for each essay and computed their averages for each L1 group: Chinese average = 134.4 vs. German average = 111.4, which is a highly significant difference ($t = -9.005$, $df = 1229$, $p < 0.001$);
- we conflated all Chinese and all German essays into one big file each and computed Yule's *K*-values for both, which supported the above impression: Yule's *K* for Chinese = 123.9 and Yule's *K* for German = 80.9.

Actually, in our data there is no correlation between the lexical repetitiveness values of all essays and their corresponding percentages of native-like genitives, and we are not implying there should be one – we are pointing out, however, that such kinds of differences between speakers/essays exist and that they can correlate with, or even have a causal effect on, learner performance (as seems to be the case in Wulff & Gries's (2015) exploration of prenominal adjective order). Thus, it is important to keep such factors controlled – if one does not do that, variability that may stem from different degrees of proficiency of speakers (lexical repetitiveness) may erroneously be considered variability due to different L1s (see Gries 2018 for much discussion).

Several observations that fell out from our analysis have implications for future corpus compilation projects, or initiatives to enhance existing corpora for that matter. For one, as we alluded to in the previous section, a potential addition to the MuPDAR(F) approach would be to either include a priori, or correlate a posteriori, any speaker information that one might deem relevant. The ICLE corpora include several variables that could be of interest (owing to the way we sampled our data, we did not investigate those here), including the speakers' age and the length of exposure to English at school, university, or in an English-speaking country. Paying heed to the major trends in individual variation research in SLA outlined above, it appears that a majority of researchers would be interested in even more comprehensive profiles of each speaker including results of test batteries tapping into speakers' aptitude, motivation, and memory capacity, to name but a few (see Möller 2017).

A maybe less obvious, but nonetheless crucial implication for corpus compilation regards the sometimes dramatic effects of differential task demands that will be manifest in the data. It is a long-established fact that different tasks and task conditions impose varying degrees of cognitive burden on L2 speakers and thus dramatically impact learners' performance across linguistic domains, from lexical diversity to syntactic complexity etc. (see e.g., Robinson 2011 for details on effects of task complexity; Lambert et al. 2017 as an example study that examines effects of task repetition; or Ong 2014 for a study investigating effects of planning time and task conditions on metacognitive processes in L2 writing). In ICLE, one can distinguish texts based on at least some task conditions, including whether the text was produced in a timed or non-timed condition, whether or not the learner was allowed to use reference tools, and whether or not the text was part of an examination – while this is not a comprehensive list of task characteristics, it is much more information that most other learner corpora provide.

Next to cognitive impacts of different tasks and task implementations, task topics are known to trigger (more or less conscious) response strategies that can influence the results of a corpus-based analysis considerably, and in various ways – some of which need not be obvious right away (Paquot 2013, 2014). To give one example from this study, we return to the finding in our study that upon examination of the noun phrases involved in non-native-like genitives, *Hong Kong* stood out as a highly favored noun phrase in the Chinese learner writing (while we could not discern any such trend in the German data). A qualitative analysis of the Chinese learner writing shows beyond a doubt that given a prompt that mentions *Hong Kong*, they are prone to referencing that noun phrases repeatedly. This not only (negatively) impacts lexical diversity scores (see Gries & Wulff 2013) and other performance measures such as overall word frequency and dispersion; what is more, since *Hong Kong* is such a culturally engrained concept, the Chinese learners consider it as more 'given', which in turn, and in fact suggesting some understanding of the *s*-genitive being correlated with discourse-givenness in native English, triggers their overuse of that noun phrase with the *s*-genitive specifically.

What is more, the task topic also triggers deployment of prefabricated language that learners have come to rote-learn as culturally desirable responses to being asked about their capital (we can infer that it must be rote-learned since various learners produce nearly verbatim passages). Shi (2004) found similar results when she investigated how task type affects the degree of lexical borrowing from source readings; among other things, she pointed out that Chinese students are significantly more likely to use material borrowed from source readings than the native English students. While such observations may be interesting from a cultural/anthropological point of view, it is likely undesirable for a linguistically oriented analysis: since the automated production of prefabricated chunks artificially boosts proficiency measures of these learners, the data do not adequately reflect the learners' genuine ability to assemble utterances on their own. In conclusion, the ideal learner corpus would comprise both culturally specific as well as more generic prompts so that researchers may choose to examine the data for cultural key words etc., but not be confined to that type of data when the focus of analysis is not on cultural influences.

In conclusion, we hope that this chapter has illustrated the usefulness of corpus-based analyses of individual variation and provides some guidance on how to approach individual variation phenomena using the MuPDAR approach. While MuPDAR is not suitable for the investigation of *all* relevant questions in learner corpus research, it is perfectly capable of being used for anything that can statistically be construed as an alternation phenomenon. This means, it can obviously handle any kind of actual alternation phenomenon (choice between two competing allomorphs, syntactic constructions, registers, modes, instructional styles, etc.). However, this also means that the frequency of any kind of lexical or grammatical choice can also be analyzed in a regression-modeling kind of approach that is conceptually extremely similar to a MuPDAR(F) analysis; see Gries (2018) for discussion of over- and underuse frequencies of the word *quite* using generalized linear mixed-effects modeling of the type used in the present chapter and further extensions. We hope that the chapter will stimulate vivid discussion among corpus developers and researchers on how to improve future corpus compilation projects with the goal in mind to make corpus linguistics a true alternative and complement to experimental studies.

References

Carroll, J. & Sapon, S. (1959). *Modern Language Aptitude Test (MLAT)*. New York, NY: The Psychological Corporation.

Chondrogianni, V. & Marinis, T. (2011). Differential effects of internal and external factors on the development of vocabulary, tense morphology and morpho-syntax in successive bilingual children. *Linguistic Approaches to Bilingualism* 1(3), 318–342.

Collentine J. & Freed, B. (2004). Learning context and its effects on second language acquisition. *Studies in Second Language Acquisition* 26(2), 153–171.

Courtney, L., Graham, S., Tonkyn, A., & Marinis, T. (2017). Individual differences in early language learning: A study of English learners of French. *Applied Linguistics* 6(1), 824–847.

Deshors, S. & Gries, S. Th. (2016). Profiling verb complementation constructions across New Englishes: A two-step random forests analysis to *ing* vs. *to* complements. *International Journal of Corpus Linguistics* 21(2), 192–218.

Dörnyei, Z. (2005). *The Psychology of the Language Learner: Individual Differences in Second Language Acquisition*. New York, NY and London: Routledge.
Granena, G. (2013). Individual differences in sequence learning ability and second language acquisition in early childhood and adulthood. *Language Learning* 63(4), 665–703.
(2016). Cognitive aptitudes for implicit and explicit learning and information-processing styles: An individual differences study. *Applied Psycholinguistics* 37(3), 577–600.
Granger, S., Dagneaux, E., Meunier, F., & Paquot, M. (2009). *International Corpus of Learner English v. 2*. Louvain-la-Neuve: Presses universitaires de Louvain.
Grey, S., Williams, J., & Rebuschat, P. (2015). Individual differences in incidental language learning: Phonological working memory, learning styles, and personality. *Learning and Individual Differences* 38, 44–53.
Gries, S. Th. (2018). On over- and underuse in learner corpus research and multifactoriality in corpus linguistics more generally. *Journal of Second Language Studies* 1(2), 277–309.
Gries, S. Th. & Adelman, A. (2014). Subject realization in Japanese conversation by native and non-native speakers: Exemplifying a new paradigm for learner corpus research. In J. Romero-Trillo (ed.), *Yearbook of Corpus Linguistics and Pragmatics 2014: New Empirical and Theoretical Paradigms*, 35–54. Cham: Springer.
Gries, S. Th. & Deshors, S. (2014). Using regressions to explore deviations between corpus data and a standard/target: Two suggestions. *Corpora* 9(1), 109–136.
Gries, S. Th. & Wulff, S. (2013). The genitive alternation in Chinese and German ESL learners: Towards a multifactorial notion of context in learner corpus research. *International Journal of Corpus Linguistics* 18(3), 327–356.
Hamrick, P. (2015). Declarative and procedural memory abilities as individual differences in incidental language learning. *Learning and Individual Differences* 44, 9–15.
Hopp, H. (2010). Ultimate attainment in L2 inflection: Performance similarities between non-native and native speakers. *Lingua* 120(4), 901–931.
Lambert, C., Kormos, J., & Minn, D. (2017). Task repetition and second language speech processing. *Studies in Second Language Acquisition* 39(1), 167–196.
Li, S. (2013). The interactions between the effects of implicit and explicit feedback and individual differences in language analytic ability and working memory. *The Modern Language Journal* 97(3), 634–654.
Liaw, A. & Wiener, M. (2015). Breiman and Cutler's Random Forests for Classification and Regression. R Package 4.6-12, retrieved from cran.r-project.org/web/packages/randomForest/ (accessed June 13, 2020).
Möller, V. (2017). A statistical analysis of learner corpus data, experimental data and individual differences: Monofactorial vs. multifactorial approaches. In P. de Haan, S. van Vuuren, & R. de Vries (eds.), *Language, Learners and Levels: Progression and Variation*, 409–439. Louvain-la-Neuve: Presses universitaires de Louvain.

Morgan-Short, K., Faretta-Stutenberg, M., Brill-Schuetz, K., Carpenter, H., & Wong, P. (2014). Declarative and procedural memory as individual differences in second language acquisition. *Bilingualism: Language and Cognition* 17(1), 56–72.

Ong, J. (2014). How do planning time and task condition affect metacognitive processes of L2 writers? *Journal of Second Language Writing* 23, 17–30.

Paquot, M. (2013). Lexical bundles and L1 transfer effects. *International Journal of Corpus Linguistics* 18(3), 391–417.

(2014). Cross-linguistic influence and formulaic language: Recurrent word sequences in French learner writing. In L. Roberts, I. Vedder, & J. Hulstijn (eds.), *EuroSLA Yearbook*, 216–237. Amsterdam & Philadelphia, PA: John Benjamins.

Prat, C., Yamasaki, B., Kluenda, R., & Stocco, A. (2016). Resting-state qEEG predicts rate of second language learning in adults. *Brain and Language* 157–158, 44–50.

Robinson, P. (ed.). (2011). *Second Language Task Complexity: Researching the Cognition Hypothesis of Language Learning and Performance*. Amsterdam & Philadelphia: John Benjamins.

Rothman, J. & Guijarro-Fuentes, P. (2010). Input quality matters: Some comments on input type and age-effects in adult SLA. *Applied Linguistics* 31(2), 301–306.

Shi, L. (2004). Textual borrowing in second-language writing. *Written Communication* 21(2), 171–200.

Singleton, D. (2017). Language aptitude: Desirable trait or acquirable attribute? *Studies in Second Language Learning and Teaching* 7(1), 89–103.

Skehan, P. (1986). *Individual Differences in Second-Language Learning*. New York, NY and London: Routledge.

Sun, H., Steinkrauss, R., Tendeiro, J., & de Bot, K. (2016). Individual differences in very young children's English acquisition in China: Internal and external factors. *Bilingualism: Language and Cognition* 19(3), 550–566.

Street, J. (2017). This is the native speaker that the non-native speaker outperformed: Individual, education-related differences in the processing and interpretation of object relative clauses by native and non-native speakers of English. *Language Sciences* 59, 192–203.

Unsworth, S. (2016). Early child L2 acquisition: Age or input effects? Neither, or both? *Journal of Child Language* 43(3), 608–634.

VanPatten, B. & Williams J. (eds.) (2015). *Theories in Second Language Acquisition: An Introduction*. New York, NY: Routledge.

Wen, Z., Borges Mota, M., & McNeill, A. (eds.) (2015). *Working Memory in Second Language Acquisition and Processing*. Bristol: Multilingual Matters.

Woodrow, L. (2016). Motivation in language learning. In R. Breeze & C. Sancho Guinda (eds.), *Essential Competencies for English-Medium University Teaching*, 235–248. New York, NY: Springer.

Wulff, S. & Gries, S. Th. (2015). Prenominal adjective order preferences in Chinese and German L2 English: A multifactorial corpus study. *Linguistic Approaches to Bilingualism* 5(1), 122–150.

Building an Oral and Written Learner Corpus of a School Programme: Methodological Issues

Philippa Bell, Laura Collins, and Emma Marsden

1 Introduction

This chapter's goal is to address issues related to the design, collection and preparation of learner corpora designed to capture second language (L2) grammatical development across a school programme. We begin by presenting a brief overview of learner corpora in Second Language Acquisition (SLA). We then present our long-term research objectives and the goals of this pilot study, which are addressed in three research questions. Our qualitative analysis demonstrates the importance of piloting before finalising the design of learner corpora as, despite the appropriateness of the tasks in terms of age, certain task design choices affected learner production. Our quantitative analyses demonstrate our tasks captured proficiency differences, defined by school grade level, when operationalised as lexical diversity and syntactic complexity. A number of other issues, which surfaced during the transcription of the oral and written data, are presented. We conclude by discussing possibilities for the standardisation of some aspects in the design and use of corpora, and the importance of extensive reporting of methodological choices if learner corpora are to be employed to their full potential in SLA.

2 Learner Corpora in SLA Research

Since the late 1980s, the field of learner corpus research (LCR) has developed, which focuses on the collection and analysis based on explicit design criteria of samples of written and spoken language by second and foreign language (L2) learners for applied and theoretical reasons (Granger et al. 2015). Concomitantly, SLA researchers have collected samples of student production using various data elicitation techniques to address important questions concerning the acquisition of L2s (e.g., Harley 1990; Muñoz 2006; Rule & Marsden 2006).

Despite a general preference in SLA research for controlled language tasks and limited sample sizes (Granger et al. 2015) (e.g., see Ellis 2008 for a summary of case studies and research into morpheme development that employed controlled language tasks), some SLA researchers have used large datasets based on semi-spontaneous elicitations more typical of LCR methodology (e.g., *French Learner Language Oral Corpora* [FLLOC], Myles & Mitchell n.d.; *Spanish Learner Language Oral Corpora* [SPLLOC], SPLLOC n.d.). Perhaps linked to the relevant ease with which large datasets can now be stored and (partially) analysed using computer programs, and the increased awareness of the importance of methodological transparency through the Open Science movement (Marsden et al. 2016; 2018), researchers in SLA and LCR are increasingly collaborating. This has led to more possibilities in terms of analysing large datasets based on SLA research objectives using corpus research tools, and will permit the present study's research objectives to be met.

3 Research Problem and Objectives

The importance of unerstanding how to maximise language learning opportunities in formal education stems from the conflicting relationship between the necessity of time/exposure for L2 development and the limited time available for individual school subjects. In limited-exposure contexts, common in foreign language school programmes (Muñoz 2006; Collins & Muñoz 2016), students typically receive a few hours of weekly language instruction spread over many years. However, much of what we know about L2 development in school-based contexts comes from specialised programmes offering extensive exposure to the target language, such as the Intensive English model in Quebec (Collins et al. 1999), immersion (e.g., Lyster 2008) or content-based education in Europe (Dalton-Puffer et al. 2010). Little, in comparison, is known about language development in the more limited exposure experienced when the foreign language class is one of many other school subjects.

We do know, however, from a substantial amount of SLA research documenting the developmental nature of L2 acquisition across learner populations and contexts (see, for example, Ortega 2009) that teaching and assessment of learning can effectively take into account interlanguage development phenomena such as backsliding and emergence (Ågren et al. 2012; Pallotti 2015), and that syllabi that conceptualise learning as occurring in a predetermined, linear fashion are inconsistent with our understanding of how languages are learnt. Alternatives to such syllabi need to be informed by empirical evidence of how L2 learning unfolds in instructed learning settings, evidence that could inform teachers in their decisions of what grammar to teach and when. However, we know surprisingly little about students' incremental L2 development in limited-exposure contexts, including the aspects of language that are learnt with relative ease and those that may require periodic and/or sustained pedagogical attention at different points in the students' learning trajectory. In the absence of such information to guide syllabus planning, the language content of school-based programmes tends to be based on perceptions of difficulty rather than on observations of learner language, and this despite calls dating back to at least 1985 (Lightbown) for interlanguage studies of instructed L2 learners, research that could provide information to better guide the selection and sequencing of grammatical objectives in L2 programmes (Ellis & Shintani 2014). Very little research has set out to describe how L2 grammar develops in speech and writing throughout compulsory schooling (primary and secondary school), with extant corpora focusing largely on either spoken (FLLOC and SPLLOC) or written language (*International Corpus of Crosslinguistic Interlanguage*, Hong 2012).

Thus the long-term research objective of this project is to understand through the analysis of a written and spoken, cross-sectional learner corpus the grammatical features which emerge, how and when they develop, and which features do not emerge and/or do not develop over the 11 years of compulsory foreign language education. The creation of a learner corpus to respond to this objective necessitates a pilot phase to ensure methodological decisions related to design, collection and preparation of the corpus are sound for our needs and for those of other researchers to whom the corpus will be made available (through the Child Language Date Exchange System [CHILDES], MacWhinney 2000). The pilot project is reported here.

Before introducing the research questions, we present and justify the basic design characteristics of the corpus.

4 Corpus Design

4.1 Environmental Variables

To understand the emergence of grammatical features across a compulsory school programme, the data need to come from an educational setting, in this case, the Quebec English as a Second Language Core Programme (Ministère de l'Éducation et de l'Enseignement supérieur 2017). The Government of Quebec oversees an eleven-year compulsory education programme starting in Grade 1, when English as a Second Language (ESL) is taught for approximately one hour per week (pupils are 6 years old on 30 September of the academic year), and thus is a limited-exposure programme.[1]

4.2 Learner Variables

A priori decisions were made concerning previous ESL experience, mother tongue and age. We restricted our study to learners who have only followed the core ESL programme, despite the existence of other programmes that provide more enriched exposure, as the core programme is the most common and is thus more representative.

We also opted to focus on francophone learners only, who constitute the majority of the school population in Quebec. Statistics from the 2013–2014 school year show there were 889,272 pupils in French L1 education, 99,450 in English L1 education and 6,456 in Cree or Inuktitut L1 education (Ministère de l'Éducation et de l'Enseigenement supérieur 2016). This decision was made to reduce potential influence on development due to other languages (Cenoz 2013). We hope to add data from these students in the future.

As LCR has tended to focus on older learners and/or only written or spoken texts, and owing to differences between educational contexts (Tono & Díez-Bedmar 2014), we also needed to decide the age at which data collection should start. Based on our research experiences with this population and discussions with the pedagogical advisers at primary school, the earliest grade in which data could be collected was suggested as Grade 5, primary (ages 10–11). It is at this time that learners are encouraged to start working with English independently, and thus may be capable of completing oral and written texts without scaffolding. Thus the final corpus will range from Grade 5, primary to Grade 5, secondary (ages 16–17). In this chapter, we report on data collected from a subset of this range, explained in more detail below.

4.3 Procedures for Choosing Elicitation Tasks

To decide the task type (genre), we firstly consulted the webpage Learner Corpora around the World on the Centre for English Corpus Linguistics website (Centre for English Corpus Linguistics

[1] The number of hours of ESL education students receive varies slightly between schools, as this subject forms part of a block of subjects that must be taught for a certain number of hours. As such, some schools choose to provide slightly more ESL instruction and reduce the number of hours for other subjects within the block (or vice versa) (Gouvernement du Québec 2017).

2017a) to extract different task types (see the Appendix). For written corpora, the most common free writing task type (as opposed to controlled writing or tests) was argumentative essays (28/175), followed by descriptive (11/175) and narrative (9/175) essays. For oral corpora, the most common spontaneous task type was interviews (18/74), followed by discussions/conversations (9/74) and narratives (7/74). As we wished to include the same genres in oral and written data collection, we chose an argumentative task (popular in written corpora) and a narrative task (popular in oral and written corpora) for a total of four tasks (two written; two oral). For the oral corpus, we also included an interview task because of its popularity amongst researchers, and because of potential influences that task condition (monologic vs. dialogic) can have on language production (Michel et al. 2007; Robinson 2005).

To find tasks from extant research that fitted our choice of genres, two databases were consulted. Firstly, an extensive search in the Learner Corpus Bibliography (Centre for English Corpus Linguistics 2017b) and subsequent consultation of publications that discussed potentially relevant tasks were conducted. Secondly, IRIS was consulted (Marsden et al. 2016). Despite there being over 3,000 materials held on IRIS, few of them had been used specifically for corpora development (as of August 2017). Certain materials could be adapted for this purpose, but if one relies on search criteria related to corpora (rather than materials used for other types of research), the initial results prior to piloting found few tasks suited to our objectives.

In terms of narrative tasks, the Frog Story (Meyer 1969) has frequently been used as an oral elicitation measure (Housen et al. 2001; Kang 2004; Pallotti 2010), so we chose to use this. As our search did not uncover a favoured written narrative, we selected one based on an image of police officers arriving at a house to speak to a mother and her son. Students are asked to imagine what has just happened, what is happening now, and what will happen. This task had already been successfully used with Quebec students aged 10–12 (Collins & White 2011), and we felt the topic could also be suitable for older learners.

Again, owing to a lack of widely employed argumentative task topics in both oral and written media, in consultation with teacher colleagues we created questions on topics we believed would be of interest to our learner population, which ranged in age from 10 to 17 years old. Thus the argumentative task asked students to respond to one of four questions on the use of cell phones in school, the existence of aliens, the possibilities of choosing one's own classmates, and the importance of vegetarianism.

For the interview, we adapted questions from Paradis (2005) and an unpublished interview protocol used with Quebec students (e.g., Collins et al. 1999). The interview began with simple personal questions (age, birthday), progressed to more general questions of personal interest (favourite holiday, choice of costumes for Halloween), then to questions relating to beliefs and attitudes (perceived differences between schools in different countries).

4.4 Pilot Phase

The next step was to verify through piloting using a subsample of the targeted population our choices relating to design, collection and preparation of this developmental corpus for young learners. We addressed three research questions:

RQ1 To what extent did the language used to provide instructions (L1 French or L2 English) affect the amount of learners' production of the L2 and L1?
RQ2 To what extent are our data elicitation tasks appropriate for learners in terms of apparent interest and different proficiencies?
RQ3 What transcription and coding issues need to be borne in mind for building developmental corpora?

5 Methodology

5.1 Data Collection

The data were collected cross-sectionally from learners at different grade levels to create a quasi-longitudinal (Granger 2002) or pseudo-longitudinal corpus (Gass & Selinker 2008).

5.2 Participants

The production data were collected in three schools – two primary and one secondary. Table 39 details the number of participants (N = 145) at each grade level, which excludes 19 students who identified English as their strongest language. A subset of eight students at each grade level completed the oral tasks.[2] We could not access students meeting our profile in Grades 1 and 2 of secondary school, as few teachers

[2] In all tables, age with respect to grade level refers to the age which the student must be as of 30 September of the academic year.

Table 39 Participants divided by grade level

Grade	N
5, primary (10 years old)	36 (13 school 1; 23 school 2)
6, primary (11 years old)	30 (14 school 1; 16 school 2)
3, secondary (14 years old)	28
4, secondary (15 years old)	28
5, secondary (16 years old)	23
Total	**145**

responded to our requests and those who did were not able to welcome us for data collection at an appropriate time (ages 12 and 13 at the beginning of the academic year). The data presented in this chapter also include some students who identified languages other than French and English as their strongest language, as this was not anticipated to have an impact on the research questions in this pilot phase (n = 8 out of 145).

5.3 Procedure

To address RQ1, we provided identical instructions either in French or English in a counterbalanced design so each pupil completed one task with English instructions and one with French. In some research, instructions are provided in the L1 (e.g., French 2006), but the majority provide them in the L2 (e.g., *International Corpus of Learner English*, Granger et al. 2009). To our knowledge, any potential effect on elicited data in terms of the quantity of L2 text produced and amount of L1 used has not been explored.

We provided four topics for the written argumentative task of which learners responded to one. We used two oral argumentative tasks. Our aim was to identify the topics that (a) appealed most to students across the age range and (b) generated the most language.

The results reported below come primarily from the written tasks, as transcription of the oral data proved unduly time-consuming for our budget constraints for the pilot phase (discussed in more detail in response to RQ3).

6 Results

In this section, we respond to the RQs and we present any adaptations made to our methodology for the main collection. All necessary statistical assumptions were met for the conducted analyses.

6.1 Language of the Task Instructions (RQ1)

To respond to RQ1, we examined the quantity of L2 text produced (Table 40) and the number of L1 words used (Table 41), as a function of whether instructions had been given in the L1 (French) or the L2 (English). A one-way ANOVA with language of instruction as the independent variable and quantity of words and number of French words used as dependent variables was conducted. No significant differences were found, and overall effect sizes as measured using eta squared were very small, explaining no variance for text quantity and 4 per cent of the overall variance for French words (quantity of words: F (1,285) = 0.12, p = 0.72, 95% CI [75.70, 86.26], η^2 = 0.00; French (L1) words: F (1,285) = 1.054, p = 0.305, 95% CI [2.48, 4.43], η^2 = 0.04).

6.2 Impact on Main Data Collection

As the results demonstrate that the language of instructions did not significantly impact the number of words produced or the number of French words used, all instructions will be provided in French to ensure students begin with the same level of comprehension. This also means the words and syntactic constructions learners produce in English in the tasks are not primed by the instructions.

6.3 Tasks and Interest (RQ2)

To address whether the chosen tasks were appropriate in terms of interest across the age spectrum, we provide a qualitative and a quantitative analysis. In terms of qualitative data, at each data collection session, the research team and the students' teacher provided their impressions of student interest. The written tasks were well received by all students insofar as all the teachers (n = 3) and researchers (n = 7) reported that students seemed to be engaged. The students appeared to be on-task, as were their questions (e.g., How do I spell 'knock'? Can we use a dictionary?). Furthermore, when we returned to complete the oral tasks with a subset of students, there were many volunteers. Their willingness to participate reinforces our belief they had enjoyed completing the written tasks. These impressions were noted across all age groups.

For the oral tasks, we used a subset of eight students per grade, chosen at random. During these tasks, the research team found the students to be engaged and interested in responding as best they could, and this despite the tasks being extremely challenging for weaker

Table 40 Quantity of text produced as a function of language of task instructions

	French (L1) instructions			English (L2) instructions				95% CI	
Grade	n	Mean	SD	*n*	Mean	SD	η^2	LB	UB
5, primary	36	51.64	41.10	36	53.47	39.62	0.04	−0.51	0.42
6, primary	31	72.71	38.90	29	65.28	33.35	0.20	−0.30	0.71
3, secondary	28	79.57	48.08	28	81.50	33.68	0.05	−0.57	0.48
4, secondary	26	104.38	33.80	28	104.96	46.29	0.01	−0.55	0.52
5, secondary	22	121.00	34.07	23	108.04	45.26	0.32	−0.27	0.91
Total	**143**	**81.94**	**46.15**	**144**	**80.03**	**44.79**	**0.04**	**−0.19**	**0.27**

Table 41 Number of French L1 words used as a function of language of task instructions

	French (L1) instructions			English (L2) instructions				95% CI	
Grade	n	Mean	SD	*n*	Mean	SD	η^2	LB	UB
5, primary	36	10.28	17.36	36	7.02	9.96	0.23	−0.23	0.70
6, primary	30	3.48	7.26	27	2.76	6.07	0.11	−0.41	0.63
3, secondary	28	1.86	1.69	28	1.57	1.85	0.06	−0.46	0.59
4, secondary	26	0.69	1.12	28	0.89	1.03	0.14	−0.68	0.39
5, secondary	22	0.86	1.98	23	1.00	1.68	0.08	−0.66	0.51
Total	**143**	**3.97**	**10.06**	**144**	**2.95**	**6.23**	**0.12**	**−0.11**	**0.35**

Table 42 Topic preferences for the argumentative written task

Grade	*n*	Cell phones (%)	Aliens (%)	Classmates (%)	Vegetarianism (%)
5, primary	36	42	25	8	25
6, primary	30	30	30	23	17
3, secondary	28	36	54	11	0
4, secondary	27	44	26	19	11
5, secondary	23	52	30	13	4
Total	144	40	33	15	13

students as they were not used to speaking spontaneously without scaffolding. No student changed his/her mind about participating or failed to respond to any tasks or questions.

Table 42 presents the topic choices from the written argumentative questions. Learners had to choose one topic, and the most frequently chosen topics, consistently across the age range, were those involving questions about cell phones and aliens.

6.4 Tasks and Proficiency (RQ2)

To understand whether the tasks were appropriate for learners at different proficiency levels, we provide qualitative and quantitative analyses. Firstly, we present three concerns with the written narrative prompt that could affect our ability to observe proficiency differences and grammatical development for morphosyntactic features. Secondly, we present word counts and results from one measure of lexical diversity and one of syntactic complexity to understand whether our tasks tap into proficiency differences across the school system. All data were transcribed using the CHAT transcription system and analysed using the CLAN suite of analysis tools, both of which form part of CHILDES (MacWhinney 2000).

The written narrative prompt was a drawing of two male police officers standing together addressing a mother and a child whose gender was not clear. Having two male police officers instead of one female and one male reduced opportunities for use of gendered determiners and pronouns. Furthermore, using a child whose gender was not clear meant it was difficult in some cases to know whether kin-different possessive determiners were being used correctly (*his mother* or *her mother* – both could be correct if the student had not made it explicit elsewhere in the discourse which gender they had assigned the child). Kin-different possessive determiner use is a known challenge for francophone learners, as French possessive determiner choice refers to the grammatical gender of the possessed noun (*sa mère* = his/her mother) whilst English possessive determiner choice refers to the gender of the possessor (White 1998; White et al. 2007). Finally, having the police officers standing together without doing obvious actions limited possible attempts at more complex language including progressive forms and subject relative clauses.

To understand whether our tasks captured proficiency differences, we initially looked at the number of words elicited by each task across the grade levels to see whether productivity increased. Table 43 demonstrates this descriptively and highlights that the narrative task consistently elicited more words than the argumentative task. A one-way ANOVA demonstrated that frequency differed significantly overall ($F\ (4,287) = 23.46$, $p = 0.000$, 95% CI [102.76, 126], partial $\eta^2 = 0.571$) with post-hoc analyses with a Bonferroni adjustment demonstrating significant differences between non-consecutive grade levels.

We also ran one lexical diversity and one syntactic complexity measure, as they are hypothesised to demonstrate growth in learner language development (i.e., proficiency) as part of the theoretical construct of complexity within the complexity, accuracy and fluency framework (Housen et al. 2012; Ortega 2003; Polio 2001). Issues abound with respect to the comparability, reliability and validity of the numerous available measures (see aforementioned publications and Norris & Ortega 2009), but to verify that our corpus captures proficiency differences in terms of complexity, the majority of measures are suitable. In what follows, we report mean number of morphemes per utterance (MPU) as a measure of syntactic complexity, which refers to the range of forms that are used during language production and gives some indication of the degree of sophistication of morphological richness/density (Ortega 2003). We report D-values (Malvern et al. 2004), which take into account the biasing effect of length (see Marsden & David 2008 for an example of this analysis using two learner corpora), as a measure of vocabulary diversity or variety (MacWhinney 2017b). Tables 44 and 45 provide descriptive statistics for the two measures.

A one-way ANOVA was conducted with grade level as the independent variable, and D-values and the MPUs as the dependent variables. The main effect for both dependent variables was significant (D-values: $F\ (4,191) = 8.58$, $p = 0.000$, 95% CI [46.55, 53.24], partial $\eta^2 = 0.15$; MPU: $F\ (4,281) = 17.88$, $p = 0.000$, 95% CI [15.47, 16.99]; partial $\eta^2 = 0.20$). For the Scheffé post-hoc analyses, alpha was set at 0.1, which is appropriate for exploratory, low-risk studies with relatively small

Table 43 Number of words by grade and task type

	Argumentative			Narrative			Both text types		
Grade	*n*	Mean	SD	*n*	Mean	SD	*n*	Mean	SD
5, primary (aged 10)	36	31.25	22.38	36	73.86	42.73	72	52.56	40.09
6, primary (aged 11)	30	51.47	22.76	30	86.77	38.80	60	69.12	36.21
3, secondary (aged 14)	28	63.00	30.53	28	98.07	43.33	56	80.54	41.14
4, secondary (aged 15)	27	98.41	37.70	27	110.96	42.67	54	104.69	40.38
5, secondary (aged 16)	23	105.69	38.83	22	123.45	40.59	45	114.38	40.26
Total	**144**	**66.12**	**41.18**	**143**	**95.94**	**44.65**	**287**	**80.98**	**45.40**

Table 44 Descriptive statistics for lexical diversity

		D-value		95% confidence interval	
Grade	*n*	Mean	SD	LB	UB
5, primary (aged 10)	29	39.58	25.93	30.89	48.28
6, primary (aged 11)	36	43.40	17.70	35.60	51.21
3, secondary (aged 14)	38	41.11	22.08	33.51	48.71
4, secondary (aged 15)	48	53.05	20.56	46.29	59.81
5, secondary (aged 16)	45	65.78	30.19	58.80	72.77
Total	**196**	**49.89**	**25.54**	**41.02**	**56.16**

Table 45 Descriptive statistics for syntactic complexity

		MPU		95% confidence interval	
Grade	*n*	Mean	SD	LB	UB
5, primary (aged 10)	71	12.49	6.00	10.96	14.02
6, primary (aged 11)	60	13.74	5.71	12.08	15.41
3, secondary (aged 14)	56	16.33	6.82	14.61	18.06
4, secondary (aged 15)	54	20.12	7.24	18.36	21.87
5, secondary (aged 16)	45	20.66	7.34	18.74	22.58
Total	**285**	**16.23**	**7.33**	**14.95**	**18.39**

datasets. We applied a correction for 10 comparisons setting the new alpha at 0.01. Table 46 demonstrates significant differences on the measure of lexical diversity between secondary 5 students, and those in primary 5 and 6 and secondary 3. Effect sizes (Cohen's *d*) range from small to large ($\geq 0.40 < 0.70$ = small; $\geq 0.70 < 1.00$ = medium; ≥ 1.00 = large; between-subjects interpretation, Plonsky & Oswald 2014) with a fairly clear progression based on grade level.

Table 47 demonstrates significant differences on the measure of syntactic complexity between secondary 4 and 5 students, and those in primary 5 and 6. Effect sizes, which are generally larger than for the measure of lexical diversity, range from small to large with a clear progression based on grade level.

6.5 Impact on Main Data Collection

Our results in terms of part one of RQ2 demonstrate that the written narrative and argumentative tasks were interesting for all ages and

Table 46 Post-hoc analyses for D-values

Grade		Mean difference between grades	Std. error	Sig. (*p* value)	Cohen's *d*	95% CI Lower bound	Upper bound
Primary Grade 5	Grade 6	−3.83	5.93	0.981	−0.18	−20.66	13.01
	Sec 3	−1.53	5.86	0.999	−0.06	−18.17	15.10
	Sec 4	−13.47	5.59	0.218	−0.59	−29.34	2.40
	Sec 5	**−26.20***	5.66	0.001	−0.92	−42.27	−10.14
Primary Grade 6	Sec 3	2.29	5.53	0.996	−0.33	−13.40	17.98
	Sec 4	−9.64	5.24	0.497	−0.96	−24.52	5.23
	Sec 5	**−22.38***	5.31	0.002	−1.23	−37.46	−7.29
Sec 3	Sec 4	−11.94	5.16	0.257	−0.56	−26.59	2.71
	Sec 5	**−24.67***	5.23	0.001	−0.47	−39.53	−9.81
Sec 4	Sec 5	−12.73	4.93	0.159	−0.50	−26.73	1.27

* The mean difference is significant at the 0.01 level

Table 47 Post-hoc analyses for mean number of morphemes per utterance

Grade		Mean difference between grades	Std. error	Sig. (*p* value)	Cohen's *d*	95% CI Lower bound	Upper bound
Primary Grade 5	Grade 6	−1.253	1.147	0.879	−0.22	−4.50	1.99
	Sec 3	−3.845	1.169	0.031	−0.61	−7.15	−0.54
	Sec 4	**−7.627***	1.181	0.001	−1.18	−10.97	−4.28
	Sec 5	**−8.167***	1.247	0.001	−1.26	−11.69	−4.64
Primary Grade 6	Sec 3	−2.591	1.216	0.340	−0.41	−6.03	0.85
	Sec 4	**−6.373***	1.227	0.001	−0.98	−9.85	−2.90
	Sec 5	**−6.914***	1.290	0.001	−1.07	−10.56	−3.26
Sec 3	Sec 4	−3.782	1.248	0.059	−0.54	−7.31	−0.25
	Sec 5	−4.322	1.310	0.030	−0.61	−8.03	−0.62
Sec 4	Sec 5	−5.40	1.321	0.997	−0.07	−4.28	3.20

* The mean difference is significant at the 0.01 level

thus no major changes are necessary. The analysis of the topics chosen for the written argumentative text demonstrated that cell phones and aliens were much more popular than classmates and vegetarianism and thus, for the main data collection, participants will be asked to respond to one of the two preferred topics.

In terms of part two of RQ2, our observations with regard to the details of the image for the narrative resulted in three changes. A female and a male police officer will be included (rather than two males), who each have distinct roles (completing an action), and the child will be redrawn to look more like a boy to increase the likelihood of kin-different possessive determiner use when discussing the relationship between the mother and son (*her son* and *his mother*).

The written argumentative task consistently elicited fewer words than the narrative task. Even though this may be an inherent difference based on genre – and therefore appropriate – we decided that asking learners to give a specific number of reasons to justify their point of view in the argumentative task may help to elicit more data. As such, 'give **three reasons** to explain your response' will be added to the argumentative task instructions.

The lexical diversity measure demonstrated mean differences between grade levels, which were significant in terms of secondary 5 students when compared to primary 5 and 6. Aside from very small effect sizes between primary 5, 6 and secondary 3, the magnitude of the differences between grades in terms of lexical diversity ranged from small to large. The syntactic complexity measure also demonstrated mean differences between grade levels, which were significant between the lowest and highest grade levels. Effect sizes demonstrated that differences were important in many cases and that there was an observed progression through the school system. Thus, our tasks permitted the observation of proficiency development overall. However, as can be seen from the very large standard deviations on the two measures, there was a lot of inter-group variation. To reduce the reliance on grade level to define proficiency (Thomas 2006), we will add an elicited imitation task as an independent proficiency measure (Ortega 2003). This task requires participants to listen to a sentence then repeat it through reconstruction not imitation, owing to a time delay. One exists that has been normed across eight languages with available information on scoring (Ortega et al. 2002). It also has the added benefit of being available on IRIS (www.iris-database.org) and so is likely to be increasingly used by other researchers, which improves the potential for comparability of our data in the future. The data from this will be plugged into analyses and used, for example, as a predictor or as a covariate when analysing performance on the production measures.

6.6 Transcription and Coding (RQ3)

RQ3 asked what transcription and coding issues need to be borne in mind for building developmental corpora that will be used for project-specific objectives and for other researchers' objectives. Transcription and coding stages of corpora building represent critical decision points that have an impact on the future utility of the corpus. To address this RQ, we document issues we encountered as we transcribed and coded the data. We hope this frank discussion is useful to illustrate (a) the complexities of building (young) learner corpora, and (b) the importance of detailed accounts of their creation so that results can be interpreted accurately and future researchers have a clear understanding of the corpus's advantages and disadvantages for their own objectives. This second point also responds to calls for methodological improvements in LCR (Paquot & Plonsky 2017).

6.7 Transcription Issues

In deciding how to transcribe the data, we found research articles do not always discuss transcription issues when presenting corpora. This is problematic, as transcribers could be making important but unacknowledged decisions (e.g., changing incorrect spelling, not transcribing foreign words), which is evident from research examining difficulties related to the transcription of handwritten essays (Somers 2005) and oral data (Ballier & Martin 2015; Jendryczka-Wierszycka 2009). Existing descriptions demonstrate how transcription conventions can impact future use of corpora (see Hilton 2008; Mitchell et al. 2008), and thus these descriptions should form part of the data attached to an available corpus. Although certain corpus-specific decisions are inevitable, the need for a standardised transcription system for LCR and SLA researchers would improve learner corpus methodology in terms of reliability and comparability across corpora (Callies 2015). SLA researchers using learner corpora appear to favour the CHAT transcription system, which has a bank of SLA corpora (e.g., BELC, Muñoz 2006; FLLOC, Myles 2002; PAROLE, Hilton 2009) and has been recommended in a number of articles (Ellis 2002; Myles 2005; MacWhinney 2017a). This is the system we use, although our fundamental point is to promote transparency and, where possible, standardisation, not this specific system. Figure 22 shows an example of a written text transcribed in CHAT.

We now discuss specific transcription issues we experienced – one based on CHAT conventions (MacWhinney 2017a) and two general issues. LCR and SLA both rely heavily on written data, but CHAT was created for transcribing spoken data in which, obviously, information about the learners' orthography is not available. Currently, automated analyses in the CLAN suite within CHILDES require accurate spelling (in order for the data to be recognised by the CHILDES dictionaries)

```
@Begin
@Languages:   eng, fra
@Participants:  TEX 1024 Text
@ID:   eng|1024p.WN|TEX||female|||Text|||
@Location:    FACE Grade 5 10/16
@Transcriber:  MCB, v-DC
*TEX:  its [:: It's] [* m] Laurent and he want [:: wants] [* m] to go
       out but the police officer don't [* sp] [:: doesn't] [*m ] want
       [: him to] [* m] because its [:: it's] [* m] dangerous for him .
%spe:  d'ont
*TEX:  her [:: his] [* m] mom want [:: wants] [* m] to résonne@s:fra$v
       [: reason with] [* m] him [: so] [*m] she say [:: says] [* m].
*TEX:  Lau its [:: it's] [* m] very dangerous for you and <you can
       te@s:fra$pron:refl faire@s:fra$v very mal@s:fra$adv>
       [: you could hurt yourself badly] [* s] .
*TEX:  but Laurent want [:: wanted] [*m] very very [:: much]
       [* s] to go out and he say [:: said] [* m].
*TEX:  please mom laisse@s:fra$v moi@s:fra$pro [: let] [* s] go to the super
       market please .
*TEX:  but her [:: his] [* m] mom don't [* sp] [:: didn't] [* m] want [: to]
       [* m].
%spe:  d'ont
*TEX:  the police officer say [:: said] [* m] to Laurent <tu@s:fra$pro
       as@s:fra$aux fait@s:fra$v une@s:fra$det bêtise@s:fra$n
       tantô@s:fra$adv> [: you did something silly] [* m] and we
       don't[* sp] want <que@s:fra$conj:sub ça@s:fra$pre:dem
       se@s:fra$pro:refl reproduise@s:fra$v> [: you to do that again] [* m].
%spe:  d'ont
*TEX:  Laurent [: was] [* m] very angry <make a grimace to>
       [:: and made a face at] the police officer and her [:: his]
       [* m] mom .
*TEX:  he cry [:: cried] [* m] and go [:: went] [* m] to him [:: his]
       [* m] room .
*TEX:  Laurent is very angry to [:: at] [* m] her [:: his] [* m] mom .
*TEX:  she not défendre@s:fra$v [: defend] [* s] him .
*TEX:  end !
@End
20nov19[E|CHAT] * 1
```

Figure 22 Example of transcription in CHILDES

for both L1 and L2 words. However, SLA research examining developmental patterns can require texts be faithfully reproduced. For example, fidelity to the learners' writing permits the data to be used for other research interests (e.g., punctuation, orthography). In our data, there were many L1 and L2 spelling errors. Thus, to ensure a true representation of learner productions, in the independent tier (the *TEX: tier), we needed to transcribe incorrectly spelt words correctly and accompany this word with a code ([* sp]). We then included a 'spelling' line (a dependent %spe: tier) under any independent tier, which provided the learners' actual spelling (see Figure 22 for examples), which considerably lengthened transcription time.

Another issue relates to transcribing punctuation and its consequences for executing 'length of unit' analyses, a frequent metric for complexity measures (Norris & Ortega 2009). Our learners often did not punctuate sentences, an interesting finding in its own right. However, length of unit analyses mean little if a learner's sentence structure does not follow a standardised set of punctuation. This also lengthened the transcription process considerably, as another dependent tier was included to document changes to a learners' punctuation. For this pilot phase, we wrote a comment under each text line in which an utterance had been divided (see Figure 22). Both of these decisions are vital steps in the transcription process and need to be documented for any corpora that are to be made available to other researchers.

A final issue relates to oral data whose transcription is much more laborious than written data, as has been discussed in depth elsewhere (Jendryczka-Wierszycka 2009). We had to restrict transcription to one grade level (secondary 3, which was simply the first transcribed), as the resource implications were too great. Dialogic transcription (the interview) was much more time-consuming than monologic transcription, with one interview lasting 10 minutes taking up to five hours to transcribe (and we had decided not to code phonetically). It has been argued that task condition (±monologic) affects development conceptualised using CAF (Robinson 2005). However, the evidence base for this needs strengthening given the significant consequences on resources (time and financial). Furthermore, more research is needed to understand whether different types of dialogic task (interview between researcher and learner vs. information-gap between students) affect production. This information is vital to decide the types of tasks to include in learner corpora (see also Marsden et al. 2003).

6.8 Error Annotation Issues

In order to document grammatical development, it is necessary to identify the grammar that learners do and do not produce, and what aligns and does not align with native (or target) norms. Initially, we wished to error code the data (see Díez-Bedmar 2015 for necessary steps for error coding). We abandoned this idea for a number of reasons that shed light on important issues if learner corpora are to further SLA research goals.

Error coding (for error analysis) involves the systematic coding of non-target-like forms in a corpus (Dagneaux et al. 1998; Granger 2015). A large number of coding systems already exist, despite several of these not being openly available (EARS, Díaz-Negrillo 2009; FreeText, Granger 2003); PAROLE, Hilton 2008; CLC, Nicholls 2003, TREACLE, O'Donnell et al. 2010).[3] In most publications, little information is provided on annotation decisions, which leads to an important methodological problem, as the authors' categorisations are understood based largely on the reader's interpretation of their categories (Meurers 2015; Myles 2015; Paquot & Plonsky 2017). Below, we highlight two concerns relating to (a) the taxonomies that *are* accessible and (b) the choice of who annotates/codes the corpora.

6.9 *Different Taxonomies*

We observed many discrepancies across error coding taxonomies at all levels of coding. For example, when coding the overall error domain in terms of grammar only (first-level coding), CHILDES covers morphology and syntax, FreeText (Granger 2003) covers grammar, syntax and morphology, and TREACLE (O'Donnell et al. 2010) covers grammar. This raises questions for people wishing to understand how errors have been coded. What do each of these terms mean? Are they independent? Does each system capture the same data, just under different headings? When considering second-level coding (a sub-code below the overall error domain), should this be done using word classes (Granger 2003), phrase types (TREACLE) or something else (CLC, Nicholls 2003)? As has been discussed elsewhere (Meurers 2015), error coding uses different systems and often entails assumptions about what the learner intended, especially when error coding is being done for specific reasons, reducing the ability to generate or test theory. In systems that code the *text*, rather than the intention, the type of grammar (i.e., the precise meta-data for tagging the text) still affects coding (O'Donnell et al. 2010).

6.10 *The Coders Themselves*

Coding is conducted by people with different backgrounds. Based on their experience, Dagneaux et al. (1998) suggested error *identification* be done by a native-speaker then error *tagging* done by a bilingual speaker of the target language and the first language of the learners.

[3] These references refer to the names of the corpora within which the employed error system has been detailed aside from EARS, which references a system that can be employed to code errors in English learner corpora.

The subjectivity that this process may entail has been acknowledged (Díez-Bedmar 2015), but we believe that using a coder who speaks the learners' language can increase the likelihood of errors being interpreted causally rather than linguistically, as the coder may rely on assumptions about cross-linguistic difference causing errors, which can lead to an overly narrow interpretation of the data, as other, non-L1 dependent explanations for 'errors' are possible (Callies 2015; Myles 2015). In our data, in response to the prompt used in the argumentative written narrative 'Do you agree or disagree?', many students wrote variants of 'I am agree' or 'I am disagree.' In French, *je suis d'accord* or *je ne suis pas d'accord (je suis en désaccord)* could suggest L1 transfer, particularly for coders who are native speakers of French. However, SLA research has demonstrated that we cannot always assume L1 transfer even when it seems evident, as observed patterns can be L1-independent (Jarvis 2000).

Other corpora, such as the CLC, has been error tagged using teachers of ESL/English as a Foreign Language, but teachers' judgements and classifications can vary widely and may not correspond to how researchers conceptualise language errors (Borg 2001; Pallotti 2015). The type of coder in terms of training, profession and language background will impact all later analyses conducted with the corpora. Furthermore, research into rater effects in language testing demonstrates biases linked to familiarity with the language background of the learners (Schmid & Hopp 2014; Winke et al. 2012). More research is needed to understand the effects of coder background to increase the objectivity of error tagged corpora. At the very least, as recommended by Díez-Bedmar, raters need to be well trained and all decisions should be noted in a 'ship's log' (2015, 45). Furthermore, information needs to be included concerning the backgrounds of all researchers involved with transcription and coding (transcribers, verifiers, coders).

Research objectives can determine decisions about error coding but, we think, some standardisation is possible. Methodological transparency, with basic agreement about and sharing of coding information, is necessary to understand the reliability, validity and generalisability of research using learner corpora. This has been flagged before in SLA research more generally (Housen et al. 2012; Larsen-Freeman 2009; Norris & Ortega 2009) and needs to continue to be addressed (Marsden et al. 2018; Paquot & Plonsky 2017).

6.11 Impact on Main Data Collection

The issues above had several consequences. For transcription, we will regularise spelling and punctuation from the outset with an added dependent spelling tier and comment tier so our deviations from the original text are clear for other researchers. Transcriber and verifier language background will be reported. For annotation, we will not include an error tier. Rather, we will rely on analyses of parts of speech, the roles of grammatical morphemes and all dependencies within utterances to identify patterns that vary across age groups. Differences can then be analysed for specific interlanguage phenomena.

7 Discussion

In this chapter, we have described our piloting, its outcomes and its effects on our main data collection. As such, we take this opportunity to make some suggestions for the future. Despite the importance of the individual context in LCR, we believe it is possible and desirable for new learner corpora to exploit existing elicitation tasks, to use similar transcription conventions and analysis tools, and to bear in mind the repercussions of each methodological decision on a corpus's future use (by the research team and other researchers).

In terms of tasks, we initially wished to use extant tasks to improve reliability and the possibility for comparisons with other studies. However, it became apparent that, despite some regularity in terms of preferred genres (e.g., interviews in oral corpora and argumentative texts in written corpora), a large number of genres has been used and there appears to be little reemployment of tasks across corpora (see *Learner Corpora around the World*, Centre for English Corpus Linguistics 2017a), with reemployed tasks being limited to international corpora (e.g., ICLE, LINDSEI). Indeed, this was one of the main rationales behind IRIS – that researchers would reuse the same or similar tasks and thus increase comparability across time and different contexts (Marsden et al. 2016). Part of this issue cannot be changed when, for example, organisations build very large learner corpora (e.g., the *Cambridge Learner Corpus*) that can then, to differing degrees, be accessed and used by researchers. However, for corpora that are built for explicit, specific research objectives, it would be beneficial, wherever possible, to use or adapt tasks that have been piloted, adapted and clearly described, especially as piloting is costly and time-consuming (as demonstrated above). Such a collaborative ethic would increase the comparability of results, and it would allow researchers to better understand the likelihood of eliciting certain types of language in specific task types (e.g., possessive determiners with our written narrative, or past tense morphology as described in Tracy-Ventura & Myles 2015). Our piloting demonstrated that two out of four potential topics in the argumentative written tasks were relatively unpopular with students. We also found that the narratives consistently elicited more words than the argumentative texts. Adaptations based on these findings mean our tasks are more likely to elicit the quantity and quality of data that we want. Creating new tasks to build corpora appears only to be warranted when research objectives focus on variability across genres and tasks, which has been acknowledged as an important research endeavour (Paquot 2015).

Aside from tasks, we believe that transcription and analysis could also be more normed. Myles (2005) discussed the immense number of possibilities available to SLA researchers through the CHILDES system. However, in the intervening years, only a relatively small number of corpora have been transcribed, coded and made available through CHILDES (28, SLABank 2017 vs. 160 on the CECL website).[4] We present CHILDES here as an option but emphasise that the important point is to begin discussions in order to understand which system (or systems) are best suited for the wide variety of LCR/SLA research needs. CHILDES has flexibility (in representing and coding learner language) and uniformity/systematicity ('by working together on a shared platform in a coordinated manner, researchers will be able to construct a rich new empirical basis for the study of SLA', MacWhinney 2017a, 254). Furthermore, CHILDES can easily be used without initial error annotation. At present, error taxonomies are varied and error coders have different profiles, increasing the likelihood that results are influenced by methodological artefacts rather than due to research design manipulation. One of the outcomes of this pilot project was the decision not to error code the data. Criticism of LCR has focused on a preoccupation for error coding, L1 transfer errors and deviations from a target-like norm (Myles 2005, 2015). CHILDES permits an open and objective approach to examining development and accuracy whereby data are first automatically annotated in terms of their morphosyntax (every word is assigned a part of speech tag and grammatical dependencies between each word are provided, and this in a number of languages, MacWhinney 2017b). Analyses based on specific research objectives can then identify specific language patterns and how they have been used, which can also be supplemented by manual annotation based on our knowledge of how certain features are used and affected (similar to the manual annotation before analysis championed by Wulff & Gries in this volume). In this way, rather than taking a perceived 'error' as the point of departure, one starts from a description of learner language. This conceptualises

[4] These numbers are counts with some corpora appearing on both. Also, not all the corpora on the CECL website are openly accessible.

development in terms of emergence and trajectories, rather than an end-state of 'mastery' (Pallotti 2007, 362), which corresponds with usage-based theories of language acquisition that take into account complex interactions between variables, such as saliency, frequency, cross-linguistic influence and processing complexity (Robinson & Ellis 2008).

Our final point relates to the sharing of learner corpora and their accompanying documentation. Each methodological decision, however simple, will affect the utility of a corpus for future use. These decisions affect the corpus's utility and can constrain it to a specific research context. Further, if these decisions are not transparent, it is difficult to evaluate the reliability, validity and comparability of results emanating from the corpus (Díez-Bedmar 2015). To illustrate this issue, we highlighted a subset of transcription decisions linked to spelling and punctuation. Our decision to indicate where transcripts deviated from actual production increased transcription costs considerably, but was justified, as it permits the sharing of our corpus through CHILDES, one of our aims. Setting this as an initial goal should, we recommend, form part of the funding budget. An additional long-term advantage is that the more SLA/LCR researchers who use the same system, the more adaptations for learner language can be integrated into the system. For example, frequent misspellings could be entered into a learner dictionary (either a general one or one linked to a specific language), which would decrease, and possibly eliminate, the need to change learner spelling on the main tier in CHAT; or an initial automatic analysis that identifies unrecognised words (already present) could create an automatic dependent tier that could then be disambiguated before automatic and/or manual annotation.

8 Conclusion

We have evaluated methodological decisions in a pilot phase to examine their impacts on learner productions, transcription and coding. We hope to have demonstrated the importance of documenting all steps in the design, collection and preparation of learner corpora. Our data and discussions have illustrated the importance of methodological transparency, as discussed elsewhere in both SLA and LCR literature (Callies 2015; Díez-Bedmar 2015; Marsden et al. 2016; Meurers & Dickinson 2017; Myles 2005; Norris & Ortega 2009; Paquot & Plonsky 2017; Pallotti 2007; Tracy-Ventura & Myles 2015). Decisions, and the transparency of those decisions, at each stage in the development of a learner corpus impact on the validity and generalisability of findings emanating from it and, therefore, affect the extent to which sharing corpora can usefully contribute to the wider Open Science movement.

References

Ågren, M., Granfeldt, J., & Schlyter, S. (2012). The growth of complexity and accuracy in L2 French: Past observations and recent applications of developmental stages. In A. Housen, F. Kuiken, & I. Vedder (eds.), *Dimensions of L2 Performance and Proficiency Investigating Complexity, Accuracy and Fluency in SLA*, 95–120. Amsterdam & Philadelphia: John Benjamins.

Ballier, N. & Martin, P. (2015). Speech annotation of learner corpora. In S. Granger, G. Gilquin, & F. Meunier (eds.), *The Cambridge Handbook of Learner Corpus Research*, 80–107. Cambridge: Cambridge University Press.

Borg, S. (2001). Self-perception and practice in teaching grammar. *ELT Journal* 55(1), 21–29.

Callies, M. (2015). Learner corpus methodology. In S. Granger, G. Gilquin, & F. Meunier (eds.), *The Cambridge Handbook of Learner Corpus Research*, 5–56. Cambridge: Cambridge University Press.

Cenoz, J. (2013). Third language acquisition. In C. A. Chapelle (ed.) *The Encyclopaedia of Applied Linguistics*. Oxford: Blackwell Publishing.

Centre for English Corpus Linguistics, Université catholique de Louvain (2017a). Learner Corpora around the World, retrieved from https://uclouvain.be/en/research-institutes/ilc/cecl/learner-corpora-around-the-world.html (accessed June 13, 2020).

(2017b). Learner Corpus Bibliography, retrieved from https://uclouvain.be/en/research-institutes/ilc/cecl/learner-corpus-bibliography.html (accessed June 13, 2020).

Collins, L., Halter, R. H., Lightbown, P. M., & Spada, N. (1999). Time and the distribution of time in L2 instruction. *TESOL Quarterly* 33(4), 655–680.

Collins, L. & Muñoz, C. (2016). The foreign language classroom: Current perspectives and future considerations. *The Modern Language Journal* 100, 133–147.

Collins, L. & White, J. (2011). An intensive look at intensity and language learning. *TESOL Quarterly* 45(1), 106–133.

Dagneaux, E., Denness, S., & Granger, S. (1998). Computer-aided error analysis. *System* 26(2), 163–174. https://doi.org/10.1016/S0346-251X(98)00001-3

Dalton-Puffer, C., Nikula, T., & Smit, Y. (eds.). (2010). *Language Use and Language Learning in CLIL Classrooms*. Amsterdam: John Benjamins.

Díaz-Negrillo, A. (2009). *EARS: A User's Manual*. Munich: Lincom Academic Reference Books.

Díez-Bedmar, M. (2015). Dealing with errors in learner corpora to describe, teach and assess EFL writing: Focus on article use. In E. Castello, K. Ackerley, & F. Coccetta (eds.), *Studies in Learner Corpus Linguistics: Research and Applications for Foreign Language Teaching and Assessment*, 37–70. Bern: Peter Lang.

Ellis, N. C. (2002). Reflections on frequency effects in language processing. *Studies in Second Language Acquisition* 24, 297–339.

Ellis, R. (2008). *The Study of Second Language Acquisition, 2nd Edn*. Oxford: Oxford University Press.

Ellis, R. & Shintani, N. (2014). *Exploring Language Pedagogy through Second Language Acquisition Research*. Abingdon: Routledge.

French, L. M. (2006). *Phonological Working Memory and Second Language Acquisition: A Developmental Study of Francophone Children Learning English in Quebec*. Lewiston, NY: Edwin Mellen Press.

Gass, S. & Selinker, L. (2008). *Second Language Acquisition*. New York, NY: Routledge.

Gouvernement du Québec (2017). *Loi sur l'instruction publique*, retrieved from http://legisquebec.gouv.qc.ca/fr/ShowDoc/cs/I-13.3 (accessed June 13, 2020).

Granger, S. (2002). A bird's-eye view of learner corpus research. *Computer Learner Corpora, Second Language Acquisition and Foreign Language Teaching* 6, 3–33.

(2003). Error-tagged learner corpora and CALL: A promising synergy. *CALICO Journal* 20(3), 465–480.

(2015). Contrastive interlanguage analysis: A reappraisal. *International Journal of Learner Corpus Research* 1(1), 7–24.

Granger, S., Dagneaux, E., Meunier, F., & Paquot, M. (eds.) (2009). *International Corpus of Learner English, Version 2*. Handbook and CD-ROM. Louvain: Presses universitaires de Louvain.

Granger, S., Gilquin, G., & Meunier, F. (2015). Introduction: Learner corpus research – past, present and future. In S. Granger, G. Gilquin, & F. Meunier (eds.), The Cambridge Handbook of Learner Corpus *Research*, 1–6. Cambridge: Cambridge University Press.

Harley, B. (ed.) (1990). *The Development of Second Language Proficiency*. Cambridge: Cambridge University Press

Hilton, H. (2008). *Corpus PAROLE. Parallèle oral en langue étrangère: architecture du corpus et conventions de transcription*. Chambéry: Université de Savoie.

(2009). Annotation and analyses of temporal aspects of spoken fluency. *CALICO Journal* 26(3), 644–661.

Hong, H. (2012). Compilation and exploration of ICCI corpus for learner language research. In Y. Tono, Y. Kawaguchi, & M. Minegishi (eds.), *Developmental and Crosslinguistic Perspectives in Learner Corpus Research*, 47–62. Amsterdam: John Benjamins.

Housen, A., Janssens, S., & Pierrard, M. (2001). The development of auditory proficiency in French and English as foreign languages in secondary schools in Flanders. *Círculo de Lingüística Aplicada a la Comunicación* 6, 46–58.

Housen, A., Kuiken, F., & Vedder, I. (2012). *Dimensions of L2 Performance and Proficiency: Complexity, Accuracy and Fluency in SLA*. New York, NY: John Benjamins.

Jarvis, S. (2000). Methodological rigor in the study of transfer: Identifying L1 influence in the interlanguage lexicon. *Language Learning* 50(2), 245–309.

Jendryczka-Wierszycka, J. (2009). Collecting spoken learner data: Challenges and benefits. In M. Mahlberg, V. González-Díaz, & C. Smith (eds.), *Proceedings of the Corpus Linguistics Conference, University of Liverpool, 20–23 July 2009*.

Kang, J. Y. (2004). Telling a coherent story in a foreign language: Analysis of Korean EFL learners' referential strategies in oral narrative discourse. *Journal of Pragmatics* 36(11), 1975–1990.

Larsen-Freeman, D. (2009). Adjusting expectations: The study of complexity, accuracy, and fluency in second language acquisition. *Applied Linguistics* 30(4), 579–589.

Lightbown, P. M. (1985). Great expectations: Second language acquisition research and classroom teaching. *Applied Linguistics* 6(2), 173–189.

Lyster, R. (2008). Evolving perspectives on learning French as a second language through immersion. In D. Ayoun (ed.), *Studies in French Applied Linguistics*, 3–36. Amsterdam: John Benjamins.

MacWhinney, B. (2000). *The CHILDES Project: Tools for Analyzing Talk. 3rd Edition*. Mahwah, NJ: Lawrence Erlbaum Associates.

(2017a). A shared platform for studying second language acquisition. *Language Learning* 67(S1), 254–275.

(2017b). *Tools for Analysing Talk Part 3: Morphosyntactic Analysis*. Mahwah, NJ: Lawrence Erlbaum.

Malvern, D., Richards, B., Chipere, N., & Durán, P. (2004). *Lexical Diversity and Language Development: Quantification and Assessment*. Basingstoke: Palgrave Macmillan.

Marsden, E. & David, A. (2008). Vocabulary use during conversation: A cross-sectional study of development from year 9 to year 13 among learners of Spanish and French. *Language Learning Journal* 36, 181–198.

Marsden, E., Mackey A., & Plonsky, L. (2016). The IRIS Repository: Advancing research practice and methodology. In A. Mackey & E. Marsden (eds.), *Advancing Methodology and Practice: The IRIS Repository of Instruments for Research into Second Languages*, 1–21. New York, NY: Routledge.

Marsden, E., Morgan-Short, K., Thompson, S., & Abugaber, D. (2018). Replication in second language research: Narrative and systematic reviews, and recommendations for the field. *Language Learning* 68(2), 321–391.

Marsden, E. J., Myles, F., & Mitchell, R. (2003). Using CHILDES tools for researching second language acquisition. In S. Sarangi & T. van Leeuwen (eds.), *Applied Linguistics and Communities of Practice*. British Studies in Applied Linguistics Vol. 18, 98–113. London: BAAL/Continuum.

Marsden, E., Thompson, S., & Plonsky, L. (2018). A methodological synthesis of self-paced reading in second language research. *Applied Psycholinguistics* 39(5), 861–904.

Meurers, D. (2015). Learner corpora and natural language processing. In S. Granger, G. Gilquin, & F. Meunier (eds.), *The Cambridge Handbook of Learner Corpus Research*, 537–566. Cambridge: Cambridge University Press.

Meurers, D. & Dickinson, M. (2017). Evidence and interpretation in language learning research: Opportunities for collaboration with computational linguistics. *Language Learning* 67(S1), 66–95.

Meyer, M. (1969). *Frog, Where Are You? A Boy, a Dog, and a Frog*. New York, NY: Dial Press.

Michel, M., Kuiken, F., & Vedder, I. (2007). The influence of complexity in monologic versus dialogic tasks in Dutch L2. *International Review of Applied Linguistics in Language Teaching* 45(3), 241–259.

Ministère de l'Éducation et de l'Enseignement supérieur. (2016). *Statistiques de l'éducation. Éducation préscolaire, enseignement primaire et secondaire*. Gouvernement du Québec.

(2017). *Programme de formation de l'école québécoise*, retrieved from www.education.gouv.qc.ca/enseignants/pfeq/ (accessed June 13, 2020).

Mitchell, R., Domínguez, L., Arche, M. J., Myles, F., & Marsden, E. (2008). SPLLOC: A new database for Spanish second language acquisition research. *EuroSLA Yearbooks* 8(1), 287–304.

Muñoz, C. (2006). *Age and the Rate of Foreign Language Learning*. Clevedon: Multilingual Matters.

Myles, F. (2002). Linguistic Development in Classroom Learners of French: A Cross-Sectional Study. Full report of research activities and results, retrieved from www.regard.ac.uk/research_findings/R000223421/report.pdf. (accessed September 9, 2017).

(2005). Review article: Interlanguage corpora and second language acquisition research. *Second Language Research* 21(4), 373–391.

(2015). Second language acquisition theory and learner corpus research. In S. Granger, G. Gilquin, & F. Meunier (eds.), *The Cambridge Handbook of Learner Corpus Research*, 309–332. Cambridge: Cambridge University Press.

Myles, F. & Mitchell, R. (n.d.). French Learner Language Oral Corpora (FLLOC). Retrieved from www.flloc.soton.ac/uk (accessed June 13, 2020).

Nicholls, D. (2003). The Cambridge Learner Corpus: Error coding and analysis for lexicography and ELT. In D. Archer, P. Rayson, A. Wilson, & T. McEnery (eds.), *Proceedings of the Corpus Linguistics 2003 Conference*, 572–581. Centre for Computer Corpus Research on Language Technical Papers, Lancaster.

Norris, J. & Ortega, L. (2009). Towards an organic approach to investigating CAF in instructed SLA: The case of complexity. *Applied Linguistics* 30(4), 555–578.

O'Donnell, M., Murcia, S., & Garcia, R. (2010). Error analysis in the TREACLE project. Paper presented at the ICAME 2010 Conference. Giessen, 26–30 May 2010.

Ortega, L. (2003). Syntactic complexity measures and their relationship to L2 proficiency: A research synthesis of college-level L2 writing. *Applied Linguistics* 24(4), 492–518.

(2009). *Understanding Language Acquisition*. London: Routledge.

Ortega, L., Iwashita, N., Norris, J. M., & Rabie, S. (2002). An investigation of elicited imitation tasks in crosslinguistic SLA research. Paper presented at the Second Language Research Forum Toronto, October 3–6, 2002.

Paquot, M. (2015). Lexicography and phraseology. In D. Biber & R. Reppen (eds.), *The Cambridge Handbook of Corpus Linguistics*, 460–477. Cambridge University Press: Cambridge.

Paquot, M. & Plonsky, L. (2017). Quantitative research methods and study quality in learner corpus research. *International Journal of Learner Corpus Research* 3(1), 61–94.

Pallotti, G. (2007). An operational definition of the emergence criterion. *Applied Linguistics* 28(3), 361–382.

(2010). Doing interlanguage analysis in school contexts. In I. Bartning, M. Martin, & I. Vedder (eds.), *Communicative Development and Linguistic Development: Intersections between SLA and Language Testing Research*, 159–190. EuroSLA.

(2015). A simple view of linguistic complexity. *Second Language Research* 31(1), 117–134.

Paradis, J. (2005). Grammatical morphology in children learning English as a second language: Implications of similarities with specific language impairment. *Language Speech, and Hearing Services in Schools* 36, 172–187.

Plonsky, L. & Oswald, F. L. (2014). How big is "big"? Interpreting effect sizes in L2 research. *Language Learning* 64(4), 878–912.

Polio, C. (2001). Research methodology in second language writing research: The case of textbased studies. In T. Silva & P. K. Matsuda (eds.), *On Second Language Writing*. Mahwah, NJ: Lawrence Erlbaum.

Robinson, P. (2005). Cognitive complexity and task sequencing: Studies in a componential framework for second language task design. *IRAL-International Review of Applied Linguistics in Language Teaching* 43(1), 1–32.

Robinson, P. & Ellis, N. (eds.) (2008). *A Handbook of Cognitive Linguistics and Second Language Acquisition*. London: Routledge.

Rule, S. & Marsden, E. (2006). The acquisition of functional categories in early French L2 grammars: The use of finite and non-finite verbs in negative contexts. *Second Language Research* 22(2), 188–218.

Schmid, M. & Hopp, H. (2014). Comparing foreign accent in L1 attrition and L2 acquisition: Range and rater effects. *Language Testing* 31(1), 367–388.

Somers, H. (2005). Learner corpora and handwriting. In V. Cook & B. Bassetti (eds.), *Second Language Writing Systems*, 147–163. Bristol: Multilingual Matters.

SPLLOC. (n.d.) Spanish Learner Language Oral Corpora, retrieved from www.splloc.soton.ac.uk (accessed June 13, 2020).

Thomas, M. (2006). Research synthesis and historiography: The case of assessment of second language proficiency In Norris, J. & Ortega, L. (eds.) *Synthesizing Research on Language Learning and Teaching*, 279–298. Amsterdam: John Benjamins.

Tono, Y. & Díez-Bedmar, M. B. (2014). Focus on learner writing at the beginning and intermediate stages: The ICCI corpus. *International Journal of Corpus Linguistics* 19(2), 163–177.

Tracy-Ventura, N. & Myles, F. (2015). The importance of task variability in the design of learner corpora for SLA research. *International Journal of Learner Corpus Research* 1(1), 58–95.

White, J. (1998). Getting the learners' attention: A typographical input enhancement study. *Focus on Form in Classroom Second Language Acquisition*, 85–113. Cambridge: Cambridge University Press.

White, J., Muñoz, C., & Collins, L. (2007). The his/her challenge: Making progress in a 'regular' L2 programme. *Language Awareness* 16(4), 278–299.

Winke P., Gass S., & Myford C. (2012). Raters' L2 background as a potential source of bias in rating oral performance. *Language Testing* 30(2), 231–252.

Appendix

Learner Corpora around the World on the Centre for English Corpus Linguistics Website

Written corpora (includes 118)		Oral corpora (includes 52)	
Type	Number	Type	Number
Essay		**Free speech**	
Essays (no further precision)	38	Discussion/conversation	9
Narrative	9	Spontaneous	3
Descriptive	11	Classroom interactions	2
Argumentative	28	**Guided speech**	
Literary	4	Interviews	18
Informative	1	Picture-based tasks	4
School Work		Role play	2
Standardised tests	4	Oral presentations	3
Exams	9	Descriptions	4
Assignments (summaries, project reports, etc.)	13	**Controlled speech**	
Recovered from class work	9	Reading	8
Other writing tasks		National tests/other tests	7
Compositions	9	Controlled speeches	1
Journals	5	Oral imitations	2
Story telling	4	Nonsense wordlists	2
Correspondence (emails, letters, chat, texting, CVs etc.)	16	**Other**	
Higher-level tasks		Narrative	7
Academic writing	8	Teacher talk/academic speech	2
Field-specific (Engineering, administration, translation etc.)	6		
Official writing (Parliament texts)	1		
Total	175	TOTAL	74

Note. Some corpora used more than one task; some did not provide any task descriptions. Terms used are taken from the task descriptions contained on the CECL website. Last updated in March 2017.

Commentary: Have Learner Corpus Research and Second Language Acquisition Finally Met?

Sylviane Granger

1 Introduction

Although learner corpus research (LCR) and second language acquisition (SLA) studies both partake of the general field of L2 studies, it must be acknowledged that they are still essentially two different worlds. The distance between the two fields was noted as early as 1999 by Hilde Hasselgård in her review of the first volume on LCR (Granger 1998): 'A question that remains unanswered is whether corpus linguistics and SLA have really met in learner corpus research. While learner language corpus research does not seem to be very controversial in relation to traditional corpus linguistics, some potential conflicts are not resolved, nor commented on by anyone from "the other side"' (Hasselgård 1999, 152). This echoed Geoffrey Leech's rather bleak observation in his preface to the volume: 'If ... we characterise the theme of this book as 'SLA meets corpus linguistics', this is not likely to be a meeting of unalloyed joy and good will. Rather, it may well be an encounter marked by some suspicion and misunderstanding' (Leech 1998, xvi).

The distance between LCR and SLA is unfortunate, as the mutual benefits of a rapprochement would be huge. Drawing on the nine studies in this volume, which rely on collaboration between LCR and SLA researchers, my aim in this commentary chapter is to highlight the areas which stand to benefit the most from a greater synergy between the two research paradigms, as well as those that hold great potential but are still waiting to be explored. After a brief overview of SLA and LCR, in which some of the key differences between the two fields are presented, I focus on three critical issues that constitute both challenges and opportunities in a combined LCR/SLA perspective, namely corpus use and design, L1 transfer and L2 development. In the last section I present some conclusions and sketch out some ideas for future collaboration.

2 Brief Overview of SLA and LCR

To understand why LCR and SLA have difficulty meeting, it is essential to review their respective research agendas, as well as the data and methods they most commonly use to achieve their objectives. Rather than present a comprehensive overview, which is well beyond the scope of this chapter, I focus on some of the features that distinguish the two fields and may stand in the way of a rapprochement.

2.1 Second Language Acquisition

The field of SLA, which concerns itself with the learning of a second language after the first, emerged in the 1970s from research on child language acquisition. Its main objective is to understand the process of L2 acquisition, rather than its product: 'The focus is firmly on identifying the nature and sources of the underlying L2 knowledge system, and on explaining developmental success and failure. Performance data are inevitably the researchers' mainstay, but understanding underlying competence, not the external verbal behavior that depends on that competence, is the ultimate goal' (Doughty & Long 2003, 4). The types of data that are most suitable for the achievement of that objective are spoken data. Myles is very clear on this point; in her view, written learner corpora are well suited for 'the investigation of the development of lexis and of discourse, or of literacy or academic writing, or to inform pedagogical grammars or learner dictionaries, but they are not the ideal window into internal learner processes' (Myles 2015, 314). As a result, 'written evidence takes a back seat compared to oral evidence in SLA research programmes' (Ortega 2012, 405).

As there are many variables that influence the process of acquisition, it is essential to control for as many of them as possible. Such a high degree of control being difficult to achieve in naturalistic settings, SLA researchers have shown a preference for elicitation and experimental data collected from a relatively small number of subjects over natural language use data. This reduced empirical basis is particularly noticeable in the case of longitudinal studies in view of the difficulty of collecting data from the same learners over time. The price to be paid is generalizability: 'It is difficult to know, with any degree of certainty, whether the results obtained are applicable only to the one or two subjects studied, or whether they are indeed characteristic of a wide range of subjects' (Gass 2013, 35). However, this is not necessarily viewed as a problem in an SLA perspective, as 'generalization is often not the goal. Rather, it is sufficient to know that a particular phenomenon has occurred' (Gass 2013, 35). The focus of SLA studies has tended to be on individual learners and the individual factors that influence L2 reception and production, such as age, motivation and aptitude. The majority of the studies describe the initial stages of learning, particularly the early acquisition of morphosyntax and phonology, 'advanced capacities' being relatively underresearched (Ortega & Byrnes 2008).

Another key feature of the SLA research paradigm is that, in keeping with Selinker's seminal (1972) article, interlanguage is viewed as a language system in its own right, with its own systematic rules. This view of interlanguage has led to Bley-Vroman's (1983) notion of comparative fallacy, which posits that comparing learner language with a target language norm is faulty as it distorts our understanding of the systematic rules that govern L2 knowledge. Although some SLA scholars have expressed a more qualified view on this issue, warnings against the comparative fallacy abound in the SLA literature (see, for example, Larsen-Freeman 2014).

2.2 Learner Corpus Research

LCR emerged twenty years later than SLA. One key fact that accounts for the main theoretical and methodological tenets of the field, but is too rarely referred to, is that LCR did not develop as a branch of SLA but as an offshoot of corpus linguistics. The idea behind the collection of the *International Corpus of Learner English* (ICLE) (Granger 1993) was to add foreign/second learner varieties to the large number of varieties of English (diachronic, stylistic, regional) that had already been collected in electronic form. The overarching aim was 'to pass on the advances made in computerized corpus linguistics to applied linguists' (Granger 1993, 65) with a view to informing SLA research and improving the learning and teaching of foreign/second languages. The focus on teaching applications was there from the very start of LCR and constitutes a key difference from the field of SLA, which, initially at least and to some extent still today, has sought to distance itself from language teaching.

LCR is clearly product-oriented. It focuses on performance rather than competence and, in keeping with the corpus linguistic principle of authenticity (Sinclair 1996), privileges the least constrained types of data emanating from (near-)natural situations where learners can use their own wording rather than being prompted to produce a specific linguistic feature. Following another key principle of corpus linguistics, it seeks to collect data in quantity (Sinclair 1995, 21) so as to achieve a high degree of generalizability. The focus on quantity has had two main consequences. First, LCR tends to focus on learner populations, often distinguished in terms of their mother tongue background (L1), rather than individual learners. Second, because of the difficulty of collecting and transcribing large amounts of spoken data, most learner corpora are corpora of L2 writing. Most case studies in LCR focus on the more advanced stages of acquisition, which are less well documented than the earlier stages. The objective is to provide a detailed picture of the features, in particular lexical, discourse and stylistic ones, that characterize these levels and inform advanced pedagogical materials.

Far from being discouraged, comparing learner corpus data with a reference native or expert corpus is one of the preferred methodologies used in LCR. Contrastive Interlanguage Analysis (CIA) (Granger 1996, 2015) is seen as a powerful means of uncovering the non-nativelike features (errors, over- and underuse) that characterize different varieties of interlanguage in comparison with a reference corpus which can, but need not, be a corpus of a native variety. It is important to note that CIA also includes a branch which does not involve any target variety but instead compares different L2 populations with each other so as to identify the features that are common to all the populations and those that are specific to one or more of them.

This brief overview shows that there are clear differences between SLA and LCR. These undeniably constitute a challenge for collaboration but, as will be shown in the following section, they are not insurmountable and can actually represent opportunities for both fields.

3 Three Critical Issues

The volume abounds in examples that illustrate the fruitful interplay of SLA and LCR. In this section I have selected three that, in my view, generate particularly promising synergies: corpus design and use, L1 transfer and L2 development.

3.1 Corpus Design and Corpus Use

Current learner corpora fall into two distinct categories. The first that were compiled and that still dominate the LCR scene today can be called *all-purpose learner corpora* in the sense that they were not collected with a particular SLA purpose in mind but as a general L2 resource. The all-purpose corpora used in this volume include the *Cambridge Learner Corpus* (CLC) (Nicholls 2003), the ICLE (Granger et al. 2009) and the *Louvain Database of Spoken English*

Interlanguage (LINDSEI) (Gilquin et al. 2010). The main advantages of these corpora are their large size and their arguably higher degree of representativeness. The following statement by Housen underlines this quantitative asset: 'computer-aided language learner corpus research provides a much needed quantificational basis' (2002, 78) for current SLA hypotheses and makes it possible to 'empirically validate previous research findings obtained from smaller transcripts, as well as to test explanatory hypotheses about pace-setting factors in second language acquisition' (2002, 108).

Size, however, comes at a cost. First, the data may not be entirely suitable for the intended purpose. Significant efforts have been made by learner corpus compilers to collect a large number of metadata so as to make clear what exactly the corpus is representative of and to ensure effective control of these variables. However, some of the variables that are key for specific SLA purposes may be missing, thereby reducing the usefulness of this type of corpus for SLA research. One solution to this problem is to compile *purpose-built learner corpora*, i.e. corpora collected with a well-defined SLA objective. This type of learner corpus holds great potential for L2 studies. It allows researchers to have much stricter control over the variables that can affect learner language. For example, in the case of the argumentative texts collected by Tracy-Ventura, Huensch and Mitchell, the topic is controlled, as are the writing conditions (3 minutes of planning time, 15 minutes of writing time; target number of words: 200). Bell, Collins and Marsden even go one step further and include a pilot stage, which makes it possible to fine-tune the variables prior to the main data collection. Another advantage of purpose-built learner corpora is that researchers can collect other data types alongside corpus data. Tracy-Ventura and colleagues avail themselves of this opportunity and collect questionnaire data about language use and reflective interview data in addition to the corpus data. L2 databases containing both learner corpus data and other data types are an ideal basis for mixed-methods approaches, as all the data are collected at the same time from the same learners. Myles (2015, 328) underscores the value of such rich L2 databases for SLA research: 'The design of this corpus – longitudinal, oral, containing a range of different tasks administered across learners and age groups and complemented by other measures as necessary (working memory scores, literacy scores) – enabled the research questions set to be investigated thoroughly.'

A second potential drawback of large corpus size is that it is difficult to reconcile a very substantial amount of data with the labour-intensive qualitative analysis needed to ensure an accurate interpretation of the data. As evidenced by several chapters in the volume, there are a number of ways of meeting this challenge. One option is to take advantage of large all-purpose learner corpora in order to extract a reduced subcorpus that is suited to answering the analyst's research questions. This option has been adopted in Ionin and Díez-Bedmar's study of article usage. The authors take advantage of two of the metadata types recorded in the CLC (proficiency level and mother tongue background) to extract a 30,000-word corpus of writing by intermediate German and Russian learners of English. The data are subsequently submitted to an entirely manual analysis of article usage. Another option is to use a larger sample from all-purpose learner corpora but reduce the amount of manual work by automating part of the analysis. Werner, Fuchs and Götz's study of tense relies on a large, c. 500,000-word corpus of German and Cantonese learner writing and speech extracted respectively from the ICLE and LINDSEI. The identification of present perfect and simple past tenses is done in two stages: first, automatic extraction from a part of speech (POS)-tagged version of the corpora, followed by manual screening and coding. Yet another option is to extract a random sample of the targeted linguistic items fully automatically from the POS-tagged version of the learner corpus. Wulff and Gries have relied on the POS-tagged version of the whole 3.7 million-word ICLE to extract 1,000 attestations of the *'s* genitive and another 1,000 of the *of* genitive.

Apart from the challenging quantitative–qualitative trade-off, there is another issue that has tended to estrange LCR from SLA, namely LCR's predilection for written data and SLA's insistence on the supremacy of spoken data. The gap between SLA and L2 writing research is so big that the *Journal of Second Language Writing* published a special issue in 2012 to explore the potential interfaces between the two fields 'whose connections have historically been minimal' (Manchón & Tardy 2012, v). There are reasons for optimism, however, as the editors add that 'closer future links can be expected on account of the growing number of publications … that have tried to build bridges to overcome the traditional separation between SLA and SLW [second language writing] preoccupations' (Manchón & Tardy 2012, v). In this connection it is interesting to note that six of the nine LCR/SLA teams in the current volume have opted to rely on written data only and that, as will be shown in the following two sections, these studies provide powerful evidence that written data can make a significant contribution to some major SLA issues. While no chapter in the volume is based exclusively on spoken data, three chapters rely on L2 corpora of both speech and writing. Such bimodal corpora allow interesting comparisons, especially when the data are collected from the same learners. This is the case in Tracy-Ventura, Huensch and Mitchell's longitudinal study of lexical diversity, which is based on data from two written and two oral tasks. The results indicate continued improvement in oral, but not written, tasks. Although this finding is intriguing and the authors can only speculate as to its causes, the study shows the potential of conjoined collections of oral and written data.

3.2 L1 Transfer

L1 transfer, i.e. the influence of learners' native language on their interlanguage competence and performance, has been the subject of numerous studies in both SLA and LCR. However, the importance they have attached to this factor over the years and the approach they have adopted to investigating it present some marked differences. Far from being an obstacle, these differences should be seen as ideal opportunities to bring together divergent but largely complementary expertise.

In SLA, the transfer pendulum has swung back and forth, shifting from a key position in the 1950s/60s (Lado 1957) to a minimal position in the 70s (Dulay & Burt 1974), before recovering its credentials in the 80s (Odlin 1989). Today, L1 transfer is generally recognized as a relevant factor in SLA. However, as pointed out by Jarvis (2000, 248), there is still a great deal of uncertainty as to the exact role it plays in L2 acquisition and development: 'it is still unsettling to witness the level of confusion that remains in the field, particularly in the form of conflicting claims made about the nature of L1 influence and its interaction with other factors'. This situation is due to the impressionistic way in which L1 transfer is established, the only criterion used being the existence of a similar form in the learner's native language. With a view to bringing more clarity to the field, Jarvis (Jarvis 2000, 252) puts forward a new definition of L1 transfer which rests on hard data rather than the researcher's intuition: 'L1 influence refers to any instance of learner data where a statistically significant correlation (or probability-based relation) is shown to exist between some features of learners' IL performance and their L1 background.' On the basis of this definition, he outlines a more rigorous methodology for establishing transfer which involves three conditions: (1) inter-L1-group heterogeneity, i.e. differences between learners of different L1s; (2) intra-L1-group homogeneity, i.e. similar behaviour across learners of the same L1; and (3) intra-L1-group congruity between learners' L1 and IL performance, i.e. similar language

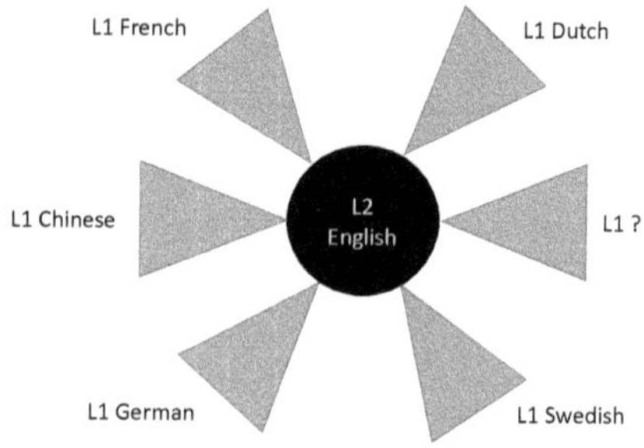

Figure 23 The International Corpus of Learner English (Granger 1993)

features in the learners' L1 and their interlanguage.[1] Jarvis's approach is highly promising, but it must be acknowledged that it has not been implemented in many SLA studies to date, and L1 effects are still often posited on a purely intuitive basis. In many studies, the L1 of the learners is not even mentioned.

In LCR, L1 effects have been at the forefront from the very start. This is clearly apparent in the way I represented the rationale behind the collection of the ICLE (see Figure 23) and the comment that accompanies it: 'Initially, material was collected from French mother tongue students only, but it soon became apparent that no definitive conclusions could be drawn on the basis of one variety of L2 English. In order to be able to distinguish those features of L2 English that were L1-dependent, i.e. the result of transfer from the mother tongue, from those which were common to all learners, irrespective of mother tongue, i.e. the crosslinguistic invariants, it was essential to enlarge the corpus and include learners from different language backgrounds' (Granger 1993, 60).

Although several other variables are recorded with each learner text, it is differentiations in terms of the learners' L1 that have mostly been focused on in LCR studies. Multi-L1 corpora such as the ICLE for English, FALKO (Lüdeling et al. 2008) for German or ASK (Tenfjord et al. 2006) for L2 Norwegian are ideal resources for establishing whether a particular feature is specific to a given L1 population or shared by many of them. They provide the necessary data to meet two of the conditions for establishing transfer, namely inter-L1-group heterogeneity and intra-L1-group homogeneity. Complementing the learner corpus with a reference corpus of the

[1] As "the three-effect requirement" is "unrealistic in many cases", Jarvis (ibid: 255) notes that the presence of two effects "may be regarded as a convincing case for L1 influence".

learners' L1 (such as the *British National Corpus* for English) allows us to meet the third condition: linguistic congruence between the learners' L1 and the L2 data. The LCR literature abounds in studies of transfer based on a comparison of two or more corpora distinguished on the basis of the L1 of the learners. Although they rarely provide a full implementation of Jarvis's model, transfer-related studies in LCR demonstrate the power of the corpus-based contrastive method to highlight L1-specific effects.

The three chapters in the volume that focus explicitly on L1 transfer demonstrate the mutual benefit to be gained from a combined SLA/LCR approach. Ionin and Díez-Bedmar investigate the article usage of learners whose native language employs articles (Spanish) as compared to learners whose native language lacks articles (Russian). The study illustrates a triangulation method that is still too seldom seen today: that of replicating a previous SLA study based on experimental data using learner corpus data (Gilquin & Gries 2009). As each text from the CLC used for the study is associated with its Common European Framework of Reference for Languages (CEFR) level, the authors are also able to examine and compare English article use by Spanish and Russian learners at two proficiency levels (B1 and B2, i.e. lower and higher intermediate). Werner, Fuchs and Götz investigate alternation between the present perfect and the simple past in L2 English learners whose native language displays this alternation (German) and another learner population whose native language lacks this alternation, with a view to teasing out L1 influence from universal mechanisms. Relying on Jarvis's (2000) model for transfer research, the study uses a multifactorial regression-based approach to explore the respective deviations of each of the two L1 populations from native usage. Interestingly, one of the factors that featured prominently in previous studies within the Aspect Hypothesis – *Aktionsart* – did not prove to be a significant variable in the learner-corpus-based study. The authors suggest that the difference might be due to the fact that the data they used represented a higher level of proficiency than that commonly targeted in SLA studies, an observation that one would do well to bear in mind in future comparisons of SLA and LCR results. The third study, by Meriläinen, aims to show how large L1-specific learner corpora can help us to better understand the interaction between universal processes and crosslinguistic influence. It focuses more particularly on the universals of simplification and overgeneralization through the lens of embedded inversion and the omission of prepositions respectively. Overall the study brings out L1 transfer as a more significant factor than universal tendencies. However, as recognized by the author herself, this result should be seen as tentative, among other things because the features examined turned out to be too infrequent to allow elaborate statistical analysis. This shows that an apparently large learner corpus may still be too small for the investigation of some linguistic features.

3.3 L2 Development

The majority of LCR studies do not investigate L2 development, a failure which has often been pointed out by SLA researchers. Myles (2005, 380), for example, deplores the fact that 'the developmental dimension is almost totally lacking' in most LCR studies. The preferred corpus design in LCR is cross-sectional, i.e. the corpus consists of L2 data gathered from different categories of learner at a single point in time. Admittedly, each study of this type enables us to see 'a slice of development' which can be used 'to piece together actual development' (Gass 2013, 36), but the corpus is nonetheless essentially static. By contrast, the focus of SLA 'is firmly on identifying the nature and sources of the underlying L2 knowledge system, and on *explaining developmental success and failure*' [my emphasis] (Doughty & Long 2003, 4). The preferred type of corpus is therefore longitudinal, i.e. consists of data collected from the same learners over a given period of time. These corpora are very difficult to collect, in particular because it is difficult to have access to the same learners for a prolonged period of time. Fortunately, the two approaches can be combined: '[O]ne can use a cross-sectional design to create a pseudolongitudinal study. In such a study, the emphasis, like that of a longitudinal study, is on language change (i.e. acquisition), with data being collected at a single point in time, but with different proficiency levels represented' (Gass & Selinker 2001, 32–33).

The three corpus designs – cross-sectional, longitudinal and pseudolongitudinal – are represented in the volume, and they all prove to be very useful for answering key SLA questions. Cross-sectional studies have often been criticized for adopting a group perspective which fails to take individual variation into account. However, if corpora are investigated not as one long text, but as a series of individual texts, this criticism is no longer valid. Wulff and Gries's study shows that, with the right statistical method, it is possible to explore individual variation in the use of the genitive alternation.

Probably thanks to the close research collaboration between SLA and LCR researchers that constitutes the hallmark of the volume, the number of developmental studies – both longitudinal and pseudolongitudinal – outnumbers the number of cross-sectional studies. The volume highlights the range of formats that longitudinal studies can take. Tracy-Ventura, Huensch and Mitchell's study spans five years and involves only three data points. By contrast, Verspoor, Lowie and Wieling's study spans only 23 weeks but involves a dense collection with that same number of data points. The two formats are perfectly in keeping with the research questions guiding the respective studies: - long-term lexical development in the former, and individual variation in syntactic and lexical development in a Dynamic Systems Theory perspective in the latter.

Also very much in evidence in the volume is the value of pseudo-longitudinal studies. They are an ideal method for identifying the linguistic features that characterize different stages of interlanguage, such as article usage at lower and higher intermediate levels in Ionin and Díez-Bedmar's study. Not only do these studies provide highly valuable descriptions for theoretical L2 research, they also have great potential for teaching, notably with regard to tailoring instructional materials to specific proficiency levels. This pedagogical value is highlighted by Bell, Collins and Marsden in connection with grammar instruction: 'syllabi need to be informed by empirical evidence of how L2 learning unfolds in instructed learning settings, evidence that could inform teachers in their decisions of what grammar to teach and when'.

One issue that remains very much open is whether longitudinal and pseudolongitudinal studies generate the same results. According to Gass (2013, 37), one can assume that this will be the case, but she cautiously adds that '[t]he extent to which this assumption is warranted is controversial'. The results of Paquot, Naets and Gries's study of verb + object structures disconfirm the similarity assumption: time does not have any effect on the collocational strength of the structures unless the proficiency level of the learners increases from one data collection point to the next. In other words, the longitudinal analysis does not display any change while the pseudolongitudinal analysis does. The similarity was also disconfirmed in a previous study of collgrams by Bestgen and Granger (2014), which also found discrepancies between the two developmental perspectives. These two studies, as well as Polio and Yoon's study in this volume, which builds on Bestgen and Granger's study, focus on a dimension of learner proficiency that has so far been underresearched in SLA, namely phraseological competence, defined as the mastery of multiword expressions, i.e. formulaic language in the broad sense. Corpora lend themselves particularly well to the investigation of syntagmatic aspects of language (collocations, colligations, lexical bundles, etc.), which can be extracted automatically thanks to a range of software tools. These multiword units can be used to design new phraseological measures involving different types of multiword units. These new measures, which straddle lexis and grammar, are fully in line with usage-based theories of SLA (Ellis & Wulff 2015) and, as shown by Polio and Yoon, are a useful complement to the traditional lexical and grammatical indices.

4 Conclusion

Have LCR and SLA finally met? The answer to this question is a resounding 'yes' . . . in this volume! In the reality of L2 studies, however, the convergence has not yet been achieved. The collaborative research conducted by the LCR/SLA tandems in this volume does not reflect the reality of today's L2 landscape. However, it provides a very rich roadmap for future L2 studies combining the two perspectives.

It is important to bear in mind, however, that 'to meet' does not mean 'to merge'. The two fields have their own research agendas and there is no reason why this should change. However, they clearly have a lot to learn from each other. SLA provides the theoretical foundation that is often rightly found lacking in LCR studies, tending to result in weak or misguided interpretation of the results, if not lack of interpretation altogether. LCR, on the other hand, offers detailed descriptions of interlanguage from a wide range of L1 populations at different proficiency levels, and the software tools and methods to extract and analyse the data. LCR studies are regularly criticized for being 'merely descriptive'. While it is admittedly desirable to go beyond description, it is equally – if not more – crucial to get the L2 facts right, and here LCR has a lot to contribute. I am convinced that the field of L2 studies would benefit greatly if SLA researchers were more familiar with the research carried out in LCR, and vice versa, resulting in more cross-referencing of each other's work in their respective publications. This view echoes Leech's (1998, xx) comment on the early 1998 learner corpus volume, which he considered to be an encouragement for 'the two research communities of corpus linguistics and SLA/ELT studies to look at one another's work, in a world where divergent, rather than convergent, trends in research thinking are all too common'.

The L2 field needs a wide range of learner corpora. The perfect learner corpus does not exist and will never exist, as no single corpus can answer all the research questions that L2 researchers aim to answer. To take but one example, for some studies it is essential to control for topic, as topic may have a determining influence on the results, as shown by Paquot, Naets and Gries's study. For other studies, for example those aimed at assessing learners' general lexical and syntactic repertoire, it is better to have a wide range of topics.

Smaller purpose-built learner corpora will probably continue to be preferred by SLA researchers, but they could benefit from also using larger all-purpose corpora as a kind of reference corpus, for example to check whether the forms and structures they investigate are specific to their data or used more generally by learners with the same L1 or proficiency level. In fact, the current volume is an invitation to rethink learner corpus collection for both LCR and SLA. One potentially very fruitful avenue for future collaborative research is the compilation of a large L2 database, whose design would benefit from insights from the two research communities. This database would contain not only written and spoken learner corpus data representing a range of carefully designed tasks, but also other data types (elicitation data, questionnaire data, aptitude tests, placement tests, etc.) collected from the same learners at the time of collection. There are many other issues – theoretical, methodological and applied – that would greatly benefit from a cross-perspective approach, and many challenges yet to be overcome. It is my hope that the collaborative endeavours at the basis of this volume will be followed by many others in the future, to the mutual benefit of the two fields.

References

Bestgen, Y. & Granger, S. (2014). Quantifying the development of phraseological competence in L2 English writing. *Journal of Second Language Writing* 26, 28–41.

Bley-Vroman, R. (1983). The comparative fallacy in interlanguage studies: The case of systematicity. *Language Learning* 33(1), 1–17.

Doughty, C. J. & Long, M. H. (2003). The scope of inquiry and goals of SLA. In C. J. Doughty & M. H. Long (eds.), *The Handbook of Second Language Acquisition*, 3–16. Malden: Blackwell.

Dulay, H. C. & Burt, M. K. (1974). Natural sequences in child second language acquisition. *Language Learning* 24(1), 37–53.

Ellis, N. & Wulff, S. (2015). Usage-based approaches to SLA. In B. VanPatten & J. Williams (eds.), *Theories in Second Language Acquisition: An Introduction*, 75–93. Mahwah, NJ: Erlbaum.

Gass, S. (2013). *Second Language Acquisition. An Introductory Course (with J. Behney & L. Plonsky)*. New York, NY & London: Routledge.

Gass, S. & Selinker, L. (2001). *Second Language Acquisition: An Introductory Course (Second Edition)*. Mahwah, NJ: Lawrence Erlbaum Associates.

Gilquin, G., De Cock, S., & Granger, S. (2010). *Louvain International Database of Spoken English Interlanguage*. Handbook and CD-ROM. Louvain-la-Neuve: Presses universitaires de Louvain.

Gilquin, G. & Gries, S. (2009). Corpora and experimental methods: A state-of-the-art review. In G. Gilquin (ed.), *Corpora and Experimental Methods. Special Issue of Corpus Linguistics and Linguistic Theory* 5(1), 1–26.

Granger, S. (1993). The International Corpus of Learner English. In J. Aarts, P. de Haan, & N. Oostdijk (eds.), *English Language Corpora: Design, Analysis and Exploitation*, 57–69. Amsterdam & Atlanta, GA: Rodopi.

(1996). From CA to CIA and back: An integrated contrastive approach to computerized bilingual and learner corpora. In K. Aijmer, B. Altenberg, & M. Johansson (eds.), *Languages in Contrast: Text-Based Cross-Linguistic Studies*, 37–51. Lund: Lund University Press.

Granger, S. (ed.) (1998). *Learner English on Computer*. London & New York, NY: Addison Wesley Longman.

(2015). Contrastive interlanguage analysis: A reappraisal. *International Journal of Learner Corpus Research* 1(1), 7–24.

Granger, S., Dagneaux, E., Meunier, F., & Paquot, M. (2009). *The International Corpus of Learner English, Version 2*. Handbook and CD-ROM. Louvain-la-Neuve: Presses universitaires de Louvain.

Hasselgård, H. (1999). Review of Granger (ed.) *Learner English on Computer. ICAME Journal* 23, 148–152.

Housen, A. (2002). A corpus-based study of the L2-acquisition of the English verb system. In S. Granger, J. Hung, & S. Petch-Tyson (eds.), *Computer Learner Corpora, Second Language Acquisition and Foreign Language Teaching*, 77–116. Amsterdam & Philadelphia, PA: John Benjamins.

Jarvis, S. (2000). Methodological rigor in the study of transfer: Identifying L1 influence in the interlanguage lexicon. *Language Learning* 50(2), 245–309.

Lado, R. (1957). *Linguistics across Cultures*. Ann Arbor, MI: University of Michigan Press.

Larsen-Freeman, D. (2014). Another step to be taken: Rethinking the end point of the interlanguage continuum. In Z. Han & E. Tarone (eds.), *Interlanguage: Forty Years Later*, 203–220. Amsterdam & Philadelphia, PA: Benjamins.

Leech, G. (1998). Preface: Learner corpora: What they are and what can be done with them. In S. Granger (ed.), *Learner English on Computer*, xiv–xx. London & New York, NY: Addison Wesley Longman.

Lüdeling, A., Doolittle, S., Hirschmann, H., Schmidt, K., & Walter, M. (2008). Das Lernerkorpus Falko. *Deutsch als Fremdsprache* 2, 67–73.

Manchón, R.M. & Tardy, C. (2012). Preface: Exploring L2 writing–SLA interfaces. *Journal of Second Language Writing* 21(4), v.

Myles, F. (2005). Review article: Interlanguage corpora and second language acquisition research. *Second Language Research* 21(4), 373–391.

(2015). Second language acquisition theory and learner corpus research. In S. Granger, G. Gilquin, & F. Meunier (eds.) *The Cambridge Handbook of Learner Corpus Research*, 309–332. Cambridge: Cambridge University Press.

Nicholls, D. (2003). The Cambridge learner corpus: Error coding and analysis for lexicography and ELT. In D. Archer, P. Rayson, A. Wilson, & T. McEnery (eds.), *Proceedings of the 2003 Corpus Linguistics Conference*, 572–581. Centre for Computer Corpus Research on Language Technical Papers, University of Lancaster.

Odlin, T. (1989). *Language Transfer: Cross-Linguistic Influence in Language Learning*. Cambridge: Cambridge University Press.

Ortega, L. (2012). Epilogue: Exploring L2 writing–SLA interfaces. *Journal of Second Language Writing* 21(4), 404–415.

Ortega, L. & Byrnes, H. (2008). *The Longitudinal Study of Advanced L2 Capacities*. New York, NY & London: Routledge.

Selinker, L. (1972). Interlanguage. *IRAL – International Review of Applied Linguistics in Language Teaching* 10(1–4), 209–232.

Sinclair, J. (1995). Corpus typology: A framework for classification. In G. Melchers & B. Warren (eds.), *Studies in Anglistics*, 17–33. Stockholm: Almqvist & Wiksell International.

(1996). EAGLES: Preliminary recommendations on corpus typology, retrieved from www.ilc.cnr.it/EAGLES/corpustyp/corpustyp.html (accessed June 13, 2020).

Tenfjord, K., Meurer, P., & Hofland, K. (2006). The ASK corpus: A language learner corpus of Norwegian as a second language. In *Proceedings of the 5th Edition of the International Conference on Language Resources and Evaluation (LREC 2006), Genoa (Italy), 22–28 May 2006*, 1821–1824. Retrieved from www.lrec-conf.org/proceedings/lrec2006/ (accessed June 13, 2020).

Commentary: An SLA Perspective on Learner Corpus Research

Florence Myles

1 Introduction

There have been repeated calls over the years for greater interaction between Second Language Acquisition (SLA) research and Learner Corpus Research (LCR), including by myself and the editors of this volume, as well as many others (e.g. Granger et al. 2015; Lozano & Díaz-Negrillo 2019; Lozano & Mendikoetxea 2010; McEnery et al. 2019). In a range of publications (Myles 2005, 2007, 2008, 2015; Myles & Mitchell 2004), I have outlined, from an SLA perspective, what I perceive to be the gaps to be bridged in order for the two fields to be engaged in useful collaboration. My task with this commentary is to assess how far these gaps have narrowed, on the basis of the chapters in this volume.

In a first part, I will briefly summarise what the data needs of SLA theorists are in order for them to investigate current research agendas and test competing hypotheses. The second part will comment on how far the chapters included in this volume have answered the calls for, on the one hand, LCR studies to be informed by SLA theoretical and empirical understandings, in both corpus design and analysis/interpretation, and on the other hand, SLA researchers to make more extensive use of learner corpora and the methodologies associated with them in their work, in order to make their findings more generalisable.

2 SLA and Learner Corpus Research

Historically, and oversimplifying somewhat, SLA researchers have been critical of LCR for producing primarily descriptive studies which extract patterns from large sets of data, and interpreting those patterns without necessarily making use of appropriate theoretical tools (Barlow 2005; Brezina & Bottini 2019; McEnery et al. 2019; Myles

2015). Consequently, conclusions drawn have not always been based on adequate data evidence. For example, studies sometimes concluded that the L1 is at the root of a given pattern when in fact learners from other L1s not sharing this pattern also produce it. Additionally, the corpora available were often criticised for not being suitable for answering many of the questions generated by SLA theory, for example by focusing on just one proficiency level and drawing conclusions about development. On the other hand, LC researchers often criticised their SLA counterparts for basing their conclusions on too few subjects, leading to problems of non-generalisability, or on non-authentic and/or experimental data, failing to reflect what learners actually do when using the L2 in less controlled contexts. Another criticism, which can be addressed to both fields, is that assumptions were often made about what native speakers would actually produce in similar contexts, not necessarily based on sound empirical evidence. Both fields have moved on substantially since these early criticisms, but it remains to be seen how far the gap has narrowed. The following will briefly review the needs of SLA theory, depending on theoretical persuasion, and in terms of metadata, corpus design, and data interpretation.

2.1 Theoretical Underpinnings

The purpose of SLA research is to understand language development in second (or third, fourth etc.) language learners: what knowledge they possess and how they acquired that knowledge. There are a wide range of different theoretical approaches which help to investigate and understand the various aspects of this multifaceted phenomenon (see e.g. Mitchell et al. 2019; VanPatten & Williams 2015) for reviews. Some theories are focused on one aspect of development (e.g. generative SLA or usage-based theories on the linguistic system; sociolinguistic approaches on the development of sociolinguistic variants or the [re]construction of identity), some adopt a broader view of language learning, incorporating its transdisciplinary dimensions, such as for example the Douglas Fir framework (Douglas Fir Group 2016) or the Dynamic Systems Theory (Larsen-Freeman 2017).

Different theories and research agendas have different data needs. To track development, nearly all theories will need data from learners at different stages of development or, even better, longitudinal data which charts the development of individual learners over time. The type of data needed will vary depending on the theory. For example, a study of cross-linguistic influence in the acquisition of a specific linguistic structure in a given L2 will minimally require: data from learners from a range of L1s (to ensure any pattern attributed to the L1 of learners is not developmental in nature, and thus shared by other learners from different linguistic backgrounds); an equivalent native corpus (to compare L2 use with that of native speakers, ideally performing the same communicative task/activity); data encompassing all the different forms and contexts in which this particular structure is used (to ensure learners are not e.g. over/under-generalising a form to inappropriate contexts). To investigate development within Dynamic Systems Theory (DST), which views L2 learning as non-linear and dynamic, datasets need to be dense and longitudinal, with many data collection points enabling to chart the complexity of the dynamic and changeable interactive forces at play over time (Lowie 2017). Research agendas focusing on ultimate attainment, i.e. the endstate of learning after many years of L2 daily use, will require cross-sectional datasets of L2 users containing language properties known to be particularly difficult to acquire, for example very subtle morphosyntactic rules (Dekydtspotter 2001; Hawkins 2008; Hyltenstam & Abrahamsson 2003), or idiomatic use of conventionalised expressions (Erman et al. 2015; Forsberg 2010). Socio-cultural theorists require rich and dense data enabling them to see development happening in real time, through the tracking of microgenetic episodes for example (Gánem Gutiérrez 2008; Gánem Gutiérrez & Gilmore 2018; Lantolf 2011). The list could go on; suffice it to say that the data needs of different SLA theories can be very different, depending on what hypotheses need to be tested.

However, these theoretical requirements have important implications both for corpus design and for the interpretation of results arising from the analysis of corpora.

2.2 Corpus Design, Exploitation and Documentation

The importance of **sound metadata** cannot be over-emphasised.

Detailed information about how the data was elicited and the tasks used is crucial. Much research has shown that different tasks can give rise to markedly different performances (Jarvis 2000; Tavakoli & Foster 2011; Tracy-Ventura & Myles 2015). For example, the amount of planning involved, the cognitive demands of the activity undertaken, whether the task involves oral or written production, all have an impact on the language produced. Additionally, learners tend to avoid producing language they are not sure of, especially when being assessed, and this can give a false impression of what they actually know.

The language background of participants needs to be comprehensively documented. What are their L1s? Do they know other languages apart from the L2 being investigated? What is their proficiency in the L2 and any other language they speak? Any investigation claiming a particular phenomenon is due to influence from the L1 needs to ensure clear information is given about other languages spoken by the participants, including other L1s (Jarvis 2000; Jarvis & Pavlenko 2008). A corpus investigation of e.g. exam scripts from a given country cannot assume that all participants will share the country's official language as L1, in our increasingly global world.

Clear information also needs to be given about transcription conventions and any annotation used, including any principled decisions taken about how to transcribe and annotate the corpus (e.g. orthographic decisions in the case of an oral corpus); handling of errors; of neologisms etc. (Bell et al. in this volume; Myles 2007). The software used for interrogating the corpus needs to be specified, including what assumptions underpin it, for example which descriptive linguistic framework is used for part of speech tagging, how sentences/clauses are defined, whether the analysis is carried out on whole words or morphemes etc.

Within the context of recent calls for open science and replicability (Marsden et al. 2018; Marsden & Plonsky 2018), sufficient information should be given to enable the creation of comparable corpora, with the modification of some specified variables enabling to tease apart the role of different factors such as e.g. proficiency, the role of the L1/L2 pair or the role of the task undertaken.

In terms of corpus design, the tasks used need to be appropriate to the theoretical framework underpinning the study. For example, if investigating the development of a specific linguistic structure, are all relevant contrasts elicited in sufficient numbers? If cross-linguistic influence is investigated, have suitable L1s and L2s been chosen to enable sound interpretations to be reached? The elicitation methods used to gather the data need to be suitable given the framework chosen, e.g. providing dense and rich longitudinal data for DST agendas or sufficient tokens of rare linguistic structures or contrasts in a generative framework. Ideally, a range of elicitation tasks should be used to enable triangulation, and to ensure that productions are not an artefact of the task and actually provide a suitable window into learners' knowledge. Relatively unplanned productions should be included, if possible oral, to avoid over-reliance on conscious monitoring of productions (for more details, see e.g. Myles 2015).

As far as the analyses carried out on the corpora and their interpretation are concerned, it is important too to bear in mind the points outlined above. For sound conclusions to be reached about the SLA process, the interpretation and discussion of the results need to be clear about the theoretical assumptions framing the study and about the predictions conflicting hypotheses might make. If the study is descriptive or exploratory in nature, its conclusions need to be careful in their evaluation of which theoretical framework best explains the results, if any, as often competing frameworks can successfully account for the same set of data, giving different explanations. The study might then point to further research which would be designed explicitly to test different hypotheses. Finally, as called for by many researchers, increasingly sophisticated tools for interrogating corpora, as well as statistical analyses and modelling, are currently available, and have opened new avenues for the full exploitation of large corpora, enabling powerful analyses to be carried out (Gries 2016, 2018; Gries & Deshors 2014; Norouzian et al. 2018; Paquot & Plonsky 2017).

In the remainder of this paper, I will provide a commentary of the current volume from an SLA perspective. How far have the studies reported taken on board the various pleas for LCR to be fully informed by current SLA theoretical and empirical needs, in terms of the criteria outlined above? I will also pay attention to the gaps between the two fields I identified four years ago (Myles 2015), to assess how far they have been filled, bearing in mind of course that nine chapters might not be representative of the field of LCR as a whole. These gaps included the relative lack of oral corpora and of longitudinal corpora; the limited range of genres and tasks used to elicit data, to enable triangulation of findings; the limited range of L1s and L2s investigated, with the vast majority of studies focusing on English L2, and with very few non-Indo-European languages included; the lack of native controls; and the overwhelming focus on advanced learners (or at least upper-intermediate – with much of learning taking place e.g. in secondary schools remaining largely undocumented).

Finally, how far have the papers succeeded in making best use of both sound SLA frameworks and powerful corpus analytical methodologies? Are the authors of the papers engaging with the research literature in the other field?

3 Commentary

3.1 Theoretical Underpinnings

Most chapters in the present volume specify their theoretical stance. Some originate clearly from SLA theory, others take as their starting point LCR paradigms, and some situate themselves at the interface between the two fields. For example, in the spirit of the volume, Ionin and Díez Bedmar set out specifically to approach the study of articles, common in both SLA and LCR research, by reviewing what both fields have found, before setting up their own learner corpus study to test the predictions of a specific semantic framework. At the root of their work is an SLA-driven agenda, and they use an already available corpus (collected for other purposes – the *Cambridge Learner Corpus*) in order to investigate a theoretical issue.

Werner, Fuchs and Götz also adopt a principled SLA-driven approach in their investigation of the role of transfer in the acquisition of temporal expressions in the L2 English of German and Cantonese speakers. The study is embedded within the extensive SLA literature on the role of transfer, broadly framed within a cognitive linguistic framework, and the role of universal principles and factors in the acquisition of this particular property. In order to test these well-known SLA questions, the authors interrogate large corpora of both written and spoken advanced learner data, and make use of sophisticated tools, both analytically and statistically. This study is a very good example of making use of available corpora to investigate research questions in a theoretically informed way while using highly sophisticated corpus and statistical analyses. It demonstrates how marrying sound SLA theoretical understandings and advanced LCR methodologies uncovers findings not available through other means, in this case by investigating in which specific linguistic environments advanced German and Chinese learners of English differ in tense use from each other and from native speakers.

Meriläinen also states an SLA theoretical allegiance, in this case to the model of cross-linguistic influence (CLI) espoused by Jarvis and colleagues (e.g. Jarvis 2000; Jarvis & Pavlenko 2008), in order to investigate the role of universals and CLI in the production of inversion in indirect interrogatives and in the omission of prepositions in Finnish, German and Swedish L2 learners of English at intermediate and advanced levels (ICLE corpus; MEC corpus). The theoretical framing remains rather vague, however. For example, the literature review claims that the interplay between universals and CLI has received little attention in SLA research until recently, when in fact a huge body of generative SLA research has been investigating it for a number of decades, in the context of Universal Grammar, parameter resetting or feature reassembly, for example (Ayoun 2003; Flynn 1996; Hawkins 2001, 2019; Herschensohn & Arteaga 2016; Hulk 1991; Liceras 2009; White 1989, 2009). Similarly, the rationale for the choice of the two structures investigated as well as for the choice of L1s could have been more clearly justified, on the basis of a detailed linguistic analysis of these structures in the languages in question.

Allusion is made to the fact that the chosen L1s have contrastive properties, but the analysis presented does not go beyond superficial observations, nor does it suggest what predictions might be made on the basis of these contrasts. Consequently, although an SLA theoretical framework is presented, it is not sufficiently fully articulated to enable sound conclusions to be reached about the interplay between transfer and universals.

Polio and Yoon take as a starting point the premise in the usage-based SLA framework that learners learn patterns and extract regularities from those patterns, in order to test the idea that comparing collocational usage in an L2 vs. a similar native corpus will allow linguistic accuracy to be measured automatically. By identifying bigrams or trigrams in learner productions which are not found in native productions and testing to what extent they are indicators of errors, and then correlating this measure with more traditional methods used to assess linguistic accuracy (on the basis of complexity, accuracy and lexical measures), they make excellent use of the sophisticated methodologies enabled by LCR techniques. Their purpose is not to contribute to SLA theory, but is more practical; their aim is to assist with a vexing issue facing teachers and testers, namely how to easily/automatically evaluate learners' performance. This method for measuring linguistic accuracy can be argued to be more valid and more principled than more traditional methods, as it relies on a probabilistic view of learning and accuracy based on large amounts of data, rather than the notoriously problematic and labour-intensive coding of errors (each error has to be coded; there are a range of possible linguistic analyses; issues of inter-coder reliability often arise).

The study by Paquot, Naets and Gries is an interesting example of LC researchers making the most of the advanced tools available for computing the frequency of statistical collocations. Their starting point is a typically LCR approach; however, they go beyond previous research which tends to treat all co-occurrences in the same way, whatever their syntactic pattern, when in fact verb + direct object structures have been found to be particularly problematic for learners of English as a Foreign Language, even at advanced levels. The aim of their study is therefore to investigate whether you can determine complexity in learner productions through measures of phraseological use (Paquot 2019, 124). The methods used are highly sophisticated, both for data handling and for analysis of a very large corpus, and enable the authors to conclude that phraseological complexity is indeed a good measure of language proficiency at advanced levels (upper-intermediate to very advanced).

Tracy-Ventura, Huensch and Mitchell's agenda is SLA-based. They are investigating the development and attrition of the lexical system in L2 learners before, during and after a Study Abroad stay, and again three years after graduating. Their study tests two theoretical frameworks of attrition (Herdina & Jessner's 2002 Dynamic Model of Multilingualism and Paradis' 2004 Activation Threshold Hypothesis), which place different emphasis on the role of exposure/use post instruction. Their SLA-driven agenda requires a longitudinal corpus gathered over four years, in order to be able to track L2 development, long-term retention and attrition, and to investigate what impacts on this development and/or attrition. The richness of their corpus, containing data from a range of tasks as well as other measures such as proficiency and L2 use at all four data collection points, enables the researchers to investigate the contribution of input and interaction to L2 development and attrition. Their contribution provides an interesting illustration of the type of corpora necessary to address specific research agendas, which could not be investigated with an 'off-the-peg' learner corpus.

Like Paquot et al., Verspoor, Lowie and Wieling attempt to find an accurate measure of development but start from an SLA rather than LCR theoretical framework, Complex Dynamic Systems Theory (CDST). This requires the use of dense longitudinal data, as in this view L2 development is construed as non-linear and dynamic, as well as highly individual, and therefore requires careful tracking over time. These contrasting theoretical approaches have important implications for the type of data required. Whereas the LCR approach of Paquot et al. necessitated a large corpus in order to run sophisticated computerised analyses measuring development (237 students; 208,000 words; data collected once a year for three years), Verspoor et al.'s CDST study had a much smaller corpus (22 learners; 36,860 words; collected weekly for 23 weeks). The focus here is on documenting change as it happens, for each individual learner, in keeping with the CDST framework. Their study shows that no two learners follow the same patterns, although there are trends across the group.

The focus of Wulff and Gries's paper is in showing how sophisticated statistical analyses including more than one predictor variable and more distributional variables can assist with the description of both native and non-native data, in this case the production of the two alternative genitive constructions *'s* and *of*. This type of approach enables sophisticated bottom-up analyses of language use based on large datasets and powerful analytical tools, allowing the comparison of native and non-native productions. The highly complex model presented in the paper, taking into account many variables which underpin native speaker choice (syntactic, phonological and semantic factors, as well as the length of the noun phrase), is able to predict with some certainty what a native speaker would produce in each context and compare it to learner choice. Interestingly, the study points out that global measures applied to the data showed non-native speaker and native speaker performing exactly the same, and it is only through a very detailed analysis that the different groups are shown to arrive at the same global measures via quite different routes.

The contribution by Bell, Collins and Marsden does not adopt a specific theoretical framework, as it is a primarily methodological paper which reiterates how important the design of any corpus is if it is going to be of any use to SLA researchers. The next section will review some of the issues they raise.

In conclusion, I think we can safely claim that, from a theoretical point of view, progress has been made. Most of the chapters in this volume have clear agendas framed within suitable theories/paradigms. These theoretical orientations of course reflect the field they belong to, with marked differences in the types of data required to address their respective agendas. The next section will discuss how far the corpora used in the various studies described in this volume have answered calls for improving corpus design and for making use of the increasingly sophisticated tools available to exploit them.

3.2 Corpus Design, Exploitation and Documentation

One early criticism of learner corpora was that the **documentation** accompanying them, describing participants, tasks, language background etc., was not always adequate. From the evidence provided in this volume, calls for fuller descriptions of corpora have been heard, and the metadata accompanying each corpus is considerably more detailed in most cases than in the early days of LCR. However, its quality still remains inconsistent (or inconsistently reported). For example, whereas the corpora originating from the Centre for English Corpus Linguistics at UCLouvain (ICLE; LINDSEI; LOCNESS; LONGDALE – Werner et al.; Meriläinen; Wulff & Gries; Paquot et al.) are now all well documented, providing information about e.g. participants' age, sex, L1 and languages spoken at home, other languages studied and language of instruction, the metadata of other large corpora is less rich. For example, the very large *Cambridge Learner Corpus* provides a profile of each candidate (sitting Cambridge English examinations) including the first language, age, sex, education history and years of English study, but it does not indicate other languages known by the participants, which can be crucial when investigating e.g. CLI. Other studies do not report on the metadata included in the corpora they use, for example Polio and Yoon, Meriläinen (for the MEC corpus), Ionin and Díez Bedmar, and Verspoor et al., who give scant details about the participants in their study. At the other end of the spectrum, some studies (e.g. Tracy-Ventura et al.) have very rich information about their participants, including, as well as detailed biographical information, a Language Engagement Questionnaire specifying their current language use in each of the languages they speak.

The **size of the corpora** used varies hugely, which is not surprising given the variety of research agendas. For example, the language feature investigated and how frequent it is will largely determine how large the corpus needs to be in order to contain a sufficient number of tokens. In the case of articles, the corpus does not need to be extensive as they are so frequent in any dataset, and Ionin and Díez Bedmar's selection from the *Cambridge Learner Corpus* only included 31,156 words across four different groups (two different L1s and two proficiencies). Size is also dependent on what annotation or coding is required by the research agenda, and whether it can be carried out automatically or not. In their case, detailed manual annotation precluded a very large size. This was also true in the case of Wulff and Gries, whose study is based on fewer than 3,000 tokens of the genitive alternation across three corpora but involved very detailed manual coding, enabling sophisticated analysis. Large corpora are used by Werner et al. (477,900 words) in their investigation of tense, by Tracy-Ventura et al. (678,208 words) for their study of lexical diversity, and by Paquot et al. in their study of phraseology (approx. 208,500 words). By contrast, Verspoor et al. use a relatively small longitudinal corpus of 36,860 words: 22 learners producing very short texts (95 words on average) once a week over 23 weeks, i.e. an average of 1,675 words per learner over the course of the project. They argue that only frequent repeated measures over the course of time can truly capture development; however, the extremely limited amount of data available per learner per data point makes it difficult to see how such very short texts on different topics can be usefully compared week by week, as different topics will elicit different linguistic features and levels of complexity (Paquot et al. this volume; Bell et al. this volume). The size of the corpus in the Polio and Yoon study is unspecified (139 essays; no mention of length).

Another plea from SLA researchers followed the large body of evidence showing that **different tasks**, e.g. involving different amounts of planning, and whether learner productions are **oral or written**, can make a big difference to the results obtained, and that therefore corpora should ideally incorporate a range of communicative activities and production modes. The plea for more oral production data, which is thought to be a better reflection of the underlying linguistic system as it precludes extensive conscious monitoring, shows some evidence of having been heard. Three out of the nine studies make use of both oral and written data (Werner et al.; Tracy-Ventura et al.; Bell et al.), enabling them to triangulate their findings and thus making them more reliable and generalisable. For instance, Tracy-Ventura et al. find clear differences between the written and oral tasks, and might have drawn different conclusions had they used only one mode of elicitation. All studies use written essays, most often argumentative, but very few studies include a range of tasks. Werner et al. also use interviews, Tracy-Ventura et al. use an interview as well as an oral narrative and an argumentative essay, and Bell et al. use two oral tasks (a narrative and an interview) and two written tasks (a narrative and an argumentative essay), all confirming previous research showing that tasks impact on productions. Because different tasks can give rise to markedly different results, it is important to repeat the same tasks to elicit productions which can then be compared across learners e.g. of different proficiencies or in a longitudinal corpus, in order to document development. This is stressed by both Tracy-Ventura et al. and Bell et al., but they are the only two studies which have fully taken account of the importance of triangulation. It has now become easier to share tasks, e.g. through IRIS (www.iris-database.org), and many researchers make use of well-known tasks such as the Frog Story or Charlie Chaplin's *Modern Times*, so the problems of ensuring we are not comparing apples and oranges should lessen in the future. These points notwithstanding, it is important that the task should fit the research agenda, for example eliciting all contexts and all forms of the linguistic structure investigated or sufficiently rich data. LCR methods should then enable researchers to track the various contexts of production; this should ideally include the omission of forms, so prevalent in learner data and often missed by computerised tools.

The vast majority of corpora to date are not only written but also **cross-sectional**, often only representing one level of proficiency, usually upper-intermediate or advanced, and this has been considered a weakness of the field. Three of the nine corpora in this volume are **longitudinal**, and this has to be welcomed. One of those is over a short period (23 weeks; Verspoor et al.) and the others are over three and four years respectively (Paquot et al.; Tracy-Ventura et al.). As SLA is primarily concerned about understanding development, the use of longitudinal data is particularly important. Three of the cross-sectional corpora used include a **range of proficiencies** (Ionin & Díez Bedmar – intermediate/upper-intermediate; Meriläinen – advanced/intermediate; Bell et al. – five grades from primary to secondary, proficiency unspecified), enabling conclusions to be drawn about development at group level. The other two corpora focus on advanced learners only (Polio & Yoon; Wulff & Gries), in keeping with their research agendas, which focus on comparing advanced learners to native speakers, in terms of accuracy in one case and the use of the genitive alternation in the other, rather than documenting development. The focus of the papers remains overwhelmingly on more advanced learners. This is undoubtedly because advanced language is more suited to corpus linguistics methodologies, e.g. for comparing with native language use, and because it is less deviant from target norms, which makes annotation and comparison easier. Corpora of beginner or lower-intermediate learners are particularly problematic to analyse, and require principled decisions about e.g. transcription, annotation etc., as pointed out by Bell et al. and others before them.

The use of **native speaker controls**, essential in the case of many research agendas, has increased, with six of the studies including them (Ionin & Díez Bedmar; Werner et al.; Meriläinen; Polio & Yoon; Paquot et al.; Tracy-Ventura et al.). **Independent measures of proficiency** are mentioned explicitly in three studies (Ionin & Díez Bedmar; Paquot et al.; Tracy-Ventura et al.), following evidence that school/university year does not equate with homogenous proficiency, as had often been assumed.

English is still by far the most **dominant** language. Only one corpus out of nine is on other languages (French and Spanish; Tracy-Ventura et al.), and even then the L1 of the learners is English. Additionally, the range of L1s of the learners of English investigated remains rather narrow, with European languages figuring prominently (Dutch; Finnish; French; German; Spanish; Swedish), with Chinese figuring in a couple of studies. It seems the call for a wider variety of typologically distant languages has not yet been fully heard.

None of the studies bar one made use of **additional data**, be it experimental or qualitative. Tracy-Ventura et al.'s participants provided very detailed information about language use, activities and networks, which enabled the authors to draw conclusions about the relationship between language attrition post-graduation and language use. Many SLA studies now make use of a range of additional data such as working memory or aptitude tests, and complement the analysis of semi-spontaneous data with e.g. psycholinguistic experiments or more focused elicitation techniques. This trend is not yet evident in the present volume. However, an increase in the use of sophisticated computerised and **statistical tools** is evident. All corpora are tagged for parts of speech or other project-specific coding, although automatic coding/annotation was not always possible. All studies make use of inferential statistics, and six out of nine resort to complex statistical analyses or modelling (Werner et al.; Polio & Yoon; Paquot et al.; Tracy-Ventura et al.; Verspoor et al.; Wulff & Gries), sometimes in a highly innovative way.

4 Conclusion

This commentary is based on the nine studies included in this volume, which give a snapshot of current work marrying the SLA and LCR paradigms. It can only therefore be considered as indicative, rather than an authoritative review of the field. With this caveat in mind, it is nonetheless evident that much progress has been made, with LCR research generally better theoretically framed, and with many of its powerful tools now being used more systematically to address complex SLA agendas.

Progress has been made in corpus documentation, corpus design and corpus exploitation. The corpora used in this volume are large, well designed and well documented on the whole, although some crucial information about learner variables is not systematically available, which can make replicability and comparability difficult.

Whereas early LCR research focused primarily on lexical or phraseological issues, the chapters in this volume encompass many aspects of language, from morphosyntax to lexis to phraseology, representing a wide range of research agendas and theoretical frameworks. The focus remains primarily on advanced learners, probably because their productions are more amenable to LCR methods, and English is unfortunately as dominant as ever. There is evidence that the importance of oral data and of using a range of different tasks is being acknowledged, although progress remains to be made in this area.

Overall, the gap between the two fields has definitely narrowed, and respective needs, strengths and weaknesses are now better understood. One area which still remains underdeveloped, however, is the sharing of resources, methodologies and expertise. Given the hugely resource-intensive nature of creating well designed corpora, it is imperative that we share not only corpora, but elicitation tasks, transcription conventions and coding tools, so that we can truly work together to the benefit of both fields.

References

Ayoun, D. (2003). *Parameter-Setting Theory in First and Second Language Acquisition*. New York, NY: Continuum.

Barlow, M. (2005). Computer-based analyses of learner language. In R. Ellis & G. Barkhuizen (eds.), *Analysing Learner Language*, 335–357. Oxford: Oxford University Press.

Brezina, V. & Bottini, R. (2019). Review of Castello, Erik, Katherine Ackerley & Francesca Coccetta Eds. (2015) *Studies in Learner Corpus Linguistics Research and Applications for Foreign Language Teaching and Assessment. International Journal of Learner Corpus Research* 5(1), 113–117.

Dekydtspotter, L. (2001). The Universal Parser and interlanguage: Domain-specific mental organization in the comprehension of *combien* interrogatives in English–French interlanguage. *Second Language Research* 17(1), 91–143.

Douglas Fir Group (2016). A transdisciplinary framework for SLA in a multilingual world. *The Modern Language Journal* 100, 19–47.

Erman, B., Denke, A., Fant, L., & Forsberg Lundell, F. (2015). Nativelike expression in the speech of long-residency L2 users: A study of multiword structures in L2 English, French and Spanish. *International Journal of Applied Linguistics* 25(2), 160–182.

Flynn, S. (1996). A parameter-setting approach to second language acquisition. In W. Ritchie & T. Bhatia (eds.), *Handbook of Second Language Acquisition*, 121–158. San Diego, CA: Academic Press.

Forsberg, F. (2010). Using conventional sequences in L2 French. *International Review of Applied Linguistics in Language Teaching* 48(1), 25–50.

Gánem Gutiérrez, G. A. (2008). Microgenesis, method and object: A study of collaborative activity in a Spanish as a foreign language classroom. *Applied Linguistics* 29(1), 120–148.

Gánem Gutiérrez, G. A. & Gilmore, A. (2018). Expert–novice interaction as the basis for L2 developmental activity: A SCT perspective. *Language and Sociocultural Theory* 5(1), 21–45.

Granger, S., Gilquin, G., & Meunier, F. (eds.). (2015). *Cambridge Handbook of Learner Corpus Research*. Cambridge: Cambridge University Press.

Gries, S. Th. (2016). *Quantitative Corpus Linguistics with R*. London & New York, NY: Routledge.

(2018). On over- and underuse in learner corpus research and multifactoriality in corpus linguistics more generally. *Journal of Second Language Studies* 1(2), 277–309.

Gries, S. Th. & Deshors, S. (2014). Using regressions to explore deviations between corpus data and a standard/target: Two suggestions. *Corpora* 9(1), 109–136.

Hawkins, R. (2001). *Second Language Syntax: A Generative Introduction*. Oxford: Blackwell.

(2008). The nativist perspective on second language acquisition. *Lingua* 118(4), 465–477.

(2019). *How Second Languages Are Learned: An Introduction*. Cambridge: Cambridge University Press.

Herdina, P. & Jessner, U. (2002). *A Dynamic Model of Multilingualism: Changing the Psycholinguistic Perspective*. Clevedon: Multilingual Matters.

Herschensohn, J. & Arteaga, D. (2016). Parameters, processing and feature reassembly in the L2 determiner phrase. In P. Guijarro-Fuentes, K. Schmitz, & N. Müller (eds.), *The Acquisition of French in Multilingual Contexts*, 215–233. Bristol: Multilingual Matters.

Hulk, A. (1991). Parameter setting and the acquisition of word order in L2 French. *Second Language Research* 7, 1–34.

Hyltenstam, K. & Abrahamsson, N. (2003). Maturational constraints in SLA. In C. Doughty & M. Long (eds.), *The Handbook of Second Language Acquisition*, 539–588. Malden, MA: Blackwell.

Jarvis, S. (2000). Methodological rigor in the study of transfer: Identifying L1 influence in the interlanguage lexicon. *Language Learning* 50(2), 245–309.

Jarvis, S. & Pavlenko, A. (2008). *Crosslinguistic Influence in Language and Cognition*. New York, NY: Routledge.

Lantolf, J. P. (2011). The sociocultural approach to second language acquisition: sociocultural theory, second language acquisition, and artificial L2 development. In D. Atkinson (ed.), *Alternative Approaches to Second Language Acquisition*, 24–47. New York, NY: Routledge.

Larsen-Freeman, D. (2017). Complexity theory: The lessons continue. In L. Ortega & Z.-H. Han (eds.), *Complexity Theory and Language Development: In Celebration of Diane Larsen-Freeman*, 123–142. Amsterdam: John Benjamins.

Liceras, J. (2009). On parameters, functional categories and features … and why the trees shouldn't prevent us from seeing the forest. *Second Language Research* 25(2), 279–289.

Lowie, W. (2017). Lost in state space? Methodological considerations in complex dynamic theory approaches to second language development research. In L. Ortega & Z.-H. Han (eds.), *Complexity Theory and Language Development: In Celebration of Diane Larsen-Freeman*, 123–142. Amsterdam: John Benjamins.

Lozano, C. & Díaz-Negrillo, A. (2019). Using learner corpus methods in L2 acquisition research: The morpheme order studies revisited with Interlanguage Annotation. *Revista Española de Lingüística Aplicada/Spanish Journal of Applied Linguistics* 32(1), 82–124.

Lozano, C. & Mendikoetxea, A. (2010). Interface conditions on postverbal subjects: a corpus study of L2 English. *Bilingualism: Language and Cognition* 13(4), 475–497.

Marsden, E., Morgan-Short, K., Thompson, S., & Abugaber, D. (2018). Replication in second language research: Narrative and systematic reviews and recommendations for the field. *Language Learning* 68(2), 321–391.

Marsden, E. & Plonsky, L. (2018). Data, open science, and methodological reform in second language acquisition research. In A. Gudmestad & A. Edmonds (eds.), *Critical Reflections on Data in Second Language Acquisition*, 219–228. Philadelphia, PA: John Benjamins.

McEnery, T., Brezina, V., Gablasova, D., & Banerjee, J. (2019). Corpus linguistics, learner corpora, and SLA: Employing technology to analyze language use. *Annual Review of Applied Linguistics* 39, 74–92.

Mitchell, R., Myles, F., & Marsden, E. (2019). *Second Language Learning Theories (4th Edn.)*. Abingdon: Routledge.

Myles, F. (2005). Interlanguage corpora and SLA research. *Second Language Research* 21(4), 373–391.

(2007). Using electronic corpora in SLA research. In D. Ayoun (ed.), *Handbook of French Applied Linguistics*, 377–400. Amsterdam: John Benjamins.

(2008). Investigating learner language development with electronic longitudinal corpora: Theoretical and methodological issues. In L. Ortega & H. Byrnes (eds.), *The Longitudinal Study of Advanced L2 Capacities*, 58–72. Hillsdale, NJ: Lawrence Erlbaum.

(2015). Second language acquisition theory and learner corpus research. In S. Granger, G. Gilquin, & F. Meunier (eds.), *Cambridge Handbook of Learner Corpus Research*, 309–332. Cambridge: Cambridge University Press.

Myles, F. & Mitchell, R. (2004). Using information technology to support empirical SLA research. *Journal of Applied Linguistics* 1(2), 169–196.

Norouzian, R., de Miranda, M., & Plonsky, L. (2018). The Bayesian revolution in second language research: An applied approach. *Language Learning* 68(4), 1032–1075.

Paquot, M. (2019). The phraseological dimension in interlanguage complexity research. *Second Language Research* 35(1), 121–145. https://doi.org/10.1177/0267658317694221

Paquot, M. & Plonsky, L. (2017). Quantitative research methods and study quality in learner corpus research. *International Journal of Learner Corpus Research* 3(1), 61–94.

Paradis, M. (2004). *A Neurolinguistic Theory of Bilingualism*. Amsterdam: John Benjamins.

Tavakoli, P. & Foster, P. (2011). Task design and second language performance: The effect of narrative type on learner output. *Language Learning* 61, 37–72.

Tracy-Ventura, N. & Myles, F. (2015). The importance of task variability in the design of learner corpora for SLA research. *International Journal of Learner Corpus Research* 1(1), 58–95.

VanPatten, B. & Williams, J. (2015). *Theories in Second Language Acquisition: An Introduction (2nd Edn.)*. Abingdon: Routledge.

White, L. (1989). *Universal Grammar and Second Language Acquisition*. Amsterdam: Benjamins.

(2009). Some questions about feature re-assembly. *Second Language Research* 25(2), 343–348.

Index

Lightning Source UK Ltd.
Milton Keynes UK
UKHW022248100321
380144UK00003B/15

9 781108 442299